W9-ARI-639

Garden Talk

Ask Me Anything

C. Z. Guest

Photographs by Elvin McDonald

UNIVERSE

To contact C. Z. Guest, go to www.czguest.com.

First published in the United States of America in 2001
by UNIVERSE PUBLISHING
A Division of Rizzoli International Publications, Inc.
300 Park Avenue South
New York, NY 10010

© 2001 by C. Z. Guest

All rights reserved. No part of this publication may be reproduced, stored in a retrieval
system, or transmitted in any form or by any means, electronic, mechanical, pho-
tocopying, recording, or otherwise, without prior consent of the publishers.

2001 2002 2003 2004 2005 2006 / 10 9 8 7 6 5 4 3 2 1

Design by Stephen Fay

Printed in China

Library of Congress Cataloging-in-Publication Data

Guest, C. Z.
   Garden talk : ask me anything / by C.Z. Guest ; photographs by Elvin
McDonald.
      p. cm.
   ISBN 0-7893-0625-5 (alk. paper)
   1. Gardening. 2. Gardening--Miscellanea. I. Title.
   SB455 .G84 2001
   635--dc21
                                        2001004599

contents

iii

To Bruce Weber,
*who changed the way the
world feels about
photography.*

introduction

I STARTED WRITING my newspaper garden columns in 1977. Since then I've written four garden planners and three books on gardening. I must say, when I was approached about writing this book, I thought to myself, how could I possibly write more about flowers and plants than I've already written? As we tossed around ideas, it occurred to me the reason my writings have stayed so popular over the years is because people like to ask specific questions and get specific answers. I've been able to do this through my newspaper columns. So we've gone through all my columns over the years and have taken what I consider to be the best and most often asked questions and I've answered them in great detail. I've also selected Elvin McDonald's most beautiful photographs of my gardens to aid in the education of my readers. I think this book will be the ultimate basic garden book.

Doing this book has been a thrill for me. It is a culmination of all my writing efforts over the years and I hope it will give the reader an easy index of answers to all their garden questions. I also hope it will stimulate gardeners to have the most enjoyment and success possible throughout their five seasons of gardening.

—*C. Z. Guest*

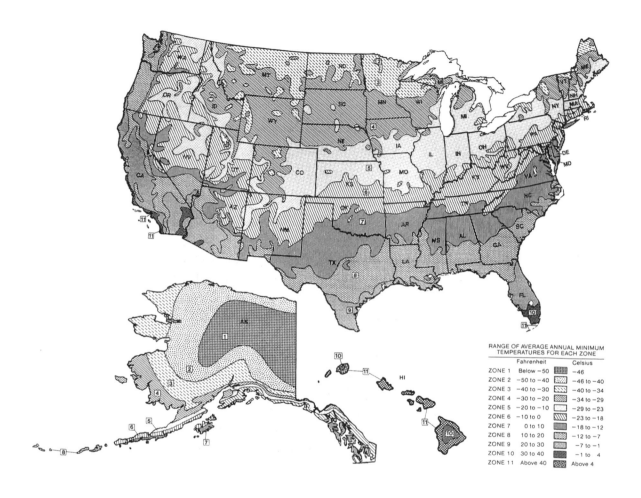

RANGE OF AVERAGE ANNUAL MINIMUM
TEMPERATURES FOR EACH ZONE

	Fahrenheit	Celsius
ZONE 1	Below −50	−46
ZONE 2	−50 to −40	−46 to −40
ZONE 3	−40 to −30	−40 to −34
ZONE 4	−30 to −20	−34 to −29
ZONE 5	−20 to −10	−29 to −23
ZONE 6	−10 to 0	−23 to −18
ZONE 7	0 to 10	−18 to −12
ZONE 8	10 to 20	−12 to −7
ZONE 9	20 to 30	−7 to −1
ZONE 10	30 to 40	−1 to 4
ZONE 11	Above 40	Above 4

U.S.D.A. Plant Hardiness Zone Map

vi

winter

WHETHER YOU'RE an experienced gardener or a beginner, winter is the time to plan and organize your garden for the following year. The experienced gardener will be thinking about how to improve the garden and planning the important changes. The inexperienced gardener has much more to think about. My advice to a beginner is to keep things simple until you know what you are doing.

What kind of flowers do you like? Do you want vegetables? Maybe a little of both? First thing to remember is that you must always plant for the area in which you live. I suggest getting a couple of garden catalogs so when the

weather gets cold and your garden is sleeping, you can leaf through them and decide what you really want your garden to look like for the next year. The catalogs clearly define the growing zones to make your choices easier. If you have a great imagination, this winter planning can be a lot of fun. Spring doesn't start until March 21, so it can seem like winter is a long haul.

There are other things to think about, too. Such as, flowers come in different colors and shapes. You may need to plan the colors to coordinate with different rooms in your house. What kind of soil do you have? Does it need any preparation before you can plant? Consider whether you want annuals or perennials. Are there any particular times in the coming year when you especially want your garden to be in bloom and look spectacular, or to have beautiful cut flowers in your house (such as someone's birthday, anniversary, etc.)? These are all questions that need to be thought out before you plant your garden. Perusing the questions, answers and pictures in this chapter will help the winter months to pass quickly and you'll be well prepared when spring arrives.

Aloe Vera

Q. *I have heard that* Aloe vera, *a medicinal plant, is also good as a cosmetic aid. Could you please tell me what part of the plant is used and how it is applied?*

A. True aloe has been grown for centuries and is sometimes known as the first-aid plant because its succulent leaves contain a sticky fluid that offers soothing relief from burns and cuts. It's said that the Roman legions carried aloe plants with them to treat wounds. Today there are many skin medications for treatment of sunburn. If you have an aloe, you can make your own skin cream. Break off some of the leaves and you'll find the center oozing with a creamy fluid. This can be applied to sunburn anywhere on your body, even on your face. It will feel cool and will draw out the heat and ease pain. I think an aloe plant would be a great present for any friend who enjoys the outdoors. The aloe is easy to grow in any frost-free, bright, sunny place. It can be propagated at any time of year from the suckers that grow at the soil line.

Annual Flowers

Unless you have actually done it before, you cannot realize what a thrill it is to plant annual flower seeds and in six to eight weeks have plants of rare beauty blooming until frost.

Annuals are not difficult to grow and the pleasure and joy they provide will reward you many times the cost and effort expended on them. Most seed packets have instructions, so you can't go wrong.

Here are some suggestions for a fabulous flower garden, a nonstop supply of annuals for cutting right up to the frost! These seeds can be sown directly into the soil: aster, baby's breath, cornflower, cosmos, dianthus, larkspur, marigold, zinnia, seabiosa, forget-me-not, nasturtium, viola and pansy.

Annuals make a beautiful border of bright, long-blooming flowers. The following are tolerant of hot, dry conditions—perfect for long, hot summers: celosia, cosmos, portulaca or rose moss, all varieties of marigold and nasturtium. (These seeds can be directly sown.)

A garden for hummingbirds and butterflies can add motion, mystery and color to the garden. Start snapdragons and salvia early indoors. These seeds can be sown directly after the last frost: cosmos, zinnia, cornflower, marigold and liatris.

Bats are among a gardener's best friends. They eat thousands of night-flying insects. To encourage these benign creatures to stay in your garden, you can create a habitat that attracts plenty of night-flying insects with the following seeds: salvia, cornflower, four-o'clocks, nicotiana, phlox and moonflower.

Annual everlasting flowers look as pretty in the garden as they do in arrangements. These easy-to-grow varieties put on an amazing display throughout the summer and will supply you with an abundance of flowers for dried arrangements to grace your house all year long. All these varieties can be directly sown into the garden: strawflower, mixed varieties of statice, starflowers and bells of Ireland.

Drying flowers is the perfect way to carry the beauty of the summer garden into winter. Many flowers are a cinch to air dry. For best results, cut flowers for drying just before each bloom opens fully, preferably in the morning after all dew has dried.

Simply strip off the leaves and bunch three to five stems together with a rubber band 2 inches from the stem ends. Suspend upside down from coat hangers, a clothes line or drying rack in a dry, well-ventilated area away from bright sun. When the stems are brittle, your flowers are ready for you to let your imagination run wild when arranging.

In addition to the varieties I've already suggested, try air drying the following: ageratum, baby's breath, celosia, larkspur, yarrow and lavender.

Dress up your shady nooks, crannies and borders with flowering annuals from early summer to frost. All these suggested seeds can be sown directly into the soil after all danger of frost is gone. Of course, if you start your seeds indoors in March, the flowers will bloom earlier when transplanted to the garden. Salvia, nicotiana, bells of Ireland, snap-dragon, viola, forget-me-not, coleus and impatiens are all good choices.

A child's garden is easy to grow with annual seeds. They will keep a child interested and teach the joy of gardening. Good choices: corn, lettuce, sunflower, marigold, tomatoes.

For an easy-to-grow herb garden, sow: basil (red- and green-leafed), borage, chives, mint, dill, oregano, parsley and nasturtium.

Order your seeds early, since some catalogs offer a discount. Or visit your favorite garden center—they will advise you for any situation.

Annuals for Transition

Annuals can bridge the transition between spring-flowering bulbs and later perennials. To fill the gaps, use dependable annuals like petunias of the floribunda or multiflora variety since lighter colors like Celebrity Mix or Light Pink Pearls produce more blooms per season than darker shades. To keep plants blooming, always cut off spent (deadhead) blooms.

Unless you already have an old-fashioned cottage garden with annuals and perennials in splendid profusion, here are some suggested favorites for you to plant this spring: zinnia 'Big Red,' calendula 'Indian Price,' cosmos long-lasting 'Heidi,' cornflower 'Blue Diadem,' marigolds in all colors and sizes. With these suggestions, you'll amply fill your vases.

Also consider such everlastings as 'Lavender Lady' and 'Strawberry Fields' globe amaranth, 'Snowflake' baby's breath and 'Bright Bikini Mixed' strawflower, statice 'Soiree Improved' and either plume or crested types of celosia such as 'Castle' and 'Chief' series; and everyone's favorite sunflowers, 'Sunburst' and 'Italian White.' These varieties are all willing bloomers over a long season.

Having a garden is like having a good and loyal friend.

Ashes

Waste not, want not. Save the wood ashes from your fireplace to spread around peonies, roses, delphiniums and lilacs. The ashes serve as a natural fertilizer and soil conditioner.

Asparagus Tips

Asparagus is a perennial and should have a permanent space in the garden.

Well-drained, only slightly acid soil (pH 6.5–6.9) is the key. Work in 5 pounds per 100 square feet of rock phosphate or calcium phosphate before planting. Each fall thereafter, putting down 2 to 3 pounds of 5-4-3 fertilizer per 100 square feet will keep the bed flourishing and vigorous.

Rows should be 18 inches apart in beds, or 4 to 6 feet apart if you want a path between rows.

To plant, dig a 6- to 8-inch-deep trench a foot wide and place a shovelful of compost in the bottom every 15 to 18 inches.

Set the crown on these compost mounds with the roots fully spread out (not doubled over).

Cover the crowns with a few inches of soil and compost mix and leave the remainder of the soil from the trench heaped between the rows.

As the ferns grow, gradually fill in the trenches until the soil surface is level again.

Avoid covering the foliage at any point. Water new asparagus beds regularly unless enough rain falls.

It's best to limit the first-year harvest to only a couple of weeks. In later years, it can be continued for four to six weeks, or until the spears start to decline in thickness to the diameter of a pencil.

Harvest before the tips of the spears begin to open—either by cutting the spears on an angle at or just below soil level, or by grasping them at soil level and snapping them off with your hands.

Bamboo

Q. *Why do I have such bad luck with bamboo in New York? Where can I find bamboo plants that will stand the winters here?*

A. There are only a few genera of bamboo that thrive any farther north than Maryland. Some species of the *Arundinaria* genus are small and hardy and can be successfully grown in a northern garden. Nitida grows to about 20 feet with graceful, arching purple canes. It's one of the hardiest of bamboos and thrives in an alkaline soil in partial shade. Another hardy and very vigorous species is the fastuosa, which grows to about 40 feet with canes marked purplish brown.

Bean Beetles

Don't let those creepy, crawly bean beetles get the best of your bean harvest this summer. Simply follow these guidelines to fight back.

First, identify the infestation. Adult and Mexican bean beetles are one-quarter-inch long, brownish with black spots and look very much like beneficial ladybugs (which you must never destroy). To be sure you're dealing with Mexican bean beetles, look for their telltale yellow egg clusters and plump yellow larvae on the undersides of leaves.

The larvae and adult beetles feed mostly on leaves and, occasionally, on beans, leaving distinctive lacy-looking damage called "skeletonizing" on those leaves.

Adult Mexican bean beetles spend the winter in nearby weeds or fields. You can prevent damage to your bean crop in spring by covering young plants with a row cover shortly after the beetles emerge from the ground.

If you do spot yellow bean-beetle eggs or larvae on the bottom of bean leaves, remove and destroy eggs and larvae immediately. If you follow this procedure once a week or so (hold a hand mirror beneath leaves to make your scouting easier), you can prevent a beetle population explosion later in the season and greatly limit the destruction.

Encourage the beneficial insects that gladly dine on the beetles. Plant perennial flowers and herbs—including Queen Anne's lace and yarrow—near your bean bed and allow them to flower. Their nectar and pollen will attract spined soldier bugs and parasitic wasps that will gobble up those beetle larvae in no time.

Bedmates, Compatible

Scientists can't explain it, but experienced gardeners have found that certain planting combinations actually enhance growth and reduce insect troubles. Keep these combinations in mind when ordering your seeds.

- asparagus, basil, parsley, tomatoes
- beans, marigolds, celery, potatoes
- beets, carrots, onions, kohlrabi, cauliflower, kale, broccoli, Brussels sprouts, turnips, cabbage
- carrots, onions and parsley (which repel carrot flies), beets, peas, sage
- corn, beans, cucumbers, lettuce, soybeans (to repel chinch bugs), spinach, squash
- cucumber, corn, radishes (to repel cucumber beetles)
- lettuce, cabbage, onions, radishes
- marigolds (which cut nematode population) anywhere
- nasturtiums, potatoes, squash
- onions, carrots, lettuce, radishes
- peas, beans, carrots, corn, potatoes, turnips
- peppers, carrots, eggplants, onions, tomatoes
- potatoes, corn, eggplants, peas
- radishes, carrots, lettuce, spinach
- squash, beans, corn, radishes
- strawberries, borage, lettuce, spinach

Beehives

Keep your beehives covered until the snow has melted and it is warm enough for the bees to leave their hives safely. If they happen to venture out while the air is still too cool, they may catch a chill and die.

Begonia, Rieger

Q. *Why do the Rieger begonias I buy from my florist start dropping flowers and leaves a few days after I bring them home? I notice that some of the leaves have splotches of white on them.*

A. Powdery mildew! To control it, you'll have to spray with a fungicide, available from the florist who sold you the begonias, or from any garden center or nursery; follow label directions. And the presence of powdery mildew suggests that the atmosphere could stand more fresh-air circulation, too. Riegers are touchy about any kind of air pollution and also tend to drop buds when moved from one environment to another, as from a greenhouse into the warmer, drier air of a house or apartment. Half-sun is needed in winter, in combination with moderate temperatures (60°–75°F), a pleasantly moist atmosphere and fresh air—but no hot or cold drafts.

Bird-of-Paradise

Q. *Every year at this time, I watch my huge bird-of-paradise put out flower heads, but only one or two are able to open. The others swell, but the case won't allow the petals to emerge. I fertilize the plant regularly and water it twice a week.*

A. Hmmm, I'm not sure what may be happening. My first reaction is to have you apply magnesium (magnesium sulfate/Epsom salts) to the plant, since this nutrient helps strengthen the flower. My other inclination is to say that the problem is genetic, but I have my doubts that the answer is that simple.

Do others in your area who are growing a bird-of-paradise plant notice the same problem? If not, are they doing anything differently in caring for their plants?

It may be that you simply need to water a little more often when you see flower stalks starting to develop and emerge. The bract from which the flower emerges is drying or becoming too tight (tough) for some reason. Try watering more often, to see if that may be a solution, but like you, I'm not absolutely sure why the flower bracts aren't opening.

Bird-of-Paradise, Nonblooming

Q. *I've had a bird-of-paradise for five years. It produces leaves but never blooms. How can I make it produce flowers? Is there anything wrong with my plant?*

A. Unfortunately, only mature plants are capable of setting the fabulous blue and orange flower spikes and it may take as long as six years.

This unusual South African native grows outdoors beautifully in California, Southern Florida and Hawaii. In colder areas it's strictly a houseplant.

The bird-of-paradise must have its cool period of rest in autumn and winter when night temperatures are around 55°F. To encourage flowering, it needs all-day sun and a rich, well-drained soil that is kept evenly moist throughout the spring and summer months (its period of active growth). Fertilize with Miracle-Gro during the growth period following directions on the label. The botanical name is *Strelitzia reginae.*

Birds

During the cold months be sure to feed the birds. A proper diet maintains weight, which insulates their bodies and helps them stay warm. Also remember that birds get thirsty, just like people. Water freezes less quickly in a clay or wooden bowl. Most birds appear to be homeless during the cold winter nights, which makes people wonder where they go. Usually, birds elect to roost in the same type of place as they build their nests during the breeding season. Unless disturbed by bullies (predators), some birds will use the same roosting spot every night.

Like us, birds have different nighttime habits, depending on the species. For instance, chickadees and other tiny-feeding birds must get settled before dusk. They head for some type of cover usually in the form of evergreen trees. Chickadee flocks fly into these evergreens and tend to perch together near the trunk to stay warm, an added protection from the wind.

Tree holes are another hot spot for nuthatches and small woodpeckers to head for the night. Others, like bluebirds for instance, may roost in tree holes or birdhouses to conserve body heat. Nuthatches and bluebirds don't mind a full house, so they may roost communally, especially on cold evenings.

Many birds fly long distances to spend the night in large communal roosts. Crows fly up to 50 miles each winter night, joining as many as 100,000 crow pals roosting in evergreens. Herons, robins and starlings also form large nighttime roosts to keep warm.

Northern bobwhites keep warm by forming a circle on the ground with their tails facing in. The circle is very snug and tight against their neighbors on either side.

Q. *How can I attract more birds to my garden? Bird feeders make such a mess, but without them the garden seems so dead and dreary in the winter.*

A. Several years ago I asked the same question. I say if your garden is beautiful in winter with lots of goodies you'll have a variety of birds. It's the perfect habitat for them.

The most important element for a winter bird garden is water. When winter temperatures plunge below freezing, birds have a tough time since they often must travel miles for water. I suggest a simple immersion water heater with a thermostat that can turn a small birdbath into a winter oasis providing water for drinking and bathing. The key to attracting birds from miles around is to keep the bath clean and filled.

Trees are essential for food and shelter. Evergreens such as spruce, juniper and pine are more than welcome. Deciduous shrubs and trees can be a source of berries, seeds and insects and convenient lookout perches from which to survey the yard for hidden predators. Holly, dogwood, sumac, crab apple and yew fruits all brighten the winter landscape and are appreciated by birds.

Meadows or unmowed areas at the edge of woodlands are particularly popular with overwintering birds because they are a great source for seeds and insects. Closely clipped lawns are least liked as they provide little in the way of food, cover or water.

And if you feed birds in winter, you have to keep it up every day. The birds will count on you.

New government regulations (thank goodness) are causing many home gardeners to reduce their use of pesticides. These gardeners have to fall back on natural pest controls, such as birds. Your garden will benefit from protecting and cultivating wild, insect-eating birds; and you'll be preserving a valuable natural resource. Your garden can't help but reap the benefits.

Never forget that once you start feeding birds during winter, don't stop until after your last frost date. Unfortunately, the birds adapt slowly and many will starve if their food source suddenly disappears.

Blue Flowers

There's something extra special about the flowers that bring the brilliant blue of the sky into the garden.

Here's my pick of the most fabulous blue bloomers, from spring-flowering bulbs to long-blooming perennials—all arranged by their bloom time to help you grow glorious bouquets of blue, cobalt, azure, indigo and sapphire. What a treat!

For an early "blue" spring, plant some bulbs right away. These powerful small clumps of color have an amazing impact that is far out of proportion to their individual flower size, simply because they will be the first things sprouting. The first flowers to poke their little noses out of the ground are usually snow crocus. Plant 'Blue Peter' and 'Blue Pearl' for starters. They will bloom in early March. Next to arrive is glory-of-the-snow *(Chionodoxa)* with its brilliant clusters of starlike blue flowers on 6-inch stems; they will readily adapt wherever planted. Intensely colored blue scillas are next to arrive; their seeds will readily spread to create a carpet of blue in your lawn if allowed to.

Then we get to the ever-popular and very fragrant hyacinths—you must choose the dark-blue variety, 'Blue Jacket,' and the long-blooming, daisylike windflower, *Anemone blanda.* Finally, in late spring, you can finish off your array of blue bulbs with Spanish blue-bells *(Hyacinthoides hispanica).*

All of these beautiful bulbs are hardy from Zones 3 through 8 except the windflowers, which are safe only down to Zone 4. All these gems are widely available at garden centers at the proper time to plant them in your area.

Some of my favorite annual blues: 'Heavenly Blue' morning glory—the name tells it all! All you have to do is find a sunny location, build a giant tepee of saplings and grow this lovely annual as a centerpiece right in your vegetable garden or any other place that suits your fancy.

They are also fabulous in containers (clay pots, etc.) for the patio or swimming pool areas. Place three or four stakes in the container to form a tepee, and before you know it the slender vines will be winding up those stakes and growing a few inches daily. The taller the stakes, the better.

Buy a pack of 'Heavenly Blue,' available at any garden store seed rack, soak them overnight to soften the hard seed coat (you can help even more if you use a knife to snip a tiny bit off the end of each seed before you soak it) and then plant only a few of the soaked seeds next to each tepee stake.

Perform the same procedure when planting seeds in a container. Morning glories have no serious disease or pest problems; they need one fertilizing in the spring at planting time.

Another super easy-to-grow annual is the cornflower known as 'Bachelor's Button.' These delightful bloomers are loaded with 2-inch-wide, deep-blue flowers. They make great cut flowers, too. Most varieties grow about 30 inches tall. You can buy all blue-flower seeds (in a packet) or a mixed bag of pink, white and blue seeds.

An added bonus is that bachelor's button will usually self-seed, so you'll have blue buttons for years to come.

Lobelia is another favorite annual of mine. The 6-inch-high plants are completely covered with brilliant blue flowers. Lobelias do extremely well in dry, western areas but don't do well in hot, soggy areas. To get the most out of these lovely plants, grow them in well-drained soil, in part shade.

Lobelia comes in compact, edging types and trailing varieties. Top edgers include the blue 'Mrs. Clibran' and 'Crystal Palace.' Trailing types such as the cascading series are perfect for windowboxes and hanging baskets.

Lobelia plants are easily spotted at garden centers. Buy plants, because they grow very slowly from seed. For growing your own, start seeds by February and try to plant four or five of the tiny seeds together to form nice clumps for transplanting.

Other blue annuals include petunias, pansies, love-in-a-mist, forget-me-not, veronica and *Salvia farinacea.* Thompson & Morgan's seed catalog lists a blue nasturtium *(Tropaeolum azureum).* It's not easy to grow, but think of how great you'll feel if you can grow it—that's the reward of taking on a challenge.

Bethlehem sage, a blue perennial, looks nothing like regular sage. Bethlehem sage forms a 12-inch-high mound of pretty green leaves mottled with silver. It remains attractive all summer long and is accented by pink to blue flowers. It's hardy from Zones 3 to 8.

Another excellent springtime blue perennial is the forget-me-not *(Brunnera).* These tiny sky-blue flowers have little yellow eyes and feature airy clusters above mounds of large green leaves. Forget-me-nots self-seed quickly, so buy just one plant and you'll soon have plenty for holiday gifts. They are hardy in Zones 3 through 7.

Virginia bluebell is one of the earliest perennials that can help ring in spring. Its 18- to 24-inch-high flower clusters start out pink but then change to blue. The plants go dormant during the summer and the foliage dies back, so I suggest interplanting them with other shade-loving perennials. Bluebells are hardy in Zones 3 to 9.

These three plants: bluebells, Bethlehem sage and forget-me-nots, prefer moist, partly shady spots, especially in the South.

Bromeliads

Q. *I understand the Silver King bromeliad I received recently in bloom will eventually send up a "pup" that will grow into a new plant. Please tell me how to handle this.*

A. First, be sure your Silver King is in a window where it receives bright light, preferably a few hours of sun; that will ensure that the pup, or offset, grows strong and has good color. Keep the growing medium in a range between evenly moist and slightly on the dry side; once a week turn the plant upside down to drain all the water from the cup, then turn it right side up and refill with fresh water. When the pup is about 6 inches tall you can remove it from the parent, unpotting the two so you can see what you're doing. Take as many roots with the new plant as possible and pot up in a suitable epiphytic or air plant mix—about equal parts of sphagnum peat moss, coarse vermiculite, well-rotted leaf mold and shredded bark, for example. Water well, then enclose in plastic for a week or two. You can repot the parent; it may send off one or more additional pups before consignment to the compost pile.

Bulbs, Spring

Spring bulb flowers are a joy. A simple pleasure, and what a fragrance! They aren't expensive, and the best part is watching them grow.

Duck inside when a florist's window catches your eye and buy a potted blue hyacinth. Get your mother some daffodils—a pot will last and last on the dining room or bedside table. Add colorful potted tulips to the sitting room and you'll see how it perks you up!

More and more top-notch American growers are growing quality cut and potted bulb flowers, making them more widely available and affordable to everyone.

It just makes sense that people look for particular flowers when they are in season and affordable, when local growers pull out the stops to supply their local markets.

Following are tips for enjoying an early spring indoors with potted flower bulbs such as tulips, daffodils, crocuses and hyacinths.

Buy potted tulips in a young stage, with buds formed but not even fully emerged. Watching them grow provides weeks of enjoyment. The flowers are the grand finale!

Potted bulbs can be enjoyed in their plastic or terra-cotta nursery pot, but also look especially attractive if repotted or double-potted.

To repot, gently tap out the nursery pot contents (keeping bulbs and soil intact, to avoid root damage) and repot in one of your own favorite containers. Your pot must have a drainage hole and saucer to collect draining water.

To double-pot, just lower the existing potted plant "as is" into a prettier container. You can use a nice container with no drainage hole (often called a cachepot) or a slightly larger pot with a drainage hole and saucer.

Water to keep soil moist but not soggy.

Bulbs, Spring—Easy Forcing

A house filled with living flowers in the dead of winter might seem like a luxury. Actually, some flowers are surprisingly fun and easy to grow indoors at this time. The process is called forcing: fooling a flower bulb into thinking it is time to bloom when it's not.

Many flowers can be forced, but bulb flowers are more easily forced than others. In fact, two bulbs in particular are so quick and easy to grow that anyone can do it and feel instantly gratified.

Amaryllis bulbs are big, and yield big beautiful flowers. They are available in prepackaged kits and also sold loose. By staggering start-up times, it's possible to have amaryllis blooming in the house from December through April.

The kits contain everything you need along with instructions. Loose amaryllis bulbs offer a wider selection of varieties and are just as easy to grow as the kits. They can be planted in any kind of container you like, but a drainage hole (and a saucer to catch the water that drains) is required. The width of the pot should be only slightly larger than the bulb itself.

Spread a shallow layer of gravel, pot shards or other drainage material at the bottom of the pot. Add several inches of soil and place the bulb, pointed end up, with the neck and shoulders of the bulb just peeking over the top of the container.

Fill in with soil and gently pat down, leaving the neck of the bulb exposed. Water well. Place in a cool, sunny spot. Water sparingly at first. After the first sprouts appear (about two weeks), water often. In about eight weeks, you'll have tall plants with huge, sophisticated flowers.

Paperwhites are especially easy to grow. They, too, can be bought as loose bulbs or as part of a prepackaged forcing kit. They are often found in displays along with gravel, containers and other bulbs for forcing.

Paperwhites are best forced in a shallow pot or bowl with no drainage holes in the bottom. Fill the pot two-thirds full with gravel, stones and fun things like marbles or polished stones. Place as many bulbs as will fit on the gravel with the pointed side up. Then fill in gravel around them, leaving the tops exposed. Add water up to the base of the bulbs and maintain water at this level.

Place the container in a cool place. Within days, roots will appear. As they grow, they will sometimes push the bulbs upward.

When the green shoots appear, move the plant to a cool, sunny spot. The shoots will develop rapidly and in about three more weeks you'll have masses of heavily scented, sweet white flowers.

Other bulbs, such as hyacinths and daffodils, are also easy to force, but require a bit more time and effort. They need to be potted and then put in a cold location for 12 to 15 weeks (a great use for an old refrigerator).

Of course, once you experience the pleasure of having a house full of easy-to-grow, super-spectacular amaryllis and paperwhites, the tiny bit of extra effort to move on to other forcible bulbs will seem well worth it!

Cacti Transplanting

Q. *Please give me tips on transplanting some cacti that I raised from seeds. Should I use a special soil? How do I avoid getting stuck?*

A. Transplanting cacti can be a painful task, so it's good that it doesn't need to be done often.

The best time to transplant cacti is when they are dormant (late winter), but the job can be done most anytime, if you're cautious with your after-transplanting care.

Wear a pair of gloves (preferably thorn-proof ones) and fold a sheet of paper into an 8 ½-inch by 2-inch strip, to use as a sling or collar to hold the cactus in place without your getting stuck.

Another option is to use ice tongs to hold and position the cactus during repotting—but if you press too hard, some of the spines may come off.

A piece of stiff paper folded into a funnel can be used to place the new soil around the plant. And, a pair of chopsticks or craft sticks will come in handy to firm the soil around the cactus, without getting your hands too close to the spines.

I do recommend that a special cactus and succulent potting soil be used, but if you've had good success with the soil you've used thus far, I wouldn't change it.

A common mistake is putting the cactus in too large a pot. Doing so will cause the plant to be more susceptible to root rot. Most cacti are happiest in a small pot, so don't repot them until they've grown close enough to the pot's edge to make watering difficult.

After replanting your cactus, don't water immediately. Allow the plants a few weeks to adjust and start to produce new roots. In fact, if you replant them during the dormant season, don't water them until you normally would resume regular watering.

A layer of stone or gravel on top of the soil looks nice, and will help keep the base or crown of the cactus dry (thus decreasing the chance of crown rot), but the gravel may make it difficult for you to tell when the cactus needs to be watered.

Central Park's Formal Garden

Six glorious acres enclosed by a wrought-iron fence, the Conservatory Garden at Fifth Avenue and 105th Street in New York is Central Park's only formal garden, containing Manhattan's most varied collection of flowering trees, shrubs, annuals and perennials.

Olmsted and Vaux's Greensward Plan for Central Park originally called for the present site of the garden to be part of a native plant arboretum. This plan never materialized, but a nursery was laid out. Huge greenhouses were built on this site in 1899 (hence the name, Conservatory Garden).

Great flower displays brought thousands of visitors to the conservatory and its surrounding gardens, but the costs of maintaining such structures were too high, and, in 1934, the conservatory was torn down and the garden built in its place.

The creation of the garden was a Works Progress Administration project, one of thousands across the country that provided employment during the Depression.

By the late 1970s, the garden had fallen into disrepair because of city budget shortfalls. Major restoration by the nonprofit Central Park Conservancy began in 1982.

It consists of three separate gardens, each with its own distinct style.

The North Garden is designed in the French style, with formal, ornate plantings. In its center stands the bronze Undermyer Fountain, known as "Three Dancing Maidens," sculpted by Walter Schott. The sloped outer beds of the garden present two dazzling floral displays each year: 20,000 tulips in spring and 2,500 Korean chrysanthemums in fall. Rose beds and spiraea hedges circle the garden's perimeter. At the northern end of the garden (at 106th Street), the Emily Mumford Gate reveals a view of the beautiful Harlem Meer.

The Central Garden is a classic Italian design, featuring an expanse of manicured lawn, a central fountain and semicircular, tiered hedges leading up to a wisteria pergola. The garden is flanked by two crab apple allees that in the spring overflow with fragrant pink and white blossoms. These trees were planted in the garden at the time of its opening in 1937, and were brought down the Hudson on barges in full bloom.

Here also is the Vanderbilt Gate, the main entrance to the garden, at Fifth Avenue and 105th Street, which was forged in Paris in 1894 for the Vanderbilt mansion on Fifth Avenue at 58th Street, and was given to the city by Gertrude Vanderbilt Whitney in 1939.

The South Garden is styled after English perennial gardens, reinterpreted with an American flair. Trees, shrubs, perennials and annuals are woven together in seemingly informal sweeps of flowers and foliage.

The Central Park Conservancy is a private, nonprofit organization founded in 1980 that manages Central Park under a contract with the City of New York. Through private donations from individuals, foundations and corporations, the conservancy provides 80 percent of the park's annual operating budget, funds major capital improvements, provides horticultural care and management, and offers programs for volunteers and visitors.

The conservancy invites all Central Park visitors to become partners in taking care of the park to ensure that it remains a beautiful place for leisure, recreation and the appreciation of nature. The garden, of course, is at its sensational best during spring, summer and fall. Don't miss a wonderful treat.

Christmas Cactus

Q. *How can I get my Christmas cactus to bloom?*

A. Give it sunlight, warmth, moisture and regular applications of a fertilizer for flowering houseplants during the spring and summer. In autumn and early winter take care that the plant receives only natural light; in other words, keep it in total darkness from sundown to sunup. Water only enough to keep the leaflike stems from shrinking, and apply no fertilizer. If possible, subject the plant to cool nighttime temperatures, ideally a range of 50° to 60° F. Given this regimen for two months, any holiday cactus will bloom—Thanksgiving, Christmas or Easter. Recent studies show that a nighttime chill into the 50s brings on bloom in these plants just as surely as do short days and long nights. Poinsettia and kalanchoe respond to similar treatment.

Q. *How do I keep my Christmas cactus blooming?*

A. Keep the cactus growing during the summer. Water it just enough so that the leaves don't shrivel—and never let your plant dry out! Pot in well-drained soil and wait until the soil is dry before watering again. In the early fall, move the cactus into a cool, well-lit room. These plants demand bright—but not direct—light, and will also thrive on artificial light.

Once indoors, the cactus must have 14 hours of darkness each day in order to bloom for Christmas (from 5 or 6 P.M. to 7 or 8 A.M.), and temperatures of 50° to 60°F, until buds form. Increase watering while the cactus is forming buds and flowering.

Christmas Roses

Q. *What is the botanical name of the Christmas rose? How should I start a bed of Christmas roses?*

A. The Christmas rose is not a rose at all, nor does it always bloom at Christmastime. It is *Helleborus niger,* a member of the buttercup family. The Christmas rose originally comes from the Italian and Austrian Alps. It has been a treasured garden plant in England for centuries, and early in the eighteenth century its magical beauty could be found in American gardens.

The Christmas rose is a hardy but very slow-growing plant. Hellebores, like other winter flowering plants, should be placed in a protected spot. They like a rich, moist soil, with well-rotted manure, leaf mold or compost.

This is truly a wonderful plant that blooms in the snow, when all else is bare and bleak. The short days and cool weather of fall stimulate growth and the buds into bloom.

Christmas roses do best in partial shade, where they are not subject to being dried out in summer. They resent being disturbed and once established should be left alone.

Citrus Houseplant

Edible and/or ornamental citrus continue to be popular houseplants, as they should be. They're showy, a fruiting curiosity, readily available at the florist or garden center, and generally do well in the house. A few points should be considered prior to their purchase.

Don't try starting your own plants from seed unless it's for curiosity's sake. They will take years to bear fruit and the plant will become too large in the meantime.

Choose plants that have been grafted onto dwarfing root-stock. Otherwise, plants may quickly grow out of scale and routine pruning will be necessary. Garden center staff should be able to advise you.

Citrus should have cool temperatures at night in winter—about 55°F, but need a bright sunny window during the day.

Although often grown solely for fragrance, pollination will be necessary if you are seeking fruit. If it's summer and the plant is "vacationing" outdoors, bees will do it; otherwise, you must "tickle" the flower with a fine artist's brush or cotton swab.

Pests can be real problems on citrus. Inspect very carefully for the difficult-to-detect scale insects and spider mites. Once your collection is infested, especially with scale, it's very tough to clean them up.

Clematis, Changeable

Q. *I have a* Jackmanii *clematis that bloomed profusely for many years until last spring. Instead of the usual beautiful flowers, it had white and lavender striped flowers with small curly, distorted petals. What do you suppose happened?*

A. I think your original plant dropped some seeds. Those seeds simply germinated into a new plant that grew up and obscured the original plant, which by now needs some pruning to bring back the kind of flowers you are used to seeing. Trying to grow clematis from seed is almost impossible, but once in a while nature takes over and a seedling develops. Most of these "volunteers" have strange characteristics and the curling you describe is no doubt a trait of the new plant. So locate the new plant and pull it up.

To get your original clematis to bloom, simply prune the lateral branches back to just above the second leaf node from the main vine because clematis plants become woody with age and often can't get nutrients to the end of their branches.

Climate Zones

Before buying plants, make sure the varieties you choose are suited to the climate you live in. Creating an attractive garden involves more than just coordinating and selecting a mix of eye-pleasing plants. It won't mean much if your plants wilt, freeze or die because of your climate.

Climate maps show low temperature extremes by zone. By choosing plants best adapted to your zone and planting them at the proper time, you will have more success. Most plants and seeds in nurseries, garden centers and mail-order catalogs will be classified by a growing zone.

Green-thumb gardeners, however, use climate maps only as general guidelines. They realize that within one square mile of their houses may be dozens of microclimates. Even within one's backyard or garden there may be a half dozen or more situations that affect the choice of plants and planting times. Consider these factors:

Exposure:

Southern and western exposures are best because they are the sunniest and warmest. So match a plant's needs to the proper exposure.

Wind:

Gusting winds can dry out the soil and endanger delicate plants. Especially the cruel winter winds in northern zones.

Elevation:

When selecting plants and their placement in the garden or yard, remember that cold air sweeps down hills and rests in low areas. These frost packets are okay for some plants, but deadly for others. Always put plants that prefer warmth on the tops and sides of hills.

Structures:

When planting, take advantage of shrubs, trees and buildings for protection. Watch carefully for the play of shadows at different times of the year, wind and snow drift patterns.

These varying situations are perfect for some plants while a disaster for others. In short, make the best use of what protection your property or garden has to offer.

Q. *Several years ago, there was a big effort to update and modernize the U.S.D.A. hardiness zone maps. I bought one from Rutgers University, but it doesn't indicate any city, counties or state boundaries for landmarks. How can I tell what zone I'm in? I live in a borderline area in Rockbridge Baths, Virginia. Could I possibly obtain a zone map just for Virginia? Do you have the same problems that I do? Help!*

A. The map you got from Rutgers is not the official map prepared by the U.S. Department of Agriculture. The U.S.D.A.'s map, which has been updated for the first time in 25 years, clearly shows boundaries, as well as each county.

According to the U.S.D.A. map (pictured on page *vi* of this book), you're definitely in Zone 6. This means your average annual low temperature is between 0° and 50°F. This is kind of a new zone because when the U.S.D.A. updated the map, they split old zones into two sections (A and B); each new half zone represents a 5-degree temperature difference instead of the old 10-degree difference. I'm sorry to inform you that there aren't any zone maps for individual states. Try calling your cooperative extension office and ask them specific questions regarding the climate in your area.

You can order a full-size U.S.D.A. map for $6.50 from the Superintendent of Documents, U.S. Government Printing Office, 8660 Cherry Lane, Laurel, Maryland, 20707.

Clivia, Nonblooming

Q. *Why doesn't my clivia bloom?*

A. Maybe it's not big enough; blooming isn't likely until there are at least 16 of the big, evergreen, strap-shaped leaves and the roots fairly jam an 8-inch pot. Provide half-sun all year; a cool, sunny window is ideal in winter, with nighttime temperatures into the 50s. In the fall and winter don't fertilize, and water less—but never let clivia dry out completely as you might the related amaryllis. Toward the end of winter or at the onset of spring, water more frequently and make applications of a fertilizer prepared for flowering plants; as the days become longer and the temperatures warmer, watch for emerging flower buds. And if they don't show, be patient; clivia is definitely worth waiting for!

Clivia, Rare Yellow from Seed

Clivia miniature 'Sahin's Yellow,' the legendary Yellow Clivia, is now available as seed.

For years, the famous yellow clivia has been the Holy Grail of the horticultural elite around the world, so jealously guarded that only the wealthiest and best-connected could ever hope to own such a precious plant. Now the adventurous gardener can enjoy these fantastic plants at a fraction of the cost by growing them from seed.

Recently, a well-known mail-order plant marketer offered vegetatively propagated clones for $900 each.

Wow! Like all clivia plants, germination is easy, plants are very easy to grow, and they live very long. Unfortunately, blooming size is not achieved until the fourth or fifth year after sowing, so one needs plenty of patience.

Seed is sold in packets of two for around thirty dollars. Seed is so rare that the supply is limited. You must order early to avoid disappointment. Seed is shipped only in March, at peak of freshness, and must be sown on arrival. Make your call now.

SOURCE: *Park Seed Co. (800) 845-3369.*

Coleus

Q. *What causes bunches of cotton to grow on my coleus?*

A. Mealybugs! They seem to favor coleus, gardenias and African violets, but anyone who grows plants soon discovers that mealybugs will attack anything, no matter how tough it may seem. One way to deal with them is hand-to-hand combat, using a cotton swab dipped in denatured alcohol. If mealybugs have become badly entrenched before you discover them on a plant, it may be better to pitch it and start over rather than fight.

Container Edibles

By filling pots and containers with vegetables or flowers, you can add color to your patio, yard, deck or swimming pool area. The rewards of container growing can be many.

Your choice of containers is as wide as your choice of plants to put in them. Planters made of redwood, cedar or clay will give you many years of service. Keep in mind that treated-wood containers are a no-no!

When choosing a container you must always consider the ultimate size of the plant to be grown in it. Too often a plant is placed in the wrong type of container, too small for the plant at maturity.

It's also important to use a good potting soil. I use a commercial Pro-Mix potting soil where all the nutrients are in the ingredients to make your plant grow to perfection.

Once you've selected your planter and filled it with soil, you can choose from a wide range of perennials, annuals, vegetables, or herbs. You're on your way to add beauty and excitement to the landscape.

Most nurseries have an excellent selection of containers and planters to choose from.

Container Gardening

Growing plants in planters, pots, urns and hanging baskets has been the fashion since ancient times. The use of containers is perfect for modern life, for not only are they fabulous-looking and practical, they are also easy to move around on your patio, terrace, deck or yard.

There are a number of wonderful candidates to choose from for your summer container garden. For sunny areas, you can't beat geraniums, lantana, heliotrope, New Guinea impatiens or the new trailing petunias.

Shady places will be perfect for Nonstop begonias, coleus, herbs of all sorts, nicotiana and caladiums. Don't forget training fuchsias from a hanging basket makes a bold statement.

There are endless ways to display flowers, vegetables and herbs. You can always put color where you want it in your outdoor living space.

Your choice of containers is endless; it's as wide as your choice of plants to put them in.

Planters made of redwood or cedar will give you many years of service. In addition, a great number of other types of decorative pots—terracotta, ceramic, concrete and plastic—can be used to beautify your surroundings.

Visit your local nursery and see for yourself the extent and variety of container plant selection.

Container Garden Doctor

Container gardening is a most popular pastime, and not just for houseplants anymore.

Cities and small towns are lined with sidewalk planters of trees, porches are bedecked with hanging baskets or mini-container vegetable gardens, and flower pots are popping up all over.

Growing plants in containers solves many problems, such as time and energy; however, space limitations may create some problems, too. If your garden isn't living up to your expectations and is performing poorly, check my list below of ordinary problems and their solutions.

Plants wilt in spite of receiving ample water.

Cause: usually, insufficient drainage. Cure: use a pre-mix soil (available at most garden centers); everything is in that soil to make your plants thrive. Good drainage is a must, so don't forget that a hole must be in the bottom of each pot.

Leaf edges die or burn, turning brittle and dry.

Cause: high salt content. Cure: leach pot by watering until water drains through the soil and out of drainage holes.

Plants are leggy, spindly and unproductive.

Cause: insufficient light, too much nitrogen. Cure: relocate your plant to more light, apply fertilizer less often and, when watering, allow pot to drain.

Plants are yellowing from bottom, show poor color and lack vigor.

Cause: too much water and low fertility. Cure: water less often and always check for proper drainage. Use a fertilizer with higher levels of nutrients. Look for higher numbers on the fertilizer bag.

Plant leaves have spots, dead dried areas and rusty or powdery areas.

Cause: plant is growing at too low a temperature (too cold) or the plant has a disease. Cure: move plant to a warmer spot. Remove diseased portion of plant and use a fungicide. If problem is too severe, simply throw away the plant.

Leaves are distorted in shape.

Cause: insect damage. Cure: an insecticidal soap spray targeted to the type of insect that's destroying the plant. Read directions on the label carefully.

Container Gardening, Materials

When planting large window boxes such as planters or cedar barrels, I have a good use for those styrofoam peanuts used in packing boxes.

Fill the bottom third of your containers with styrofoam peanuts. You save by not having to fill all of the container with soil mix and the container won't be so heavy, either.

Cut Flowers

Steps to Lasting Bouquets
You can keep fresh flowers lasting longer with these four easy steps:

1. Always start with a clean vase.
2. Remove all leaves that will be under water. Submerged leaves will decay and create bacteria, shortening the life of your bouquet. Besides, they make the water smell bad.
3. Re-cut the stem of each flower under water using a sharp knife or scissors. This prevents air pockets from forming, which block water uptake to the flowers. Re-cut stems every two days. Always cut the stems at an angle under water to lessen trauma to the blooms. Smash the woody stems of roses and lilacs for greater water absorption. I singe my lilacs' stems with a match; they seem to last longer (just as you do with poppies).
4. Add fresh flower food, available wherever fresh flowers are sold, to the vase water. Display flowers in a draft-free location away from harsh sunlight or heating vents. Change the water every day and re-cut stems every two days. Don't use tap water if you have a water softener; the flowers don't like salt.

Daffodils can be deadly to other flowers because they secrete a poison in the water. After trimming, leave them on their own for a whole day and do not cut again before combining them with other flowers. A special cut-flower food is available for daffodils, and this enables them to be mixed in with other cut flowers immediately.

Keep them away from fruit, as it lets off a gas called ethylene that accelerates the aging process of flowers.

Put a drop of bleach in the final rinse when you wash vases to keep the growth of bacteria at bay.

Cyclamen

Winter got you down? Need a little color to boost your garden or house? Why not consider cyclamen?

These winter bloomers with eye-catching flowers that seem to be reaching to the sky are perfect for a winter pick-me-up.

Cyclamen flowers offer instant color when purchased in already-blooming 4-inch or 6-inch pots, and many varieties are fragrant. You can buy them in garden centers, or even as potted plants in grocery stores and at the florist.

Cyclamen will bloom throughout winter and well into spring in some areas. They are perfect when grown in containers in partially protected patios or porches. They can also be used as scented houseplants when kept in a cool, lit area. Even better, since cyclamen are tuberous-rooted perennials, they'll come back year after year.

Goldsmith Seeds, one of the world's largest wholesale producers of hybrid flower seed, has a cyclamen variety to fill your needs. Whether it's florist-quality, large-flowered cyclamen ('Sierra'), an intermediate type with a smaller plant habit and flowers ('Laser'), or a miniature type ideal for patio containers ('Miracle') this company has the cyclamen for you!

'Sierra, ' 'Laser' and 'Miracle' are all bred to have their "shooting star" flowers bloom atop their attractive marbled foliage. Flowers bloom early and often all winter long. Many colors have also been bred specifically for fragrance, which is an added benefit when used as houseplants.

Cyclamen are hard to beat for winter, since they are just as much at home in containers as in-ground planting in mild climates. They can be planted in rock gardens, in naturalized clumps under trees and as carpets under camellias, azaleas and large noninvasive ferns.

Cyclamen combine well with other winter-blooming bedding plants in mild climates, including pansies, violas, calendula, primula and snapdragons, or you can mix up a large container of cool-season bedding plants using cyclamen as the featured attraction, and place them on your patio.

Daylily, the Incredible Edible

Q. *Are daylilies really edible?*

A. Nearly all parts of this incredible plant are edible.

Enjoy the first, spring shoots in a salad and the peppery stamens as sprouts. Or harvest the open blossoms in the morning after the dew has dried, then dip them in batter and stir-fry.

The blossoms also make marvelous and easy garnishes for salads, soups and sauces.

The most succulent daylily form, however, is the bud—it should be picked the day before bloom, when it is sweet and crunchy and at its peak of edibility. Use the buds in salads, soups or as garnishes. For colorful sushi, substitute a clean daylily bud for fish.

Caution: Never confuse daylilies *(Hemerocallis)* with true lilies *(Lilium)*. True lilies grow from bulbs—not rhizomes—and are not for eating.

Deer, and Mesh Fencing

The deer problem in the United States has accelerated in recent years due to the ever-increasing suburban sprawl. With their once-bountiful grazing areas rapidly diminishing, deer are being forced to find alternative sources of food. This in turn puts many people in areas with high deer populations in an awkward position because their estates and gardens are at risk of being damaged and/or destroyed.

Benner's Gardens has come up with an amazing polypropylene plastic mesh fence that keeps deer out. The lightweight, high-strength fencing is virtually invisible and has solved the deer predicament without detracting from the appearance of the land.

In areas where there are few or no trees, pressure-treated 2x4s, 4x4s, fiberglass or metal posts can be installed for support. Distances between these types of posts will of course vary. The fencing is staked to the ground with metal pins every 12 feet to keep the deer from pushing their noses underneath.

To ensure the immediate success of a newly installed system, it's recommended that 12 long white streamers be attached to the fencing (at a height of 4 feet) at 12-foot intervals. The streamers need only be left up for a month or so, but are most important because they warn the deer that there is now a barrier present, and keep them from running into the fencing. The deer will then reroute their paths to bypass the protected area.

By providing a unique product that keeps the deer out without changing the appearance of the property, Benner's mesh deer fence has helped many gardeners maintain their sanity.

Q. *Where should deer fencing be installed?*

A. The Benner's deer barrier fencing should be situated around the perimeter of the area you wish to protect. The barrier should be attached to existing trees when possible. Additional wooden, fiberglass or metal posts can be added for support where necessary.

It's very important to completely enclose the area you are protecting. If this is not done, the deer may reroute their paths and enter the property from the unprotected direction. They will then be trapped inside the fenced area and, of course, attempt to escape.

Q. *Is it possible for deer to damage the fencing?*

A. If deer suddenly become frightened and do not see the fence and run into it at full speed, they could damage it. This is a very infrequent occurrence, however, and typically happens when the entire area has not been enclosed. In this situation, the deer enter from a portion of the property that has not been fenced, become scared and attempt to escape by running in the other direction and into the barriers.

Virtually no damage to fencing or plant material has been reported by property owners who have completely enclosed the area to be protected.

Here is another solution that never seems to fail; in fact, it's surefire. Tiger dung!

Just pull up at the back door of the tent or arena when the circus comes to town and most trainers or handlers will let you shovel all the dung you want for free. I've been told on absolute authority that no deer will cross a dung line. It's certainly worth a try.

Earthworms, Growing

Q. *The worm box I've had for several years recently developed fruit flies by the millions. I've tried covering the bed with both window screening and newspaper to no avail. Do you have any ideas?*

A. Fruit flies always seem to be attracted to the food scraps that are fed to worms that they in turn are transforming into fabulous compost. For control, be sure your worm box has ample, moist bedding for you to totally bury the scraps each time you put them in the worm box. Since fruit flies tend to stay toward the top of the bedding, this will prevent them from reaching their food source. Placing a thick layer of newspaper over the bedding can make an even more effective barrier. Tear the paper into strips, crumple those strips up and place them on top of the bedding to a depth of at least three to four inches. Don't moisten this layer (like you did the bedding when you started the box), then push the newspaper out of the way when you bury the food scraps in the bedding.

So what about all those fruit flies you already have in your worm box? Be assured that they aren't bothering the worms one bit. However, if you've had it with getting flies up your nose every time you open the worm box, a few rounds with a vacuum cleaner can help reduce the adult fly population immediately.

Another technique: Fruit flies are easily lured into a beer trap; simply nestle a cup of beer or wine into the middle of the worm bed and the flies will drop right into the beer and drown themselves. What a way to go.

February Tips

Stay off your lawn during periods of little or no snow. Excessive traffic will injure frozen turf.

If not already done, order seeds at once. The more planning and preparation you do now, the easier your spring gardening chores will be.

Check mulches placed around plants late last fall to see if they are still in place.

Yearly pruning of fruit trees, especially apples, should be done now through mid-March.

Even though this is a good time to prune, try to keep away from certain trees and wait until they come into full leaf later this spring. These "bleeder" trees are maple, beech,

dogwood, elm and sycamore.

Allow cyclamen, poinsettias and other Christmas flowering plants to bloom as long as they like. Fertilize every 2 to 3 weeks with a liquid food and place in a cool spot for the night.

Now is a good time to make cuttings from geranium stock plants; they will then be ready for setting out in the garden after May 15.

Monitor indoor humidity—most houseplant problems are due to neglect, rather than disease. Low humidity is the big problem in most apartments and houses in winter. This causes leaf drop or browning leaves. Increase air humidity in the room with your plants and it will reduce the problem.

Even when it's cold and bleak outdoors, an impatient gardener knows how to hurry the arrival of spring by forcing out-of-season plants and flowers to brighten dreary winter days and bring a promise of warmer days to come. Forsythia, pussy willow, apple, plum and peach branches are all good candidates for forcing.

Many flower plants sold to be displayed indoors are not worth the effort or space they occupy once their bloom fades and should be discarded. Some, however, like the narcissus, crocus, tulips and hyacinths you forced for the holiday season, can be stored in a cool, dry place until they are replanted in the garden with the rest of your fall bulbs.

Visit garden shops now to see what's available for early planting. Asparagus roots, onion sets and strawberry plants come in about now. And if you're lucky enough to have a greenhouse or cold frame, you should start your seedlings and cuttings now—flowering annuals, beets, tomatoes, celery, leeks, lettuce and onions are good choices—so you'll have a head start on outdoor planting when the threat of frost is over. Keep a fan going in the greenhouse after seedlings begin to poke through the soil, to keep plants from damping off or developing mildew. And don't place fluorescent lights too far above the seedlings or they'll get spindly.

Fern, Boston

Q. *Why do my Boston ferns always look pale and scraggly, with hardly any new fronds?*

A. Sounds like a face-lift is needed! Cut off all dead growth. Transplant to fresh soil using a mixture of two parts sphagnum peat moss to one each of packaged, all-purpose potting soil, coarse vermiculite and clean, sharp sand (or perlite). Check to be sure your ferns are receiving bright light or even a little direct sun. During the winter heating season, be sure to protect from drafts of hot, dry air; temperatures on the cool side, say into the 50s at night, up to around 70 on a sunny day, are ideal in the winter. During the spring and summer, make regular applications of an all-organic fertilizer such as fish emulsion. You should also inspect your ferns for any signs of insects, such as the cottony white mealybug or brown scale; the latter forms a raised bump, oval-shaped and about ⅛-inch long, that is juicy if you squeeze it. Spray at weekly intervals with insecticidal soap.

Ficus Tree

Q. *Why is my* Ficus benjamina *suddenly losing lots of leaves? It's been growing in the same spot for almost a year, and this is the first sign of trouble.*

A. It's entirely possible that nothing is wrong with your tree; the healthiest ficus in the world has to have a little rest during the course of a year. Leaf drop such as you describe often precedes a period of active new growth. The main thing is not to panic when a ficus starts dropping leaves. Check the soil; it should feel moist. When you water a ficus, be sure that the entire ball of earth in the container is moistened. If water remains in the saucer, pour it off after an hour or two (if the tree is too heavy to move, use a bulb baster from the kitchen to suck off the excess water). There are other problems that could result in leaf loss; these include use of the tree's soil by a cat as a litter box, a reduction in the amount of light it has grown accustomed to, or letting the soil become bone-dry or too wet.

Fireside Gardening

After the holidays, millions of home gardeners review their successes and failures of the previous year. When you're sitting by the fire looking out at the winter scenery, surround yourself with as many gardening catalogs as possible.

Most of the people who order from seed catalogs grow flowers as well as vegetables. In winter the days are short, the skies are bleak and the weather is usually cold. But a home gardener can look out the same window over the same ground and see his or her garden for all the four seasons.

Gray days simply fade away for gardeners who start annuals indoors in winter. So once you've decided what flowers and vegetables you are going to grow in your garden, it's best to quickly order the desired seeds.

Before ordering from a catalog, take time to read the descriptions inside. These helpful guides are designed to give all sorts of details to aid you in selecting the best seed and plant varieties for a more productive and successful garden. You must always plant for the area you live in.

Try to use all the seeds you order within a year. It's best not to save leftover seed, as this almost always results in poor germination.

Fish Fertilizer

Q. *What is fish fertilizer?*

A. Fish fertilizer is an all-natural, organic concentrate made from oceangoing fish. It contains all the nutrients that plants need for healthy growth—nitrogen, phosphorus, potassium—and 19 trace elements, including copper, zinc and iron. It also includes 11 vitamins and folic acid.

Q. *How does fish fertilizer improve the soil?*

A. Fish fertilizer is a naturally slow-releasing organic fertilizer that clings to soil particles through microorganisms in the soil. The plant can then feed itself naturally. Fish fertilizer also promotes soil activity, builds humus content and encourages earthworms to populate the soil.

Q. *With a name like "fish fertilizer" doesn't it smell fishy?*

A. Fish fertilizer is made from seagoing fish. This results in a product with a less offensive smell. Fish fertilizer is deodorized to keep the smell to a minimum. Garden tests in which fish fertilizer has been diluted at the proper rate indicate the odor dissipates within 24 hours after fertilizing.

Flower-Buying Tips for Men

Trying to make an impression on someone special? Here are a few tips on the ins and outs of flowers and romance.

First date: A mixed bouquet of soft, romantic and fragrant flowers—freesia, godetia, white roses, anemones and seeded eucalyptus.

You're special: After six months of dating, send the same type of flowers you sent her on the first date.

I'm sorry: Roses, or a big bouquet of her favorite flowers.

Anniversary: Red roses, one for every year of marriage, or have the florist re-create her bridal bouquet.

A marriage proposal: An all-white bouquet of flowers associated with weddings, including some fragrant flowers—gardenia, dendrobium orchids, stephanotis and ivy (symbols of fidelity and happiness in marriage).

Color: Softer pastel shades of pink and purple rank highest among women.

Scent: Make sure the bouquet contains several exceptionally fragrant flowers, such as lilies, freesias, gardenia or jasmine.

Flowering Maple

Q. *How do you control whiteflies on flowering maple without hurting the plant's leaves? I've found the plant doesn't take soap sprays very well.*

A. Whiteflies can really devastate flowering maples *(Abutilon)*. I suggest you spray with neem, which will stop the insects' life cycle, and alternate sprayings with an insecticide such as pyrethrum or acephate (orthene) to control the adult whiteflies. You could also alternate with an insecticide soap, which shouldn't cause trouble with the plants if it's applied as directed.

Be sure that the temperature is between 60° and 85°F when you apply the product. When using homemade soap sprays, don't use dish soaps containing harsh grease-cutting compounds, and don't make too strong a mixture.

In addition, sticky yellow squares or strips placed close to the plant's canopy will also help draw and trap adult whiteflies.

It's true that flowering maples can react to soap sprays, so neem may be a better choice.

Flowers, a Stylish Addition to the Home

Spring bulb flowers are smile-makers: a great pleasure, a lovely self-indulgence and not expensive.

Pick up a bunch of tulips on the way home or when visiting a friend after work. When a florist's window catches your eye, duck in and buy a chunky potted blue hyacinth. Get your loved one a jaunty potted daffodil—it'll last for several weeks. Add a vase to your breakfast table—a single stem of a fragrant lily puts one in a good mood.

Why now?

In Europe, cut flowers are a part of daily life, a weekly purchase all year round, but too often cut flowers here are seen as rare treats for special occasions. That's so ridiculous! A bunch of tulips costs maybe $7 to $10—there must be millions of Americans who spend that much weekly on junk food.

Wouldn't more Americans find flowers of interest if we could buy them in more places? With better quality and more affordable prices? I think so.

Recent market research shows that approximately 45 million U.S. households now purchase flowers at least once a month, up from 31 million a decade ago. Part of the reason for the increase may be the larger role that supermarkets and mass merchandisers now play in cut-flower demand.

In the case of tulips and other bulb flowers, a big factor is that more professional growers in America are growing and supplying local markets with a greater variety and volume of cut and potted bulb flowers, especially during their peak season.

For shoppers, peak seasons are the best time to buy many fresh products—whether spring flowers or summer melons—because that's when you get the most varieties, best quality and best prices.

For cut and potted tulips, daffodils and other spring bulbs, the peak season is January through May; for lilies, May through September; for irises, May through June.

Fluorescent-Light Garden

Q. *What is meant by the term "fluorescent-light garden"?*

A. Good question. The answer is: any table or shelf over which is placed a commercial or industrial reflector having two or more fluorescent tubes. These may be 20, 30, 40, or 74 watts, ranging in length from 24 inches to 36 inches to 48 inches to 96 inches, respectively. Two tubes in a reflector will light a growing space 12 inches to 18 inches below, approximately 18 inches to 24 inches wide and as long as the tubes. For good general growth of foliage and flowering plants, as well as for starting seeds and bulbs, most fluorescent-light gardeners use an automatic timer set for 14 to 16 hours of light out of every 24. Fluorescent-light gardens can be installed as part of a wall-storage system, taking the place of books on some shelves; they are also available in stacks of shelves so that it is possible to have four shelves of plants from floor to ceiling in an area that might otherwise be dreary or wasted, such as at the end of a dark hallway..

Forcing Branches

Cut some dogwood, forsythia, or quince branches and put them in a large vase filled with warm water. Springtime will get an early start.

Place bouquets of flowering branches inside the front door to greet visitors or on the dining room table as an interesting centerpiece.

Selecting the Branches:

Whether you fill every room in your house with flowering plants or limit your indoor garden to select window sills, the plants you choose and how you arrange them can make all the difference in the satisfaction they provide.

Since flowers and attractive foliage are the primary goal, you should know what to expect of a plant before you choose one. If colorful flowers are your objective, branches cut from forsythia, flowering quince and daphne are some of the best choices. In as few as two weeks, forced buds formed on last year's branches will produce an array of vibrant blossoms ranging in color from yellow to pink. Trees and shrubs that flower early in spring are generally the easiest to force.

Forced branches from budless trees and shrubs such as Japanese maple, however, will produce only leaves. Plants such as these should not be overlooked for forcing, though, as bountiful green foliage creates a vibrant atmosphere in any room of the home.

Remember to consider the shape and size of branches when selecting plants for forcing. Choose branches that have an attractive yet suitable shape for transplanting indoors. Plants that are too large and cumbersome for limited indoor space will appear awkward and overgrown, detracting from the beauty of the home rather than enhancing it.

Transplanting:

Like people, branches need to feel at home. Transplanted branches need an environment with appropriate temperatures, light, water and humidity to provide desired blooms and leaves. Although plants are highly adaptable, the closer you can come to creating the environment that each plant finds ideal, the more they will flourish and blossom.

Cut branches such as mock orange, kerria and pussy willow have a high success rate when transplanted and forced indoors. No longer subject to high winds, driving rain, or wide-ranging temperatures, plants will thrive in the consistent and stable conditions of their new home. For instance, plants receive a regular supply of food and water, while the threat of disease and insects is reduced.

Technique:

The first step for successful forcing is careful stem-end preparation. Make several 2-inch to 3-inch cuts up the stem from its base to increase plant cell exposure and maximize their absorption capacity.

Damaged or smashed stems severely diminish the number of plant cells available for water and nutrient absorption, which results in limited blooms. Crushed stems are also displeasing to the eye when placed around the home in floral arrangements.

Once stems have been cut, branches need to soak in a warm-water bath for two to three hours. Soaking the branches softens winter bark formed around buds to protect future blooms from cold weather and other harsh elements. A warm soak also removes excess dirt and debris. Clean, soft buds and branches facilitate the forcing process and minimize stress on blooms and leaves.

Now ready for the final phase of forcing, prepared branches should be placed in a container of water and set in a room with a constant temperature of 65° to 75° F. Water branches as necessary and continue to mist buds to prevent dehydration and hardness. This "greenhouse" effect along with minimal maintenance will produce vibrant and colorful flowers and leaves in one to five weeks.

Once branches begin to bloom, arrange flowers and plants as desired. Forced leaves and blossoms can be kept healthy and fresh-looking with daily fresh lukewarm water in the vase.

Homeowners will delight as they see the fruits of their labor blossom before their eyes. Simple to do and easy to care for, forcing branches results in endless combinations of indoor flowering bouquets limited only by the gardener's imagination.

Fragrance

Q. *What are your favorite plants and flowers for fragrance?*

A. For bouquets: roses, peonies, lilies, lilacs and freesias. In plants: the sweet olive *(Osmanthus fragrans)*, scented-leafed geraniums (mint, rose, nutmeg, apple, lemon, coconut and many others), *Lavandula dentata* (a lavender that grows better indoors than the hardy type), gardenia, citrus, bulbs (narcissus, daffodils, hyacinths), jasmine, hoya, lemon verbena and some cyclamen, even in the new mini-varieties.

Fuchsias

Q. *Is it possible to grow fuchsias indoors?*

A. Yes, but only if you have a space that might be called a garden room, sun porch or greenhouse. Fuchsias demand fresh, circulating air, not too warm, not too cold, bright light and some direct sun—but again, not too much or the leaves will burn, not too little or there'll be no flowers. One somewhat less finicky variety is the honeysuckle fuchsia *(Gartenmeister Bohnstedt)*, which can be a nearly ever-blooming greenhouse shrub.

If you were wondering how to handle summer hanging baskets of fuchsias through the winter, here's the procedure: bring indoors before frost; reduce watering so that the soil is damp but neither moist, wet, nor dry; withhold all fertilizer; cut back all stems 6 inches to 8 inches from the soil; set in bright light (sun if you have the space) or in a dark place—in cool temperatures, say around 50°F. The idea is to keep the fuchsias alive but hibernating until about March, at which time they need more warmth, full sun and that fresh, circulating air we talked about earlier—in other words, the "works"—to bring on strong new shoots and blooms by June.

Geraniums

Q. *How come my geraniums grow lots and lots of leaves but produce no flowers?*

A. They need to go on a diet of little or no nitrogen, more phosphorus and potash (a 5-15-15 fertilizer, for example, or one with a similar ratio); you might even try one of the fertilizers made specifically for geraniums. Also, be sure that your geraniums are receiving at least a half-day or more of full, direct sun, and that nighttime temperatures drop at least ten degrees.

Geraniums, Scented

Outdoor uses: Traditionally grown as houseplants, scented geraniums are also useful in the garden. In frost-free areas, they may be treated like ordinary perennials and renewed from cuttings *only* when the plant grows too woody. In northern zones they should be planted in containers (tubs, pots, etc.) and over-wintered indoors, or otherwise treated like annuals. Scented geraniums are marvelous placed on a sunny porch or terrace. The heat of the sun releases their perfume (which ranges from rose-scented to spicy to pungent) and fills the air with titillating fragrances. An open-air potpourri! These lovely plants are a cinch to raise; they require almost no effort with the exception of a very few cultivars.

Culture: Soil, equal parts of a good garden soil, peat moss and sand, with proper drainage.

Watering: Only when soil surface dries.

Harvesting: Dry leaves for potpourris. Drying should be rapid to prevent molds. Remove leafstalks and spread out leaf blades to dry. Leaf blades should never overlap.

Light: As much sun as possible. Keep them cool, preferably not above 70°F.

Disease or pests: Scented geraniums are not bothered much by either, since most diseases are caused by too much moisture. To discourage fungi (disease) during mid-winter, avoid poor ventilation and dampness. Propagation is best done by stem cuttings.

SOURCES: *Logee's Greenhouses, 55 North Street, Danielson, Connecticut, 06239. Well-Sweet Herb Farm, 317 Mt. Bethel Road, Port Murray, New Jersey, 07865.*

Q. *I enjoy the fragrance of scented geraniums, but they turn black at the base and on the stems; then wilt and die.*

Could you tell me how to properly care for them and what is causing them to turn black and die?

A. Scented-leafed geraniums are grown for their aromatic leaves that can be fruity, spicy, floral or pungently scented.

Grow scented geraniums in full sun and in a lean sandy soil and allow the soil to dry between waterings. Keep the plants warm, but give them cooler, drier conditions during winter. Cool nights are needed to promote flowering during the winter through spring months.

Since most scented geraniums do not tolerate high humidity or frequent rainfall, move the plants indoors during the summer.

The black stems, wilt and plant death are caused by a crown rot, which causes the plant's growth to stop, lower leaves to yellow and foliage color to pale. Eventually the plant will wilt and die. Sunken, brown areas can be seen at the ground line at the advanced stages of the disease.

Usually the plant can be salvaged from cuttings taken from uninfected growth. A systemic fungicide may also help prevent crown rot.

This disease results from the plant being exposed to excess moisture either through watering or wetting of foliage. If you can locate the plants where they are exposed to warm, dry air during summer, the disease shouldn't be a problem.

Gerbera Daisies

Q. *My gerbera daisies have a white growth on the leaves, and older leaves have turned brown. Should I be concerned?*

A. Yes, you should be concerned, but don't become alarmed. The white growth is powdery mildew, a common disease during the spring and fall months. You shouldn't have to worry about it during the summer, but if it appears again spray the plants with a fungicide such as terraguard or fine sulfur.

Although it's normal for gerbera daisies to drop their lower leaves, the situation you described is not normal. This is particularly true since the new growth is starting to pale.

The combination of symptoms you describe could signal that the plants are succumbing to a crown-rot disease.

If the gerberas arc mulched, move the mulch away from the plant's crown. If you've been watering to keep the soil moist, allow it to dry a little more between waterings.

Germination of Seeds, Indoors

Once you know germination requirements for the seeds you wish to plant, all you have to do is find a good location around your house for germinating almost any type of seed. Many tiny seeds like steady warmth, so for best results I suggest the top of a refrigerator; it's given me great results. Another ideal spot is under a grow-lamp, though a countertop in your bathroom or kitchen works well, too, if these rooms are kept warm. The use of a heating cable, one strand under each tray, can provide bottom heat for speeding the germination of warmth-loving seeds. These cables come in various lengths, with or without thermostats. Other seeds like a cool spot. A cold frame or raised protected bed outdoors during cool weather, an attic in winter, or a closed room (during cold weather), or a basement or a north-facing windowsill, all have worked marvelously well for me. These locations can also be used to satisfy any initial chilling or freezing that is required by a specific type (this fact appears on the seed packet). Of course, your freezer or refrigerator can do the same. Once seeds have been sown, check the moisture of your planting medium daily; if it feels dry, sprinkle the top gently, or better still, water from the bottom with water at room temperature. Allow the water to soak up until the surface becomes moist, for a constant moderate degree of moisture.

Keep your seed trays out of direct sunlight, which is often too hot and drying, until the seeds have emerged. Then be sure to furnish additional light. The baby plant embryo then breaks out of its seed coat, and the first stem rises out of the soil. The first leaves that appear on most seedlings are the so-called seed leaves (cotyledons) which often bear little resemblance to the later leaves. Shortly after the first true leaves (which are more or less typical of the plant) appear, the seed leaves will drop off—don't worry when this happens; it's a natural procedure. With some types of plants like lilies and corn, the first part to appear is a true leaf that will continue growing.

Growing on to garden-size plants may take only a week or it may take several months depending on what you're sowing. Your seed packet instructions and cultural index on most seed catalogs will give you detailed information about each variety of plant.

Watering: After your seedlings are established with healthy roots spreading through the Pro-Mix, they will need a drier medium and less frequent but more concentrated feedings. Let the surface Pro-Mix become dry to the touch between waterings (lower layers should never be allowed to dry out). Fertilize once a week, increasing the dosage to ½ teaspoon per gallon of water.

Pinching: If plants get too tall before planting time (outdoors), pinch them back. Leave plenty of foliage and some branches so growth can continue, but pinch off just above a lower leaf or branch. A small pair of pruning shears does a better job than fingers!

Suggestion: Sow your seeds in "Park starts" (available from Park Seed Co.). They are the product of the most up-to-date plant-growing practices and will enable you to grow strong healthy seedlings with minimum effort.

Germination Problems

Q. *Each winter, I start many vegetable seeds indoors under lights. They grow in a soilless germinating mix, in a warm room, after germination. The lights are only a few inches above the tops of the seedlings. Even though the seedlings grow straight initially, they flop over before they straighten themselves out, leaving a crook in the stem. What's wrong?*

A. For seedlings to grow properly, keep the lights on for 16 hours a day. Even though the lights may be only a few inches from the seedlings, and if you haven't changed the fluorescent bulbs in several years, the light quality and intensity may have diminished so much that the baby seedlings aren't getting enough to grow straight and strong.

Seedlings placed in a 72°F room will grow swiftly but produce weak, spindly stems that are more likely than not to fall over. Also, if you don't plant the seeds deep enough the roots aren't growing far enough down in the soil to support the stems.

Plant broccoli, tomatoes and eggplants ½-inch deep, while peppers should be planted ¼-inch deep. Always check the depth of the seeds after watering, since soil washes away from the seeds, leaving them shallower than they were originally planted. It is best to water seedlings from the bottom of the pot.

Gloxinia

Q. *How should I care for a gloxinia received in bloom?*

A. Keep the soil evenly moist and place the plant where it receives bright light but not much direct sun. When the last blooms fade, discard the plant—unless of course you're a serious indoor gardener or would like to be, in which case follow this procedure. Place the gloxinia in a half-sunny window or 5 inches directly beneath the tubes in a fluorescent-light garden. When there are no more flower buds, set the plant away to rest in a dark place at moderate temperatures (60–70°F); the old leaves will wither and dry, at which time they can be removed. After a rest of 8 to 12 weeks, bring back to a sunny, warm, humid window or light garden; resume watering, and when growth becomes active, begin regular applications of fertilizer. You can propagate gloxinias from leaf cuttings, just like the related African violet, or from tip shoots; in either case, a mixture of equal parts sphagnum peat moss and coarse vermiculite (or clean, sharp sand) makes a surefire rooting medium.

Greenhouse, Best and Worst Crops

Excellent: Leaf lettuce, Swiss chard, spinach, celery, mustard greens, cress, basil, fennel, parsley, to name a few.

Good: Leeks, green onions, cherry tomatoes. I think they are worth the effort.

Poor: Corn, carrots, melons, squash, beans. These crops are best grown in the garden.

To eliminate disease and weed problems when starting seeds, use a Pro-Mix commercial soil.

Groundhogs Predict Sun, Fun and Flowers

As most Americans know, Groundhog Day is February 2. It's on this day—during the dreary winter season when many people are craving warmer weather—that the chubby rodents from all around the United States are called upon to predict either an early or late spring on the basis of their shadows.

If a groundhog emerges from his burrow on a sunny day and sees his shadow, the legend goes, it's six more weary weeks of winter. However, if the day is overcast or stormy and he doesn't see his shadow, spring is just around the corner.

Recently, Groundhog Day has been growing in reputation and popularity, perhaps inspired by the successful 1993 movie *Groundhog Day*. Many people are turning the day from a passing curiosity into a cause for personal celebration. And why not?

As Americans seek new occasions to celebrate (just look at what's happened to Halloween!), Groundhog Day is emerging as the newest seasonal occasion to generate some extra fun. So let your imagination go wild! Another activity coming to the fore is the exchange of colorful flowers, especially tulips, everyone's favorite—the symbol of spring.

In America, tulip sales have begun to climb during the weeks before and after the groundhog's big day. Giving tulips in celebration of spring seems to be catching on. On dreary winter days, who doesn't get high from bunches of vivid red, yellow, orange, pink or pastel flowers? They provide instant fragrance and an early promise of spring. They lift the spirit!

The Groundhog Day celebration is rooted in European lore. According to legend, if the weather was fair on the mid-winter feast day of Candlemas, winter would return in force. But if Candlemas proved a dreary day, then spring would come early that year. It is likely that the Roman legions, during their northern European campaigns, carried this tradition to Germany. It was there that the marmot and shadow were added.

Preserved from generation to generation, the idea was eventually exported to America along with German immigrants. Here it survives to this day as an event increasingly important on the calendar of every fun-loving person!

Herbs as Living History

The herb garden is truly a magic spot that has satisfied the spirit and soul of many people down through the ages.

Although the discovery and first uses of herbs are unknown, it is believed that they have been used for centuries throughout the world for a multitude of purposes. When herbs were first added to food, it may have seemed like magic that such a tiny bit of leaves could cause such fabulous changes in flavors.

Herbs must have appeared to possess special powers, and it is no wonder that they quickly became the stuff of myth, magic and ritual. Here are some facts:

The first written record of the use of herbs goes back to the time when the pyramids of Egypt were being built, more than 4,000 years ago. The ancient Egyptians used herbs for medicinal purposes, in religious ceremonies and for cosmetic benefits. In fact, wreaths of basil have been found in the pyramids' burial chambers.

Early civilizations such as those in China, India and Egypt used herbs in their daily lives to flavor food and for medicinal purposes. Greek athletes celebrated victories with crowns of bay and parsley. In India, native ginger was used not only to flavor and preserve food but to treat digestive problems.

Early uses of herbs also involved perfumes, deodorants and fumigants. The ancient Romans revered in scenting their baths with lavender and other aromatic herbs.

In the time of Charlemagne, the floors of stone castles were strewn with fragrant herbs (known as strewing herbs), and gentlemen carried herbal nosegays to clear their nostrils of the unpleasant odors they encountered daily.

Herbs have been used in literature for centuries. With the Renaissance and the advent of printing mania, many collections of herbal lore were written. "There's Rosemary, that's for remembrance," Shakespeare reminds us with the line from *Hamlet*.

When the colonization of the New World began, herbs accompanied the first settlers, who fell back on reliable remedies and flavorings from their distant homeland.

Many plants used by American Indians proved helpful and were gladly adopted by the settlers. Every homestead had an herb garden, and carefully packed seeds were carried westward.

You can almost say that herbs have governed our lives. Today herbs are widely available to everyone and are prized for their aromatic, culinary and medicinal uses. Herbs are a delight for the senses, bringing color, fragrance and freshness to every place they're used.

Herbs can add a new dimension to ordinary dishes and complement exotic food, and few things match the fun of gardening when combined with the pleasure of flavoring a meal or scenting the house with an herb you have grown in your own garden.

Herbs, Growing Indoors

It's easy to grow many varieties of herbs indoors. Here are some with the best track record:

Parsley: Sow seeds in a deep container since the plant has a long taproot and needs some extra space. Germination is slow, 9 to 21 days. Harvest by cutting the outer leaves; the plant grows from the center. Parsley likes full sun in an east or west window.

Chives: It's best to separate a section of an established plant because it takes too long to grow a cultivatable clump from seed or buy a new small cluster for your indoor garden. For best growing conditions, put them in a sunny window.

Sage: Easily grown from tip cuttings. It can tolerate dryness and warmer daytime temperatures better than other herbs. Place sage in a south window.

Thyme: Start new plants by placing non-woody cuttings in a moist, sterile mix until roots appear, then pot up in a Pro-Mix commercial soil. If you pot a garden-grown thyme plant for the winter, check carefully for insects before moving indoors. Thyme likes full sun but will grow in an east or west window.

Bay: This herb grows beautifully in a container and can be trained into a standard. Bay will thrive in an east or west window. A slow grower, it's dormant in winter and requires less watering than other herbs, so water only when the top of the soil is dry. This herb is really a small tree that can grow 5 feet tall in a pot. When you see roots coming out of the drainage hole, it's time to put it in a larger container.

Rosemary: Never let rosemary plants dry out completely or they'll die, especially in winter when the plant begins to produce new growth. Water well, but as with all plants be sure they drain properly. Propagate by cutting or layering to produce plants faster than growing from seed. Rosemary loves a southern exposure.

Holly

Q. *I had a nursery plant a holly tree last year. The new holly had red berries when the men planted it, but the berries turned black and fell off. I called the nursery, and they promised to look at it but never showed up. What is wrong?*

A. Your tree is lovesick—she needs a boyfriend. A holly tree must have a male counterpart for pollination. The male trees are pollen-bearing and never have berries. Only the trees with the female flowers will fruit. I suggest you go right out, purchase a male holly tree and plant it next to the pining female. You should have berries next year.

A Holly Fan, by George!

George Washington was a horticulturist, and is said to have liked holly. He recorded in his diary that, in the early part of 1785, he spent several days planting holly trees at Mount Vernon. Washington's set of false teeth was reported to have been made of the hard, grained holly wood.

Houseplants

Shower houseplants with tepid water once a month to keep the leaves shiny clean and to discourage insects. At the same time, remove old flowers and dead leaves.

Plants that are resting should be kept damp and without fertilizer; it's good for their diets. Pinch off the yellow leaves—new ones are on the way.

Q. *How often should houseplants be misted, syringed or washed under a spigot?*

A. Keep in mind that hairy-leafed or fuzzy-leafed plants such as gloxinias, African violets and streptocarpus (Cape primrose) are prone to getting ugly water marks on their leaves if you mist or syringe them with cold water, so use lukewarm water at all times. Glossy-leafed plants, however, do splendidly with a monthly sponging or syringing, but washing with a spigot full out can drown any plant!

Q. *How can I prevent pests from getting a start on my houseplants?*

A. Make it a habit to inspect all plants weekly. Plants that are infested with bugs must be segregated. Pick off all dead flowers and leaves—these are great hiding places for pests. Sponge with soap and lukewarm water at monthly intervals to check for such deadly pests as red spider, mealybugs and scale. Segregate any new plants initially and promptly throw out all plants that simply cannot be saved.

Q. *How does one go about getting the tiny, sticky, hairlike seeds of the African violets or calceolaria from their packets into the dirt of started pots? I'm all thumbs.*

A. Tear open the packet and use a pair of tweezers to pull out the seeds gently. This is the surest way not to lose any.

Q. *The new leaves on my potted plants sometimes turn a light green and stay small. What can I do to stop this?*

A. This is probably due to lack of food. Nutrients can be dissolved by too much water or poor drainage. Although plants need water to survive, the roots need air, too. If the soil is kept too wet, the air spaces fill up with water and the weakened roots can easily die. Plants with diseased roots do not absorb as much water as they did when they were healthy, so the soil stays wet and the plants cannot get the nutrients they need to thrive. Discard severely wilted plants and those without white root tips. Do not water less severely affected plants until the soil is barely moist. To prevent the problem, pot plants in a light soil with good drainage.

Q. *What kind of houseplants do well with hardly any direct sun?*

A. That depends upon the temperature you maintain. Hot, dry rooms will kill any-thing, but if the temperature is moderate and you have fair humidity, you can grow ferns, ivy, aspidistra, snake plants, rubber plants, philodendrons, many large-leafed begonias as well as tropical foliage plants and bromeliads. Keep your night temperature down to 55°F if possible and your plants will stay vigorous. Remember that hot or cold drafts will make plants lose leaves and buds.

Q. *Are there any houseplants a beginning gardener can raise from seed?*

A. Raising houseplants from seed is a rewarding hobby. With very little expense and a small amount of time, you can have all sorts of delightful varieties of plants in every size (stan-dards, miniatures), shape, color and fragrance. African violets, aloe (mixed species), cactus, cineraria, fuchsias, geraniums, gerbera, gloxinias, impatiens, kalanchoe, primula, wax begonias and other flowering plants can all be started from seed. Be sure to use plant markers to keep the names straight.

Q. *What should I feed my plants and how often?*

A. Most plants need additional food in periods of major growth as well as feeding every three to four weeks in periods when growth slows down. Fertilize with an all-pur-pose plant food that contains equal quantities of the three nutrients most needed: nitrogen (to prevent stunted growth and yellowing of leaves), phosphates (to develop a root system and promote luxurious flowers) and potash (to strengthen stems and promote bloom), vital in making plants resistant to diseases.

Q. *I'd like to buy a gift for an avid gardener. Are there any special tools you'd recom-mend?*

A. These are what I consider the essential tools for indoor gardening. Put them in a basket, tie on a cheery bow and you have the perfect present.

- Hand fork, for loosening soil around potted plants.
- Light trowel, for transplanting.
- Tweezers, for pulling tiny seeds out of packets and catching pests.
- Alcohol and cotton swabs, for hairy-leafed plants and to control mealybugs.
- Sponge, for cleaning foliage.

- Sprayer and duster (camel-hair brush), for applying pesticides.
- Safer Agro-Chem's Insecticidal Soap, for controlling whiteflies, spider mites, aphids, mealybugs (use only on ornamental houseplants).
- Twist-Ems, for tying and staking.
- Plant Markers, for identifying varieties.

Remember, clean and wipe your tools with an oily cloth after using. Then store in a high place away from tiny hands.

Q. *Are there any common houseplants that bloom in the winter?*

A. African violets, wax begonias and shrimp plants give constant bloom. Paperwhite narcissus and French-Roman hyacinths can be started for succession and are long-lasting. Also try scented geraniums, amaryllis, jasmine, azaleas and chrysanthemums. If there is sun, tree-form geraniums or lantanas make a handsome grouping. For most flowering plants, sunshine is the key. Of course, many lovely pre-potted bulbs available at garden centers are especially cultivated to bloom at Christmastime, such as amaryllis, narcissus, hyacinths and crocuses. These fragrant bulbs will last several weeks and require only a little watering.

Q. *What are the best containers for all types of houseplants?*

A. Most plants grow well in both clay and plastic pots as long as cultural care is satisfactory. Plants in plastic pots need less water than those in clay. During the hot, sultry months (July and August), plants potted in clay dry out fast, especially if they're sitting in direct sun. They may need two daily waterings—morning and evening—to survive wilting and heat stress. Whatever type of container you use, be sure there are drainage holes in the bottom.

Q. *What houseplants need the least attention? I'd like to have the green of plants in my home, but I don't want to spend a lot of time caring for them.*

A. The following plants grow easily indoors: spider plants, grape ivy, cast-iron plant, dracaenas, philodendron, piggyback plant, ferns, ponytail, snake plant, jade plant, lipstick vine, wandering Jew and wax plant.

Here are some simple steps to ensure that your indoor plants remain healthy.

Basic watering: Always water thoroughly and deeply, until it runs out the bottom of the pot or container. Empty the saucer of excess water. For pots 5 inches in diameter or less, water again when the surface feels dry to the touch. For larger containers, water when it feels dry 1 inch below the surface.

Temperatures: Temperatures are all-important. A nighttime temperature from 65° to 70°F is perfect to keep plants healthy. Temperatures typically rise 10 degrees during the day.

Light requirements: Low light examples: 10 feet, or more, away from a window where there's no direct light, or directly in a north window with obstructions, or in a hallway.

Medium light examples: 4 to 10 feet away from an east, south or west window, or directly in front of an unobstructed north window.

High light examples: 4 feet or less from unobstructed south, east or west windows. Bright direct light or sunlight.

Houseplants, Individual Care

Aglaonema (Chinese evergreen). Low light. Warm temperatures (70°F). Keep dust off leaves. Can grow directly in water. Propagates easily by cutting stems into pieces. Watch for scale and mealybugs. For control, spray with an all-natural insecticide soap, according to directions on the label.

Araucaria heterophylla (Norfolk Island pine). High light (turn plant frequently). Prefers cool temperature, but tolerates 65° to 70°F temperatures. Do not remove terminal tip. Be wary of an invasion of mites.

Asparagus densiflorus Sprengeri (asparagus fern). High light. Cool night room temperatures (55° to 60°F). Likes additional humidity. Best as a filler and good for planters. Keep soil evenly moist.

Aspidistra elatior (cast-iron plant). Low light. Temperature not critical, just keep dust off leaves. Good filler plant in a grouping or small floor specimen.

Brassaia actinophylla (schefflera). Medium light. Warm room temperatures (70° to 75°F). Does best being pot-bound. Keep leaves free of dust. Accent plant in planters or large specimen. Spider mites can frequently be a problem; a natural spray for mite control is the key.

Chlorophytum comosum (spider plant). Bright light and average house temperatures are required for proper growth. Plantlets form from runners, making this a spectacular hanging specimen. Short days during fall are necessary to initiate runner formation on stubborn plants. Do not overpot or allow your plant to dry out.

Chrysalidocarpus lutescens (areca palm). Medium indirect light, normal room temperature. Keep soil barely moist. Repot infrequently (may slow down growth, but so what). Grows tall fast and can be pruned back. Most graceful of palms, but intolerant of low light. Examine periodically for spider mites and then spray for control.

Cissus rhombifolia (grape ivy). Medium light, but easily conditioned to low-light situations. Prefers cooler room temperature, but tolerates higher. Keep leaves free of dust and avoid overwatering; soil should be kept barely moist. Never let the plant dry out.

Crassula argentea (jade plant). High or medium light. Prefers cool temperature (55° to 65°F). Will not put up with overwatering. Can be cut back and easily propagated in many ways. Ideal for planters and pots of all varieties, sizes and shapes. Keep away from drafts. It is normal for this plant to lose its lower leaves sporadically. Poisonous to humans and animals, so take care, especially with children.

Dieffenbachia (dumb cane). Medium to high light, warm indoor temperatures (65° to 75°F). Will not tolerate overwatering. Can be cut back and easily propagated in many ways. Keep away from drafts. Just like the jade plant, it's normal for this plant to lose its lower leaves sporadically. Poisonous to humans and animals, so again I say, take care.

Dracaena fragrans 'Massangeana' (corn plant). Culture same as for *Dracaena deremensis,* but will produce only one side when cut back. Grows fast and very large.

Dracaena marginata. Medium light. Normal room temperature (60° to 65°F) at night. Accent plant. Develops into large specimen, but rarely branches.

Epipremnum aureum (pothos). Medium light, but will tolerate lower although loses colorful leaf markings. Warm room temperature (70°F). Although a hanging plant, it can be trained into many interesting forms, so let your imagination run wild.

Ficus benjamina (weeping fig). Normal room temperature (65°F), medium to high light. Any variation to lower light will trigger leaf drop. Prune carefully in March, and avoid fluctuations with watering—keep soil evenly moist.

Hedera helix (English ivy). Prefers high or medium light, but will survive low light. Low temperature (45° to 55°F) will control mite attacks. Syringe frequently to remove dust accumulating on leaves.

Philodendron scandens (heart-leaf philodendron). Low to medium light. Warm night temperature (70°F). If grown on a totem, try to keep sphagnum moss moist. Never hesitate cutting the plant back. Propagates easily from leaf or tip cuttings. Useful as a hanging or trellis plant and as a ground cover in planters. One of the most adaptable group of plants for indoor life.

Phoenix roebelenii (pygmy date palm). High light. Thrives in normal room temperatures. Encourage a winter rest period (50° to 55°F) and keep the soil evenly moist, but never soggy. Repot every two to three years, using a Pro-Mix professional soil. Feed regularly. This plant requires a winter rest period. Watch for spines along the main branches.

Pteris (brake or table fern). Medium to low light, low night temperature (50° to 55°F). Keep soil moist. There are many species and varieties of dwarf ferns. I recommend them for their slow growth and adaptability to the home. They are the perfect houseplant.

Sansevieria trifasciata (snake plant). Low to medium light. Normal room temperatures. Use in dish gardens or as multiple specimens. Overwatering and drafts are the only known problems. Overwatering rots the roots.

Spathiphyllum. Low light (will flower in medium light). Provide warm room temperature and no drafts. Great filler plants for planters. Never allow the soil to dry excessively. An exceptionally good houseplant, large- and small-leafed varieties among the best.

Houseplants, Problem-Solving

Indoor plants have become a part of the décor for homes, offices, churches and public buildings. With this surge of popularity, problems inevitably come up.

Light problems. Find out what level of light intensity your plant requires for adequate growth. Ask yourself: How close is the plant to the window; does the window face north, south, east or west; do trees shade the house or does an overhang, porch, tree, or awning shade the window?

Water problems. Ask yourself about the watering techniques being used: how much; how often; how large is the pot; is there a drainage hole in the container; what type of soil is used; is the water allowed to accumulate and remain in the saucer? Carefully examine the roots, soil and drainage conditions. You can tell if the plant has been overwatered by smelling the soil. If it's musty, you know it should be dried out. And if the roots don't cover the whole soil ball, it's evident that watering may be the problem. If a plant has been overwatered, the roots will be rotted, brown-tipped, sparse and present only at the top of the soil ball. If underwatered, the soil may be powder dry and live roots will only be on the top of the soil ball. This is because there isn't enough moisture in the lower portion of the ball to sustain growth.

Temperature problems. Don't take it for granted that the temperature remains constant in all parts of your home. Fluctuations can cause foliage or growth problems. Most foliage plants require temperatures around 60°F for best growth and maintenance. Hot drafts from heat registers, radiators or blowers can dry out plants or cause watering problems due to varying conditions of drying. Cold drafts from open doors, windows or air-conditioning vents can also damage plants. Plants are like people, they hate drafts.

Humidity problems. Most large foliage plants are grown from one to two years in greenhouses or humid, shaded areas. These plants are then put into a house with restricted humidity. Plants are quite adaptive to changes, but too abrupt a change will be reflected in leaf drop or loss of plant color. New structures must be seasoned. These often are the hardest places to keep plants because they may have low humidity.

Gas problems. Unburned cooking or heating gas can cause damage to plants that lose their leaves easily (i.e., ficus, orange). Fumes from improperly vented furnaces, stoves or burners can also cause difficulty.

Houseplants, and Goldfish Fertilizer

Get a pet goldfish. It's a great source of houseplant fertilizer: *goldfish water!* Since a fresh bowl of water is necessary daily to keep a fish healthy, happy and swimming, the used fish water (already at room temperature) is just perfect for your plants. The water is rich in fish manure, and the uneaten fish food is an additional source of nutrients for plants. The water rivals commercial fish-emulsion fertilizers, and it's also a great motivation to keep the fish bowl clean!

Humidity

Winter heating often dries your skin, and it may also cause dryness in your plants. To prevent drying and provide humidity, place pebble trays filled with water under your plants. Group moisture-loving plants in the same room and operate a humidifier for them.

Jade Plant

Q. *For the past three years I have had a lovely jade plant that has been doing nicely. Is there any way I can force it to branch out? It's starting to grow long and leggy.*

A. The best way to encourage your jade plant *(Crassula argentea)* to branch out is by pruning and providing plenty of sunlight. Clip or pinch off all the long, leggy branches and shape the plant the way you want it to grow. With the cuttings (best between May and July) start new plants by simply inserting the individual mature leaves into some potting soil. In a few weeks roots will form, and eventually a small rosette will appear at the base of each leaf.

January Tips

Send for free seed catalogs now.

Think about last year's successes and failures, and take the time to learn about gardening topics that concerned you during the past growing season.

Gently remove snow that piles on branches of small trees and evergreens—wet, icy snow can be heavy for tender limbs and cause plant injury.

Stay off the grass; it is easily damaged this time of year.

Check, repair and oil garden equipment, if you haven't already done so.

Substitute coarse sand or wood ash for rock salt on frozen walkways, to protect adjacent plants from salt injury.

Keep houseplant leaves from touching freezing windows.

Prune old, neglected apple trees. Pruning the aging apple trees is largely a job of renovation followed by renewal of fruiting wood. The pruning must be moderate and be spread over a two- or three-year period to avoid excessive growth (or injury) to large limbs from sudden overexposure to sunlight. Such pruning consists of gradually lowering tree height to 18 feet or less, removal of surplus scaffold limbs and the elimination of weak wood.

Re-pot houseplants. Houseplants often need re-potting when they become pot-bound. You can easily tell when this has happened to a plant: It produces little or no new growth, and it dries out quickly even after frequent watering. The roots of such a plant usually protrude from the drainage holes. Use a Pro-Mix soil when re-potting your plants, available at most nurseries and garden centers.

To prolong the life of a flowering poinsettia, keep it evenly moist and protect it from becoming chilled or sitting in any draft. It delights in full sunlight and a temperature range of 65° to 72°F. When the colorful bracts begin to fall, set the plant in a lighted place where the temperature will not fall below 55°F, and keep the soil barely moist. When the danger of frost has passed in the spring, sink the pot up to its rim in the soil outdoors in a location where it will get full sunlight, preferably morning sun.

Mail-Order Gardening

It's well-known that Thomas Jefferson was an early fan of mail-order gardening. His journals document his detailed orders and exchanges of flower bulbs, seeds and plant material with friends and nurserymen in America, France and England.

Today, mail-order gardening is booming, as hundreds of garden catalogs tempt America's estimated 75 million home gardeners with the promise of garden glory seemingly leaping off the pages. Whether it's plants, perennials, bulbs, tools, tubers, garden décor, yard furnishings or books, there is a mail-order firm that can fulfill your heart's desire!

To gardeners of Jefferson's era (who would have swooned over today's color catalogs), the ease and speed of modern mail-order gardening would probably blow their minds! Try to imagine explaining to 18th-century people (whose routine mail-order transactions took at least five months on average) that people today can order overnight deliveries by phone, fax or the Internet. Wow!

For modern-day flower fanciers, the following is a list of American mail-order companies that carry flower bulbs for spring planting, plus other seasonal plants or gardening products:

Antonelli Brothers Inc., *Santa Cruz, California (888) 423-4664. Tuberous begonias, plus other plants, bulbs, begonia supplies.*

Breck's Dutch Bulbs, *Peoria, Illinois (800) 722-9069. Flower bulbs, Dutch floral gifts and gardening ideas.*

W. Atlee Burpee & Co., *Warminster, Pennsylvania (800) 888-1447. Complete line of gardening products, including seeds, plants, bulbs, nursery stock and gardening merchandise.*

Dutch Gardens, *Lakewood, New Jersey (800) 818-3861, www.dutchgardens.com. Flower bulbs and perennials.*

Geo. W. Park Seed Co., *Greenwood, South Carolina (864) 223-7333. Full assortment of flower bulbs, seeds, perennials, roses and vegetables.*

Henry Field Seed & Nursery Co., *Shenandoah, Iowa (800) 798-7842. Full line of flower and vegetable seeds, starter sets, flower bulbs, trees, fruits, shrubs, perennials, hard-to-find items.*

Holland Flower Market Ltd., *Marysville, Ohio www.hollandflowermarket.com. Full assortment of flower bulbs.*

Jackson & Perkins, *Medford, Oregon (800) 854-6200. Roses, perennials, indoor plants, bulbs, gifts and furnishings.*

Klehm Nursery, *South Barrington, Illinois (800) 553-3715. Estate peonies, tetraploid hemerocallis, fancy hostas.*

Quality Dutch Bulbs, *Easton, Pennsylvania (800) 755-2852. Full assortment of flower bulbs.*

Robinett Bulb Farm, *Sebastopol, California (707) 829-2729. Specialty bulbs, including California natives.*

Schreiner's Iris Gardens, *Salem, Oregon (800) 525-2367, www.oregonlink.com/sca/iris. Tall bearded and dwarf irises.*

Spring Hill Nurseries Co., *Peoria, Illinois (800) 544-0294, www.springhillnursery.com. Complete assortment of flower bulbs, perennials, flowering shrubs and roses.*

Thomas Jefferson Center for Historic Plants, *Monticello, Charlottesville, Virginia,*
www.monticello.org. Selected plants and flower bulbs known to have been grown by
Jefferson, plus other period plants. To receive catalog, send $1 to TJCHP, Box 316,
Charlottesville, Virginia, 22902.

Thompson & Morgan, *Jackson, Mississippi (800) 274-7333. Flower and vegetable*
seeds, small plants, flower bulbs, including rare seeds.

Wayside Gardens, *Hodges, South Carolina (800) 845-1124. Ornamental plants,*
including hardy perennials, bulbs, shrubs, trees, houseplants, indoor bulbs and gar-
dening supplies.

White Flower Farm, *Litchfield, Connecticut (800) 503-9624,*
www.whiteflowerfarm.com. Flower bulbs, perennials, shrubs, gardening tools and
supplies.

Many mail-order gardening companies are actively involved in recycling programs in
their hometowns as well as donating plants and material to help replenish the earth.

A source guide to gardening and landscaping by mail: Mail-Order Gardening Association, P. O. Box 2129, Columbia, Maryland, 21045 (401) 730-9713.

Mail-Order Gardening Catalogs

Mail-order garden catalogs contain an amazing amount of valuable growing (and
choosing) information—if you know how to read them, of course.

Variety name: You'll notice that some varieties (often very old ones) are known by
several names.

Usually, the most common name is listed first, with others afterward. So if you can't
find a particular variety by the name you know, describe it to the company and ask if it is
sold under a different name.

Open-pollinated varieties are those whose seed comes from pollination that occurs
naturally in the field. For example, if you save the seeds from an open-pollinated variety
that you have grown in your garden and plant them, you'll get the same variety as the parent plant (in most cases).

Open-pollinated varieties often improve—and are more adapted to local conditions—if you keep saving and planting the seed from your best plants. Gradually, you can

create a strain well adapted to your garden conditions.

You should not, however, re-plant the seeds of hybrid varieties. Hybrids are identified in seed catalogs by the symbol "F1" or the word "hybrid" spelled out in the variety description—it's the law.

Hybrids are created by using the pollen of one variety to fertilize the flowers of another variety of the same basic kind of plant (two varieties of corn, for instance). Thus, the resulting seeds are not exactly like either parent. If you save seed from hybrid plants and plant it, the new plant won't be the same as the plant that produced that seed for you originally.

Days to maturity: Most catalogs indicate "the days to maturity" of each of their varieties. To use this number, first determine whether the number of days indicated refers to seeds sown directly into the garden (crops such as corn, lettuce, spinach, carrots or beets,) or whether that number of days refers to the time it takes a six-week-old transplant to mature (crops such as tomatoes or peppers that are usually started inside and then transplanted to the garden).

Vegetables started indoors need a week or so to sprout, then another six weeks to grow to transplant size—then the number of days listed in the catalog comes into play. Add those seven weeks to the listed "days to maturity" and you have the number of days it will really take to go from a planted seed to harvesting your crop.

Whether you start your seed indoors or outdoors, remember that the "days to maturity" listings are loose guidelines at best. Many factors can affect the actual number of days it takes a variety to mature; for example, weather conditions, your garden's degree of shade and sun, and the time of year you plant the crop.

Disease resistance: Catalog descriptions often indicate a variety's ability to tolerate or resist disease. But be careful, because those two words have distinctly different meanings.

"Tolerant" means that the variety in question will probably not suffer from a disease as much as another variety that lacks tolerance altogether. But it can still get (and suffer from) the disease. "Resistant," on the other hand, a stronger word, means the variety in question probably won't catch the disease at all.

If a variety description lacks the terms "tolerant" or "resistant," don't just assume it's susceptible to disease. It just may not have been evaluated yet.

Disease-resistance ratings are conveyed only after trials in which a dozen or so leading commercial varieties, grown side by side, are doused with disease organisms and then compared at weekly intervals. Those showing little or no infection are labeled "resistant"; those with slightly high levels of infection but that still look pretty good are considered "tolerant."

Many heirlooms and other varieties sold in small quantities have never been tested this way, so gardeners have to rely on the advice and experience of others.

Vegetable harvest: I stress that regular picking is the number-one way to prolong your vegetable harvest. You should pick at least every other day.

Beans, for example, should be picked before their pods swell up with seeds. When seeds finish developing inside the pods, it sends a signal to the plant that it can stop producing because it has succeeded at its job of reproduction.

But if you keep picking before those seeds mature, the plant will make more beans to make more seeds. Besides, when beans get bigger, they don't taste as good. Cucumber plants are another good example—the more you pick, the more they produce.

Mazes

Q: *What do you know about mazes?*

A: You'll be amazed at what I'm about to tell you. There's a new trend sweeping the Midwest and western United States. Farmers are having fun with their corn planting all the way from Illinois to Hawaii. In order to attract tourists who are driving through miles and miles of monotonous farmlands, farmers have planted their corn in artistic patterns to create mazes. From the ground it still looks like a cornfield but from the air you can see the various shapes and murals that are growing out of the land. Passersby are encouraged to stop and try to figure out the maze. If they reach the center, a cool refreshment is waiting. All this is being done to try to raise money for local charities throughout western America. In Idaho there is a cornfield solar system; in Kansas a five-acre turtle; and in Missouri there is a cornfield maze with a sun, fish and outline of the state. People are flocking to see it. What a great idea—something fun for the farmers and tourists too.

Q. *What is the history of the maze? When did they begin?*

A. In ancient times the maze was called a labyrinth. Who knows why they were created in the time of the Greeks and Romans? My theory is that they were a hiding place for lovers—the king, the noblemen, anyone who wanted to escape from prying eyes. During the sixteenth century labyrinths turned into mazes and became popular in gardens, created by evergreen shrubs and hedges. The garden maze, according to the *Encyclopedia Britannica*, is "an intricate network of pathways enclosed by hedges or plantations so that those that enter become bewildered in their efforts to find the center or make their exit." The great thing about the garden maze (if you've ever been in one) is that at the center there is usually a delightful place to sit and relax—sometimes even a fountain to enjoy a cool drink of water. After a nice rest the hard part is to find your way out!

Oak Trees

After the driveways, streets and parking lots are cleared from the recent snow, take a look around at the surrounding landscape.

The oaks look nice with snow on the branches because they have dark-colored bark, making a nice contrast. Some of these large trees have seen a lot of snows.

In the Midwest you can get a rough estimate of a shade tree's age by measuring all the way around its circumference at about five feet above the ground. How many inches you get in the measurement will be about the number of years old the tree will be. There are slow- and fast-growing trees and some trees grow in better or worse conditions, so you may need to add or subtract a little.

White oaks are among the oldest living things in the Midwest. Many are over 200 years old.

The white oak is the name of a species of oak and of a division in the oaks. There are five groups of oaks nationwide and over 500 white oak acorns ripen in only one year, have no hairs on the inside of the acorn shell (not the cap) and can often be eaten. Red oak acorns are on the trees for two years and are very bitter. They must be ground up and rinsed several times to make them edible.

White oaks are more tolerant of our high-pH limestone-based soils than the red oaks. The most common white oaks used in landscaping are the white oak, English oak and the bur oak. All grow to be very large and sometimes do not fit into the scale of a small landscape.

They grow more than 60 feet tall and often grow wider than that. Some very large specimens are more than 100 by 100 feet. Some varieties have been selected to grow in a columnar form. They may be 50 feet tall and only 10 feet in diameter. Fall leaf color tends to be dark red, maroon and dark brown.

The pin oak is very sensitive to high-pH soils. It cannot get iron out of the soil and it develops yellow leaves. Adding fertilizer may help the trees. It should not be planted in most subdivisions where the soil has been removed and replaced.

All oaks mentioned are natives that prefer full sun, well-drained acidic soil and lots of room. They grow better if they have loose soil and bark mulch for the roots. They get few insects or diseases. Some may have odd-shaped growths on the leaves and stems which can be from insects or diseases, but are just unsightly, not harmful.

If you have the room and good soil, an oak is one of the best trees you can plant for a long-term investment. Once established, they tend to grow fast for the first few decades so do not worry that they will not be a good return on your investment.

Orchids

Q. *How do you take care of an orchid plant—a beautiful white one of the corsage type? Should it be indoors or out—say, a patio open on top but sheltered on the sides?*

A. Your orchid plant is a Cattleya. Orchids, like people, can sometimes be temperamental; some need to be pampered more than others. During cold weather your Cattleya must be kept indoors. Keep the potting mixture damp by watering once or twice a week. The leaves will stay green all winter long, but you won't see blooms again until spring. Once the weather starts to warm up, around the end of May, hang your plants outside and start fertilizing once a week. The Cattleya should be kept in only partial sunlight. When it blooms again, the flowers should last at least three weeks, and as they die down, the cycle starts all over again.

Q. *Could you provide information on growing Cattleya orchids? I have two that are turning black and dying.*

I re-potted them in new orchid bark, watered them with distilled water and fertilized with a water-soluble fertilizer.

Should I mix the bark with peat moss?

A. I suspect your orchids are succumbing to disease caused by the potting media staying too wet.

Cattleyas need very warm temperatures to thrive, so when winter conditions are cool, it's best to keep the plants on the dry side. Cattleyas are adapted to being dry at the roots between waterings, so pot them in very porous, free-draining soil, the most popular being coarse fir bark or a mix of dark and tree-fern chunks.

So, no, don't mix peat in with the bark. Once temperatures warm and the plants resume active growth, continue normal watering and fertilizing.

Give Cattleyas bright light, with some sun, but not direct midday sun. Indoors, an east, west or shaded south window is ideal. Give the plants day temperatures around 80°F and night temperatures no lower than 55°.

Fertilize Cattleya orchids with a high-nitrogen product every two weeks during the growing season. Decrease the frequency to once a month when plants are not growing. Every two to three months use a bloom-enhancing fertilizer instead of a high-nitrogen one, to promote flower development.

Flush the potting soil with clear water once a month to prevent salt buildup in the soil.

Orchids, Care of

Orchids compose the largest group of flowering plants in nature, and they are very popular these days all over America. Here are tips on growing them at home.

Watering: Use tepid water to keep orchids growing in potting media moist below the surface. Allow epiphytic orchids—those that grow on other plants—to dry out below the surface between waterings.

Potting media: Orchids tolerate a wide variety of potting media including fir bark, tree fern, perlite, charcoal, stones and sphagnum moss. Any combination of these is acceptable. Some terrestrial orchids need more moss to retain moisture.

Pots can be plastic or clay. Clay pots dry out faster, so orchids potted in them have to be watered more often. Pots must have at least one or two holes at the bottom of the pot; having openings at the sides to ensure proper drainage is good, too.

Charcoal or Styrofoam "peanuts" must be put in a sterile pot for drainage before adding the medium. Always wait until a plant has flowered before re-potting it. It also is necessary to re-pot if the potting medium breaks down (becomes soggy).

To re-pot, shake all the old mix off the roots and cut away all dead parts with a sterile tool. Divide plant if necessary, leaving four healthy growths to each division.

Summering outdoors: When the danger of frost has passed, orchids thrive outdoors on a porch or under a tree if they are raised off the ground to receive light and ample sun. Once the temperature reaches about 90°F, mist the leaves several times a day to avoid sunburn. If you feel thirsty, maybe your orchids need a drink, too.

Vacation care: Water all plants thoroughly and provide less light. If plants are growing on a window sill, provide a curtain to cut down the sunlight. Reduce light to about eight hours a day if you are using artificial lighting. Reduce night temperatures to slow growth.

If you plan to be gone more than four weeks, have a friend water your collection once a week.

Orchids, Growing Inside or Out

Orchids comprise the largest flora of any flowering plant in nature. There are around 35,000 uncultivated species and as many hybrids, located on every continent except Antarctica.

These diverse and highly evolved plants are called orchids because of their flower structure. All orchid flowers have three sepals and three petals. One of the petals is called the lip, or labellum. It has a different shape than the other two petals and is very showy.

Protruding from the center of the flower are the male (stamen) and female (pistil) reproductive organs. They are wedded together.

There are two kinds of orchids: epiphytic and terrestrial.

Epiphytic orchids are not parasites, although they anchor themselves to other plants, tree limbs or rocky places for support. They take their nourishment from the air, rain and debris that fall on them and store it in a "pseudobulb" (the thickest portion of a stem, but not a true bulb).

Terrestrial orchids grow in the ground in the top layer of humus or moss. They have no pseudobulbs to store water, as epiphytic orchids do. Their leaves rise from an underground rhizome (a root-bearing horizontal stem that, in orchids, usually lies on or just beneath the ground surface). They remain damp at the roots.

There are two growth patterns of orchids. Smypodial (a form of growth in which each new shoot arises from the rhizome of the previous growth) orchids have a main stem that stops growing at the end of each season. A new lead branch grows from the base, developing its own pseudobulbs and, eventually, its own flower.

Monopodial orchids have a main stem that grows steadily from the center each year and produces flower stalks at the axil (the crotch between the stem and leaf) of the leaves or opposite them.

Growing Orchids in Home Conditions

Light: Plants should be placed in an east, south or west window and protected from direct noonday sun. Orchids are variable in their light requirements, depending on genera and variety. Plants that need high light, such as *Cymbidiums*, can be placed close to the window.

This protects other plants that need medium light, like *Cattleya*, by blocking direct sunlight. *Phalaenopsis* is an orchid that needs low light. If only a south window is available, a sheer curtain helps prevent scorching during months when the sun is low in the sky.

Artificial light: Provide artificial light only during daylight hours to initiate flower buds during their growing season. Varieties with lower light requirements bloom better in this type of environment. For best results, use wide-spectrum fluorescent tubes such as grow lights. Warm and cool white tubes used together are also satisfactory.

Temperatures: A minimum-maximum thermometer helps check daily temperature fluctuations. A differential between night and day temperature of at least ten to 20 degrees is a must for good growth.

Warm-growing orchids should have a day temperature of 72° to 80°F with sun, and night temperature to 65°F. Day temperatures for intermediate-growing orchids should range from 68° to 70°F with sun, and night temperatures should be around 60°F.

Cool-growing orchids require a day temperature of 65° to 70°F with sun and night temperature of 50° to 55°F.

All varieties tolerate higher temperatures in hot summer weather, but additional shade and misting is necessary to keep them cool.

Ventilation: Orchids need good air movement to prevent fungi and keep leaf temperature low on sunny days. Small fans placed near the growing area or a distant window opened a crack (except in very cold weather) supply much-needed moving air.

Humidity: Forty to 60 degrees is a suitable range and can be checked with a hydrometer (an instrument that measures humidity). Use a humidifier or put plants on gravel in trays containing water. Pots should not touch the water. This permits weekly drying out of epiphytic plants and prevents rot.

As the water evaporates, a humid microclimate is produced around the plants. A bright room that can be closed off from the rest of the house is an ideal area for growing plants indoors.

Fertilizer: Orchids thrive if fed regularly during the growing season. Use high-nitrogen food like 30-10-10 at one-quarter the recommended dose once a month for the first six months after blooming. Then switch to a high-phosphorus fertilizer like 10-30-20 at one-quarter the recommended amount.

Palms, Indoor

Q. *I've had it with* Areca *palms; they just turn yellow and die back, either from red spider mites or too much heat, I think. Is there a better palm?*

A. Yes, the kentia *(Howea),* which costs more money but is worth every dollar. Give it half-sun, keep the soil evenly moist and apply fertilizer regularly. Keep the fronds clean, either by wiping between pieces of moistened paper toweling or by giving the plant a shower. Red spider mites cause green leaves to go splotchy yellow, then turn grayish brown and die; shake one over a sheet of paper, and if red spider mites are the culprits, you'll see little dark specks begin to move across its surface. Treatment involves the use of a miticide such as insecticidal soap sprays; you can also improve the atmosphere by increasing humidity and fresh-air circulation, and taking care that the plant's soil does not dry out severely on a recurring basis. Two other excellent palms for indoors are the lady palm *(Raphis)* and the dwarf palm *(Chamaedorea elegans bella).*

Peat Moss

Sphagnum peat moss: Sphagnum peat moss consists of naturally occurring organic matter made up of partially decomposed plants. These structures contain hollow cells that hold water, nutrients and air, and when added to compacted clay or sandy soils, assist plant root growth.

Potting mixtures: Potting mixtures must drain well, and at the same time keep roots moist, retain nutrients and resist compaction. An all-purpose potting soil mixture would contain one-third sterilized garden soil (sell-sieved), one-third sphagnum peat moss and one-third vermiculite. There are plenty of peat-based specialty potting mixtures that provide a good base for any plant type.

Composting: Peat moss helps produce better compost by speeding up the process, reducing odors and controlling air and water in the compost pile. Mix ½-inch layer of peat to every 41 inches of compostable materials, being sure to slip over the top layers of organic materials every week or so. Add water when needed to keep the center of the pile moist.

Amending gardens: When adding compost to the garden, blend with equal parts of peat moss. The two complement each other with unique benefits for your garden. Peat decomposes slowly (over several years versus several months for compost) ensuring longer-term organic matter in the soil, balancing the nutrient-rich but faster decomposing compost and reducing compost's tendency to compact.

Eliminating thatch: Compacted soil in lawn areas creates an environment for thatch. To prevent or relieve thatch and promote deeper grass root growth, aerate the lawn and apply a top dressing of peat moss. The best times of year to aerate are mid-spring, after the ground is reasonably dry, and early fall.

Perennials

Perennials are plants that survive cold winters and continue to grow for years and years. Unlike woody trees and shrubs, most perennials die back to the roots in fall and send up new shoots each spring.

Perennials offer a breathtaking parade of lovely blooms from spring through fall, in an amazing range of colors, sizes, shapes, habits and heights. Of course, many kinds are excellent for cutting. Since most perennials show color for only two to three weeks, a successful perennial garden depends on a careful selection of varieties that bloom at different times. Many gardeners use favorite annuals and spring-flowering bulbs, interplanted with perennials, to enhance the garden.

Perennial plants are easy to grow in any good garden soil and once they are established require little or no care. Every two to four years, most types of perennials should be "divided"; by that I mean roots dug up and separated into small sections and re-planted. This small effort yields many new plants to enlarge your garden, or to give to friends.

Perennials, New

One, *Achillea* 'Anthea,' belongs to a genus of perennials that derives its name—as well as supposed magical healing powers—from Achilles, the heroic warrior of Greek mythology. Another, *Hebe* 'Margret', attracts butterflies and will bloom from early summer to late fall.

The third, *Heuchera micrantha* 'Bressingham Bronze,' is known more for the deep purple color of its foliage than its flowers. Whether planted together or individually, they bring beauty and charm to any garden.

These new varieties were selected for North America from more than 5,000 exclusive perennial varieties made famous by Alan and Adrian Bloom, a prominent father-and-son team of horticulturists and their Blooms of Bressingham Ltd., one of Britain's largest nursery companies.

Named for Adrian Bloom's sister, *Achillea* Anthea is noted for soft, beautiful yellow flowers, which lend magic to the legend that Achilles used poultices of yarrow (or *Achillea*) to heal his wounds during the Trojan War.

Another delightful specialty are *Heuchera*, known for their flowers and foliage. A robust variety of unsurpassed beauty and form, 'Bressingham Bronze' offers the deepest purple, most stable leaf color of any plant in this genus. Fine, off-white flowers form in late spring to midsummer and can be used for arrangements or drying.

A dwarf hybrid of *Hebe* 'Margret', another good choice for the garden, has deep evergreen leaves and bright blue flowers that fade toward white as they mature. The flowers form flowering spikes resembling those of the genus *Veronica*.

'Margret' is normally hardy in Zones 8 to 10 and does best only in a limited area of the United States along the less humid West Coast in partially shaded areas. The relatively slow-growing plants require little maintenance and range in size up to 16 inches wide.

'Anthea' and 'Bressingham Bronze' both are hardy in Zones 4 to 8 with 'Anthea' liking full sun and 'Bressingham Bronze' full sun to partial shade. At 30 inches tall and 12 inches wide, 'Anthea' fits beautifully into rock gardens or can be used as background plantings for island beds and borders. 'Bressingham Bronze' can be expected to reach 24 inches tall and 12 inches wide, ideal for border edgings or as a specimen plant in island beds.

Pest-Resistant Gardening

The average home gardener is unfamiliar with alternative pest-control methods. They're uneasy to try something they haven't seen. To that, I say, "Why not plant a more pest-resistant landscape?"

So many fabulous quality plants are available with pest-resistant traits that it's a shame they are not planted more often.

For example, try planting silver linden, red oak, Chinese elm, Kousa dogwood, or flowering crab apples to name a few. Although landscape gardeners are now being educated about the importance of planting pest-resistant trees and shrubs, many unfortunately still place a higher priority on other tree characteristics.

Color, form and flowering still rate high on the list. Hardiness is critical, too (for northern dwellers), as is the plant site itself and weather conditions, such as wind and sun exposure. So you see how pest resistance is often lost in the shuffle.

Robert Mower, professor of horticulture at Cornell University, says, "There's not as much pest-resistant planting as there should be. I haven't seen major changes in the choice of landscape plants in fifty years. Somehow, we need to convince the rest of the world that it's the way to go."

Keep in mind that many of our popular traditional plants have disease and insect problems now that they didn't have 25 years ago. A scarcity of pest-resistant trees has also contributed to the problem. Nurseries and garden centers have not always carried an inventory of such plants, but public interest is building to inspire them to diversify.

Of course, the greatest advantage to pest-resistant trees is good plant health without the use of pesticides. Proper setting comes into play, too. Having the right plant in the right place is the key.

Try to remember that although native plants are usually your best choice, not all native plants are guaranteed to be resistant to insects.

In addition, your landscaping area can be very different from the native habitats of the trees. So be careful when selecting hemlocks, birches and crab apples. Hemlocks are readily attacked by the wooly adelgid, so you might want to think of another conifer. Birches are susceptible to the birch borer but resistant birches are available.

Spring or fall is the perfect planting time; conifers should be planted by the end of September; deciduous trees can be planted up to mid-September. Water your plants consistently so that the roots will become well established before dormancy sets in. I also recommend mulching with several inches of bark and protecting the trunk with a plastic sleeve.

Native versus Non-native

A native plant grows naturally in your climate or in a climate and site similar to the one in which it is found. While a non-native plant may not grow naturally in your climate, many non-native plants are well adapted to thrive in different parts of the country.

Both native and non-native plants can be excellent choices. The most important thing is to select plants based on your area's specific climatic requirements, rather than focusing on the geographic region where the plant originated.

Another way to create a tough garden that will withstand your climate is to select "cultivars." A cultivar is a cultivated variety—a plant that has been grown and bred for specific characteristics by nursery professionals.

If you're looking for a flower with a particularly strong fragrance, ask your nursery professional for a cultivar that meets your needs.

Creating a lasting home landscape is easy when you choose quality plants over often inferior plants that seem like excellent money-savers, but turn out to be money-guzzlers when they die early. Quality plants may cost slightly more, but that's because they have received the best care from growers and nursery professionals before they reach you.

SOURCE: *American Chestnut Council*

Pine Cones

Q. *How does a pine cone grow?*

A. Oranges, apples and pears are fruit, and fruits contain seeds. If you open the fruit you can see the seeds. A pine cone is just like a fruit, since it also contains seeds and, when ripe, it opens by itself. You can see the seeds resting in the scales that make up the pine cone.

When an apple seed is planted, an apple tree grows; and when a pine seed is planted, a pine tree grows.

Fruits come from flowers. Flowers have two important parts—pollen and ovules. Seeds develop when the pollen combines with the ovules. The fruit grows to hold and protect the seeds. Pine trees are different; they don't have flowers, but instead they have pollen cones and seed cones. The seed cone has ovules which become seeds.

In the spring, the pollen cone releases pollen. Pollen looks like a fine powder—it blows easily in the wind. When pollen lands on the ovules of a seed cone, pine seeds develop and the seed cone grows larger. The scales are tightly closed around the cone and protect the seeds growing inside it. At first the seed cone is like a tiny ball on or close to the top of a branch.

Depending on the variety of the pine tree, the cones take two to three years to finish growing. After the cone is all grown, it dries out and the scales spread apart. The seeds rest on the top side of the scales. Each seed has a thin papery covering that acts like a wing. The seed is carried through the air, and when it lands on the ground it sprouts. If all goes well, someday it will be a tall pine tree.

Make a Bird Feeder

Stuff a pine cone with pieces of bread or moist crackers. Intermix seeds and crumbs. The cone can be rolled in honey or molasses and then heavily sprinkled with birdseed and small crumbs. Hang out of reach of cats and squirrels. Do not paint the pine cone or use glitter or glue. These may injure birds.

Planning Ahead

To have a good garden, you must organize well, and winter is the time to do just that. If you wait until spring, you will be too busy, and it will be too late. Start by making notes of what you want your garden to be season by season for the whole year.

When you're sitting by the fire looking out at the winter scenery, surround yourself with as many garden catalogs as possible. My two favorites are Burpee and Wayside Gardens. Leaf through the catalogs carefully, looking at the pictures, and decide what kind of flowers and vegetables you like.

It's a good idea to have your season-by-season plan prepared by the end of December. Write down in your garden planner the flowers and vegetables of your choice, when to plant, their growing needs, height, and when and how long they bloom or produce vegeta-

bles. This is a big job that takes a lot of careful consideration. Yet, once you've completed your schedule, you're on your way to being well organized.

Once you've decided what flowers and vegetables you are going to grow, it's best to order the seed quickly through catalogs. It's important to act early because many of the seed companies offer discounts to those who order by January or the beginning of February. It pays to be an early bird!

After the seeds arrive, you may start your vegetables and flowers in flats in the greenhouse or wait until spring to sow outdoors.

A good potting mixture that I use for seeds is a commercial sterile potting soil such as Pro-Mix, available at nurseries and garden centers. It's pre-mixed so all you do is pre-moisten it well with warm water, then pot up your seed.

Try to use all the seeds you order within the year. It's best not to save leftover seeds, as this almost always results in poor germination.

Poppy, Iceland

A great springtime flower is the Iceland poppy. Scatter some seeds anywhere you wish—roadside, field, wild garden or along the driveway. You can even scatter the seeds over snow-covered earth! Nature will do the rest.

Pot Cleaning

Keep empty clay pots cleaned and stored together, outdoors if possible. The winter freezing will automatically sterilize them, making them ready for use in the spring. The same holds for utilitarian plastic and wooden containers. Indoors, try soaking pots in a mixture of water and household bleach (1 teaspoon bleach per quart of water).

Potpourri, Revitalizing

Q. *Is there a way to give old potpourri a fresh smell?*

A. Essential oils such as rose, lavender and tea olive are available (send for the catalog of Caswell-Massy Co., 575 Lexington Avenue, New York, New York, 10022) to give your old potpourri a boost. Remember, with these oils a little goes a long way.

Do as I do, and add also petals that are sweet-smelling (violet, rose, lavender) or colorful (blue delphinium). Pinch off the dead leaves from scented-leafed plants, such as lemon, nutmeg and rose geraniums, not to mention rosemary and lemon verbena.

Potpourri blended this way becomes the most personal creation of a fragrance that is uniquely yours.

Potting Soil

Q. *What kind of soil is best for all types of container gardening?*

A. For best results, choose a commercial Pro-Mix soil developed specifically for houseplants. The ready-to-go mixture is specially prepared containing all needed nutrients and is available in most garden centers and nurseries.

Potting-Soil Danger

Legionnaire's Disease, the nasty pneumonia-like bacterial disease usually contracted by inhaling mist from contaminated water sources, can apparently be transmitted by potting soil.

Open bags of soil carefully and wet down the soil to avoid inhaling any airborne particles. To be safe, wear gloves and wash your hands thoroughly after handling potting mix.

Anyone with a weakened immune system or chronic lung disease, or anyone middle-aged or older, is likely to be more susceptible to the disease.

Raccoons

An open-door approach should prevail at a wildlife pond. Even if your pond contains no fish, raccoons associate water with feeding because they like to "rinse" their food before eating.

Raccoons are blessed with dexterous hands, so you can imagine the mischief they can create. To keep these amazing animals at bay, here are some deterrents that work for me.

Sprinkle baby powder or cayenne powder (raccoons don't like the feeling on their paws).

Plant prickly bushes or ones that are hard to walk across (juniper, ferns).

A low-voltage electric fence or a large, hungry dog outside at night may keep them away.

If these tips don't work, try coyote urine. What a stench this vile smelling potion makes—a few drops on a scent dart should do the trick. This potion will definitely send deer and raccoons packing.

Gathered on certified farms, this exotic perfume is available in bottles ranging from 8 ounces to 1 gallon. Bobcat and fox urine are also available. They make great gifts for the gardener who has it all. For information, contact J&C Marketing Inc., P. O. Box 125, Hampden, Maine, 04444 (800) 218-1719.

Reproduction, Plant

The word *monoecious*, from the Greek *mono* for one, and *oikos*, for house, means having male and female reproduction parts on the same plant. Most fruit and vegetable plants are monoecious because each plant comes equipped with all the reproductive organs needed to produce pollen and egg—in other words, seeds and fruit. Many monoecious plants self-pollinate, so they don't require any help from insects such as bees.

Dioecious plants are different. They have male and female reproductive parts on separate plants. For pollination to succeed, both a male and female plant must be within the flight pattern of the pollinator. The pollinator must visit both plants in the right order and deliver the pollen from one to the other.

For example, asparagus and kiwi vines are both dioecious plants. Growers take advantage of this trait and develop the male asparagus plants because they tend to grow larger, thicker stalks, while female asparagus direct all energy into seed and fruit production.

Another example is greenhouse cucumbers. These plants have been bred to produce only female flowers that need no pollination, and thus are perfect candidates for an indoor bugless culture. If female flower-producing plants even ventured outdoors in the garden to be bedmates, the result would be horrendous.

Roses as Cut Flowers

Love roses? You are not alone. Americans bought more than 1.2 million stems of fresh-cut roses last year.

A recent survey by the Gallup Organization revealed that more than 19 million American households have rosebushes in their gardens. While roses are beautiful on the bush, they're even more gorgeous in your home.

Fresh-cut roses look best in vases that are about half as tall as the flowers. Cut your flowers to fit the vase and always cut them under water.

To give a simple bud vase arrangement a finished look, tuck a few small leaves at the rim and tie a pretty ribbon around the neck of the vase.

Try floating just one or two garden roses in a crystal bowl for a gorgeous, eye-catching display.

For a special celebration, create an all-rose bouquet. Combine stems of hybrid tea roses and spray roses with daintier sweetheart or miniature roses. Choose roses of different colors, but colors close to each other on the color wheel—peach, yellow and pale pink, or cream, champagne and blush pink. Lavender, deep rose and hot pink are another good combination.

If a rose wilts prematurely, it usually means the lowest one-inch of the stem is clogged with bacteria or an air pocket has formed and the flower isn't drinking water. To remedy this, re-cut the stem under water. Then submerge the whole rose in warm water until it revives (about two hours).

Roses, Hardy

Q. *For years I have grown roses, concentrating on the Spartan because of its sturdy nature. What are other tough varieties of roses suitable for the Midwest?*

A. There are roses for every purpose, and many varieties are tough enough to take your winters. Try the tall-growing 'Betty Prior' or the medium-height 'Fashion.' If you like climbing roses, the 'Mary Wallace' is a lovely pink June bloomer that does well even in Maine. A good hardy garden shrub is the Damask rose. It's one of the oldest roses in cultivation and is second only to the cabbage rose in the intensity of its fragrance. The *Rosa rugosa* hybrids are definitely tough and are often planted near the sea.

Roses in Containers

America's most beloved flower, the rose, is often overlooked as a container-gardening candidate. Growing these colorful, fragrant and cherished plants in pots is surprisingly easy and creates endless possibilities for a beautiful landscape design. Many home gardeners have excellent success growing beautiful roses in containers on sunny decks, terraces, balconies or ledges.

Whether you prefer the classic hybrid tea, compact floribunda, majestic tree rose or space-saving miniature, all rose types can be grown successfully in containers when properly planted and maintained.

The best containers for roses are wood or unglazed ceramic. A pot should provide good drainage and comfortably accommodate the plant's roots. Containers should be at least 10 inches in diameter and 12 inches deep for a miniature rose; 16 inches in diameter and 18 inches deep for a tree rose.

Planting mix should be three parts sandy loam soil to one part organic matter. Add about half a cup of bone meal or superphosphate fertilizer at planting time.

Form a mound of planting mix on which the plant's roots will rest, and position the plant so that the crown is an inch or two below the rim of the container. Fill the container with planting mix, press down gently and water well.

Container roses should be watered twice weekly and fertilized once a week with a liquid plant food after the new growth is off to a good start. Of course, during the hot months of July and August, more water is necessary.

Roses require six hours of sun daily, but roots must be kept relatively cool in the heat of summer, by using techniques such as mulching.

Wintering container roses is a snap. Simply move the container into an unheated shelter when the temperature dips below 28°F. Keep the roots barely moist and do not fertilize. When the weather warms up, bring your pot into the sun, prune and watch the amazing process repeat itself year after year.

Sage, Keeping Blue from Turning Yellow

Q: *I received a plant called blue sage, but it isn't one of the outdoor flowering sages. The plant didn't have a care tag, so I'm not sure how to care for it. It has lovely blue flower spikes.*

The problem is that the foliage is yellowing. I fertilize it regularly, but it hasn't helped. It's in a south window, so it has plenty of sun. Could you help?

A. I suspect from the way your plant is acting it's not one of the tropical salvias (sage), but instead is *Eranthemum pulchellum*, which is often sold as blue sage. This plant needs moderate light, average soil and moderate to warm temperatures and even moisture.

Eranthemum bears blue flowers from late fall through spring on 3- to 4-foot plants. *Eranthemum* doesn't need bright light, and if the light it gets is too strong the foliate pales. I suspect this is why the foliage is yellowing.

If you move the plant so that it's near (but not in) an east or west window, it will do much better.

This is an easy plant to grow, but keep it a little drier during the winter, to avoid disease problems. Plant *Eranthemum* outdoors in moderate shade in rich, well-drained soil.

Seeds, Tropical

Q. *On a visit to the Bahamas my husband and I picked up many different kinds of seeds, in particular when we visited some of the beautiful public gardens. How should we go about planting these? They are of many sizes and shapes.*

A. Remove husks and shells; soft-skinned coverings may respond to soaking overnight or for 48 hours, after which time the seeds can be rinsed clean in water. Use a clean planting medium, that is, one that is "sterile" or pasteurized; a mixture of equal parts sphagnum peat moss and vermiculite is excellent. Scatter the seeds over the surface by kind, and cover each to the depth of its own thickness. Moisten well, then set to sprout in a warm (65°–75°F), bright spot. In order to ensure uniform moisture conditions, enclose the entire planting, container and all, in a plastic bag; gradually remove this, having first punched some holes in it so as to allow the seedlings ample time to adjust to the open air. When large enough to handle, or as they begin to crowd, transplant to individual containers. You're in for an exciting adventure. Enjoy!

Shady Gardens

Q. *I have two rather unprosperous borders that get very little sun yet have to be planted with flowers each year to give the backyard a little color. Can you think of anything easy that will do in such a situation except for begonias?*

A. How about the jewel-flowered impatiens? They're fabulous for shady gardens. Also give them the company of fancy-leaf caladiums, hardy hostas, hardy ferns, trailing vinca and English ivy, blue and white browallia, and the charming annual wishbone flower, torenia. In early spring, enjoy sweet violets, lily of the valley, pansies, violas and many beautiful primroses.

Snow Plantings

Q. *A friend of mine told me that a certain variety of annuals could be planted on snow and the seed would nestle down into the soil and germinate as the snow melted in the spring. If this is true, what seeds do you suggest?*

A. Yes, it's true. The hardy annuals to sow on snow are: bachelor's buttons, sweet peas, larkspur and Shirley poppies. These annuals can be sown now either on top of snow or open ground. You can also sow these seeds in fall!

Soil Testing

Want to have your soil tested? To do so, you have to go out to the garden and collect a sample. How you collect this small amount of soil is important if you want proper results.

Wait until the soil to be tested is moist, but not soggy. Scrape away any surface debris and then cut a V-shaped wedge 6 to 7 inches deep into the soil with a clean shovel; then cut a ½-inch slice from the smooth side of the hole you made. Cut out a 1-inch vertical cone from the center of that slice. Then repeat the same process in a couple of other places.

Mix the soil together thoroughly in a clean plastic container using a clean trowel; then measure out the amount of soil requested by the lab from the mixture. Don't touch the soil with your hands, it could contaminate your sample and throw off results.

Your local cooperative extension agents usually offer inexpensive soil testing, but be sure they can provide organic advice for any corrections the test deems necessary. Also, ask the extension agent to tailor such recommendations to the size of your garden; that is, the amount of amendments (mulch, fertilizer, compost, etc.) that you should apply per 100 or 1,000 square feet, instead of per acre.

The term "pH" refers to the acidity or alkalinity of the soil.

Sweet Alyssum

For all its versatility, sweet alyssum is still easily cultivated. With improved quality and a wider color range, sweet alyssum can be found in window boxes, blooming in hanging baskets, tumbling over walls, brightening outside containers, filling in nooks and crannies in rock gardens, and growing as ground cover beneath taller plants.

Sweet alyssum's combination of beauty, hardiness and versatility make it a popular selection. The lovely blooms and scent can add a great deal to a container or garden.

Sweet alyssum is a seaside plant with small, honey-scented white flowers and downy, lance-shaped leaves with a grayish or whitish cast. The plant is native to much of the Mediterranean area.

Sweet alyssum's legend as a cure for rabies grew during Elizabethan times. Herbalists included it in their lists—one writing that it was so powerful it would counteract the bite of a mad dog "by being presented only to the diseased person, without any internal or extended application."

Some old folktales claim that sweet alyssum can keep witches and evil spirits away, and in some parts of southern Italy and Greece a spray of sweet alyssum was brought into the house from meadows where it grew wild to guard the household from evil.

Sweet alyssum is attractive in almost any type of container. The profuse blooms and fresh scent will boost your well-being. Just imagine:

- A lovely basket, spilling over with a dozen clusters of pink and white alyssum
- A window box planted with contrasting colors, such as the classic pink geraniums and white sweet alyssum, accented with rose-pink 'Rosie O'Day' alyssum
- A row of pots and planters with alyssum tumbling over the sides
- Dainty and colorful sweet alyssum among herbs

You can sow seeds directly in the containers or transplant sweet alyssum from the garden. To transplant, lift clumps of sweet alyssum in the early fall, before the first frost. Provide cool nights, full sun and good air circulation, and keep soil evenly moist. A sunny porch would be an ideal spot for sweet alyssum.

You may want to plant a new crop in August, especially for winter blooming. Take advantage of the flower's fragrance by planting them higher up where their scent, as well as their blossoms, will be more noticeable.

Thistles

Q. *I intend to plant thistle against a garden wall. I have clipped and collected the heads of thistle for seeds. Please advise how to plant the seed (scatter or dig in?) and at what time of year.*

A. Thistles are generally unwelcome intruders in the garden. They are really prickly herbs, some of which are biennials with alternate or basil leaves—irregularly toothed or lobed with strong spines at the outer edges. There are four varieties of thistles for your guidelines:

Tall thistle: A biennial weed native to the eastern and central United States with alternate leaves, prickly, white and woolly beneath, and with a tap root. Purple flower heads bloom during August and September. Not as dangerous a weed as the Canada thistle.

Canada thistle: A vicious perennial weed that spreads by seed and creeping roots, introduced from Europe and Asia and common, especially in grain fields in southern Canada and central and northern United States. Lavender flowers are about 1 inch across and appear from July to October. It's one of the worst weeds in the United States because of its creepy rootstock and should be vigorously dug out wherever it grows.

Bull thistle: A biennial weed from Europe and Asia, common throughout North American oilfields and in rich soil, with pinkish-purple flowers that bloom from June to October. The leaves are extremely thorny. Fortunately, this weed does not last long in cultivated fields.

Swamp thistle: A vigorous plant growing in swamps and low, wet pasturelands. It blooms from July to September.

For more details I suggest calling your local extension service.

Tips for Winter

- Buy those houseplants that are easy to care for and can tolerate the normally difficult growing conditions found in most apartments and houses.
- Poinsettias that have finished flowering should be allowed to dry out. Store them on their sides in a greenhouse or in a cool cellar (55°–60° F) and cut back sparingly.
- Cinerarias and greenhouse primulas should be fertilized weekly the minute they show buds and their pots are filled with roots.
- During the cold winter months be sure to water plants with room-temperature water, especially African violets. Do it early in the day so they can dry off before night. Violets won't bloom if temperatures fall below 60°F or if they get insufficient light.
- Keep cyclamens moist (and I don't mean soggy) because if allowed to go dry they will "plop" over completely. To revive a dry plant, set the pot in a pan of warm water up to its rim, and put in a cool room for about one hour. The plant should perk up immediately unless it's been allowed to remain dry for an intolerable length of time.

Tips from Folk Wisdom

January
- Two full moons in a month bring on a flood.
- If the wind veers from north to northeast in winter, intense cold follows.
- If on a fair day in winter a white bank of clouds arises in the south, expect snow.

February
- Thunder on Shrove Tuesday fortelleth wind, store of fruit and plenty.
- Dry Lent, fertile year.
- When the sky seems full of stars, expect rain, or in winter, frost.

March
- In western Kansas it is said that when the moon is near full it never storms.
- Brisk winds from the south for several days in Texas are generally followed by a "Norther."
- If you plant onions on March 21, you may expect a good crop.

April
- If the horns of the moon are turned downward, it is a sign of rain.
- A wet Good Friday and a wet Easter Day make plenty of grass, but very little hay.
- Excessive twinkling of stars indicates heavy dews, rain and snow, or stormy weather in the near future.

May
- The later the blackthorn bloom after May 1, the better the rye and harvest.
- A hot May makes a fat churchyard!
- If a woman crosses your path when you're going to fish, you won't catch any fish.

June
- Butchering should be done on the first Friday in the new moon.
- If a stray cat comes into your house immediately after you move in, keep her for good luck.
- Calm weather in June sets corn in time.

July
- If it rains on the first Dog Day (July 3), it will rain for 40 days after.
- The roses are said to begin to fade on July 22.
- If a blue color predominates in a rainbow, the air is clearing.

August
- August sunshine and bright nights ripen the grapes.
- To cure rheumatism, put a copper penny in your shoe.
- On Whay Day in August observe the day the first heavy fog occurs, and expect a heavy frost on the same day in October.

September
- September rain is good for crops and vines.
- Shave for the first time at the new moon if you would have a heavy beard.
- Always leave by the door by which you enter.

October
- When stars flicker in a dark background, rain or snow soon follows.
- When the hoarfrost is accompanied by an east wind, it indicates that the cold will continue a long time.
- If it rains while a couple is being married, they will have sniveling children.

November
- Flowers in bloom late in autumn indicate a hard winter.
- Thunder in November, a fertile year to come.
- Crows cawing louder than usual is a sign of rain.

December
- Burning wood in winter "pops" more before snow.
- When there is a spring in the winter, or a winter in the spring, the year is never good.
- Marry in a snowstorm and you will become rich.

Tools

Be sure that all garden tools and machines are cleaned, oiled and greased to prevent rust. Get this work done on a day when the weather is bad, and you will find your spirits lifted considerably.

Tools with smooth wood handles are kindest to your hands. Paint the handles your favorite bright color to make them easier to spot in the garden.

Tree Care in Winter

The tree-filled landscapes of winter can be mistakenly thought to be asleep, but they're not. They are simply counting the days until spring.

Most of the growing points in trees are protected inside tight little jackets called buds. Only in spring will it be apparent whether the tree has put aside enough resources for a new season of growth.

Winter is a difficult time for trees, because they must stand in the face of drying and cold winds, sleet and snow. Food is carefully conserved for the coming needs of spring, while water continues to move through the tree until it freezes. Any hungry creature needing a meal chews and nibbles on the resting buds and twigs. Trees stand alone to survive all the circumstances that the winter season can generate.

What can you do to help our valuable trees? Here are a few tips that can help a tree be more efficient and effective in surviving the winter and thriving in spring. These winter techniques can pay off in a large way, yielding healthy and structurally sound trees.

The six critical things to do for your trees this winter are:

1. Add thin layer of composted organic mulch that blankets the soil surface. Mulch protects and conserves tree resources and recycles valuable minerals.
2. Properly wrap new trees that have not developed a corky bark and could easily be damaged. Mechanical injury from the environment—including chewing, rubbing and gnawing by animals—must be prevented.
3. Remove or correct clearly visible structural faults and deadwood. Try to make small pruning cuts that minimize the exposure of the central heartwood core on branches.
4. Perform limited pruning of declining and poorly placed branches. Pruning should conserve as many living branches as possible, with only a few selective cuts.
5. Fertilize in small quantities. Essential elements added over a mulch layer will help provide a healthy soil environment for root growth. For the winter months, choose a fertilizer with a low nitrogen content, to slow growth.
6. Water where soil and trees are cool but not frozen, and where there has been little rainfall. (Winter droughts call for watering, the same as summer droughts.) However, it's easy to overwater in winter, so take care!

For trees, wonderful springs come from well-tended winters. Help your trees emerge from winter for a healthy, vigorous spring.

Helping Trees in the City

Though city street trees endure stress like disease, temperature extremes, vandalism and drought conditions the year round, the winter season brings with it a more serious problem—damage from rock salt!

Rock-salt applications to roads and sidewalks can result in stunted growth, a decline in vitality and high levels of sodium and chloride ions in the spring spa of certain trees.

To protect street trees from this damage do not pile snow or salt sidewalks around the tree pit or trunk and carefully remove plowed snow from the tree pit. Do not nick the tree trunk with the snow shovel!

During periods of thaw when the air and soil temperatures are above freezing, water the tree to leach out salts. This should be done during early March. Wrap the trunk of trees smaller than 12 inches in diameter with burlap. Start at the soil line and work up to the lower branches. Use twine to hold the burlap. This will protect the tree from damage, especially from frost cracks. Be sure to remove the burlap in early April.

Underground Damage

Q. *I wintered my carrots in the garden under hay mulch. When I went to harvest them, many had been chewed off underground. What animal is doing this, and what do I do to stop it?*

A. Rodents, or most likely rot, are destroying the carrots. If the parts of the carrots left in the hole are slimy, it's no doubt a rot such as pyhthium is attacking your carrots.

If the crowns appear eaten, especially around the top of the root, then it's almost certain that moles or mice are the culprits.

If the problem is rot, the main cause is soil that is too moist. If there's a dry spell during winter, cover the patch with plastic and then pile the hay back on top. The plastic helps protect the carrots from the elements and provides a better growth environment.

During a mild winter, the rodent population soars. Moles and mice look for a safe winter haven, and your hay-covered carrot bed is the perfect spot!

Traps and deterrent sprays aren't too effective if you're losing the whole crop, so I suggest digging up the remaining crop and storing it in a cool (35° to 40° F) basement in boxes filled with moist sand. They should be okay for the rest of the winter.

Next season, plant your crop away from the house foundation or rock walls, and line the bottom and sides of the patch with hardware cloth.

Valentine Customs

Even before there were romance novels and the Romance Channel, there was the holiday of love and romance, Valentine's Day.

Contrary to what many believe, Valentine's Day is not just about greeting cards. Its origins stretch back to Imperial Rome.

In Roman times, the goddess Juno was honored in an early spring festival. Juno was the deity young women prayed to when hoping for true love. Pagan practices also provided Lupercus, a god for young men, who was also honored with a spring festival. A special feature of the Lupercan festival was its annual lottery in which young men drew the names of available young women; the girl they chose would be their partner for the festival, and often the arrangement led to marriage.

Just as the modern date for Christmas was adapted from a Roman winter solstice ritual, modern Valentine's Day was, in 3 A.D., a replacement for the Roman spring festival.

St. Valentine, as legend has it, was a Catholic priest who performed secret marriages for young lovers, despite a decree from the emperor Claudius banning the institution of Christian marriage. The priest lost his head in the process, and as a result February 14 comes down to us as a celebration of both the saint and romantic love sanctified.

Today, Valentine's Day is observed mainly through the exchange of gifts. The custom ranges from puppy-love cards given to kindergarten classmates to diamond earrings, rings or bracelets given by husbands to their wives.

Candy is another Valentine favorite. While chocolates may tip the scale in these fitness-conscious days, those little candy hearts are really cute, low-cal and delicious! Irresistible!

Of course, red roses are the traditional flowers of the day. So popular have roses become that I suggest buyer beware. Many retailers jack up the price of roses before Valentine's Day; thus the increasing popularity of red tulips.

Other gift ideas include CDs, live pets and, of course, lingerie! A quiet evening, perhaps some candlelight or champagne, seems the perfect bridge between the days of romance of ancient Rome and those of our times.

Water-Wise Gardening

The long drought across the United States may have ended (California comes to mind), but the need for water-wise gardening has not. Even gardeners who dwell in humid eastern areas have come to expect water restrictions during dry summers.

Keep in mind our supplies of clean, fresh water are dwindling everywhere. Using this precious resource as efficiently as possible just makes good sense no matter where you live and garden. For example, traditional overhead watering should be avoided because 50 to 60 percent of the water is lost to evaporation and run-off.

Here are some guidelines to help you make the best use of water in your garden.

1. Start with good soil preparation. Adding organic matter will increase the water-holding capacity of light soils and improve drainage in heavy ones.
2. Choose plants that tolerate dry soil or drought conditions. Specific choices will depend on the climate of your area. The extension service of your local garden nursery can help you choose plants that are well adapted to your area. Garden for the area you live in and by that I mean plant native plants. Of course, if you have a greenhouse or lean-to, you can grow anything you desire, especially if you live in a northern area.
3. Landscape with water conservation in mind. A windbreak of drought-resistant shrubs and trees planted on the windward side of an exposed site can reduce the water needs of the other plants in the garden.
4. Use intensive planting methods in the vegetable garden. Closely spaced plants in beds will shade the soil surface, reducing water loss.
5. Use mulch to reduce moisture loss from the soil. It will cut down on your weeding chores at the same time.
6. Drip irrigation will put water right where it's needed, with little lost to evaporation or run-off. Whether it's in the flower or vegetable garden or around individual trees and shrubs in the landscape, drip irrigation helps give plants the optimum amount of moisture while using water most efficiently.
7. If you use sprinklers, water either first thing in the morning or in the evening to reduce water loss by evaporation of the heat of the day, especially during the hot months of July and August. Apply water only as fast as the soil can absorb it—otherwise you'll lose a lot as run-off.
8. Reduce the size of your lawn. Even in humid climates, lawns need frequent watering to keep them lush and green through the heat of summer. Keep only as much lawn as you absolutely need for children and dogs. But those of you that need all the lawn you've got and could still use some more, try planting some of the new varieties of drought-tolerant turf grasses that have been developed recently. Suggested improved varieties of tall fescue grasses include Falcon, Mustang and Olympic.

Whiteflies

Q. *I have tried everything to get rid of whiteflies on most of my houseplants. Nothing seems to work. Please help me!*

A. A combination of insecticide-soap spray, sticky traps and persistence is the key to getting rid of this nuisance.

Hang a few yellow sticky tapes around your plants, to capture as many adults as you can (even if you don't catch all the whitefly adults, this is a good way to monitor their presence).

Spray your plants thoroughly when you do spray—over and under—don't miss a spot! Spray every few days for a month, because new whiteflies are hatching all the time, and you have to keep up with their pace. Keep in mind, many mature insects are in the pupal stage during which sprays don't work.

The key is to eliminate all the life cycles of whiteflies over a period of time, so that no stage is ever left behind to reproduce.

Do be careful about bringing in new plants. Inspect them carefully, then rinse off the leaves with a soapy sponge (do not use detergent), and keep them separated from other plants for several weeks.

Winter Gardens

In places where winters are freezing and snowy, most gardens are silent except for hungry birds and a few lonely squirrels looking for nuts. But what has happened to the other garden creatures like butterflies, spiders, frogs, ladybugs and earthworms? And where are all those buzzing bees and chirping crickets?

Many of your garden guests are sleeping in a deep, coma-like rest called hibernation. They don't drink or eat; they hardly even breathe. For instance, if there's a frozen pond in your garden, the frogs are hibernating deep down in the muddy bottom, waiting for the ice to thaw. Earthworms are sleeping, too, curled up underground. When the cold weather is over, they will push back up to the surface and go back to work by loosening up the soil and depositing nutrients in their wake.

Honeybees spend their winter in hives. Last fall, some of the females mated; then all the males died. So now the only bees alive in the hive are the queen bee and the fertilized females that mated. In spring, the females will lay eggs that hatch into larvae inside the hive. The larvae will develop into males and females so that, once more, the hive will be jammed again with buzzing honeybees.

Ladybugs, also, are hiding in the garden; they might be huddled together under a pile of leaves or a fallen log. Often thousands of ladybugs rest in one hideout.

Last autumn, some butterflies left the garden and flew to warmer weather. But many just stayed home. Look closely at garden wells and tree trunks and you might spot a chrysalis (cocoon) attached to one. Inside the chrysalis, a butterfly is developing. When the weather gets warm, the chrysalis will split open, and the new butterfly will pop out and fly away.

If you're lucky and you keep your eyes open, you may find some cricket eggs this winter. Tree crickets like to make holes in a slit along a tree branch. They lay pinhead-sized eggs in them.

Last but not least, garden spiders last fall were busy constructing their winter haven, papery-looking egg sacs about marble-size. Then they attach themselves to weeds or tall grasses. Baby spiders hatch inside the sacs and are smart enough to spend the winter there. When the warm days of spring arrive, they'll break out of the sacs—all ready to weave their own webs.

Just remember: your winter garden is full of life; but right now the DO NOT DIS-TURB sign is up. To survive the cold, your garden guests must be left alone to sleep and dream so that, when spring comes, they'll be up and ready, making your garden the best place in town.

Winter Room with a View

If you're tired of looking out on a gray and lifeless landscape during the chilly days of winter, follow my advice: Plant a colorful tree, vibrant shrub or winter-hardy annual in the fall and watch your garden come to life.

One popular way to create winter color is through the use of a variety of ever-greens. There are a number of possibilities and a garden center or landscape profession-al can help you make selections based, in part, on a particular tree's foliage and bark col-ors. When planting with winter color in mind, don't overlook ornamental kale, pansies, perennials or herbs.

Deciduous holly is always a good idea. You must get a male and female because if you have one without the other—no berries! Their berries are even more showy in the winter-time after their leaves have dropped.

There are a number of winter-hardy annuals to plant in the fall, such as foxglove, Canterbury bells and dusty miller. Ask the experts at your local garden center for annuals that will flourish in your wintertime soil, sun, wind, moisture and temperature conditions.

If you're too busy or unsure about what or how to plant your landscape, consider calling in a local landscape professional; they're just waiting to help you.

Winter Suggestions

- Great cooks have secret recipes and so do gardeners. The best amaryllis breeder we know gave us his "secret" potting mix: 1 part each of clean, sharp sand, well-rotted leaf mold, well-rotted cow manure and sphagnum peat moss.
- Try a drop of glycerin in your birdbath; it will keep the water from freezing. A mirror on the bottom will also keep it warm.
- Waste not, want not. Save the wood ashes from your fireplace to spread around peonies, roses, delphiniums and lilacs. The ashes serve as a natural fertilizer and soil conditioner.
- To keep fresh-cut flowers from drooping, try adding 2 tablespoons of vinegar and 3 tablespoons of sugar to each quart of warm water. Keep at least 3 inches or 4 inches of this mixture in each vase. Changing the water and recutting the stems every day or two also helps.
- Spring can come early for those with a greenhouse, cold frame, sunny window or fluorescent-light garden. Start seeds and cuttings now and get a head start on outdoor planting. When deciding what to plant, select for your area. Check with your garden center or contact your county agent through your State Agricultural Experiment Station.
- "Squiggly" packing foam makes a great drainage material for potted plants. It's especially effective for hanging planters because it's lightweight, does not retain water and is usually available free from appliance stores!
- When making a terrarium (bottle garden), it's the dickens keeping the sides of the bottle clean. Use a very dry soil (most important) and after planting, use a cooking bulb, baster-type, to drip water down the inside of the bottle. It will clean the sides while adding moisture at the same time.
- Use your indoor garden light for double duty. Use it as a room safety or night light. This helps offset the cost. Use a timer to prevent long and costly light periods. The cost of using a timer is well spent if it prevents long light periods because of forgetfulness. Saving energy saves money!

Yeast

Researchers report that fine-grained or pelleted dried yeast makes a perfect fertilizer for greenhouse grown potted plants over a period of at least two months following application. Yeast has all the ingredients—nitrogen, phosphorus and potassium—needed to make plants thrive.

Application should be $1/17$ to $1/3$ ounce of yeast per pot. Plants used by researchers included chrysanthemums, zonal geraniums and poinsettias.

Previous page: C. Z. with grandsons Gregory and
Winston at peony time. Above: Over the years the
yew hedges around the kitchen garden have been
selectively trained and clipped to form a grand arch
over the entry from the topiary garden. Blue
Siberian iris bloom with peonies. Opposite, top to
bottom: Pink azaleas grace the stables. A collection
of old colored glass bottles filled with cut flowers
from the greenhouse, ready to be placed around
the house to make the rooms come alive. The
kitchen garden also provides lots of flowers for
cutting: here, orange lilies, Gloriosa daisies and
white 'Annabelle' hydrangeas.

This page, clockwise, from top right: Late summer harvest: beets and parsley have been hosed off right in the garden. Rhubarb chard is one of the most decorative vegetables, also tasty and full of vitamins. Yellow zucchini is a recent introduction for summer squash lovers. Opposite page, from top: Lettuce, carrots and radishes are sown in the spring and again in late summer for a constant supply of fresh vegetables. Nasturtium flowers are edible, adding color and a slightly peppery taste to salads. Sweet peppers, sweet onions and spinach, freshly picked and ready for the cook.

Above: Old camellia bushes and a glory bush stand outside the greenhouse. Right: Debudding peonies means removing from each stem all but the largest bud. The same technique is used for dahlias to produce grander flowers. Opposite page, clockwise from top: Beets and peas enjoy a refreshing shower from the irrigation system. In late fall the raised beds are mulched with pine needles or sown with a winter cover crop of ryegrass, which acts as green manure when turned under in the spring. C. Z. can't resist pulling a weed with her assistant Lyle. Pine needle winter blankets for the peony beds.

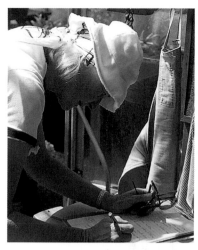

Opposite: Snow drapes the statue of Diana. This page, clockwise from top left: C. Z. lists supplies and seeds needed for the new season. A rare orchid in the library. C. Z. and Tiger celebrate a surprise snow in late April. Poinsettias and amaryllis on the mantle in front of a painting of C. Z. and her children, Alexander and Cornelia. C. Z., Venus and Tiger frolic in the snow-covered allee of linden trees. A holiday wreath of blue spruce and pine cones.

Opposite, top: All-white flowers picked from the garden and ready to be put in vases for a dinner party. Opposite, bottom: If you want beautiful hydrangeas, keep the hose handy, otherwise they wilt quickly and become de-hydrangeas. This page, clockwise from right: In late summer the lindens in the allee begin to shed older leaves. Freesias are favored for exquisite, unique fragrance. Asters give fall color and look beautiful in bouquets. Luncheon is served on the rose garden terrace. Next page: C. Z. with homegrown sweet corn ("how sweet it is") and her devoted assistant Tiger.

spring

The hardest thing about spring is waiting—waiting for its true arrival. The first warm day doesn't count. You have to wait until the frost is really out of the ground. Try squeezing a handful of soil; it should crumble apart rather than clump damply. How exciting! It's finally time to plant and you're so well organized after the long winter that you know exactly what you want to plant, where and when.

You can go out now and uncover any shrubs, trees (fruit and otherwise), perennials and berries that you had covered in fall for winter protection. Of course, you know by now the pH of your garden soil and you have everything

ready to go. You'll need to clean your garden and till the soil in the beds, get your tools organized and decide which fertilizer should be used. I suggest C. Z. Grow! If you're planting roses before you get started, make sure you have proper drainage; roses need it to thrive. In addition to roses the following season, we will talk about planting flowers and vegetables, annuals, perennials, shrubs and trees. You'll learn everything you need to know to go about preparing your garden and getting it off to a great start in the spring.

Annual Flowers

What is an annual? Simply speaking, an annual flower is one that completes its life cycle (from germination through flowering to settling seed) in one year or one growing season. In other words, an annual is any plant bought at the nursery in spring that dies in the fall. Of course, there are many exceptions to this rule, and many variations.

The exceptions are due mostly to climate, since many plants we grow as annuals in North America are perennials in milder climates. For example, there are tender perennials such as wax begonias, salvia, verbena and geraniums, which are usually easy to care for, long-blooming and adaptable. California poppies, which most of us grow as annuals, may thrive for several years and attain great size in a warm climate with dry soil.

Hardy annuals: Sown in early spring, these relatively tough customers will mature and bloom in summer. They set seed if you allow them to do so and then die away. Hardy annuals can take considerable cold, and frost too. Most can be sown directly into the garden.

In most places, the next planting after spring is fall—October in northern states. Hardy annuals include sweet alyssum, larkspur, stock sunflowers, California poppies, Shirley poppies, nasturtium and sweet peas. Rule of thumb: most self-seeders can be assumed hardy.

Half-hardy annuals: These plants are a bit demanding and like to be snug in warm greenhouses until the nights are truly warm (over 60°F). They prefer loose, fluffy soil, plenty of water and fertilizer given early and often. Half-hardy annuals also germinate, flower and die all in one year, but they require a longer period of growth.

To give them a good start in life, sow half-hardy annuals indoors and then move them cautiously into the garden only when all danger of frost has passed.

Half-hardy annuals include many summer bedding plants, such as cosmos, begonias, zinnias, marigolds, petunias, phlox, lobelia, salvia, heliotropes, dianthus and verbena.

Tender annuals: These are flowers that originated in frost-free tropical climates and can't tolerate frost at all. They also dislike chilly days and nights, and refuse to grow until the weather warms up. Dahlias, zinnias and portulaca are examples of tender annuals.

Annuals: What a Bargain!

Of all the major groups of plants, annuals have as much to offer as any—if not more. Annuals add color, texture, fragrance, beauty and form to the garden, asking little in return.

From the fuzzy foliage of 'Dusty Miller' to the French marigold variety 'Aurora Red' and rich jewel hues of coleus, annuals offer many diverse colors and qualities. A gardener bringing home containers of bedding plants can create a fabulous landscape in much the same manner as an artist with an assortment of paints.

With loving care, annuals are effective in borders, beds, window boxes, along walls, trellises and fences. They can also edge a walkway, blend beautifully with perennial plantings, brighten a shady nook, shield spent bulbs or add zest to a vegetable patch.

There are a few guidelines for setting out tender bedding plants. Before you bring them home, plan what to put where and then prepare the soil. Limit plantings to four to six species with no more than three basic colors. Put the taller plants in back, lower growers in the middle and at the edge.

If you have some strong colors that don't blend, simply plant white or blue flowers between them in large groups to serve as a neutralizer. Delicate pastel shades are best in the foreground, while deeper and stronger colors such as purple and red are perfect for shaded or distant places.

Impatiens: The most popular bedding plant. Versatile with single or double blooms and thrives in shade. Use as a ground cover, in a bed, in a tub or in a hanging basket. Wide range of colors, such as white, pink, red, orange or multicolor. The New Guinea impatiens are taller with fewer but larger blooms and variegated foliage. These beauties require more sun than the standard impatiens. Good choices: 'Tango' and 'Spectral.'

Cosmos: Showy, long-lasting and grows rapidly, comes in white and several bright colors with yellow centers, grows 2 to 8 feet high. Sow seeds directly into the garden (after the frost is out of the ground) in a sunny location. Thrives even in poor, dry soil. Excellent choices: 'Bright Lights,' shades from yellow or orange; 'Versailles,' a Japanese strain bred for commercial-quality cut flowers; 'Sonata,' a white flower. These lovely flowers attract butterflies and birds to the garden.

Marigold: Sun-loving and long-flowering. The seeds are easy to handle and start to germinate swiftly. Four common categories and recommended series include 'Signet,' feathery-leafed, compact plants with thumbnail-size single blossoms; 'Gem' series French or dwarf, generally no more than 12 inches tall, double-flower heads and many warm colors; 'Aurora' series triploids, 12 to 18 inches tall, flowers all season; 'Nugget' and 'Fireworks' series, tallest variety with large, coarse leaves and huge 4- to 5-inch blooms. The perfect annual for a children's garden.

Alyssum: Ground cover for edging or drifts in a formal bed, extremely hardy, tolerates hot and cold temperatures, fairly drought-resistant, compact and very fragrant with pink, white or purplish flowers. Plant in full sun. Good cultivars: 'Pastel Carpet,' 'Rosie O'Day,' 'Snow Crystals' and another favorite of mine, 'Carpet of Snow.'

Geranium: Brilliant colors, marvelous as bedding plants, in pots, as borders or as shrubs of ever-cascading varieties over window boxes and hanging baskets. Most types grow to 30 inches and don't mind neglect. Don't overwater; simply let the soil dry to about 1 inch deep, then water thoroughly. Start seeds about 12 to 14 weeks before the last frost date. Suggested varieties: 'Orbit' or 'Multibloom.'

Petunia: Recently edged out as a favorite U.S. flower. Easy to tend, long-flowering and versatile. The perfect bedding plant for window boxes or in hanging baskets. Seeds will germinate in 10 to 12 days with heat and light. Start six weeks before planting. There are many sizes, shapes and colors from which to choose.

Zinnia: The perfect annual for a child's first garden and for yours, too, with large, easy-to-handle seeds that can be sown directly into the garden bed. All colors except blue. Flowers range in size and shape from 1-inch singles to pompons 6 inches across. Many All-American Selections winners include 'Ruffles,' 'Peter Pan,' 'Dasher' and 'Border Beauty.' Plant in masses in the cutting garden. (My favorite is 'Envy'—it's green!)

Containers: The best candidates for container culture are annuals with shallow roots and long-flowering seasons. Geraniums and dwarf zinnias are good choices for one-variety containers.

Hanging baskets look their best if they contain only matched plants, while window boxes make a great show with a minimum of three species. For example, odd numbers of plants make pleasing arrangements. Use single colors or simple combinations and stagger the plants and rows of plants within the box for a luxurious appearance.

Ground covers: Cover the ground quickly with trailing annuals. Such plants spill over the edges of walls, paths, trellises and fences or screen the pool or patio for privacy. I suggest nasturtium varieties such as 'Climbing Mix' and 'Double Gleam'; they are foolproof, inexpensive, lush and instant trailers and climbers. They can blanket the ground before slower-growing perennial ground covers.

Other spreading annuals include zinnia 'Mandarin Orange' and portulaca 'Wildfire,' both of which thrive in poor, dry soils. 'Heavenly Blue' morning glories are a perfect solution; they create a luxurious wall of flowers from midsummer to frost.

Unless you already have an old-fashioned cottage and garden with annuals and perennials in splendid profusion, here are some suggested favorites for you to plant this spring: zinnia 'Big Red,' celosia 'Indian Prince,' cosmos long-lasting 'Heidi,' cornflower 'Blue Diadem,' marigolds in all colors and sizes. With these suggestions, you'll amply fill your vases.

Consider such everlastings as 'Lavender Lady' and 'Strawberry Fields' globe amaranth, 'Snowflake' baby's breath and 'Bright Bikini' mixed strawflower statice 'Soiree improved' and either plume or crested types of celosia such as 'Castle' and 'Chief' series; and everyone's favorite sunflowers, 'Sunburst' and 'Italian White.' These varieties are all willing bloomers.

Artificial Light's a Natural

Q. *My sunny window space is limited. Can I grow flowers and vegetable seeds under artificial light?*

A. Yes, of course you can grow vigorous seedlings under artificial light. Just make sure to keep the lights on at least 16 hours a day. This way, you'll have better, healthier seedlings than if you put the plants on a windowsill that receives insufficient natural light.

Berry Good Advice

Blackberries do best in full sun and prefer a slightly acidic (pH 5.5 to 6.5) compost-enriched soil that drains well. The berries spread rapidly, so give them plenty of room to grow. Harvest when the stems separate easily from the cone.

Blueberries, like their berry cousins, prefer an acidic compost-enriched soil that drains well. Keep soil moist but never soggy. Ripe berries drop off the vines when touched. Vines take two to four years to begin bearing fruit.

Raspberries prefer full sun and well-drained soil rich in organic matter. Give them plenty of room to spread. Summer-bearing varieties produce a big harvest midsummer into fall.

Strawberries prefer full sun and fertilized soil that's slightly acidic (pH 5.5 to 6.5) and drains well. Strawberries bear fruit the first season.

Bouquets for Spring

Exotic floral arrangements no longer need to be the exclusive property of embassy balls and White House galas. By following the same basic steps as professional designers, you can make beautiful fresh flower arrangements for your house.

First, decide where you will place the arrangement—in the dining room, kitchen counter or living room. When purchasing your flowers, choose varieties and stem lengths that will fit the "scene" and use different types of flowers such as:

- Several "mass" flowers with a round shape, such as roses, carnations or gerberas.
- A few tall, linear flowers like gladiolus or liatris.
- Filler flowers (stems with a lot of little flowers) like statice or wax flower.

Each of these types has a particular role to play in an arrangement. Mass flowers are the focal point of color and interest in the bouquet. Tall flowers add height at the center of the bouquet. Filler flowers give your bouquet fullness. Include in your selection some flowers that have their own natural foliage, such as chrysanthemums and feverfew.

For a beautiful bouquet, you also must have some stems of foliage or "greens." The foliage expands an arrangement, giving it a full, lush look. Ask your florist for more unusual types of foliage, such as myrtle, asparagus and eucalyptus.

At home, select the container that will fit the mood of the occasion, the location and the flowers you have selected. The possibilities are endless from an antique white teapot for garden roses to a silver urn for gladiolus and lilies. Make sure the container has a neck and bowl large enough for the stems to fit loosely.

The container must also be the right size to give your flowers the best display. A good rule of thumb is that the height of the vase should be about half the stem length of the flowers or a little less. For example, a stem of roses 24 inches high looks best in a vase that is 12 inches high.

Now you are ready to start arranging the flowers.

Put warm water and a packet of fresh flower food in the vase. Put the foliage in first. Prepare the foliage stems by stripping all leaves from the section of stems that will be underwater. Cut the foliage stems to the right length by making a diagonal cut at the bot-

tom with a sharp knife. Place the stems of foliage in the vase, creating a framework or a grid that will hold the flowers in place.

Next, prepare the flowers by stripping all foliage from the section of stems that will be underwater. Place mass flowers in the container first. Arrange them in groups of three, placing each flower the same distance from the others, like the points in a triangle. Then, add linear flowers to give height and width to your arrangement. Next, add stems of filler flowers to fill in spaces between the flowers and foliage.

Finally, stand back and review your work from a distance of several feet. If any flowers appear to be out of line, you can make adjustments by cutting stems shorter, if necessary.

Long-Lasting Cut Flowers

Always cut stems at an angle under water to lessen trauma to the blooms. Smash the woody stems of roses and lilacs for greater water absorption. I singe my lilac stems with a match; they seem to last longer (just as you do with poppies). Remove all leaves that are below the water line to stop decomposition, odor and bacteria.

Change the water every day and re-cut stems every two days. Don't use tap water if you have a water softener; the flowers don't like salt.

Keep flowers out of sunlight and heat (for example, not on top of the TV).

Put a drop of bleach in the final rinse when you wash vases to keep the growth of bacteria at bay.

Boxwood

Q. *The leaves of my English boxwood have turned a reddish-bronze color. I noticed the problem last year, and it seemed to get progressively worse as time went by. How about the newly developed leaves? Will they turn colors too?*

A. Some bronzing of boxwood foliage is normal because of winter burn. However, spring growth should emerge a healthy green. If not, there are two possible reasons.

It may be caused by poor drainage or drought. Bronzing caused by drought can be reversed by giving your boxwoods ample water throughout the growing season, especially in late fall. Poor drainage is more difficult to cope with, but I suggest mulching around the plants.

Another cause of bronzing is a disease caused by the Volutella fungus. The problem is more commonly seen in boxwood varieties that have a light growth. Thinning interior branches and removing infected stems will slow the progress of the disease. Or simply pull out the diseased boxwood and plant a nonresistant variety.

Bulbs after Spring Bloom

People often wonder what to do when tulips, daffodils, hyacinths and other spring-blooming bulb flowers have faded. Here are some tips that should come in handy.

After spring-flowering bulbs have faded, snip off the dead flowers so they won't go to seed. But let the green foliage die back naturally—a process that generally takes about six weeks.

A deadheading exception: Daffodils do not require deadheading, though many people choose to do so because they think their gardens will look more attractive. Large naturalized beds of daffodils can be left as is after blooming and suffer no ill effects.

Avoid the urge to tidy up bulb plantings after they bloom by tying up the leaves with string or rubber bands, as some people suggest. The six-week leaf die-back time is a critical work period for leaves busy with photosynthesis (the process by which plants use chlorophyll to produce the starches that re-charge the bulb with food for next year's bloom). The leaves must be free to soak up sunshine during this crucial period.

If dying foliage seems unattractive, the best solution is camouflage. Interplant with hosta or other leafy perennials. They will grow up and around fading bulb plants and disguise the dying foliage of the bulbs.

Remember, some bulbs (such as tulips and hyacinths) do not always come back. If the variety you planted wasn't a variety marked "good for perennializing," then it's probably best to treat them as annuals. Compost or toss them after bloom and re-plant new bulbs in the fall.

Planting indoor-forced bulbs (potted daffodils, crocuses, etc.) in the garden after they've faded is never a sure thing. Unlike bulbs planted in the ground during the fall planting season—or even spring-planted pre-sprouted "bulbettes" which can mature in place in your garden—forced bulbs that have bloomed and faded indoors have been through a pretty exhausting process, and they may or may not re-bloom in the garden the following year.

Bulbs like crocuses and daffodils, which are good at naturalizing, generally do well when they are planted outside after forcing. Just plant them out in the garden when they're finished flowering. Give them water and some slow-release bulb food. Then wait until the leaves brown and die back before chopping them off at ground level. No guarantees, but there's a good chance they'll do fine and come back, if conditions for re-blooming are generally good in your area.

It's a different story with bulbs such as tulips, which do not readily come back when originally planted in the garden in fall. With these flowers it's generally not worth the trouble to plant them outdoors. The same is true of paper-white narcissi. These should be enjoyed during the initial indoor bloom—then composted and just tossed out.

Forced hyacinths may come back in the garden, but not with the same full, robust blooms that they had in their first year. (This is also true of hyacinths planted in the garden.) For these bulbs, it would be a matter of preference. If you don't mind the smaller blooms, fine—otherwise, forget it.

Cauliflower: Why Not in a Container?

Plant one to two cauliflower plants per 5-gallon container. Tie the large outer leaves together over developing cauliflower heads to prevent discoloration. Plant some petunias or geraniums around them as colorful companions.

Chamomile, Tea and More

Chamomile is more than just a tea. Cultivated for centuries in Europe and honored by the ancient Egyptians, it's one of the most versatile herbs for healing the body and soul.

There are two types of chamomile with medicinal properties. German chamomile

(*Matricaria recutita*) is a 1- to 3-foot-tall re-seeding annual with a dreamy apple fragrance and is the one usually found in tea bags and other products.

Roman chamomile (*Chamaemelum Mobile*), a low-growing perennial, is perfect for a ground cover and is hardy in U.S.D.A. Zones 6 through 9. It gives off a heady apple scent, but yields a more bitter taste.

Both plants are similar in that they produce feathery leaves and dainty flowers with white petals and yellow centers.

Harvest chamomile in full bloom throughout the summer, making sure all dew has evaporated first. Spread the flowers sparingly on a screen or cloth and let them dry in the shade. Discard any stem or leaf parts and store flowers in an airtight container away from light, heat and moisture.

When drunk as a tea, chamomile helps to alleviate insomnia and to calm the nerves. It will also relieve nausea and indigestion. Dab a moist tea bag on skin inflammations and bacterial infections—it feels great on a hot summer day.

To make the perfect pick-me-up, pour 1 cup of boiling water over 1 tablespoon of fresh or dried flowers. Let the tea steep ten to 15 minutes, but cover to prevent the escape of medicinal magic. For insomnia, sip the tea before going to sleep. For digestive problems, drink three to four cups several times a day, between meals.

Both Roman and German chamomile thrive best growing in full sun and fairly light, sandy soil. Sow seeds outdoors in early spring or late summer by scattering them. Keep the soil moist but not soggy.

When the seedlings are 1 to 2 inches tall, thin them out so that they are 8 to 12 inches apart. For a ground cover, thin Roman chamomile seedlings to 4 inches apart.

Weed carefully, since you must avoid disturbing the shallow roots when using a hoe.

Clematis

If you want your clematis to give spectacular bloom, situate the roots in cool shade but give the vine lots of sun. The same idea applies to certain lilies, in particular the late-summer-blooming *Speciosum rubrums* and *auratums*.

Composting

Despite all its benefits—both for the environment and for your garden—composting can seem to be more trouble than it's worth. Many gardeners who faithfully compost kitchen scraps and lawn clippings find the process takes too long and, when it's done, there just isn't enough compost for an entire garden. You can avoid this and other common composting problems by adding peat moss to the compost bin and when mixing compost into the soil.

Spring is an especially good time to "renovate" an existing compost pile since the compost material has had plenty of time to decompose over the winter. While it takes some elbow grease, the entire composting process is easier when you incorporate peat. In the compost bin, peat helps produce better compost by speeding up the process, reducing odors and controlling air and water in the compost pile. Start by mixing a half-inch layer of peat to every 4 inches of compostable materials, being sure to flip over the top layers of organic materials every week or two. Keep the center of the pile moist, not soggy, by adding water when needed.

Q. *I've never composted before. Is it difficult?*

A. Composting is as easy as boiling an egg! Just add water, some shredded clippings, leaves, kitchen wastes—and stir. Cook until it's done, then serve up a fantastic flower or vegetable garden.

Q. *What do I use for kitchen scraps?*

A. Be sure your kitchen scraps include only vegetables, fruits, bread and pasta. Don't use bones, fats or meat, because proteins don't degrade well and may attract animals.

Q. *Do I add leaves, clippings and waste in any particular order?*

A. Any order you choose is fine. Simply add different materials in layers. Each layer should be 8 inches thick. Then water each layer until it's like a squeezed-out sponge.

Crabgrass Prevention

It's that time again to give some thought to preventing crabgrass from invading our lawns. We must fight back!

The best way to combat this problem is to know what to do before the enemy invades your lawn. For starters, long-term grass control depends on the use of the right grass in the right place, planted at the proper time with adequate mowing, fertilization, watering and disease and insect control. Having a healthy, vigorous lawn is the first line of defense against crabgrass.

Keep in mind that not all crabgrass preventers can be used on all varieties of grass. As for timing, it's best to apply a preventer when the forsythia bushes are in full bloom. Using a pre-emergent crabgrass preventer is the best way to prevent the invasion of crabgrass.

If your grass is growing under drought conditions, it's advisable to water the lawn the day before applying the application. You must always read the label carefully and follow the manufacturer's instructions. To be on the safe side, ask your garden center or extension center for advice on what products are best for you in relation to the variety of grass you have.

Cucumbers

If you live in a zone where the growing season is short, start your cucumber seeds indoors four to six weeks before it's time to set out transplants. When setting out transplants, cover the baby plants with "hot caps" or plastic to protect them from frost.

Don't worry about the failure of the first early flowers to set fruit, because the male flowers open first. About a week later you'll see flowers with baby cucumbers at their bases. The male flowers supply the pollen that is transferred by insects to the female flowers.

It's important to pick the fruit as soon as they reach usable size. I can't stress this enough, because even a few fruit left to mature on the vine will completely stop the setting of new fruit. Invite friends and neighbors to share your harvest if you can't keep up.

Disease resistance is important in cucumbers; sow these newer "types": 'Meridan' (Cornell); 'Marketer' Hybrid (Cornell); 'Marketmore' (Cornell); 'Triumph' Hybrid (All-America Selection). Do not pick cucumbers until the leaves are dry in the morning, as disease is easily spread by disturbing wet or damp foliage.

For a continuous supply, there must be at least two plantings between May 1 and July 10. If a few radish seeds are sown in each hill, they will germinate quickly and attract all the insects. As soon as the cucumbers appear, pull up the radishes and destroy them, including the insects!

Cut Flowers, Long-Lasting

Whether you are arranging them for your house or to give to a friend, follow these tips to make cut flowers last longer and look fresher.

1. Harvest either early morning or evening; never but never cut flowers in midday sun!
2. Carry a pail with water and place each flower (especially roses) into it immediately.
3. Cut at a slant to maximize the water-absorbing surface and to prevent a stem from resting flat against the bottom of the pail. It's usually best to cut stems a bit longer than you think will be needed.
4. Back in the house, fill a clean, deep container with tepid water, re-cut each stem and place in the container. Leave the flowers in a cool, dark place for several hours, even better overnight if possible.
5. Always handle flowers carefully by their stems at every stage. When you lay them out on a table, let the heads hang over the edge to prevent crushing.
6. As you make arrangements, re-cut each stem once more on a slant to the desired length and remove all leaves that will end up below the waterline of the vase.
7. Change the water every day or two and, as they fade, remove dead flowers.

Cuttings, How to Take

Take 3 to 4 inches of vigorous terminal and lateral shoots with a sharp knife and dust the cut ends with rooting powder. Insert several of these cuttings into sterile rooting media such as vermiculite and peat, and place in a sterilized container with a drainage hole.

Enclose the plant in a plastic bag to simulate a greenhouse effect. Make sure the medium is moist, but not wet. Place the little greenhouse in ample light, but out of direct sunlight, and wait for several weeks for the cuttings to root. Once rooted, move to maximum light and coolish temperatures.

Cuttings, Time to Root

Recycle last year's potted plants: Fuchsias, geraniums, begonias and other outdoor bedding or container plants that have been living indoors all winter should be attended to now. Whether growing in a greenhouse, sunny window or under lights, my advice is to propagate new plants from these. No matter how good they look now, the plants that result from the new rooted cuttings will be far healthier and better-looking than the old ones.

Dandelions: Eat Them!

Biblical scholars say dandelions were probably one of the common herbs of feasts and daily life. Since then they've been popular throughout most of the world as medicine and food. All parts of the dandelion—leaves, flowers and roots—are edible, each in its own season and in its own way.

Young spring leaves are delicious as cooked greens in salads, baked dishes, or in gravy spooned over potatoes. Pick tender leaves before the flower buds and the greens taste bitter.

Harvest dandelion greens throughout the summer by cutting the leaves back to the top of the root, then simply snip off new growth. Cut the greens with a bit of root attached; it helps hold the leaves when washed before use.

Harvest the roots during fall and winter months. Roasted, cleaned and ground dandelion roots make a great caffeine-free base for cold and hot drinks.

If you're like most people, you probably have more dandelions than you can use. If dandelions don't grow where you live, they will grow easily in your garden. They thrive in most climates (except extreme heat) and in almost any soil. They're one of nature's most prolific weeds; at least 25 dandelion species exist around the world, while only a few are common in the United States. Dandelions are the only herb that has been found on the margins of desert water holes.

Lawn dandelions fall into two categories: healthy ones and the others. The best way to get rid of the healthy ones to is eat them before they flower or set seed.

The others, including those that have been contaminated with car exhaust, road salt or chemicals, should be dug up and composted. Avoid eating plants growing close to neighbors' yards or close to streets that have been treated with chemicals.

Also, be careful where you harvest dandelions for consumption. If the taproots of mature plants are not removed to a depth of at least 12 inches, the plant will return. Dandelions can be easily dug up in damp soil. Simply pull the leaves to one side, plunge a trowel or a dandelion digger straight down into the soil along the root as deep as possible, push the handle down and pop up the root.

People in France, Britain, Russia, China and elsewhere consume them as well as raise them commercially. Growing dandelion greens generates millions of dollars a year in the United States. Most greens are grown in Texas, Florida, California and New Jersey, and are shipped all over the country. A company in Wilton, Maine, has been growing dandelion greens since 1886.

You can harvest fresh dandelion greens all winter long. Plant several dozen roots in large containers with drainage holes in the bottom and place them on a south-facing windowsill. You'll get a nice bunch of fresh greens every two weeks.

Seeds for wild species and several hybrid dandelions are available from some of the finest seed houses in the country, so read your catalogs carefully.

Make the perfect liquid fertilizer by placing a handful of dandelion leaves in a pint of water, bringing it to a boil, covering it and letting it cool. After cooling, strain the liquid off, dilute with 4 tablespoons water, add a tablespoon of liquid soap (not detergent) and use immediately as a leaf spray.

Day lilies

You can plant day lilies in spring or fall since they tolerate a wide range of growing conditions. Some bloomers are better than others, such as 'Happy Returns,' a compact 18-inch yellow variety that will bloom all summer long. It is a true yellow and will blend beautifully with other flowers.

Edible Flowers

Edible flowers add a distinctive flavor and a splash of color to all kinds of foods. But you can't eat just any flower. Some are poisonous. Even edible flowers may be contaminated by chemicals. Don't eat flowers you buy from a florist, greenhouse or a roadside vendor. There's a long list of flowers that aren't edible, such as buttercup, lily of the valley, foxglove, periwinkle, oleander, delphinium and daffodils, so memorize these names for safety's sake!

For edible flowers, you need to either grow your own or buy them in the produce section of your supermarket. They should be labeled as "edible flowers." Only eat flowers if you're absolutely sure they are safe.

You can grow edible flowers in the kitchen garden outside your back door, such as marigolds, nasturtiums (enjoy the leaves and the blossoms), borage, pansies, violets and roses. Fertilize your flowers as you would a vegetable garden. Then, when harvesting, wash them well and gently pat them dry.

Evergreens

Q. *I want more evergreens; when should I plant, how large can they be at planting and what is most hardy? Also, what kinds of bushes fit in with forest shade? Are forsythia and lilacs possible, and can you suggest others?*

A. I've planted many pine trees around my house on Long Island, and I've found the Japanese white pine to be very satisfactory. It is a hardy species with wide-spreading horizontal branches—wonderful windbreakers.

Another type you might like is the hemlock. It is hardy and one of the fastest-growing of all evergreens. Any tree can be as large as you want at planting, but to be realistic, trees over 5 feet are too difficult to do yourself, and it gets too expensive to have someone plant them for you. Whatever you decide, be sure to plant in the early spring. As for your bushes, forsythia and lilacs are great starters—they both do well in half-shade. There are a few other good shade dwellers; among them are some species of rhododendron (including azaleas), mountain laurel, barberry, box huckleberry, holly and witch hazel.

Fertilizer

Q. *What is the best type of fertilizer to use when starting a garden?*

A. One of the best fertilizers is horse manure. For many people, especially city dwellers, this form of organic fertilizer is becoming scarce and too expensive to buy. The best way to prepare a new garden is to work up the soil, then apply fresh horse manure and turn it under immediately. The mixture of soil with manure slows down the fermentation and lessens the danger of overheating. Water this soil well and turn it over several times to create a rich humus excellent for planting any vegetable or flower.

Fig Trees

Q. *Is there any way we can grow a fig tree outdoors in upstate New York?*

A. The common cultivated fig (*Ficus carica*) was originally native to the Mediterranean area. It is but one of the many species of the large tropical genus *Ficus*. This variety of fig is the species that I have. I find it is the hardiest type and gives me the best results. If you provide good winter protection for your tree you should have good luck. The tree should be laid down in winter, particularly if the temperature is likely to drop below 10°F. If this doesn't do it, I suggest you keep your fig trees in tubs, like I do, and move them inside to a cool, moist place in winter (I use an empty stall in my stable).

Fruit Trees

Q. *I have a few apple, peach and pear trees at my country place. Please tell me when, how and with what to spray and maintain them.*

A. Flowering fruit trees are delightful but need plenty of maintenance. They require pruning, feeding, watering and constant vigilance against disease and pests. They need lots of sun and fertile, deep, well-drained soil. Mulching and watering become crucial during the dry months. In March, on a non-windy day, they should be given a dormant spray, which should be repeated every ten days to two weeks until the blossoms appear. This treatment will kill off any diseases or insects that have been living off the tree during the winter. After the blossoms fall, start spraying again every two weeks until after the tree fruits. This may sound like a lot of work—and it is; but healthy trees provide spectacular blooms, fragrance and delicious fruit. For more precise spray recommendations for your climate, contact the agricultural extension agents in your state.

As for pruning, cherry, apple and pear trees need only light pruning of damaged or inferior twigs and branches, but nectarines and peaches are just the opposite; if not pruned regularly, they can easily get out of hand. Remember that last summer's new growth will produce this year's fruit and flowers. Always leave some of the previous year's new growth, or your tree will not produce fruit. Like peaches, apricots and plums grow quickly, but like apples their fruit is produced on slow-growing short spurs. New branches that are too straggly or long can be removed completely without the loss of the entire fruit crop, but do try to leave at least a piece of each new branch.

Gladiolus

Q. *I have planted gladiolus for several years, and each year I dig and store the bulbs over the winter, then plant them again in the spring. I started with several different colors, but this year I noticed that most of them are white. Did the original plants change to a different color? Why do I have so many plain white flowers?*

A. Your situation reminds me of the glads my mother planted. She started with several varieties but, eventually, most of the plants she grew ended up flowering white. This didn't happen because the bulbs (corms) reverted or regressed, but because the white-flower types were hardier and more vigorous. Each year she lost some corms during winter due to rot, and each year she planted some of the smaller corms that were produced with the previous season's corms.

As you may have guessed, most of the corms that were lost due to rot were the fancy types, and the regular corms and the small corms were white. So each season the white lived and propagated themselves while the fancier colors did not produce as many offsets and often didn't store through the winter. Hence, the white glads prevailed.

Gypsy Moths

Q. *What's the history of gypsy moths?*

A. The gypsy moth caterpillar (*Lymantria dispar*) is an example of an introduced pest (and what a pest!) that has wreaked havoc in the United States since 1868, when a few moths were brought to Massachusetts from France by a professor who thought he could make a hybrid moth to produce silk.

Unfortunately, their cage was broken open by a windstorm, and the caterpillars—hairy, brown with blue and red tubercles—escaped, prospered and fed on many deciduous and evergreen trees, with a particular preference for oak trees.

These pests are so voracious that a single caterpillar can eat and destroy a square foot of leaf surface within 24 hours. For instance, evergreens may be killed by a single season's defoliation; other varieties of trees may die, too, after successive defoliations.

Massachusetts has spent a fortune trying to eradicate this pest, and for many years a barrier zone confined them east of the Hudson River. Now, however, the gypsy moth (appropriately named) has moved on and is a menace to New Jersey, New England, eastern New York, eastern Pennsylvania, and has been spotted in Virginia and other states.

Gypsy moth caterpillars attack trees and occasionally vegetables and other plants if they're really hungry. Caterpillars are 2 inches long with conspicuous blue and red markings. A large aerial spray program using DDT was launched in 1957 but had to be given up because of public outcry against the use of chemicals.

To prevent further spreading, it's vitally important that individuals cooperate in observing quarantine regulations. The tan egg clusters with a feltlike texture about 1 inch long may be attached to almost any object but are especially visible on tree trunks and limbs.

Don't try to bring Christmas trees or other plants out of the regulated areas without inspection. Check your automobile or trailer if you have vacationed in gypsy-moth-infested areas. The U.S. Department of Agriculture is releasing parasites for control of gypsy moths and experimenting with sex attractants in traps.

I have had many letters from readers requesting guidelines so that the home gardener can control a gypsy moth infestation. You can have your shrubs and trees sprayed with BT (*Bacillus Huringiensis*) in mid-spring just after the eggs hatch. In the fall and winter, when the tan egg clusters are most conspicuous, you can scrape them into a can and burn them in the fireplace, where they will pop like firecrackers.

In late spring, when the large caterpillars are crawling up tree trunks, they can be trapped by wide bands of overlapping burlap wrapped around the trunks. The caterpillars that are most active at night hide in the burlap during the day, so it's a cinch to collect and drop them into containers of kerosene.

If you need assurance, call the extension service in your area.

Healthy Garden

Weeds, insects and diseases top the gardener's list of problems. What causes plant diseases? Parasitic organisms called pathogens cause diseases. Pathogens include three main groups: bacteria, fungi and viruses.

Fungi are the largest cause of plant diseases. They're responsible for rusts, molds, wilts, cankers, leaf spots and mildews. Since fungi can't produce their own food, they're quite content to sap the nutrients made by green plants. These nasty microscopic fungi are reproduced by minute spores that drift in the air constantly. Most fungi live on decayed or dead matter, while some owe their existence to living plants.

Bacterial diseases include scabs, blights, soft rot, galls and visular wilts. They're all killers. Bacteria invades plants through wounds, natural openings caused by weather, careless gardening or insects. Bacteria can survive for years in soil. Often they stay dormant during winter and emerge in the spring. Blights kill plant tissue. Viruses are extremely tiny. You can only see them through a microscope. Viruses are responsible for stunt, leaf spot and ring spot. As a virus multiplies, it usually spreads to all parts of the plant. Therefore, once a plant becomes infected there is no cure, unless it recovers through its own healing process. Most viruses are introduced to plants by insects, mostly leafhoppers and aphids.

Naturally, I understand that it's impossible to keep your garden completely free of insects and disease, but good cultural practices are a must for healthy, vigorous plants.

Helpful hints:

- Give your plants a good start. Healthy, happy plants have a better chance of surviving if attacked by diseases or insects.
- Choose disease-resistant varieties, check your seed catalogs for these types.
- Provide proper spacing and watering. Plants need ample sunlight and proper ventilation.
- Provide proper drainage. Stagnant water encourages root rot and weakens plants, which makes them more susceptible to disease.
- Eliminate diseased plants and debris. Garden refuse harbors disease pathogens. It's best to dispose of it by burning.
- Be careful not to injure plants when cultivating, since injuries weaken plants. Remember, viruses enter plants through wounds made from careless gardening.
- Keep tools and clothes clean; they can harbor disease pathogens.
- Control insects that transmit diseases. You can do this with beneficial bugs like praying mantis, ladybugs, lacewings, fly trichogramma wasps and parasites. Always read chemical labels carefully before applying dusts or sprays to your plants. Remember, less is better than more!

Heeling-In

If some of the shrubs or trees you ordered arrive before the ground is quite ready for planting, you can dig a trench in a protected area and plant them there temporarily (for a week or two). This is called "heeling in." When the ground is ready, move them to the desired location, and they will be in fine shape.

Heirloom Gardening

This spring, plan an heirloom garden of the nineteenth century.

Thanks to horticulturists' careful documentation of old garden designs, plans and preservation of heirloom seeds, you can easily re-create the garden of your dreams that typified the beauty of early American gardens.

Flower types that are considered heirloom or antique are usually at least 100 years old. Some younger types also qualify if they have strong heirloom tendencies. Here are some characteristics that make heirloom flowers more of a treat to grow than their hybrid cousins:

- They are often hardier and more disease-resistant. They are survivors in the truest sense, having been around for so long!
- They are easily pollinated and usually self-seed, making them simpler to grow.
- They retain the characteristic for which they were originally propagated; for example, for their unique scent. Newer hybrids, which are mostly developed for height and color, cannot compete with the fragrance of heirlooms.

Old-fashioned vines and roses have many forms and habits that contribute to growing marvelously well anywhere in the garden.

Here are my guidelines for re-creating the look of a garden from years gone by.

Plant a doorway garden in front of the house and feature your favorite fragrant, showy flowers and spring bulbs. In the backyard, create the same atmosphere—only let your imagination run wild! Express yourself with favorite plants, no matter their size, shape or color.

Frame the yard and house with a fence or hedge and add old-fashioned shrubs like mock oranges, lilacs and hydrangeas. Train climbing plants on trellises, fences, porch posts and railings. Try climbing roses, morning glory, clematis and trumpet vines for a profusion of color.

Take care when watering your heirloom jewels. Moisture that stands and clings on the leaves and plants can be a breeding ground for diseases and germs. If you can, avoid using overhead sprinklers to water flowers. If you do have overhead sprinklers, water early in the morning on days with a sunny forecast, so the leaves will not stay wet. Many gardeners rely on soaker hoses or other drip-irrigation systems that bring water directly to the plants' roots.

Plants dislike cold baths as much as you and I. So, if you can, use lukewarm water—particularly with tender seedlings. Staking is important for many tall-growing heirloom flowers such as hollyhocks, dahlias, delphinium and lilies. As you plant, place a stake next to the heirloom so you won't be disturbing the plant as it grows.

When propagating self-seeding perennials, let them do their thing by scattering their seeds on open ground in midsummer. Foxglove and feverfew are among the many perennials that self-seed by this easy process.

Other heirloom flower varieties of interest include the crocus, daffodil, cornflower, sweet pea, pansy, iris and phlox.

Herbs—for Garden and Kitchen

If you want to add a personal touch to your garden, as well as to your cooking, there's nothing like herbs. When we think of herbs we usually picture formal gardens planted in intricate designs, but actually herbs perform beautifully mixed into the average flower garden and added to border plantings. If you are really cramped for space, by all means grow your favorite herbs as close to the kitchen door as possible so the cook will remember to use them.

Outstanding features of most herbs are their texture, leaf color and shape. Color may range from gray to green to silver to the variegated types. Some varieties such as mint, thyme and borage-scented geraniums have bright blooms, which also add to the beauty of your garden.

A rule of thumb is to grow your herbs in a sunny, well-drained bed with at least a half day of sun. Regular watering is especially important during the hot months of July and August so your plants don't dry.

Just as herbs provide a delicious dimension to cooking—meals would certainly be dull without them—basil, sage, thyme and oregano (to name a few) are familiar to every cook. However, there are many other fabulous herbs that are not as famous but are equally useful in the kitchen.

Look for a large and varied selection of unusual herbs in the annual and perennial department of most nurseries and garden centers. Most well run nurseries have a staff only too happy to answer all your questions and help you choose the best herbs for your garden.

Invasive herbs such as tansy and mint should be planted in pots so they don't invade their neighbors' territory. In other words, they are not good "bedmates" since they will aggressively spread and overtake anything that stands in their way.

Some herbs make great bedmates for roses and do exceptionally well in the shade of their foliage. I recommend the following herbs for contrast or ground cover in the rose bed: leeks, garlic, chives, lavender, foxglove, purple sage and English violet.

Herbal Essence

To discourage moths, hang dill in the closets and place it in drawers. For those interested in fertility and a long life, the herb caraway is the answer.

Instead of smoking, chew anise leaves. Herb tea made from rosemary leaves will improve the memory.

Herbs in Pots

Herbs are so delicious and deliciously scented that they should be close by, where you can snip and sniff at them at a moment's notice. The best news is that growing herbs in pots is easy.

Herbs love container life. The ones that thrive in the dry soils of the Mediterranean do especially well in pots or raised beds.

Because herbs such as rosemary and oregano do best in soil that is well drained, pots are the perfect place to grow them. In fact, many herbs will do better in a pot than in your garden.

Where should you begin? Herbs require a sunny location—and the hotter, the better. Patios and deck planters are great for herbs.

Your potted herb garden should receive at least six hours of sun a day and should be placed in a well-protected area so that drying winds don't wilt newly planted seedlings.

Use potting soil, then add some sand to ensure the soil drains well. How can you tell if your soil is well drained? Spray the garden area with a hose. If the water pools, then you need to improve the drainage of your soil by adding more sand.

How much should you water? As a general rule, herbs like their soil on the dry side. If the surface of the soil is dry to the touch, then it's time to water. Err on the side of dryness if there's any question.

Some herbs, such as basil and mint, have a tendency to get a little too tall and leggy. To encourage bushier growth, pinch off the growing tip just above the first set of leaves. This makes new shoots sprout from the stem, giving you more leaves to harvest.

Growing these wonderful plants in pots allows you to have fresh herbs that are ready to be clipped into salads or soups, or onto pizzas or focaccia breads.

Set a mixed-herb pot in the center of a table as you would with other seasonings such as balsamic vinegar, salt, pepper and olive oil. By using fresh herbs right from the pot, you capture their best flavor.

Keep in mind that herbs generally taste their best if you harvest them just before the plant begins to flower.

Horseradish

I simply adore fresh horseradish sauce, so I grow my own horseradish roots—but never in the garden where they can become an invasive pest! Instead, I plant them in a large container on my sunny patio. It's really the easiest way!

I start with a few store-bought pieces of roots or crowns. Many supermarkets don't carry horseradish year-round, but most sell it during the Easter and Passover holidays.

Next I fill a 10-inch container with a Pro-Mix commercial potting soil, making sure there are ample drainage holes. After watering the soil thoroughly, I push a few crowns in just below the soil line. Roots will sprout in a week or two if you keep the container indoors in front of a sunny window until the last spring frost passes. Water only if the soil dries out.

Once the plants are moved outdoors, I water often, especially during the hot months of July and August. I fertilize every two weeks.

After the large leaves die down in fall, I knock out the rootball and break off the white roots, leaving a few small pieces of root in the soil to sprout next spring.

Finally, I wash and peel some of the roots, whip together one cup of cut-up roots with 1½ cups of white vinegar in the blender and add salt to taste. Then I bottle and refrigerate it. It's simply out of this world!

No More Tears

Many readers have asked me for ideas on how to grate horseradish sans tears. By far the most popular suggestion was to go outside and cut—not grate—the roots into chunks and let a blender or food processor do the work with some white vinegar. After blending the roots to the consistency you desire, simply pour the mixture into glass jars.

Very important: Don't stick your face right over the blender as you remove the lid. Other suggestions:

- Freeze the roots before cutting them.
- Use a table fan to blow the fumes away from you.
- Stick a piece of bread in your mouth.
- Look at something that's green. One of my readers swears this works for her when she's chopping onions. I'm always open to other tried-and-true suggestions.

Housekeeping in the Garden

One of the most important measures for controlling plant diseases and insect problems in the garden is good housekeeping. The potential for plant diseases spreading from spores that over-winter on fallen leaves, branches and plant debris is enormous because next spring it is these spores that become the source of the new infection.

So be ahead of the game and reduce this threat by raking up any fallen leaves and removing all infected branches and plant parts as this season comes to a close.

When removing diseased branches, do it during dry weather and always cut back into strong, healthy wood. Never compost or mulch with any infected debris. Disease problems in the vegetable patch or flowerbed that cannot be taken care of through cultural practices should be removed immediately.

If crops are rotated (a must), certain insects will likely starve if their food source is not available. Where crop rotation is not feasible, the idea of container gardening, planters and raised beds should be explored.

Houseplants

On warm spring days open your windows to give house plants a breath of fresh air. Don't overdo, or they will be chilled—and who wants to catch cold this time of year?

When moving indoor plants outdoors for the summer, expose them gradually to more light otherwise they will sunburn. Evening temperatures should be around 60°F or above before you make the move.

Insect Problems Solved Naturally

Many people ask me, "Why are there no insect problems in your garden?" Of course, they want a simple answer like, "I use this special new natural organic insect repellent." (I'm working on one for next year.) But I couldn't give them an answer like that because it doesn't exist, not for the time being.

So, until then, I keep my garden very, very clean. All fallen leaves are raked up. While there are many insects buzzing around my garden, there haven't been many harmful bugs in it for years.

Here's what I do: I simply throw on the compost, plant seeds, pick vegetables and pull weeds, keeping every bed as tidy as possible. The best advice I can give you is to do the same.

Manage the garden by timing plantings to avoid pest cycles, choosing resistant types and using cultural techniques such as interplanting and keeping the garden spotless. All of these are a part of successful gardening.

It's really learning the total approach to maximum resistance using nature's own ways of preventing harm to plants. Applying plenty of compost makes plants so healthy, and bugs simply don't like the way they taste.

Principles of Disease and Insects

Fungi and insects are not the real cause of plant diseases since they only attack unsuitable varieties or crops grown imperfectly.

The method of protecting crops from pests by means of chemical powders and sprays is unscientific and unsound because, even when successful, such procedures merely preserve the unfit plants and obscure the real problem: how to grow a healthy harvest.

Burning diseased crops is an unnecessary and wanton destruction of valuable organic matter. Nature simply doesn't do that, so why should we?

Thousands of gardeners use these principles successfully. You, too, can be part of this effort by switching to the organic pest-control approach in your garden. It's just that simple. Carefully selecting varieties of plants that you know are the most resistant to the problems in your area is the key. Remember, sickly plants become especially appealing food for marauding insects and disease organisms, so don't give them the opportunity.

Ivy, English

Q. *My wife and I are trying to get some ivy growing up the wall of our patio here in New York City. Can you give us some help?*

A. In the city, your best bet is to use common English ivy (*Herdera helix*), one of the hardiest of all climbing plants. For the patio you'll have to start your ivy in large pots or planters, one at each end of the wall. Put a trellis of thin canes up against the wall and, as your ivy grows, train it any way you like. In two or three years your wall will be covered—and what a pretty effect that will be for your patio! You shouldn't have any trouble getting the ivy to grow—just keep the plants moist throughout the year and feed with a weak liquid fertilizer at monthly intervals from April to September. Also bear in mind the old saying about newly planted English ivy: The first year it "sleeps," the second it "creeps," and the third it "leaps."

Juniper Ground Cover

Q. *I noticed what looked like tiny pieces of gravel or dirt on my ground-cover juniper. The smaller branches on the juniper are dying. I shook the stuff off the plants and stirred up a lot of ants. Are the ants nesting on the plants and damaging them? How do I control the ants? Help!*

A. First, check the junipers for scale insects. I have seen where ants have moved scale insects throughout an evergreen and then basically camouflaged the scale insects with debris. The ants then feed on the honeydew excreted by the scale insects.

Look along the plant's smaller stems and leaves. The scale will be green, tan or reddish brown, and oval or round in shape. It wouldn't surprise me that this is what's going on.

To control scale insects, use an insecticide soap with applications of neem. Follow label instructions, particularly those related to temperature restrictions, when using the product. Regardless, never spray plants in the heat of the day.

You could also use a systemic pesticide such as acephate (Orthene) or dimethoate (Cygon), but check the label to be sure the product is safe for junipers. When you treat for the scale insects, the ants will also be controlled or move away.

Kids and Gardening, a Perfect Match

Children love to watch things grow. Don't worry about neatness and rules, just let them do and grow what they like and they'll get hooked on gardening.

Ask children what their favorite vegetables are. Steer them toward those that are easy to grow and can be eaten raw.

Carrots and sweet corn are favorites with kids. Carrots take off a little slow, need frequent watering and need to have 2 inches between each plant. Corn grows tall and can't be overwatered. You'll get one or two ears per plant. Keep plants close, as corn pollinates by wind. Kids also like tomatoes, especially the cherry tomatoes that are more their size.

Watermelons and pumpkins are great fun for kids to grow. Some other fun veggies: lettuce (try to get different colors), peppers (sweet, not hot), okra, herbs and broccoli.

A child's garden should be the way the child wants it. Forget about neat rows and endless planning of what should go where. To maintain children's enthusiasm about gardening, let them do it their own way—planning will come later. Weeding is a basic chore and should be learned at an early age so the child doesn't get into bad habits. Gardening for children should be fun, not work (at least from their viewpoint).

Getting Started

A good starting point for your child's garden would be to simply ask what their favorite vegetables are. Children will want to plant something they can eat raw, rather than having to wait for it to be cooked. If they say peas, think of snow peas or sugar snap peas that can be picked and eaten.

Carrots are usually a favorite with children. I'm not sure why; perhaps it may have to do with Bugs Bunny. And carrots can be eaten raw. You can even over-winter them because they get sweeter (in some areas).

Growing Tips

Carrots: Carrot seeds can be directly sown into the garden once the weather is favorable, although carrots do prefer cool temperatures. They can be slow to germinate, so be patient. Carrots mature in about 65 days. Keep the plants well watered or their growth will be retarded and a strong flavor will develop. They should be thinned to one plant every 1 to 2 inches because crowding will produce lots of foliage but no root.

Carrots are also adaptable to containers, provided the containers are at least 4 inches deep. One of the neat things about carrots is that they can be harvested over a long time; they won't spoil if they stay in the ground. Carrots can also be shared with wildlife, such as neighborhood rabbits and squirrels (which adults may consider to be pests in the garden, but children view differently). If a child does want to share the bounty with nature, you may want to suggest a feeding area well away from the garden to discourage animals from becoming too much at home.

Corn: Corn likes the hot days of summer and will mature in 60 to 85 days. One corn plant will produce only one or two ears, so plan accordingly. Because corn grows so tall, plant it on the north side of your garden so it doesn't shade other plants. Most kids enjoy corn on the cob and the plants grow tall fairly quickly. There are a wide variety of sweet corn types available in addition to the standard yellow hybrids, plus there are novelty corns such as bicolored and popcorn varieties. Corn plants need to grow close together (like blocks) so that they can be pollinated by the wind. Grow only one variety of corn or you may get mixed kernels on an ear. It's difficult to overwater corn, so pour it on.

Tomatoes: Tomatoes are another favorite, especially the cherry types like Sweet 100. I recommend varieties that can be eaten in one or two bites.

Tomatoes can be grown from transplants or from seeds sown in the garden. Choose early maturing varieties (50 to 60 days after transplanting) if possible. Tomatoes come in a wide variety of shapes and sizes, most of which are also readily adaptable for container growing. Cherry tomatoes for salads or to eat fresh from the garden are popular with children, as are huge types whose slices can rival the size of the beef in a hamburger. Children are usually fascinated with the concept of the biggest or smallest, so a combination of these might be a good idea.

Watermelon: Children love to eat watermelons. I recommend smaller ice-box types, such as Sugar Baby and yellow varieties, rather than the standard red. Watermelons and other melons from seeds or transplants are great fun to grow, but be prepared to give them space, somewhere around 9 square feet for each plant.

The vines can be rigged with a support system using a cloth sling tied around the melon (when it grows) for support to keep the stem from breaking. Expect to get two to three melons from one plant. There are newer hybrid varieties that have shorter vines, so if space is a consideration, look for restricted-vine varieties.

Pumpkins: And, while children may not think of a pumpkin as a vegetable, growing their own jack-o'-lantern can be a real experience. They like to see who can grow the biggest (zucchini is popular for the same reason).

I recommend two varieties of pumpkins: the medium-size 'Autumn Gold', a 1987 All-America Selections winner that children like because it only takes six weeks to turn orange. Youngsters don't like to wait too long for an orange pumpkin. I also recommend the 1- to 2-pound 'Baby Bear' (a 1993 All-America Selections winner). Sketch on a face when the pumpkin is small so the face will grow with the pumpkin.

Lettuce: Lettuce is a good children's crop, especially the different colored ones. I have a red-leafed one that I keep growing just for that reason. Many children like peppers, too, but plant the sweet ones, not the really hot ones. If they handle hot peppers and then rub their eyes, it can really hurt. I recommend the 'Gypsy' peppers, a 1981 All-America Selections winner. They produce so much, while a newer, sweet variety called 'Jingle Bells' is very popular, too.

Other kinds: Broccoli is another good choice. Children think it looks like little trees. Vegetables with unusual colors are popular: red lettuce, yellow watermelon, purple beans.

What about spinach? I grow some spinach and I always put a picture of Popeye next to it. The children laugh, but they still don't like it!

Kids Can Grow at Gardening
The future greening of America depends a great deal on our children learning how

to garden and appreciate the wonderful benefits nature offers. Second-grade teachers throughout the country say it's amazing how much children can learn from growing flowers. Young students take great pride in doing something others can see and enjoy.

For example, I had no idea how teaching children some basics about gardening could be so much fun and how it could lead to learning about so many other subjects. In the United States, 27,000 youths are learning firsthand about growing Dutch flower bulbs. The generous support of three international gardening organizations has enabled teachers throughout the United States to take learning beyond the classroom.

Each grant recipient received 252 assorted Dutch bulbs directly from Holland. Complete instructions and tips for classroom activities involving the study of bulbs were also sent. The selection of flower bulbs, chosen by Dutch bulb experts, included tulips, crocuses, hyacinths, muscari blues, paperwhites and amaryllis.

This hands-on program has made learning fun for the children. And their enthusiasm for learning seems to grow right along with the flowers and vegetables they planted. Students are learning how flowers grow and how to plant vegetables, but that's just the beginning. The garden grant has opened the door to future lessons in art design, history, math and even geography. The program has great potential for introducing the fun and healthy benefits of gardening to all school-age youths. I believe providing flower bulbs is a good start for making gardening in the classroom a year-long activity.

Planting and caring for bulbs and watching them grow and develop into colorful blooms can bring joy to children as well as adults. I believe school-age children become better people through their positive experiences with gardening. Gardening helps youths gain a better understanding of the cycles of nature and, perhaps even more important, it helps them learn about discipline, working as a team, patience and taking part in neighborhood beautification.

Project for Kids

Set up a windowsill herbal barbershop. Plant thyme, chives, basil, parsley or other fragrant herb seeds in tiny pots with drainage holes. Let your child make funny paper faces to tape on the pots. When the herbs start growing, your child will love giving them haircuts. Use the clippings to season your cooking.

Landscaping Problems Solved

It's hard to accept that despite the time, effort and money you've spent, sometimes the only way to correct your mistakes is to replace a shrub or tree.

Let me help you make this tough decision easier with the following reasons to consider replacing a plant:

The plant has grown completely out of scale with the site. For example, the pine tree you brought home has become an eyesore, encroaching on your walkway and whacking you in the face or back every time you try to get into the front door. Rather than resigning yourself to a life of pruning, simply pull it out and ask your nursery or landscape professional to suggest a more suitable alternative.

A shrub or tree just looks lousy. A sun-loving shrub in a shady spot languishes, simply refusing to bloom and thrive. Be understanding; relocate it to a sunny area and watch it do its thing. If that's not an option, remove it and replace it with a shade-loving shrub or tree.

Live trees in a state of decline can pose serious problems for your house or your neighbors' homes. Trees die for a variety of reasons, including damage to roots from disease or construction. Although the decline can take years, you should consider certain problems such as: Is the tree weighted heavier on one side than the other? What is the tree's proximity to your house, or your neighbor's? If removal is needed, consult a professional arborist or a garden center person.

Looks tell it all. As you make improvements to your house, you may need to make improvements in the landscape. Could be those pink azaleas clash with your home's new shade of paint. And maybe you've added details to your house that call for a more dramatic landscape. If you're uncertain about where to start, a landscape professional can be of assistance with your choices and ideas.

If you find yourself spending a lot of time trying to keep a plant alive, it's often easier to simply eliminate it—chuck it out!

Renovating Your Landscaping

What if you're trying to sell your house in a competitive real estate market and the yard could look better; or you've just moved into a new house with a dreary, empty landscape; or you need more sun in the kitchen and better wind protection on the north side of the house? Then again, you may have plenty of trees, shrubs and flowers, but they suddenly look haggard and have overgrown their boundaries. What to do?

If you face these situations and have decided to get help from a landscape professional, here are some guidelines to follow:

Time is money for you and the landscape professional. The more prepared you are, the easier it will be to find a contractor. It is important to realize there are difficult disciplines in the landscaping business.

Landscape designers can give you a blueprint of your property that shows the precise location of each plant you choose. The plan is to help the contractor make the blueprint come true. Or, you may decide to carry out the plan yourself.

If you want one company to do the whole project, consider a design-build company. Some garden centers can do this for you.

Whatever approach you take, split your budget into two categories: design and landscape.

Professional landscape contractors can help schedule your project because they are experts in such matters. Spring and early summer are the best times to install such things as pools, walkways, decks, tennis courts and a garden because that way you don't subject tender, young plants to the midsummer heat.

Above all, hire a professional. Finding a top pro doesn't have to be difficult. A good first call would be to the neighborhood garden club or professional landscaping association. Nurseries can provide referrals, too.

When considering a company, ask for references. Most professionals have portfolios with pictures of projects they've done. Whatever you do, think carefully about what you want—then go for it!

Lawn-Mowing Basics

Q. *Is it possible to cut any grass too low in a single mowing?*

A. Yes! Never remove more than one-third of your grass height at one time. Cutting your grass too short can severely limit its ability to manufacture food and resist invasion of weeds.

Q. *How often should I mow my lawn?*

A. Mow often enough that only a small portion of the grass is lost at any one clipping. Ideally, mow once a week so that no more than one-third of the leaf blade will be removed.

Q. *Do I need to mow my grass as often in the spring as in the fall?*

A. No, mowing frequency varies by season. In the spring, most established lawn should be mowed as soon as the grass turns green and begins to grow. In summer, close mowing (especially during the hot months of July and August) can weaken some grass types.

As autumn approaches, cool-season grasses begin to grow faster and produce more clippings, while warm-season grasses begin to slow down.

Simply adjust your mowing habits. In warm climates, grass should be mowed at the normal heights throughout the winter months.

Q. *What is thatch?*

A. Thatch appears right at the soil surface and looks like a layer of straw. It's composed mostly of grass parts that live underground, but it also includes lawn clippings and other undecayed material.

In healthy soil, plant parts decompose quickly into humus. However, in soil that is compacted, over-fertilized, overwatered or underpopulated with soil insects (the good guys) or earthworms, you end up with thatch.

Q. *How can I remove my thatch?*

A. You'll need a mower that has a de-thatching attachment. The large amount of organic material brought to the surface from using a de-thatcher should be immediately removed from the lawn. This will eliminate raking and get your lawn off to a healthy start by removing thatch buildup. Then re-seed the lawn, and water.

Q. *When should I de-thatch my lawn?*

A. The best time to do this chore is just before a lawn has its most vigorous growth of the season. That means de-thatching warm-season grasses at the beginning of warm weather in late spring. The prime time for de-thatching cool-season grasses is late spring or early fall.

Smart Mowing

A mower that recycles is best. If you do not have a recycling mower, mow frequently enough that the clippings will not exceed 1 inch in length. Lawn clippings make great mulch.

Never shear off more than one-third of the height of the leaf blade of your grass, so mow high and mow often.

Early evening is the best time to mow—grass can recover before the next day's hot sun. Keep the mower blade sharp and do not mow wet grass.

Lettuce, Early

Most types of lettuce are ideal for planting or sowing at this time of year. Sow loose-leaf, nonheading types such as 'Bibb' or 'Rosette.' All work well and are best grown from seed sown directly in the garden as soon as the soil can be worked.

Lilacs

Lilacs herald spring all over the world as they have since the sixteenth century by blooming early and showing off fabulous fragrant flowers. Lilacs make attractive hedges and durable landscape features.

Plants do best in sunny locations where soil is fertile; they grow leggy and bloom sparsely in dense shade. They need an alkaline soil, thriving best where winters are cold. The lovely spring blossoms vary in color: lavender, white, pink and purple in single or dou-

ble blooms. The leaves are heart-shaped. Bushes grow from 3 to 4 feet, depending on the variety. Although lilacs are mostly problem-free, use the following guidelines for growing great plants.

Plant bare root-stock in early spring. Fall to spring is the best for planting balled and burlapped stock and containerized shrubs. Water new bushes each week through the season if no rain falls. Keep in mind that established plants will tolerate some drought. Lilacs take two to three years to begin producing full-size flowers in their true color.

Pruning is most important the first three or four years after planting. Deadhead faded flower heads before seed sets to improve the following year's blooms.

Renovate old or overgrown shrubs by cutting one-third to one-half of the older growth to within 2 to 3 inches of the base. Over several seasons, gradually prune out remaining old stems and the suckers at the base of the shrub. After blooming, do your pruning; pruning too late removes next year's buds as lilacs set their buds by the end of July.

Lily, Easter

Q. *What can you tell me about the Easter lily and its care?*

A. The Easter lily was a symbol of purity long before Christian times, and in later years an emblem of Christ's resurrection. In some countries lilies are dedicated to St. Catherine or Venus. During the thirteenth century it was believed that lilies and laurel juice could be concocted into a powerful charm for use against enemies. The lily is also considered one of the oldest plants known to man. Lilies were and still are used for ointments, salves and cosmetic purposes. Today, lilies have become flowers for every garden; the new hybrids are superb. Their exotic colors and varieties are incredibly beautiful, especially the oriental ones from Japan and Korea. I often arrange cut lilies in tall bottles of different sizes, shapes and colors that I collect on my travels to Europe. They are unbelievably diverse, blooming from early June through September. Plant lilies in your garden in autumn or early spring. If someone gives you a lily for Easter, plant it in your garden after it blooms and you'll see it again next year.

Mole Crickets

In North America, there are several species of mole crickets. They are closely related to field and house crickets, but they live underground and have wide front legs perfect for digging.

Peak egg-laying season is in May and most hatch in June. By October, the crickets are mature and over-winter as adults. Adult crickets die soon after they mate and lay their eggs.

Mole crickets do their damage by tunneling through the earth, leaving trails of dead grass. Their tunneling disturbs the soil around grass roots. During drought periods they will tunnel as deep as 2 feet! Crickets feed at night in warm weather and after rain. During the day they retreat to underground burrows.

In spring, the male cricket makes a trilling sound to attract mates. Male crickets love to spread their wings and fly, mostly in spring during the mating season. They can fly more than eight miles a night.

Mole crickets like to dine on the dead roots of turf grass, seeds, insects and dead plant debris. The Southern mole cricket is also cannibalistic! Mole crickets, especially the Southern and tawny species, are very destructive when they form large groups, as they do in sandy soils along the Gulf and Atlantic coasts from southern Texas to North Carolina, Georgia and Florida. These states really take a beating!

Their tunneling wreaks havoc in vegetable gardens, yards, golf courses and athletic fields.

Suggested control: Apply Steinernema, a species of beneficial nematodes, in spring or fall when mole crickets are in their adult stage. These nematodes are available from catalogs and garden supply stores.

It's also a good idea to consider planting St. Augustine grass in areas of infestation because it stands up better and does not show the ravages of mole crickets like other turf grasses.

Natural enemies of mole crickets: birds, spiders, fire ants, red foxes, raccoons, skunks and armadillos.

Passion Flower

Q. *I was enthralled with the description of the passion flower in your question column in the paper recently. However, you referred to the ten petals as the ten Apostles. I was under the impression the number of Apostles was twelve.*

A. The inflorescence of the passion flower is said to be symbolic of aspects of the Passion of Christ. The ten petals were seen as the ten good Apostles (excluding Peter and Judas); or, according to other views, the Ten Commandments. The five upper petals were linked to five main events: birth, suffering, death, interment and hell. The tri-colored corona represents the purple cloak in which Christ appeared before Herod. The center of the corona is white; Jesus was sent back to Pontius Pilate (by Herod) in a white cloak. The brown interior, the seamless linen cloak. The stigma, the sponge and below the stigma, the five wounds. The cross of the stigmata symbolizes the three nails with which Christ was nailed to the cross, and the stalked ovary represents the Lord's goblet.

The passion flower vine is one of my favorites for summer blooms outdoors. I plant mine in a big pot (18-inch diameter) with a trellis to climb on. It likes sun, lots of water and C. Z. Grow fertilizer.

Peat Pellet Magic

Last year, millions of home gardeners used a trick for seed-starting, rooting and cutting that professional growers have known for years. The trick? Sowing, rooting and growing in peat pellets.

They learned that growing in peat pellets creates the perfect environment for your seedlings and cuttings that helps them get off to a good healthy start. They learned that pure sphagnum peat moss pellets, such as Jiffy-7 plant starter pellets, retain moisture and have plenty of air pockets to let young roots breathe.

As the young roots grow, they poke right through the tray, which greatly increases the whole root area. Mature plants grown in peat don't suffer transplant shock, since they can be set in the garden pot without disturbing the tender roots.

To start, drop the pellets in warm water and let them expand fully, to about 1⅝ inches high. Then, make a small hole with a pencil in the top of the pellet. Place two or three large seeds in the hole and cover them with peat. Smaller seeds should be pressed into the surface without making a hole.

Place the pellets in a tray in a warm spot, away from drafts; then cover the container with transparent wrap to keep humidity high.

Keep the seed flat out of direct sunlight; however, when seedlings appear, remove the cover and move the seedlings to a cooler spot, but one in which they'll get at least six hours of sunlight.

Snip off all but the most vigorous seedling in each Jiffy-7. When the pellets become light brown, mist or gently water them.

Apply diluted fertilizer three to four weeks after germination. Check the label for the proper application for each plant.

Harden the plants by exposing them to cooler outdoor temperatures for several days before transplanting.

When it's time to transplant, set in, pot and all, just below the soil surface and cover the pot with soil. Tomatoes should be planted deeply, since they'll root along the stem, resulting in a more vigorous plant.

You can also make identical copies of your favorite houseplants by rooting them in peat pellets. Clip the parent plant stem just above a leaf node (the spot where the leaf forms on the stem). Remove the bottom leaf. Trim the cutting stem just below it. (If you're rooting African violets and gloxinia, trim the leaf stem close to 1 inch and insert the leaf stem.)

Poke a hole in an expanded pellet, insert the stem in the hole and press together to secure the cutting. Cover the cutting tray with transparent plastic and make sure the cuttings don't touch the bag or the greenhouse sides. Remove the cover after one week.

When roots grow through the pot sides, transplant, pot and all, into a larger container.

Those who start a garden from seed or root their own cuttings enjoy seeing them develop into mature, healthy plants. Gardeners experience the warm glow that comes from starting from scratch. What is more fascinating than watching your plants grow? Buying transplants has become very expensive, and growing your own seeds is easy and fun.

Peonies

Now is the time to fertilize peonies and other herbaceous, hardy perennials—when the first shoots pop out of the ground. Where fertilizer is concerned, it always pays to observe this rule: Apply at the rate recommended on the product label; any variance should be toward less rather than more.

Perennials, Propagating

Q. *I'd like to try propagating ornamental perennials from root cuttings. What perennials can be propagated this way? Can you explain the basics?*

A. Propagation by root cuttings is often used by many gardeners when propagation by other means is too slow or unsuccessful. Like other methods of propagation (leaf or stem cuttings), it's perfect for increasing stock of plants that don't come true from seeds, or from plants that don't produce seed. Root propagation is usually slower than making leaf or stem cuttings, taking at least four to six months before propagated plants can be placed in their permanent places.

Perennials that can be propagated include anemone, globe thistle, phlox, bleeding heart and primrose, to name a few.

In January, February and March, given favorable conditions, roots can draw upon the stored starch from the previous season to begin growing. Dig up the plants you want to propagate, cut off several roots close to the plant's crown where they are the largest. Do not remove more than one-third of the entire root system. Replant the parent plant.

Carefully lay out the cut roots as they were growing on the plant. Cut the root pieces into smaller sections about 1½-inches long. Be careful to keep the right side up.

Fill a grow flat a with sterile commercial Pro-Mix soil, making sure of proper drainage. Bank up one side of the flat with soil to a 45-degree angle and lay the root pieces on the bank with their tops up.

Cover the cuttings entirely with the soil mix, with the top of the cuttings near the surface and their bottoms about a half-inch below the soil surface. The top of the root piece will produce new shoots, while the lower half will generate a root system. Cuttings will produce shoots faster if soil and air temperature are at least 60°F. Keep the cuttings moist but do not overwater. When the new shoots appear, start fertilizing with Miracle-Gro.

Transplant new plants into individual containers when the root system has sufficiently formed to support the growing shoots.

Planting Delays, How to Overcome

Timing in gardening is everything. You just received the daylilies and gladiolus that you ordered by mail and the backyard is already crowded with shrubs, so you can't plant right now and you won't have time this weekend. And freezing rain is predicted to boot.

What you do during the critical days between the time you receive your plants and the time you plant them can mean the difference between their success or failure. Planting immediately is best. But if planting must be delayed, you can take several steps to ensure your plants' survival and health.

First, open the package and check to see that your order is correct. Be sure to open anything wrapped in plastic to allow air circulation. Don't be alarmed if on nursery stock you find last year's foliage and stems withered and brown (the plants are dormant, after all), but they shouldn't be broken or shredded, and there should be no signs of mold or decay.

Keep bulbs such as daffodils and tulips in a cool, dry spot with good air circulation. Whether the bulbs are packaged in plastic or paper bags, open the bags and spread the bulbs in a single layer. Be sure they do not get wet. Avoid temperature extremes and changes that could cause sweating and subsequently promote the growth of mold on the bulbs.

In contrast, keep lilies in the dark. Moisten them with an occasional sprinkle of water. Don't let them dry out because they may sprout. Caladiums, dahlias and other bulbs that are not winter-hardy should also be moistened lightly.

Rhizomes such as irises can be kept in their original packing material as long as you open the shipping container. Simply store them in a lighted area, but out of direct wind or sun.

Bulbs can be held longer than most plants, depending on the time of year. For spring bulbs, an extended holding period of three to four weeks won't hurt so long as you plant before they sprout. Fall bulbs, however, can suffer from a long delay; they should be in the ground and growing during that time.

Many perennials, trees and shrubs are shipped bare root or without any soil around the roots. Since these plants are shipped dormant, you'll usually find no signs of life in the upper part of the plant. Do check the plant's roots when your package arrives. If the packing material around the roots is dry, trickle in a little water, enough to moisten, but not soak, the roots.

Unfortunately, nurseries sometimes prove more prompt than Mother Nature and plants may arrive while your garden soil is still half-frozen and soggy. Digging soil in that condition will destroy its structure and you may have to wait several weeks before it dries sufficiently to be worked. During that time, provide your bare-root stock with temporary houses to keep them healthy.

The best option is to "heel them in." Dig a trench a half-spade deep in a well-drained, sheltered area—the side of a south-facing slope is ideal. Fill the trench with a mixture of one part builder's sand and one part peat moss. Dormant perennials can also be planted like this or they can be planted in pots.

Balled and burlapped stock should also be heeled in outdoors with wood chips or leaf mold if you cannot plant it within a week or two of purchase. Water the stock every day if the temperatures are above 80°F or every other day if temperatures are in the 60s or 70s. Keep plants in containers, watered and away from extreme temperatures. Try to store them in a protected area outdoors, in bright light but away from direct sun. Don't keep them in a warm, balmy area indoors.

For container stock planted in midsummer, cut tops back by one-third to prevent dieback. Ready-to-plant boxes don't usually need to be opened, but do need water frequently. Bare tree roots should also be soaked again before planting.

When planting bare-root stock in its final resting place, it's important to not let exposed roots dry out. Carry the plants to the garden in a bucket of water and don't remove them until you are ready to set each one in the ground. Once they are planted, water them well. Follow your supplier's directions for your newly planted surgery stock from this point.

Small perennial plants can be covered for two or three days with an overturned bushel basket. Shielding the plants from the wind protects against dehydration until the roots awaken.

Poison Ivy

Q. *Our property is rampant with poison ivy. I sprayed with over-the-counter weed killers to no avail. Is there a remedy?*

A. I'm glad to answer this question—I really know how uncomfortable poison ivy is. I'm usually covered with it all summer long because our six dogs run in the woods and I pick it up from them. However, unless you have six dogs, there is a remedy! Amitrol is a herbicide specifically for controlling poison ivy when in full leaf. You can get it in spray cans for spot control of plants or in larger quantities to be mixed with water for wide application. The product is often labeled "Poison Ivy Control" and is packaged under several different brand names. Good luck!

Pruning Time Is Now

Now is a prime time for pruning. Major renovations are best accomplished when a plant's metabolism is on the rise, as it is in early spring. A tree or plant will best close its wounds during this period. In contrast, during bug break and leaf formation (as well as when the leaves are falling), plants are susceptible to injury.

Now is also when you have a clear view of the branch structure of deciduous trees. Leaves don't mask the tree's shape. But if you don't know the meaning of such terms as "branch collar" and "branch bark ridge," you may wish to consult some horticulture resources at your library or elsewhere.

Cornell University has published *Pruning: An Illustrated Guide to Pruning Ornamental Trees and Shrubs*. To receive a copy of this 28-page illustrated publication, send a check for $5 made out to Cornell Cooperative Extension, to Pruning Book, CCE of Nassau County, 1425 Old Country Road, Building J, Plainview, New York, 11803-5015.

Rhododendrons

Q. *My favorite rhododendron bush was damaged three years ago when a tree branch fell on it. I cut off the broken limbs and it seemed to do better. However, it produces lots of new growth but no flower buds. How can I encourage my rhododendron to bloom once more?*

A. Perhaps your plant hasn't flowered because of the abundance of new shoots that emerged as a result of your pruning. Research has shown that an increase in the number of leafy shoots results in the production of fewer flower buds. In late spring, selectively thin out the weakest shoots on each branch to encourage flower buds to develop on the strongest ones.

Once the rhododendron blooms, don't forget to deadhead the spent blooms. This is the key to keeping your plant blooming profusely because if it goes on to produce seed, the plant may end up becoming too exhausted to develop flowers for next season.

To keep your rhododendron in tip-top shape, maintain the correct soil pH: between 4.5 and 6.

Roses

For centuries, the beauty and fragrance of roses have captured the imagination of people the world over. They are a part of history, as evidenced by their presence in the Garden of Eden, ancient Persia and the Hanging Gardens of Babylon.

These days, roses remain just as popular, from the Rose Bowl to giving roses as a present on Valentine's or Mother's Day. Everyone loves a rose, the most popular flower in the world.

Roses are readily available at nurseries and floral shops, but how do you grow the perfect rose at home?

There are more than 100 rose species and thousands of varieties. Blooms come in a rainbow of colors ranging from red to lavender to white, or, in some cases, two or more colors in a single blossom.

There are miniature roses that are perfect ground covers or easily grown in containers and disease-resistant, hardy floribundas, commonly used as barriers, borders and along pathways. They grow 3 to 5 feet tall and with blossoms up to 5 inches wide, hybrid tea roses are the most prized and popular of roses grown today.

Planting Tips

If you are seriously considering growing roses, consult a gardening friend to determine which type you would like to raise and to learn if it will thrive where you live. Still not sure? Consult your local landscaper or ask for help at the local nursery.

Roses require at least six hours of sun daily, so pick a planting side with easterly exposure. The site should be slightly sloped to ensure maximum water drainage. Plant roses away from other shrubs and trees so there's no competition for moisture and nutrients.

Rose bushes are sold either in containers or bare-root. Bare-root roses need to be planted immediately after purchase. Prior to planting, soak the bare roots in a bucket of water to protect roots from drying out. Container roses can be planted at your convenience and needn't be presoaked.

Well-aerated soil is the best growing environment for a newly planted rose bush. Add peat moss if needed and then apply a fertilizer.

Next, dig a planting hole 1½ feet deep and 2 feet wide to provide enough space for good drainage and root spreading. Begin planting bare-root roses by creating a firm mound at the bottom of your planting hole. Gently spread the roots over the mound and check that enough stem will be above the surface. Then refill the hole with soil, firmly anchoring the plant. Water promptly after planting and water regularly throughout the growing season. Roses need plenty of water, especially during the hot months of July and August.

As you can see, roses are rather easy to grow. And, as you know, the results are usually beautiful. So why not try growing the perfect rose at home this season?

Roses as Carpeting

Just in time for the new millennium, Anthony Tesselaar International is introducing the fourth in its highly popular series of Flower Carpet easy-care ground-cover roses. These red Flower Carpet roses have unprecedented natural disease resistance and high performance, and for this reason more than five million of them have been sold in the United States.

All Flower Carpet roses are sold in a distinctive pink pot, with instructions for planting and care on a booklet-style label. A complementary sachet of time-released rose food is attached. Gardeners wishing to locate a nearby retailer can call (800) 580-5930. The suggested retail price is between $12 and $16.

A prolific bloomer, this rose features wide-open, softly ruffled blooms in sprays that gently cascade over the pot or along the ground. Its tight, compact buds are deep red with golden stamens. Each flower is about 2 inches across and softens in color as it ages. This multicolored effect, punctuated by the prominent golden yellow stamens, adds a lot of character to the bush.

Red Flower Carpet is easy to care for, exhibiting its impressive levels of natural resistance to black spot and mildew, has a long bloom season and produces a vigorous bush and glossy green foliage with burgundy margins. Bushes stand 24 to 32 inches tall, with a spread of about 3 feet.

The plant establishes itself easily and is quick to flower. Its long bloom season extends from mid-spring through fall. It is winter-hardy in Zones 5 through 10.

As with other Flower Carpet roses, this new one does not require routine dusting or spraying, tricky pruning, deadheading or special handling of any kind. All it needs is water, fertilizer and a good cut-back in later winter or early spring.

In full sun, well-watered, a mature bush can produce up to 2,000 flowers per season. In partial shade (4-5 hours of sun per day) or good filtered light, these roses still bloom prolifically, though in reduced numbers. They perform beautifully in landscapes, flower beds, mass plantings, large patio containers and hanging baskets.

Flower Carpet roses are also available in white, pink and apple blossom.

Roses from Cuttings

Q. *I have tried unsuccessfully several times to root roses. Could you please tell me the best way?*

A. If you've been trying to root cuttings of certain modern roses, it's no wonder that you've been having a rough time. Grandifloras, hybrid teas and floribundas are usually pampered rose plants that have been grafted onto the sturdy rootstock of a stronger rose.

So, even if you do get a cutting to sprout, it would not have as strong a root system as the original plant (which was actually a combination of two different roses) and probably won't survive more than a couple of years.

For example, old garden roses practically root themselves because they are already growing on their own rootstock. Some people just stick such cuttings in the ground to let them take root. It's that simple.

The best time to take cuttings for most of the country is late spring, after the first round of bloom (rose propagators in the north should take cuttings in the fall).

Take a stem, cut about 6 inches off the tip and strip off the bottom leaves, leaving a few at the top. The angle of the cut doesn't matter. Put the cutting in a moist medium and be sure to keep it moist until rooting occurs.

Commercial breeders use a mist bench to root their roses and so can you. Simply use clear plastic to make a little tent over the container in which you're going to place the cuttings you wish to root. Don't place your cutting in direct sunlight. Keep it where temperatures will be moderate. Again, keep the medium moist, lift the cover and mist the cutting three or four times a day, replacing the cover each time.

I root my rose cuttings in plastic bags in a very light, damp soil mix. I seal the bags and put them in a bright, cool spot and wait for roots to fill the bag; then I move the rooted cuttings into pots. When the rooted cuttings are actively growing, you'll see new leaves begin to emerge.

Just keep the little plants in their pots until they're on the verge of becoming rootbound.

If you've been growing the cuttings indoors, gradually accustom them to the great outdoors by hardening them off for a week or so; then plant the roses in their permanent home. April and May are the best months for this.

Seedlings

To avoid leggy, spindly seedlings: sow thinly. If leaves overlap when seedlings sprout, thin immediately; provide full light as soon as seedlings emerge; do not overwater; keep temperatures on the cool side once seedlings emerge; and provide good air circulation, but avoid drafts.

Seeds

The seed is an amazing curiosity that holds the secrets of life. Some aspects of the seed and its means of survival still remain a mystery. Learning more about the seed can help gardeners improve their own germination successes.

For instance, when you look at a seed, you are looking at the seed coat. A distinct "fingerprint" for the plant species, many garden seeds can be identified by their shape, size and seed coat.

Variations of the seed coat are many, including some that are thick and hard, while others are thin and papery. Just as people wear coats for protection against foul weather, seed coats perform much the same function—protection against entry of parasites or injury, and, in some seeds, protection against extreme temperatures.

Inside the seed coat is the embryo, an immature plant with all the parts of the adult plant. A close look shows leaves and a root. Although they are not the "true leaves," and the root may be a mere speck, they are the beginnings of a plant.

The names of the embryo parts express the immature nature and eventual purpose of each part. The seed leaves inside the embryo are called the cotyledons and their point of attachment to the axis divides the embryo into halves. The area above the seed leaves (epicotyl) is the immature stem; below the seed leaves (hypocotyl) becomes the embryonic root. The endosperm is like a picnic basket, storing food that will nourish the embryo during its early stages of development.

Germination is a fascinating process. Seeing that tiny seedling emerge from a dry, wrinkled seed coat, watching its growth and transformation, is observing the mystery of life unfolding.

It starts with "digestion." A growing embryo uses only water-soluble food, so the first sign of germination is the absorption of water—lots of water. This activates an enzyme, respiration increases and protoplasm is duplicated. The seed is alive and growing.

Soon the embryo becomes too large, the seed coat bursts open and the root tip of the growing plant emerges. The root emerges first for good reason—not only will the seed be anchored in place, but also the embryo can now absorb water and nutrients from surrounding soil before there is a stem.

I've talked about the seed and how it comes to life, but before the seed germinates it is either in a state of dormancy or quiescence. Both terms refer to a living seed suspended for a period of time in a sheltered place, waiting for conditions to be right to grow and change. Dormancy is caused by internal conditions, whereas quiescence is caused by external conditions— such as the lack of moisture or oxygen, improper temperature or light.

Seed dormancy is a complex phenomenon. It protects the life in the seed from an adverse environment. The causes of seed dormancy are varied, complex and still being studied by researchers. When you purchase seeds from reliable seed companies they will be prepared for germination, or specific instructions for germinating the seed will be provided.

The garden seed is an individual, mysterious package of life. Once that small particle of life becomes activated and a growing plant emerges, the excitement has only just begun.

Seed Fact Trivia

• Only 3 percent of the plants cultivated in 1900 are still available today.

• Wheat seeds provide more food for the world than any other plant or animal.

• Seeds of grain plants provide 75 percent of the diet of people outside the United States.

• An average of 38 million American households spent an estimated $600 million on seeds during each of the past five years.

• Approximately 25 percent of the plants grown from seed include turf grasses, while another 25 percent are vegetable plants. Almost half of all the non-hybrid vegetable varieties appearing on the market ten years ago have been dropped from mail-order catalogs.

Soil Preparation

Every gardener dreams of a garden bursting with succulent vegetables and glorious flowers spring through fall.

To cut down on the weeding, watering and fertilizing necessary to make that dream come true, garden from the ground up and properly prepare the soil.

Unless you are planting a large area, hand dig peat moss into existing vegetable and flower beds. Be careful not to disturb plant roots. For best results, dig 1 inch of peat moss into the top 6 inches of soil to condition the beds for existing plants or new transplants.

Checklist for creating new garden beds:

1. Outline the area for your new garden bed with string.
2. Cut away the sod, saving it for lawn patches or the compost pile.
3. Dig or rototill 2 inches of peat moss into the top 6 or 8 inches of soil. Consider adding organic matter, such as compost, for nutrients.
4. Add bedding plants, perennials or seeds and water gently over a period of one to two weeks.

The most common causes of plant failure are planting too deep, poor drainage, infertile soil, drought and spray damage and foreign material in the soil.

Always set plants at the same depth. Make sure the roots are covered; if they're too shallow, the sun will bake the roots, and plants usually die immediately. If planted too shallow in the fall, frost can heave the roots of perennials right out of the ground. Foreign materials in the soil such as buried concrete around newly built dwellings restrict root growth, and a plant may die.

Compacted or hardpan soil can kill plants because excess water simply won't drain away, and roots cannot penetrate hardpan soil. Infertile soil may also kill plants. Some soil is so poor that it will not let anything grow except weeds.

The best remedy is to deeply till the soil, fertilize it and plant a cover crop, such as white clover. Plant this cover in spring and plow under in fall. Several years of this practice will add enough humus and nutrients to the soil to support plants. This way the soil will be fertile and healthy once again.

Drought can also kill plants. Few plants, trees and shrubs can get by with less than 20 inches of rainfall each year. Unfortunately, even evergreens or other well-established plants ten or more years old can be killed in a drought. Remember, water your ornamental plants every few days if you don't have rain.

Spray drift kills plants, too. This type of damage often occurs in small towns or near the edge of large towns where farmers spray crops with chemicals. The spray can drift several miles on a windy day. There isn't much you can do about this. However, I do suggest visiting the farmers and convincing them that the way to go is with an organic soap spray. Chemicals are no longer acceptable, and it's about time they know it.

Your garden soil has a way of telling you it needs attention. Slow growth and slimy plant stems may be a sign of nitrogen deficiency, especially if the leaves are fading and yellow. If growth is slow and plants don't set fruit and mature properly and the undersides of leaves are a reddish purple color, the problem could be phosphorus deficiency. If older leaves turn yellow at the edges and the plants are stunted with weak stems, they may not be getting enough potassium.

Spring Planning

Spring, without a doubt, is the most exhilarating time of the year. The season's thrill exists for everyone but, for a gardener, it is also the busiest time.

After a long winter, whether you're starting a new garden or continuing one that's already established, you're eager to get going. There's lots to be done, and you'll have to hurry to keep pace with nature.

I want to stress the importance of having a plan before spring planting time arrives.

In the fall and winter, plant bulbs of tulips, daffodils and other narcissuses, hyacinths, crocuses and snowdrops. These can begin blooming as early as March.

All of these are perfect as cut flowers indoors. Another way to enjoy them is to dig up the bulbs with some soil and pot them just as they are about to bloom.

My favorites are the marvelously colored tulips, like the subtle 'Apricot Rose' or the almost glow-in-the-dark orange and yellow 'Easter Surprise,' which bring the feeling of springtime right into the house.

Read carefully any notes you made over the winter about starting your garden. You should have written down what you want to plant and when, but if you haven't now is the time to decide what your preferences are.

The next important step, as you begin planting, is to keep good records. Label your garden beds so that you know what you have planted and where you have planted it. Make rows 12 inches apart for both flowers and vegetables. Sow seeds evenly down the row, and give your young seedlings ample room to grow into maturity without crowding.

First watering should be very gentle, otherwise you will wash the seeds away. In fact, one of the biggest hazards of spring is too much rain. Proper drainage in your garden beds is crucial, since tender growth will drown if left standing in a pool of water.

When shopping for flowers, keep the size of your garden in mind. Choose those that will bloom for a long time and give you great rewards for your time and effort. Consider petunias, alyssum, shasta, daisies, geraniums, marigolds and salvias. These are my alternatives for impatiens and begonias.

If your garden life is limited, choose vegetables that will produce the greatest yield for your time and effort. Plant cucumbers, corn, squash, peas, lettuce, tomatoes and string beans; then choose the crops you simply wouldn't want to be without.

Hybrids are usually a little more expensive, but they usually provide healthier, stronger, more disease-resistant plants and yield bigger flowers or more abundant crops. They are bred especially for use in home gardens, and nearly all of them perform well over the country.

Perennials are a good investment for your garden. They provide continuous blooms, year after year, and most kinds are easy to care for.

Every two to four years you can divide your garden so you'll be able to expand your garden at little or no effort.

Perennials are convenient, since when the flowers have finished blooming for the season and start to die back, you just cut the plants down to a few inches and forget about them until next spring rolls around. Then they will sprout and bloom again.

Spring Scents

Early spring smells of damp earth and blooming spring bulbs. A flower that smells marvelous to you may not seem so sweet to your best friend. Keep in mind that a few flowers just plain stink—at least to some people.

Flower fragrances are for attracting insects and birds, not people. Birds and insects called pollinators find flowers by their color, smell, shape and pattern. Pollinators spread the flower's pollen from flower to flower. With the help of pollinators like bees, flies, hummingbirds and butterflies, flowers make seeds that grow into new plants.

Many people love the smell of violets, and so do bees. They are attracted by the bluish color, too. The shape of violet flowers helps bees find the nectar, which is the food the pollinators want.

Have you ever smelled skunk cabbage flowers? To us, they smell like rotten meat. Flies love that smell. Parts of the flowers are even the color of rotting meat and heat up, spreading the odor. Look for skunk cabbage when there is still snow on the ground—the flowers are warm enough to melt nearby snow.

Strawberries

Strawberries are a fabulous fruit and the most popular one grown in home gardens. You can harvest more strawberries per plant than any other berry. They are also versatile; you can grow them in their own beds or plant them along with perennials or annuals. They also thrive in tubs, patio containers, windowboxes or in hanging baskets on a porch or balcony.

Plant strawberries in beds or rows 12 inches apart, spreading the roots apart carefully. Be sure to set the plant's crown at soil level. Too deep and the plant will rot; too shallow and it will dry out. To help plants get established properly, set each plant over a small amount of soil, gently spread the roots over it and fill in over and around the roots. Keep the strawberries moist while planting. The parent strawberry plant usually sends out runners the first year, and if you're lucky may bear some fruit. The second and third year they'll bear larger crops. After that, for better yields, cut back or simply remove older plants.

Allow new plants borne from runners to become the bearing ones in the future seasons.

Strawberries need only periodic care. Luckily, older plants send out runners to establish healthy baby plants for your future crops. Healthy baby strawberry plants make great Christmas, anniversary or birthday presents. To stop weeds, keep the beds well mulched and moist.

Strawberry cultivars to plant are very specific to region, so buy your plants at a local garden center.

- South: 'Sunrise,' 'Dixiland,' 'Surecrop' and 'Marlate'
- Northeast and Midwest: 'Midway,' 'Fletcher' 'Sparkle.'
- West: 'Rainier,' 'Puget Beauty'
- California: 'Tufts,' 'Tioga,' 'Shasta'

Strawberries, Alpine

Plant some *fraises des bois* (alpine strawberries) now; you'll enjoy them all summer. Since their ever-blooming, ever-bearing habit depends on soil that is rich, well drained and evenly moist at all times, be sure to mulch well with salt hay.

Thyme

Plant several kinds of creeping thyme between brick or flagstones along your terrace or garden path. They will scent the air as you walk along them. This herb also makes a good-smelling groundcover for container gardens in town or country.

Tomatoes, and Vitamin C

Tiny tomatoes pack a bigger wallop of vitamin C than their larger counterparts. Researchers at Rutgers University looked at the vitamin C content of 36 tomato varieties and found that cherry tomatoes like 'Tommy Toe,' 'Peacevine' and 'Sweet Chelsea' had more vitamin C per ounce than larger varieties.

The absolute champ of these teeny-weeny varieties is 'Chapis Wild,' with an astonishing 84.5 milligrams of vitamin C per 100 grams of tomato.

Transplanting

Doing your transplanting on cloudy days will lessen wilt and watering, as the ground is usually damp. It generally pays to reduce the top parts of a plant to about the same extent as roots lost in the transplanting process.

Tree Pruning—Proper Cuts Are a Must!

Pruning is the most frequently performed tree service and one that evokes quite a bit of misunderstanding. Pruning is defined as the removal of tree parts; therefore, one must always keep in mind that a valid reason to prune is essential. Some reasons are for tree health, safety, size, shape, electric-line clearance, repair of storm or other damage, selective pruning to clear land or open vistas and enhancement of flower, nut or fruit production.

Before any cuts are made, the objective should be well defined so the work can be properly planned. For the well-being of the tree as well as the safety of the pruner, the proper tools have to be on hand and they must be sharp and in good operating condition. It's always a mistake to "make do" with what's on hand. The list of operator safety rules is almost endless; that's why I rarely suggest that a homeowner or nonprofessional prune trees on a do-it-yourself basis. Tree pruning is one procedure that is best left to professionals for safety reasons alone.

In cutting all but the smallest twigs, the correct procedure calls for the cuts. The first is an undercut, the purpose of which is to prevent the bark from ripping down the stem as the branch falls. The second cut is made above the undercut, a couple of inches further out. The third cut is most important; it's made to remove the stub which, if left, could become an opening into the tree for disease and decay problems. The final cut must be made as close to the branch bark ridge (or branch collar) as possible without damaging the live tissue of the ridge (or collar) which contains essential chemical barrier zones to fend off decay.

Most tree owners are amazed at the amount of dead wood and brush that can come out of a properly pruned tree. Most trees can't survive removal of more than about one-third of their canopy at a time because pruning of live tissue also removes a lot of foliage that is essential in the process of manufacturing the sugars and starches that sustain the plant.

If you have questions about tree pruning, be sure to consult the F. A. Bartlett Tree Co.; they are the best in the business. For an office in the area you live in, consult the Yellow Pages of the phone book.

Tulips

Q. *My tulips grew green leaves but no flowers this year. Why?*

A. If tulips produce leaves but no flowers, there are generally two reasons.

If the tulips were planted just last fall, it probably means that the bulbs were exposed to a fertilizer with a very high nitrogen content, such as a lawn fertilizer. Nitrogen promotes vigorous green growth—but too much can inhibit flowering.

If the bulbs were planted several years ago, they may just be running out of gas (in regression).

Technically speaking, tulips are perennials, which means they should naturalize (come back) each spring. But actually, most tulips only behave this way when grown under climatic conditions (cold winters and hot, dry summers) of their original native habitats in the steppes of Russia, northern Turkey and elsewhere. In most U.S. home gardens, tulips do not find these conditions.

Bottom line: Count on tulips for a terrific first-year showing—and enjoy future appearances as a bonus.

Vegetables: When to Plant

Vegetables may be roughly grouped for planting according to hardiness and temperature requirements. Planting dates revolve around the dates of the last frost in your area. The spring frost-free date is usually two to three weeks later than the average day of the

last frost, just about the time the oak trees leaf out.

Very hardy: Plant four to six weeks before frost-free date. Includes broccoli, cabbage, lettuce, onions, peas, potatoes and spinach.

Hardy: Plant two to four weeks before frost-free date. Includes beets, carrots, chard, mustard and radishes.

Not cold-hardy: Plant on frost-free date. Includes beans, squash, sweet corn, New Zealand spinach and tomatoes.

Requires hot weather: Plant one week or more after frost-free date. Includes lima beans, eggplant, melons and cucumbers.

Medium heat tolerant: Good for summer planting. Includes spinach, squash and sweet corn.

Hardy plants for late summer or fall planting: Plant six to eight weeks before first fall breeze. Some northern areas may be too cold. Includes beets, kale, collards, lettuce and mustard spinach.

Top 10 nutritious vegetables: Broccoli, spinach, brussels sprouts, lima beans, peas, asparagus, artichokes, cauliflower, sweet potatoes and carrots.

Wildflowers

Wildflowers are among nature's greatest treasures. They are low-maintenance, simple and abundant, and they provide a changing panorama of colors, shapes and sizes. It is this informal spontaneity and the changes that occur as the growing season progresses that make them so delightful to the viewer. No wonder wildflowers have become popular.

Growing wildflowers is a cinch. Wildflowers grow in their natural state with little human interference. They are not bred or cross-bred the way annuals and perennials may be. Read seed-packet and plant-label descriptions carefully to avoid disappointment. Many perennial wildflowers will not perform until they have been established in the garden for a year. Some wildflowers are biennials, blooming every other year, and some are annuals, which must be re-planted each year as there is no guarantee that they will re-seed themselves.

Deciding which wildflowers to grow in your garden depends on where you live and where in your garden you want to grow them. Today's marketplace abounds with choices, often right at local nurseries, garden centers and mail order seed sources. Wildflowers can be purchased as seeds or plants, as a single species or in mixes. It is important to note that the botanical reference to genus and species is given in wildflowers listings, as some do not have true variety names, and the "common" names may differ from one area of the country to another. *Centaurea*, for example, commonly known as 'cornflower,' is also called 'Bachelor's Button.'

When choosing wildflowers it is best if you know the botanical names of what you want and then check the packaging. By law, wildflowers must be listed by genus and species, so checking these shouldn't be too difficult.

Seed packets offer choices in individual species or mixes, so you can select exactly what you want, or blend your own custom mix. Individual plants are often available at retail outlets and through mail-order catalogs. A newer innovation in wildflower planting is the development of started, growing plants that look like a piece of sod. The "sod" is simply placed on prepared soil and kept watered, or the mats can be cut apart and the pieces spaced out in a bed.

If you want only a few specific wildflowers, purchasing growing plants or buying seed packets may be your best choice. Started plants offer the advantage of avoiding the germination stage and give you a better idea of what the adult plant will look like.

Mixtures are a popular way of purchasing wildflowers. While started-plant mixtures are available, seed mixtures are more common and have the advantage of combining a wide range of species. Mixtures come in combinations that will do best in sunny locations or shady locations and are usually clearly designated for certain regions of the country. They have been specially blended with annuals and perennials that are suited to a particular area, which takes some of the guesswork out of what will grow where. Some of these mixtures produce flowers in shades of specific colors or a combination thereof.

Windowboxes

Q. *What is the best combination of spring and summer flowers for sunny windowboxes facing west in New Jersey?*

A. Lantanas, geraniums, petunias and nasturtiums come to mind. Get potted plants from your garden center; they are usually in flower at spring-planting time and will bloom until frost. They will stand heat but do best when well watered and pruned to stop lanky growth. They prefer full sun but can be grown in partial shade. Why not try dwarf marigolds and verbenas as well—they come in so many different colors, shapes and varieties.

Wood, Arsenic-Treated

Many wooden decks, playground equipment, picnic tables, docks and raised bed frames are leaking toxic levels of arsenic into American backyards.

Adults and children alike can ingest harmful levels of arsenic when they play or are near such structures and then put their hands in their mouths. Also, the soil and growth pattern of nearby plants can be impaired.

All this is happening because almost all wood that has been sold to consumers for outdoor use for the past several decades has been treated with a chemical called chromate copper arsenate (CCA). The industry label is "pressure treated"; but in fact it has been saturated with a deadly chemical containing arsenic!

A report from the Connecticut Agricultural Experiment Station (published in *Frontiers of Plant Science,* vol. 51, no. 1, Fall 1998, pp. 6–8) has confirmed what I already know and have previously reported. Dangerous levels of arsenic, as much as ten to 35 times above legal limits, are leaking from CCA-treated wood; and potentially dangerous amounts of arsenic easily rub off whenever the wood is touched by human hands.

Although arsenic is a natural substance found in tiny amounts in most soils, it's also a deadly poison! It's so deadly that the current limit for arsenic in drinking water is 50 parts per billion; in fact, several studies indicate that this limit should be lowered even further.

Long-term exposure to low arsenic levels such as the amounts released from CCA-treated wood can also cause other problems such as vomiting and nerve and blood-vessel damage according to the "Toxicological Profile for Arsenic" published by the U.S. Department of Health. Of course, in the past the treated-wood industry has denied the hazards of arsenic-treated wood, but those dangers are now obvious thanks to honest research conducted by independent scientists such as those mentioned above. If the industry doesn't stop selling CCA-coated wood soon, it could possibly face the same kind of legal nightmare the tobacco industry is experiencing.

It's time for the nation's home gardeners (big-time consumers) to launch a full-scale boycott of CCA-treated wood. When you buy wood for garden and outdoor projects, demand that your supplier provide non-arsenic alternatives. The best and safest choices include untreated rot-resistant woods like locust, ash, cedar or wood treated with alkaline copper quat (ACA), a copper-based chemical that does not contain arsenic or chromium. Chromium is another toxin that leaches CCA-treated wood.

If you already have an arsenic-treated deck or other structures, you can prevent further leaching or rubbing off of the arsenic by painting the structure with one of several coatings tested by the Connecticut Agricultural Experiment Station. Polyurethane enamel, acrylic stain, alkyl-resin stain and spar varnish will substantially reduce leaching of arsenic from the CCA-treated wood surface, making it safer.

You can just use cheap wood to make raised beds for your garden and replace the frames after five or ten years, or you can buy raised-bed kits made of recycled plastic shaped like landscape timbers. You can use concrete or cinder blocks, or simply not frame your beds at all and plant lettuce on the edges (you gain a lot of space that way).

summer

JUNE 21 IS THE BEGINNING OF SUMMER. By now your hard work pays off and you start to see the fruits of your labor. This is a time of great satisfaction. There is nothing more enjoyable than watching a garden grow. Summer means a time of maintenance for your garden. Weeding, staking, pruning, battling the pests and insects, and watering are all part of your daily chores. It's important now in the summer to keep up your garden journal. Make notes of things that are growing as you thought they would, and start to think of any changes for next time around. As summer progresses, your vegetables will

be a great source of enjoyment. It's so much fun, whether you're serving two or 22 people, to have succulent vegetables right off the vine.

Your cut flowers are a joy, too. Beautiful, colorful bouquets can fill many rooms in your house. Of course, the most popular flower in the world, the rose, makes my favorite bouquets. Their fragrance and gorgeous colors mix beautifully with almost all other flowers. They are not as difficult to grow as most people think. And this goes for orchids too—another of my favorite flowers. By the end of the season you should be confident enough to grow any sort of flower you want, even if it does come with the myth of being difficult to grow.

African Violets

Q. *Can you tell me why my African violets die in the center and the outside leaves keep growing? I have had wonderful luck with more than 50 different kinds and colors, but suddenly this summer every one is affected, and I am about to throw them out.*

I have several new leaves rooted from these plants. Will they be affected, too?

A. Check your plants and see if you have mites or mealybugs. If so, spray with Safer's Insecticidal Soap, reading the label carefully. Failure to bloom may be caused by several factors: lack of humidity, lack of light, stale air, hot or cold drafts, overwatering or underwatering. Baby plants (called suckers) that form at the base of old leaves are best removed immediately, as soon as you're sure they aren't flower buds; otherwise, you'll have few flowers on your plants.

When moved, African violets may "sulk." Relax, they'll recover! For best results, place your plants in a pot or tray on moist stones.

Beekeeping

Notes from a Beekeeper

"As a beekeeper with 40 years of experience, I would like to share several observations so your readers understand the function of honeybees. They are truly amazing.

"It is true that in the fall most of the males (drones) die. They are forced from the hive by the workers and perish outside. This is done to conserve during the winter months.

"The only purpose of the drones is to mate with a virgin queen. The only fertilized female in the hive is the queen. The other females (workers) never mate and do not lay eggs under normal circumstances. In the unlikely event that the queen should die and the workers would be unable to raise another queen, workers have been known to lay eggs because of the stress, but these eggs produce only drones. Under these circumstances the population will gradually diminish and the colony will perish.

"It may be of interest to know that a queen is fertilized only once in her lifetime, from which she may lay millions of eggs over a period of several years. A still unexplained phenomenon is that the queen lays both fertile and infertile eggs at will: The fertile egg producing a female worker and the infertile egg producing a drone. The drone has no father and has no lineage to the drone that fertilized the queen."

Bruce Burney
Applegate, California

Bird-of-Paradise

Q. *Last year a friend gave me a bird-of-paradise (Strelitzice reginae) in a container, but it never bloomed. I keep it in a solarium. What's my problem?*

A. You may have a young plant. A bird-of-paradise must be at least five years old and rootbound before it will bloom. When your plant reaches 1 to 2 feet tall, the roots will crowd the pot and "pups" (offshoots) begin to form on the main crown; that's when the "bird" is close to blooming.

This is a great plant because it's so easy to grow. Place it in a pot in full sun and feed with a 10-10-10 fertilizer once a month from spring to fall—but no feeding in winter!

When blooms appear, switch to a high-bloom fertilizer, a 10-20-10.

Once the "bird" starts to bloom, it will continue sporadically all year. Flowers will last at least a month on the bush, and one to two weeks if cut for arrangements.

Birds, Attracting

Why do some people seem to have their property full of birds, while activity around your feeders is negligible to none?

It is as simple as S-W-F: shelter, water and food.

Take a good look at your backyard from the perspective of your feathered friends. Do you have different types of feeders, placed at different heights to accommodate the way birds feed in the wild? Are there shrubs and trees to provide nesting sites as well as protection from predators? Is there water available for drinking and bathing? We all love to bathe.

Think about your yard and plan for diversity—small and tall trees, shrubs, bushes and native grasses. Talk to an expert at your local nursery, lawn and garden store or county extension service before making new purchases.

You want plants that are suited for your area and for conditions that will provide food, nesting sites or shelter for the birds.

Evergreens, including juniper, spruce, hemlock and pine, are marvelous nesting and escape sites for the birds.

Fruit-bearing trees such as crab apple, cherry, hawthorn and mulberry produce food attractive to a wide range of bird species.

In your flower garden, plant asters, bee balm, coneflower, mums and pinks, all perennials that will come up every year. Popular annual flowers attractive to birds include bachelor's buttons, coreopsis, impatiens, phlox, sunflower and zinnias.

Encourage growth of wildflowers in your yard, too, to attract a number of wild songbirds as well as to enhance your landscape with color.

Add new feeding stations each year to accommodate the needs of your resident birds. Even relatively tiny suburban yards can become the perfect habitats in a way that works for the birds, for you and your budget.

The goal of the National Bird-Feeding Society is to make backyard feeding and housing better for people and birds.

Providing food, water and shelter helps birds survive; it benefits the environment and supplements wild birds' natural diet of weed seeds and insects.

A happy bird will stick around.

Birds, and Eggshells

A study by the Cornell Lab of Ornithology in Ithaca, New York, suggests that wild birds relish crushed eggshells.

Recent studies show that some birds are not getting adequate calcium from natural resources, mainly because acid rain is leaching calcium deposits from the soil. The lab asked bird lovers to put out the eggshells and watch what happened.

The project was a smashing success, with many birds eating the shells—a year-round project to keep our feathered friends healthy and happy.

Bulbs for Summer

No matter how big your garden, or whether or not you have a sunny location, there's a plant for you. Not all varieties require lots of water; some plants do well in shade. A little bit of research will ensure that you find the best possible match for your growing conditions.

So velvety, so lush, so over-the-top! Tuberous begonias are attracting a tremendous following, being one of the few brilliantly colored summer flowers to bloom abundantly in deep shade or filtered light.

If treated well, these voluptuous nodding flowers in the richest shades of deep to pastel red, pink, apricot, white, yellow, champagne, orange and bi-colors, will bloom all season long.

Pineapple lily, or eucomis, is an extremely tropical plant. A pineapple look-alike, it is topped by a 15-inch spire of tiny greenish-white flowers and a base of strappy green leaves. The plants bloom in July and August, but even after flowering continue to hold their own in the garden. Plant in groups in full sun or shade; they're perfect for garden or summer.

Lilies, so spectacular in summer, are almost as easy to grow as planting a pink flamingo. Just stick them in the ground and admire! In fact, lilies are so unfussy they don't care whether they are planted in spring or fall.

These hardy perennials will return year after year, so plant them in garden beds or containers. The Asiatics bloom early to mid-summer, the Orientals bloom later. They thrive in full sun or partial shade.

These three summer bulbs are top performers, known for their fine foliage: elephant ear, caladium and canna.

Elephant ears can be used as stage setting for "instant tropics." The plant stands 3 to 5 feet tall with huge green leaves that unfurl to look just like, well, elephant ears! Plant in containers or the garden, in shade or partial shade.

Caladiums bring cool leafy softness to any setting, whether planted in beds or containers, or in combination with other plants. Best in deep shade or filtered light, caladiums sport glorious swaying leaves in a wide range of colors.

Canna have a distinctly upright lushness with foliage in dashing shades of green, brown, burgundy or multicolored stripes. They also sport flamboyant blooms atop 3- to 5-foot plants. Canna thrive in full sun and hot weather.

Those Wily Chipmunks

Q. *Chipmunks keep taking small bites out of my tomatoes and other vegetables from my garden. I've tried everything, including human hair, soap spray, netting, etc., to no avail. Last summer, I trapped about 40 chipmunks and released them in a wooded preserve about 10 miles from my property. This year, I see more of them and they look just as hungry. Will this ever stop? Do you have a solution?*

A. I know this will amaze you, but here goes. You're probably trapping the same chipmunks over and over again! ABC Humane Rescue in Arlington Heights, Illinois, suggests taking the trapped chipmunks at least 20 to 40 miles away to a rural area for release. Five or ten miles is simply not far enough. However, trapping is the best way to go, and I suggest Sherman live traps (the same traps for moles). The traps you need are 3 inches by 3½ inches by 10 inches.

Sherman traps are most effective when you position them so that the entrance looks like a natural cavity—for example, poking out of a leaf pile. Chipmunks hunt by smell and, of course, they are very curious. A good bait is a mixture of greasy peanut butter, oatmeal and something fruity. Other delicacies they enjoy include beans, acorns, nuts, peas, raspberries and blackberries.

If your dogs and cats are good hunters, maybe they can control these rascals. My dogs, unfortunately, are no good at this type of hunting because they are too large for the tiny spaces chipmunks can fit into.

To successfully fence these devils out, you have to enclose your entire garden with a 6-foot fence made from one-quarter-inch mesh hardware cloth, sunk at least a foot into the soil (so chipmunks can't dig under it) with plastic bird netting across the top from side to side.

Two no-no's: Never use mothballs, moth flakes, or any form of this extremely toxic substance in your garden or anywhere else because they are dangerous to pets. Also, chipmunks and squirrels that are biting tomatoes and other fruits are doing so to quench their thirst. So before you do anything, install a birdbath or other water source. They might just leave your tomatoes and fruits alone.

For more information, contact H. B. Sherman Traps, Inc., P. O. Box 20267, Tallahassee, Florida, 32316.

Composting

Getting to the top of the heap, the compost heap, is key to having a great garden. Compost piles are very useful and simple to make—simply toss in anything, as long as it's organic matter and not an animal product.

Rotten and Ripe

Leaves: The leaves of one large shade tree can be worth as much as $35 in terms of humus and plant food. Pound for pound, the leaves of most trees contain twice as many minerals as manure. Two things will guarantee you success in composting leaves.

First, add extra nitrogen by supplementing manure in a mixture of five parts leaves to one part manure. Second, shred or grind your leaves.

Grass clippings: Clippings are valuable when left on the lawn, but they may also be used in other garden areas and, of course, are indispensable to the compost heap.

Weeds: Weeds with phosphorus, nitrogen and potash content similar to other plant residues can provide ample humus for the soil. Weed seeds will be killed by high temperatures in the compost pile, and weeds that sprout from the top of the heap can be easily turned under.

Garbage: Organic refuse is a neglected source of compost material that is particularly rich in nitrogen and other nutrients essential to soil-building and plant growth.

Manure: Use manure from animals that eat only plants. Manure contains about one-third of the total nitrogen, one-fifth of the total potash and nearly all of the phosphoric acid voided by animals. But it is because of its large bacteria population that manure is so valuable in the compost heap. Manure provides the necessary bacteria to break down other materials.

Straw: Straw will add little nutrient value to the compost heap, but it's used mainly because its bulk adds considerable organic material. Most farmers offer bales of spoiled hay to gardeners at nominal costs.

Composting Additives

Bone meal: Because of its high nitrogen content, a sprinkling of bone meal will stimulate bacterial growth.

Rock phosphate: This additive is an excellent natural source of phosphorus for fertilizer use.

Soil: The heap itself should be built on freshly dug earth with the soil, of course, loosened. Soil should also be layered with other materials.

Wood ashes: Ashes are a valuable source of potash for the compost heap. Wood ashes should never be allowed to stand in the rain, as the potash leaches away.

How to Make a Compost Pile

To make a small clean-smelling compost pile from kitchen and yard waste, cut the bottom out of a trash can (or use a wire enclosure) and set on the ground.

Pile a day's kitchen waste on the bottom. Shred or break up large pieces; avoid large amounts of any single material.

Cover with a layer of dry leaves, grass clippings and soil. Keep pile loosely packed and exposed to air.

Repeat layering daily. Keep pile damp.

An offensive odor means the pile is packed too tightly or the wrong materials have been used. Earthworms or other small organisms are beneficial.

Materials take six to eight weeks to break down.

Don't use pet feces, large amounts of grease or fat, charcoal, synthetics, floor sweepings, diseased plants, bulky materials, large amounts of meat, cheese or milk products.

Gather your materials for composting at a ratio of five parts vegetable matter to one part nitrogenous animal matter, such as manure.

Shredding is another must, because this will make the compost material break down faster. This can be easily accomplished by tipping a rotary lawn mower against your pile of debris.

Start building layers. First build a "hot" layer of manure and garbage about 1 to 2 inches thick, followed by a foot or so of green matter. Then sprinkle on additives such as bone meal or potash, and top this with an inch of soil. Then start layering the same way over again until the pile reaches 5 feet. The pile can be as small as 3 feet high and still work.

Cover the heap with straw or dirt, then water. Do so frequently, as the secret is to keep the heap moist, but not soaked.

If you turn the heap twice within the first two weeks, you'll have compost before you know it. The turning-over exposes air to all parts of the pile and brings slower decaying surface materials to the "hot" center of the heap. After that, a monthly turning is sufficient.

Crown Imperial Bulbs

Q. *Last season, after a wet spring, my crown imperial bulbs were late in coming up. And when the plants finally reached about 14 inches, they turned yellow and fell over. Unfortunately, no flowers developed. What happened?*

A. I think you may have a drainage problem, so perhaps a soil test is in order. Before planting crown imperial bulbs, turn the soil over to about 2 feet, work in coarse builder's sand to ensure good drainage and enrich the soil with compost. Then plant your bulbs 4 to 6 inches deep as measured from the bulb top, and 10 inches apart in partially shaded, slightly acid soil (pH 6.4). No fertilizing is necessary at planting time.

Simply water the bulbs well after planting and, if autumn rains fail to fall, soak the bed deeply to keep it moist. Keep in mind that seed-setting robs the bulb of food, so remove fading flowers. Although the dying stems and leaves are unsightly, never cut them down before all of the green is gone.

Like all bulbs, they need to store all the leaf-manufactured food they can get for proper growth and flowering the next year. Weak growth and yellowing of these temperamental plants may have been due to an unfavorable pH.

Cucumbers

Q. *This summer I am planning a garden. My only problem is cucumbers. My garden area is a plot of fertile land in direct sunlight. Can you please give me some helpful tips on cucumber growing?*

A. Make your first sowing when danger of frost is past. Rows can be 4 to 5 feet apart, with a plant every 2 or 4 feet in the row. Cucumbers grow best in a fertile, light, well-drained soil.

To keep vines productive, pick before cucumbers are too mature. For nice, straight vegetables, plants grow best on a trellis.

Suggested types are Bush cucumbers, which take about one-third the space of the usual vining types, and the Burpless hybrid, which is easily digestible, juicy, crispy and delicious.

One can obtain these from W. Atlee Burpee Co., 300 Park Avenue, Warminster, Pennsylvania, 18974.

Delphinium

When spikes of delphinium flowers start to fade, cut them back to the ground, mulch with rotted compost or manure and water well. They will send up strong new growth and more blooms in a month or so.

Dill

Dill (*Anethum graveolens*), a member of the carrot family, has been a favorite culinary herb for centuries. It is valued for its flavor, leaves and its pungent seeds.

The word *dill* comes from an old Norse word "dilla" that means "to lull." The plant is often used in tea to treat insomnia and digestive problems. In the Middle Ages, it was regarded as a charm against witchcraft. In modern times, its essential oil is used in pharmaceuticals, cosmetics and liqueurs.

Dill is a delightful herb with many culinary uses. Native to southern Europe, it is a staple in "green cooking." It is common in Scandinavia and Germany as well.

Fresh or dried, dill leaves add a distinctive flavor to salads, fish, vegetable casseroles and soups. Used whole or ground, dill seeds add zest to breads, cheese and salad dressings. The herb is also used for pickling cucumbers, green beans, carrots and beets.

Dill plants are annuals—they die back each year, but will over-winter in the soil to pop up the following year.

In the garden, dill attracts beneficial insects, including bees, parasitic wasps and tachinid flies. In orchards, it attracts insects that control codling moths and tent caterpillars. Whenever dill blooms, it contributes to the welfare of neighboring plants.

Common dill grows 3 to 5 feel tall, but dwarf versions grow from 24 to 36 inches.

When dill matures, it develops tiny yellow flowers that bloom in flat, lacy clusters resembling airy umbrellas. They eventually develop dark-brown seeds that are narrow, ribbed and flattened. About one-sixth of an inch long, their pungent flavor is similar to caraway seeds.

Properly placed and planted, dill is so fast-growing that some of its foliage is mature enough to be harvested in only eight weeks. Plan to sow several crops in succession, three weeks apart, to assure a supply over the entire growing season.

Dill does best in full sun. While it's fairly tolerant of poor soil conditions, it prefers a sandy or loamy soil that drains well. It is a light feeder, so extra fertilizer is not necessary in reasonably fertile soil.

To sow seeds directly into the garden in rows, make ¼- to ½-deep indentations in the soil to guide planting. Then dribble the tiny seeds through your thumb and forefinger into the indented rows. Firm soil over the rows of seeds and water gently. Expect to see sprouts in ten to 14 days.

To plant seedlings, choose an overcast day so they will not have to cope with hot sun as they overcome transplant shock. Dig holes in the prepared soil in the planting area about the size of the containers the seedlings are growing in. Space the plants 8 to 10 inches apart if harvesting seed.

Gently pop each seedling from its container by tapping it on the bottom of the pot. Take great pains to avoid disturbing the taproot that has formed. Set a plant in each hole and firm the soil over the root's ball and around its stem to support it. Water immediately and shade new transplants from bright sun the first day or two while they cope with the shock of transplanting. Depending on the variety, these fast-growing dill plants will grow to maturity and set seed in about 60 days.

Dill leaves taste better picked just before the flowers form on the plant.

Dry Growing Season, Preparing for

Toil in the Soil

The key to water conservation is to improve your soil. Experts tell us that rainwater can slice through pure sand at the rate of 20 inches an hour, stealing with it everything plants need for survival. To prevent this from happening to you, add lots of compost and peat moss to your garden beds. Soil with an abundance of organic matter slows the transition of water from the soil to the subsoil, therefore giving plants a chance to absorb what they need.

Planning Your Crop

In garden planning, concentrate on plants that can handle dry spells, such as beets, broccoli, carrots and onions. Just plant fewer of those that require frequent watering.

It's so tempting to plant all the latest varieties in the spring, even though they'll produce enough food to feed the whole neighborhood. Take stock of what your needs are and don't exceed your calculations. For instance, two or three hills of cucumbers and half a dozen tomato plants will easily meet the needs of a family of four. Bush varieties are another good choice. They grow low to the soil and lose less water through transpiration than those that spread rapidly or twine up to the sky like pole beans. Check descriptions in seed catalogs for varieties that need little space and can tolerate dry conditions.

Place plants close together. Leaves from neighboring plants help to shade the soil; it also helps conserve moisture and reduce weed growth. Plant tomatoes about 18 inches apart and beans about 1 inch apart.

Mulch the garden well. Mulch prevents moisture from evaporating from the soil's surface and it reduces competition from weeds. Don't mulch with peat moss when it dries; it forms a mat on top of the soil that easily sheds water. Always thoroughly work peat moss into the soil. I like wood chips for mulching or a thin layer of grass cuttings.

You should weed continually. Don't allow them to compete with your plants for moisture or anything else. Smother them, yank them out, just hang in there. They are tough customers.

Reduce water evaporation by watering your garden early in the morning or late afternoon, the time when the least amount of water will evaporate from the leaves. Give your garden beds a thorough soaking rather than several light waterings to encourage proper root growth.

Drip irrigation is more thrifty than sprinklers. To set it up, consult your local expert. They will advise you to install a drip system to allow different beds to be on separate cycles, since watering needs for various plants differ—and a system that delivers one rate of water to your entire garden can be wasteful.

Large, luscious, bushy tomatoes lose a lot of water through their leaves. Once the fruits reach full size, strip off most of the leaves to reduce evaporation. That will keep water going to the ripening plants.

As soon as a vegetable or fruit is ripe, remove it from the plant.

To keep plants productive, keep harvesting. Any plants that are nonproductive and past their prime, it's off to the compost pile or chipper for them. Some plants may need more attention than others, but once you adapt your own system of checking your plants it won't take more than 15 minutes a day.

Water Wisdom

A first-year garden needs more continued watering than an old garden because the plants' roots have not established themselves. So push back a little mulch once or twice a week to check whether the soil is dry. To test the soil for planting, squeeze a handful of it. If it sticks together, it's too wet for you to work. Tender loving care is the key to your first-year garden.

Espaliering Basics

A fruit tree or shrub trained to grow against a trellis (or other type of support) for decoration is called an espalier. An espalier can give a garden a fabulous focal point: a fence or patio divider; act as a garden; and perform as a living shield to discourage graffiti. Because it is rather flat, an espalier takes up little space. For best results, plant espaliered shrubs against a south-facing wall.

Fruit trees that have been espaliered produce more fruit because plants are more open to sunlight.

European gardeners discovered this technique centuries ago when they planted espalier groves to gain maximal fruit yields in minimal spaces.

The first step is to choose a suitable location against a fence or wall. If you want to plant a shrub, the most popular varieties for training are holly, camelia, azalea, gardenia, ivy, rose and bougainvillea, to name a few.

The pruning and tying of branches must be done correctly, so it's best to consult an expert. I suggest buying shrubs that are already trained into a specific design, or you can do the training of the greenery against a form or flat surface.

Espaliered fruit trees will be vigorous whether trained against a flat surface or grouped in a row to form a living fence. Apple and pear trees are most popular, since their spurs produce fruit for years. Nectarine, peach, cherry and pomegranate trees can also be espaliered beautifully.

However, it's wise to consult an expert when deciding which variety is appropriate for local weather conditions and which will train best for the shape you have in mind.

It takes three years for most fruit trees to reach maturity and the desired shape if the proper spraying, pruning and fertilizing have been tended to. You'll be amazed at the amount of fruit: up to 70 apples on one mature espaliered tree, as all the branches will be exposed to the sun.

Shrubs and trees in an espaliered form may be purchased at your local nursery or by mail through catalogs.

Farming Lore

The best of various vegetables were often edged with flowers to repel certain insects or destructive nematodes (worms). Marigolds were a favorite in England for protecting tomatoes and potatoes. Foxgloves were used to stimulate the growth and improve the disease resistance of many different garden plants. It was believed that this gave apples, toma-toes and potatoes great storage life.

Chamomile was considered a physician of the plant kingdom and would be set out near a fragile or dying plant until its health was restored. However, the chamomile was removed as soon as the plant recovered, since it was thought that prolonged treatment made the patient dependent on the doctor.

Garden for Cut Flowers

One of the best reasons for having a flower garden is having the ready supply of flowers just waiting to be cut for vase and container. However, when the gardenia is looking especially dazzling, nobody wants to spoil the effect by cutting the finest blooms. So, what to do? This is especially true when company is expected for the weekend.

The obvious solution, of course, is to plant a separate group of flower beds for cutting. You can accomplish this by digging a new bed in a part of the garden where they will complement the landscape or, better still, by using part of the vegetable garden.

Flowers can be a crop, just like vegetables. The more they are cut, the more blooms they will produce. This applies especially to annuals.

A carefully planned cutting garden can provide flowers throughout the growing season. The same applies to flowers grown in winter. All of this can be accomplished without disturbing your display garden.

Ideally, a cutting garden should be in full sun. Well-drained soil is a must for success. If these conditions can't be met, plants that will grow in partial shade or moist soil can be grown. Don't give up if you can't find a sunny, dry spot.

When conditions are marginal due to excessive moisture, building raised beds could solve the problem. A 12-by-24-foot rectangle makes a good-size cutting bed large enough to plant a generous selection of annuals. Of course, there are a large number of plants that can be grown in much smaller plots. Don't feel the cutting garden has to be huge, since there are tricks for getting the most out of a small space. The garden bed doesn't have to be square or rectangle. Just choose a shape that works for you, but keep it simple. Remember, this is a working cutting garden (similar to a kitchen garden); anything fussy will make harvesting difficult.

Once you've decided on the site, preparing the bed is next. Assuming the area is presently lawn, the best thing to do is to remove the sod, leaving as much topsoil as possible. Dig or rototill to loosen the soil and add a lot of manure and compost to make it even lighter. Next, add a dash of organic fertilizer made especially for flowers.

In choosing flowers for the cutting garden, start with varieties you are familiar with. Choose colors based on personal favorites and compatibility with the colors used in the house.

A variety of colors is usually best. I always plant a lot of white flowers, including fillers like baby's breath and statice. White blends perfectly with other colors, brightening dark arrangements and softening intensely colorful ones.

Another consideration is the shape and size of your blooms. Here again, a mixture is best. It should include eye-catchers like tall spikes, daisylike blooms and dainty fillers.

And the leaves (foliage) play a big part, too. Some plants have marvelous leaves that look great in arrangements. Coleus and amaranthus come to mind. The ideal cut flower has a tall, stiff stem, a lovely fragrance and lasts at least a week after being cut. Oriental lilies, peonies, asters, Shasta daisies and hydrangeas come to mind. This is what florists insist upon because the time between cutting and selling can be several days, with a lot of handling in-between. This is where home gardeners have an advantage over florists. Their flowers are fresh.

You can also experiment with favorite types considered too delicate for the florist trade. For instance, cut a bunch of daylilies for a special event in the evening, knowing the blooms will be wilted by the next day.

Even though height is not always crucial, a bowl of short-stemmed flowers makes a nice table arrangement that won't obstruct a dinner partner's view. And a small bouquet of roses, violets or lily of the valley can be a delightful touch for a bedside table or bathroom.

Perennials or annuals? The ultimate cut-flower garden should have both. But for beginners I suggest starting with annuals. They are a cinch to grow from seed, mature swiftly and bloom for a long time—and some even re-seed themselves and show up again the following spring.

There are many annuals that make the perfect cut flower. Annuals provide blooms all through the growing season, from early summer through fall, in a nice mix of shapes and colors for bouquets. They will last at least five days after being harvested, often longer.

Tips on Cutting Flowers

When and how you cut flowers makes all the difference in how long they will survive in water. Early morning, late evening or on overcast or misty days when plants are full of water are the best times to gather bouquets. Use clean, sharp pruning shears (they should feel comfortable in your hand) to cut the stems. Don't pluck the flowers by hand, since you can easily damage or uproot your precious plant.

I like to carry a bucket of water into the garden, especially during the hot days of July and August, so I can plunge the cut stems immediately into the bucket. You can also take a shallow basket lined with a damp cloth and sprinkle a little water on the flower stems.

After picking, strip all the lower leaves that would be underwater and trim the stem shorter, if needed.

Many people like to do a little "basic conditioning" with their flowers before arranging them. They will look better and last longer if you do. Here's how to do it:

To condition most kinds of flowers, such as perennials, annuals and bulb flowers, plunge them neck deep (never cover the flowers!) in a pail of lukewarm water and let them soak overnight or all day. You can do this indoors or in a shady spot.

For flowers that have milky sap, such as poppies and daffodils, hold their freshly cut stems over a candle flame for 30 seconds. Then place the flowers in tepid water.

For flowers with woody or tough stems that often wilt fast, such as lilacs, roses or hydrangeas, simply make a clean diagonal cut across the bottom of the stem, then slit the stem lengthwise for an inch or two, scraping the bark off the slit area. For a minute or so, dip the base of the woody stems (inch deep) in scalding water.

The last step is to condition the flowers by immersing the stems in a pail of warm water all day or overnight.

For best results, basic conditioning should be done the day before you arrange the flowers. That's what I do, and the flowers last for at least a week.

When caring for a bouquet, one should remove any faded or wilted flowers, pronto. Check the container or vase daily and add water as needed. Some flowers drink more water than others—roses and peonies are continually thirsty, for example. After each use, be sure to wash vases or containers thoroughly, washing away any smelly residue. They should be pristinely clean at all times.

Gardening for Health

Push yourself: In nineteenth-century England, the original push-type lawn mower was advertised as an amusing, useful and healthy exercise for country gentlemen. Today, health and fitness go hand and hand, and experts agree that lawn-mowing and other gardening activities are good aerobic exercises.

Sustained activities such as pushing a mower, weeding a flower bed, or trimming a hedge force your heart and lungs to supply more oxygen to muscles and other body tissues. Regularly making your heart and lungs work harder increases your endurance by one-third or more.

Aerobic exercise also is a safe, effective way to lose weight. In one hour, a 156-pound person can burn about 500 calories trimming shrubs or weeding, or 240 calories raking leaves or planting seedlings. Not bad!

Health and fitness experts suggest spending 45 minutes four to five days a week doing some form of moderate aerobic exercise.

It's best to choose several activities you enjoy. Mix up strenuous chores like digging and hoeing with pruning or trimming.

Grasshoppers

The cure for grasshopper invasions is "grasshopper puree." Take a dozen grasshoppers, large to medium, dead or alive (fresh is best!) and place in a blender with enough water to thin them down. Blend at high speed for several minutes.

Sprinkle the result with a watering can onto plants you wish to protect, or strain through a fine sieve and then spray on—either method does a great job. Grasshoppers will not eat anything sprayed with this concoction.

Reapply after rain. You can use the same process with other bugs that nibble on your plants. Summer bugs hate to eat their relatives.

Harvest: Best Time to Pick

Deciding when to harvest your vegetables and fruit is just as important as any other decision you make concerning your garden. It would be a shame to get great seeds, properly water and fertilize and watch over your bounty only to ruin your harvest because you picked too early or late. Follow the procedures below and you won't be kicking yourself later.

Corn: Corn is ready to eat when the silks have dried to within a half-inch of the tips of the ears and the kernels in the third row down from the top yield a milky (rather than clear) juice when pressed with your thumb.

Tomatoes: Tomatoes should be picked just as they begin to change from orange to red. Keep them at 59 to 70 degrees in normal room light (no sunny windowsills) for four to five days until they finish ripening to full red.

Of course, you should never put tomatoes in the refrigerator. Temperatures below 50 degrees in the fridge change the aroma volatiles that are major components of a tomato's flavor.

Melons: Cantaloupes and most other melons prefer to tell you when they're ready to be picked—so learn their language. Look for an unusually long stem with a small leaf where the vine joins the melon. When the melon is ripe, that small leaf will be paler than all the other leaves on the vine. Most melons are referred to as slip-type by growers because the melon separates (slips) from the vine as it ripens. Most of the melons you see in supermarkets are picked at the quarter-slip stage when the contact point between the vine and the melon is a quarter of the way dried.

However, home gardeners should wait until their melons reach the full-slip stage when the contact between melon and vine is completely dried and the melon lifts away from the vine without any tugging.

Beans: Start harvesting your patch when the bean seeds just begin to show through the first pods, then pick at least every other day after that to make sure no beans get too mature. Pick string beans first thing in the morning because if you wait until afternoon or evening you may get soft, limp beans.

Peas: Pick your peas before the top of the pod dries out completely. The pod should look fat and the stem end will have a few small white flakes or a light powdery coating on it. Open one or more pods and look at the peas before you pick the whole crop. If the peas are small and irregularly shaped, they're just not ready. When they're plump and nicely round, they're perfect.

Carrots: A carrot's color is the best way to know when it's ripe. For instance, if it's pale orange, it's not sweet enough. How can you tell the color of a carrot that's growing underground? I say scratch a bit of soil away around the top of one side of the carrot. It doesn't hurt the carrot at all.

Cucumbers: The best measure of a ripe cuke is its size. Slicing cukes should be picked when they are about 6 inches long and firm; picklers get picked at about 4 to 5 inches. Don't let them get bigger than that because left on the vine too long a cuke gets mushy, fat and seedy. If you see yellow on them at all, the boat has sailed!

Potatoes: Potatoes will be tasty and big enough to eat three weeks after their above-ground flowers first appear; these are the tender little spuds home gardeners call new potatoes. For bigger, heartier ones, wait to dig until the above-ground green leaves die back at the end of the season. Be very careful when digging up potatoes, especially the tender young ones, because they don't store properly if at all wounded. If you do happen to cut or scratch more than you can eat immediately, simply store damaged spuds in a jar of water in the fridge until you can eat them.

Broccoli and cauliflower: Pick the flower heads while they are still tight and hard for broccoli, and rock hard for cauliflower, to get full flavor and firm texture. If you're not going to put the heads right into the pot or freezer, immerse the stem end in a pitcher of water and keep it in the fridge until you're ready to eat it. Treat it like a cut flower. This way, a cauliflower or broccoli can be kept in good eating condition for a week or more.

Squash: Be patient with your winter squash—wait until the skin is fully colored and the stem begins to turn brown instead of green. Buttercup varieties will turn dark-green all over—no light-green spots left at all when they are ready to be harvested.

Once your winter squash are fully matured, I recommend removing them from the vine and curing them a month or so before eating. Put them in a cool, dark spot where they can finish ripening and sweetening up.

Watermelon: There is a tendril right where the stem of the melon joins the vine (looks like a little pigtail); when that tendril withers, your watermelon is ready to be harvested.

You can try all of your other tricks (tap or thump) but until that tendril dries out, the watermelon is not ready. I like to give my melons a thump to be sure. Green melons sound like rapping on a small hand box. Ripe melons have a sound like rapping on a human chest, overripe melons sound like rapping on a stomach. Take heed that a small, ripe melon's thump may be higher pitched than a large, unripe one. Experience with each type being grown is essential.

I harvest my vegetables, for example, when they are the smallest and most succulent, like peas, lettuce, most delicate baby corn, asparagus, limas the size of cuticles, tiny sweet radishes. Everything is so fresh! This can be accomplished if you plant about every two weeks—in other words, keep your produce coming.

Herb Planter

Parsley, sage, rosemary and thyme—whatever your favorite herb, it is quick and easy to grow at home. In about an hour, you can fill a beautiful planter with a handy supply for all your cooking needs. Here is what you'll need:

- A decorative planter. A strawberry pot is ideal. The protruding pockets allow herbs to cascade from all sides for an attractive display.
- Potting mix. To make sure your herbs grow, you need to create healthy soil. Use a top-quality potting mix containing peat moss. Yard soil tends to retain too much water and can lead to rotting roots. Poor-quality mixes allow water to drain too quickly, which can dry roots out.
- Herbs. Approximately eight different kinds.
- Small stones.
- A cardboard tube.

Once you've gathered these supplies, creating the herb planter is easy. Just follow these steps:

Add about 2 inches of peat-based potting mix to the bottom of the strawberry planter. Stand the cardboard tube upright in the center of the planter. Work it into the potting mix so that it remains upright.

Fill the pot with mix up to the first pockets. Insert plants in the first tier of pockets, then fill with mix up to the next tier. Insert the next row of plants and repeat the process until all the pockets are planted.

Save the tallest herb, such as chive and parsley, for the top of the planter. Leave about 1 inch between the potting mixture and the planter rim to allow for watering. Fill the cardboard tube with small stones and then carefully pull the tube out. The remaining column of stones allows the water to reach all of the herbs.

Most herbs are sun lovers, so place the pot in a sunny spot on the patio that is nearby and convenient for picking. The herbs should be ready within a few weeks. Remember to water the planter frequently to keep the soil moist, but not wet to the touch, and sprinkle them with a fertilizer every two weeks.

For best flavor and fragrance, harvest the herbs before flowers bloom and pick them in the morning.

Houseplants: Best Soil

Q. *Can you tell me what the best soil is for houseplants?*

A. Here is a good potting mixture that I use: one part good potting soil, one part vermiculite or perlite, one-half part coarse builder's sand and a little cow or sheep manure. Mix and add the following for each 6-inch pot you use: 1 tablespoon dolomite lime, 1 tablespoon osmocote fertilizer and 1 tablespoon bone meal.

Another good choice is ready-to-go sterile Pro-Mix potting soil available at nurseries and garden centers. Everything you'll ever need for plants is in this mixture, so all you have to do is pot up your tiny treasures.

Iris Society

Q. *For someone who is interested in acquiring and growing irises, would you recommend joining the American Iris Society? Its address is P.O. Box 1003, 717 Pratt Ave. NE, Huntsville, Alabama, 35801.*

A. Certainly! The more knowledge you acquire, the better you'll be at your craft. Plant some irises next spring—the Dutch iris, which will bloom toward the end of the tulip season, and the *Reticulata* group are among the earliest blooming of all the spring bulbs.

Dutch irises can also be forced in the fall by planting in pots, cooling at about 48°F for six weeks, then growing indoors at 50° to 55°F.

Kale, Ornamental

Plant seeds of the highly ornamental flowering kale and decorative cabbage now. Cool autumn weather will bring out maximum foliage coloration. Pot up the most beautiful from the garden when hard freezing is expected and enjoy them indoors.

Lawns

Is your lawn looking blue? Have you noticed it doesn't bounce back after a get-together? Chances are it may just need a little watering. From cool Kentucky bluegrass to the warm-season Bermuda, there are more than 100 lawn grass varieties to choose from and I offer these guidelines to growing and maintaining a vigorous and healthy lawn.

When is the best time to water? If you walk out your door and your lush green lawn has changed to a blue-green or a light brown, or when you walk across your lawn and your footprints remain in the grass, chances are it is time to water.

Without adequate water, grass loses its vigor, making your lawn susceptible to weeds and yellowing. Additional factors to consider when watering include: soil, temperatures, wind, rain and even the type of grass.

How do I control weed growth in my lawn? You can reduce the risk of weeds by watering sensibly, fertilizing properly and by mowing at the right height.

Why should I fertilize my lawn? Fertilizing maintains good color and density and helps grow a strong lawn that can withstand threats from weeds, insects and diseases. Look for three ingredients in the fertilizer you choose: nitrogen, for quick greening and top growth; phosphorus, for root and stem growth; and potassium, for general

health and resistance to stress and diseases.

When is the best time to mow? Cutting is one of the easiest ways to maintain a beautiful lawn and should be done when the lawn is dry. Never cut more than one-third of the grass blade height and alternate your mowing direction. How often you mow depends on the climate, watering, fertilizing and again what type of grass is in your lawn.

Help—my lawn is full of insects. You can reduce the risk imposed on a lawn by most invaders through proper maintenance like watering, mowing, fertilizing and the use of an insecticide. Use an all-natural insecticide. Remember, always identify the problem pest in your lawn before applying any product—and read the label carefully.

What can I do to avoid lawn disease? Help prevent lawn disease by choosing a grass variety adapted to your area and climate, and remember proper maintenance like watering and fertilizing. Mowing properly will also help avoid lawn disease; grass cut too short uses energy and nutrients stored in the roots, making your lawn susceptible to disease.

For more information on identifying symptoms and finding solutions for your lawn, most garden centers or nurseries have experts who will help solve your problems.

Lawn-Keeping

Q. *How much grass does the average lawn produce?*

A. A half-acre lawn yields about 3 tons of grass clippings per season. That's enough to fill over 450 bushel bags.

In fact, clippings and other yard waste constitute 20 percent to 50 percent of what is dumped into the nation's landfills.

To eliminate waste, I suggest mowing with a mulching mower, which cuts and re-cuts clippings into tiny pieces that are injected deep into the turf, where they form a nutrient-rich mulch.

Q. *What should I do with all my grass clippings?*

A. Your best bet with grass clippings is simply to leave them where they lie.

Grass clippings less than 1 inch long filter down to the soil surface and decompose swiftly while forming a nutrient-rich mulch.

The longer clippings tend to remain above the lawn, giving the yard an unsightly appearance and smothering the grass beneath. This is where a recycler comes into play—a must for the home gardener.

Q. *How low should I cut my grass?*

A. It usually varies by regions and by grass type.

For instance, creeping bent grass spreads by stolons and should be mowed below half an inch. If you mow this variety too high, thatch problems may develop.

Canada bluegrass won't tolerate close cuttings and needs to be kept about 2 ½ inches high to survive.

Grasses are divided into two types: cool-season and warm-season varieties.

Recommended mowing heights for cool-season grasses are as follows: Kentucky bluegrass, 3 inches; tall fescue, 2½ inches; and annual ryegrass, 2 inches.

Recommended mowing heights for warm-season grasses are these: St. Augustine and centipede, 2 inches; Bermuda grass and zoysia, one-half inch apiece.

Mice

Q. *Can you please help me? Last summer my garden was destroyed by moles. They ate all the roots of my peppers, chicory, celery, escarole, peanuts, eggplants. You name it, they ate it. Never have I had so much trouble with moles. I am so disgusted. Is there any way I can get rid of them? I would appreciate any advice you can give.*

A. I think you may be unjustly blaming moles for the damage done to your garden. The real culprits are probably meadow mice. True, moles are an irritation to gardeners in that they create unsightly ridges or mounds underneath the lawn or garden. However, moles can be an asset. They feed mostly on small animal life such as insects and earthworms and are not known to feed on vegetation. They devour pests that could be potentially harmful to a garden. Now, to put the blame where it is due, the meadow mouse and/or pine mouse is usually responsible for damage to vegetation, orchards and shrubbery. The only really effective remedies are first, watchfulness, and second, poison. Mice are very canny and have been known to refuse poison if it is unskillfully prepared. I've had the most luck with this method: insert minute doses of strychnine into raisins and drop them into the rodents' pathways. Say goodbye to mice and hello to a healthy garden. If you really have your heart set on exterminating the moles, I suggest mole pellets (available at any garden center) placed at the mouth of each pathway.

Moles

One of the most interesting and humane ways to chase moles from a garden most likely has its origins in Ireland. Empty beer bottles were buried in mole runs with the open necks protruding above the surface. As the wind blew across the mouths of the bottles, it created a ghostly wailing that echoed through the earth and caused the moles to imagine banshees were haunting the area. Naturally, that particular area would get a bad reputation among other moles, and they would avoid it for generations. It's worth a try!

Moss: How to Grow

Q. *I would like to start moss growing between the bricks in my new patio. Do you know a source for moss?*

A. Exhibitors at flower shows use moss, as do growers of bonsai, for a soil cover. A local florist can probably help you find a source, or perhaps try a flower market. Of course, you can depend on Mother Nature and collect some moss in the wild, where it reproduces by wind-blown spores falling on moist soil.

Once you have the moss in place, keep the soil-filled cracks between the bricks moist. A weak manure tea is ideal, but plain watering will suffice. (Manure tea is made by wrapping well-rotted manure in cheesecloth and soaking it in water for at least 24 hours.) Moss likes acid soil, so never add any lime. If weeds appear, pull the seedlings by hand. Don't use a weed killer because it may kill the tender moss.

Natural Gardening

Keep a healthy garden and insects, fungi and diseases will be hard-pressed to gain a foothold.

Three steps to a healthy garden:

1. Throw on the compost. Compost enriches the soil and makes plants so healthy that they become distasteful to insects and resistant to diseases.
2. Choose seeds or plants that are naturally resistant to bugs and ailments. Choose those suited to your area. Time plantings to avoid pest cycles.
3. Good maintenance: Weed often and keep the garden tidy. Refuse draws varmints and fungi. Water and fertilize properly. Pick vegetables when they are ripe and do not let them decompose in the garden—this invites trouble.

Perennials: Late Summer Planting

Late summer is the time to plant many of your favorite perennials.

Many perennials will often fare better in cool autumn temperatures than they will in the late spring when they face the scorching sun and heat of the summer. Fall-planted perennials establish strong root systems fueled by the more forgiving late-summer sun, then go quietly to sleep, dormant with the frost.

Two popular perennials can be planted right now. Plant peonies in your sunny border and hostas in your shade garden.

Beauty and Fragrance of Peonies

From delicate single-flowered beauties to dense, petal-packed double flowers, all peonies carry the same calling card—an unmistakable fragrance. If you want more of these easy-to-grow, hardy flowers in your garden next summer, now is the time to plant them. Try the following varieties.

Single-flowered peonies have large, flat bottoms, often with contrasting stamens. 'Krinkled White' has pure-white petals with dramatic yellow stamens, and 'Friendship Hybrid' has bright-pink petals edged in white. For deep-colored peonies that look great in bouquets, try 'Loretta Frank,' a dark-pink peony with a yellow center, and 'Mahogany,' a deep-red peony with touches of white.

Semi-double-flowered peonies have the delicacy of single-flowered forms and lovely contrasting centers. 'Miss America' is an American Peony Society gold-medal winner with milk-white petals surrounding a golden-yellow center, and 'Buckeye Belle Hybrid' has dark-red petals that set off a sunny center. Or try the exotic 'Marie Jacquin,' whose cupped flower resembles a water lily.

Double-flowered peonies are packed with petals. Clip them for bouquets and their lovely fragrance. Plant several for a full range of colors. 'Mrs. Bryce Fontaine' has stunning crimson petals. Minuet bears light-pink flowers. 'Mrs. James Kelway' blooms white with a pink cast.

Hostas Brighten Shady Spots

Hostas are the mainstay of shade gardens. In the early spring, they send up green rocket-like shoots, which unfold into large, heart-shaped leaves. Their foliage is colorful and textural. Hostas prefer semi-shady locations. Try the following popular varieties.

'Wariegatal' is a large-leafed hosta with thick, blue-green leaves that are generously etched at the edges in a creamy yellow.

'Sum and Substance' has huge, rounded, puckered leaves and grows up to 3 feet tall.

'Love Pat' is the hosta for which many aficionados search—a blue hosta. Its thick, green leaves have a quilted appearance.

'Halcyon' is a blue-leafed, short hosta that looks great in the front of a border or edging a path. It grows to 18 inches and has very beautiful, pale blue-violet flowers.

'Elegans' (*Hosta sieboldiana*) has earned a reputation for being beautiful and hardy. It has huge, roundish leaves that are very textural and turn more blue-green every year.

'Frances Williams' is an old friend of hosta gardeners. It grows up to 36 inches tall and spreads out 4 inches wide and adds light to the shadow with its green-yellow leaves.

'Gold Standard,' as its name implies, is something special. The golden-green leaves are edged with dark green and add light to shady spots.

Phlox: Summer Glory

Phlox, an easy-to-grow, native plant, has been cultivated for centuries.

Gardeners often call phlox the best of all perennials. The phlox family includes some of the most widely grown garden favorites; among them the creeping phlox or modern phlox.

Wonderfully fragrant and long-blooming, these beauties come in a medley of colors, ranging from palest pink to ruby red.

Set out new plants in either fall or late spring and they will self-sow in late summer, if seed pods are allowed to ripen on the stalks.

Sow fresh seeds a quarter-inch into the soil in full sun, as soon as trees leaf out.

Powdery mildew often afflicts phlox, so keep your plants a few feet apart and take out about a third of the total stalks to allow good air circulation and to strengthen the flowers. Cut down the stalks in fall so mildew-resistant varieties 'David' (white), 'Eva Cullum' (pink with red eye) and 'Franz Shubert' have their best growth.

Divide clumps of perennials and phlox every three years to keep them vigorous. Cut back the plants a third after they flower and then dig them up and divide.

Many phlox self-sow and then turn magenta color. To prevent this, deadhead often. This will encourage more flowers and branching. Always pinch back the weaker stems to prolong flowering.

Cut phlox make fabulous bouquets—they last long and are very fragrant.

The name phlox comes from the Greek word meaning "flame." *Phlox paniculata* is commonly known as summer phlox or garden phlox. The low-growing variety *Phlox divaricata* is called woods phlox.

For successful growth, the soil should be moist, but well-drained. It should be deeply cultivated and enriched with organic plant food, as phlox are heavy feeders. Set plants 18 inches apart in sun or light shade. Deadheading faded blooms will encourage a new crop of flowers later in the season. Few plants demand so little attention.

Rosebushes, Care of

Most shrub roses are "self-cleaning," meaning their fading flowers drop and the plants generally look neater. Deadheading or cutting off blooms is not necessary. Prune to shape or to cut flowers for indoors any time of year. In spring, remove dead wood.

If you live where winter temperatures are 20°F or above, plant at the container depth so that the bud union or grafted roses (the swollen area between the roots and where the plant branches) is at soil level. Where winter temperatures range around 20°F, set the bud union deeper—2 inches or more below the soil surface.

In climates where winter temperatures drop below 20°F, choose nongrafted roses grown on their own roots.

"Own root" roses are more likely to survive and re-grow after a severe cold. Plant "own root" roses at the previous soil line indicated by the color change on the thick shank above roots.

Climate will affect rose performance. Roses growing in sunny temperature regions tend to become larger than stated in some catalogs.

Suggested varieties to choose from: 'Bonica' (pink), 'Queen Margrethe' (pink), 'Baby Blanket' (pink), 'Snow Shower' (white), 'Sea Foam' (white), 'Aspen' (yellow), 'Ralph's Creeper' (red), 'Augusta' (blends) and 'Central Park' (blends).

Roses, Sunblaze: The Love Flower

From small apartments and townhouse gardens to country estates and office complexes, 'Sunblaze' roses are proving that America's national flower makes a big impact, indoor and out.

A blazing ball of color, these 'Sunblaze' roses grow only 18 to 24 inches around. Their compact size makes them the perfect alternative as a container plant for the home or office, on balconies or windowsills and as the ideal garden companion for decks, patios and perennial beds.

Many homeowners and gardeners have traditionally shied away from miniature roses because they think they are too difficult, delicate and dainty. I say, on the contrary, these more robust 'Sunblaze' roses are as hardy as any grandiflora rose, tougher than a hybrid tea and take up half the space in the garden.

What makes these roses so exceptional for indoor or outdoor use is their compact growing habit, versatility and easy care.

Doubling their enjoyment, these showy roses make very gratifying plants for the home or office and are a dazzling gift that lasts forever, indoors or out. On Mother's Day, tell her how much you love her with 'Golden Sunblaze,' known as the "best yellow in its class" and the traditional rose for friendship. One of the newest and more disease-resistant varieties, these bright-golden flowers hold the unfading color for an exceptionally long time. For the devoted red-rose lover, 'Red Sunblaze' with its velvety, vivid-red petals is the perfect anniversary gift. Plant these bushes outdoors and create a loving memory garden.

These beautiful 'Sunblaze' bushes are easy to grow indoors, requiring little attention. Give them six hours of sun, adequate water, proper drainage and regular feedings, and these stylish beauties will reward you with a showy display indoors for weeks.

Once enjoyed indoors, move them outside for all-season color either in containers on a deck, patio or in windowboxes, or planted as you would any small landscape plant in a border, perennial bed or foundation garden. They make great hedges, look spectacular in mass plantings and are excellent fillers at the base of larger plants.

Originally introduced in 1982, 'Sunblaze' roses now come in 15 varieties, ranging from scarlet red and hot pink to golden yellow and elegant white. They form a uniform ball covered with bright, blazing blooms balanced by attractive, lush foliage. With little care, these plants keep their compact shape and bloom all season.

'Sunblaze' roses are now available almost year-round in most plant shops, florists and fine garden centers. They come with easy instructions and fit nicely in any situation. They are a gardener's joy, giving long-lasting, all-season beauty and color.

Seed Chilling

If you live in a warm winter area or if you want to plant in spring or summer, you can provide a period of moist chilling by placing already sown pots of seed in the fridge for six weeks. Stratify the seeds between layers of damp sand in a plastic bag in the fridge. As soon as they sprout, sow the seeds in the garden.

Shade Gardening

Q. *My son is looking for something to plant that will grow quite tall and quickly afford privacy in his shady yard. It gets very little sun in that spot. Can you suggest something for him?*

A. Aquilegia, campanula, decentra, digitalis, ferns, hosta, lily of the valley, trillium and viola are the principal shade flowers. There are many varieties. Impatiens, numerous in color, are shade-tolerant.

For taller plants, you have a wide choice from such things as holly, mountain laurel, azalea, blueberries and rhododendron. The combination of these plants should make an attractive planting.

Shade Helps

During the hot summer months, flowering plants not only appreciate a cool, shady area, but they'll put on a better showing with it. In any climate, plants in warm spots, like close to a house foundation, will bloom longer if they receive afternoon shade. So, if you are designing an inviting area for shade plants, make it a protected spot—the best choice is on the eastern side of trees or the house.

Soil

The most overlooked aspect of gardening is the care of soil. Good soil is the key to thriving plants and a great harvest. Good soil has plenty of organic matter in it, plus it has a pH level that plants desire. Your soil probably is not ideal because most soil isn't. But you can take steps to make it healthier.

How much organic matter do you have?

First, determine if your soil has enough organic matter by conducting either one of these simple tests:

For a very general assessment of your soil, pick up a handful of soil and squeeze. If the soil clumps together, it is clay-based. If it falls apart, it's a sandy soil. It's likely that you'll find that your soil is either sandy- or clay-based. Unfortunately, neither type is optimal.

Perform a more scientific analysis by taking a 3-inch sample of the soil from your garden. Place it in a jar of water, close the lid and shake vigorously until the contents dissolve. After a few hours take a look as the clay collects at the bottom, silt at the top.

Compare your results to the composition of ideal loamy soil, which has at least 20 percent organic material (by volume) plus 10 percent to 50 percent sand, at least 30 percent silt and 10 percent to 25 percent clay.

If you have trouble differentiating between layers, let the first test be your guide.

Typically, soil has either too much clay or too much sand. In either situation, working organic peat moss into the soil will improve it. Dig 2 inches of peat moss (or peat moss combined with compost) into the top 6 inches of soil. When mixed with heavy clay soil, peat creates air pockets that give roots room to grow and breathe. In sandy soil, peat moss retains the water and fertilizer that usually drain away too quickly.

What's your soil pH? A measure of how acidic or alkaline your soil is taken by measuring its pH. The pH scale goes from 1 to 14, with 7 being neutral. Numbers lower than

7 indicate an acidic soil; numbers higher than 7 reflect an alkaline soil. Most plants prefer slightly acidic soil with a pH between 5.5 and 6.5. Knowing your pH is important because some chemicals taint pH levels and because you can take steps to improve your soil's pH.

The first step is determining your pH level by using one of the following methods.

Call your agricultural extension service or garden center to request a soil-testing kit. You'll return the sample to them for analysis.

If your pH is not in the "ideal" range of 5.5 to 6.5, you'll want to ask at your lawn and garden center about specific additives to improve your soil. For example, adding peat moss will help lower the pH.

When discussing your soil's pH, be sure to indicate the type of plants you'll be growing because some plants actually prefer a pH that's not in the ideal range.

With proper soil maintenance, your garden will mature beautifully each year. You'll enjoy watching the colors, textures and shapes change throughout the season, and your garden will be the envy of your neighborhood.

Soil, Organic

Research shows that organic soil helps plants keep bugs at bay. In a recent study, tests on soil samples from two adjacent Ohio farms—one that had been organic for more than 25 years and the other with a soil that had received chemical fertilizers for years—found that European corn borer moths lay 18 times more eggs on sweet-corn plants grown on chemically farmed soil than on organically managed soil. It was also found that many insects are put off by the complex starches and proteins in plants with a good mineral balance.

Plants growing in chemical soil lack proper mineral balance, while organically grown plants can easily absorb the right balance of minerals, making them less attractive to pests. In my book, chemicals should never be used in the garden, greenhouse, patio, or wherever there are flowers and vegetables. Remember, experienced organic gardeners take care of their plants and soil in a way that doesn't allow disease and insect problems to occour in the first place.

Healthy plants are rarely attacked by insects.

The use of pesticides is controversial to everyone, not only gardeners. Increasing concern for environmental issues, such as water contamination, is converting people to chemical-free gardening. Remember, chemicals are poison.

From reducing insects to increasing soil nutrients, organic remedies are gaining more acceptance, not only in the United States, but throughout the world. Good garden cultivation and sanitation are the best ways to control pests and diseases. Remember to rotate your crops, remove diseased and dying plant material, and water early in the morning to maintain healthy garden plants.

With good housekeeping and a little patience, you'll find that having a garden is like having a loyal friend. All the love and tender care you put into it will be returned. I hope you have the same pleasure and fulfillment from your garden as I have from mine.

Strawberries, Ideal for Impatient Gardeners

If you happen to be an impatient gardener, you might consider planting strawberry plants. They will yield fruit within a year or two after they are planted, long before fruit trees or berries are ready to harvest. And they can be grown in the tiniest garden or container and thrive.

Strawberries have been around since prehistoric times, when early man dined on wild varieties. Romans were the first people to cultivate strawberries. Today there are two basic kinds: the June bearers which produce a crop in June or July, and the ever-berries which yield two crops—one in June or July and another smaller one in late summer or early fall.

You must choose a variety that is suited to your area. (For example, ever-berries thrive only in areas with long summer days.) For best results, you should also choose a strain bred for disease resistance.

As you examine the different varieties in catalogs, you need to consider what you are going to use them for at harvest time. Some make better jellies and jams, while other varieties are best for freezing.

Tips to keep in mind at planting time:

1. Proper drainage is critical for choosing a site for your strawberry patch. If you have clay soil, work in plenty of compost and sand. Do this several months in advance of planting.
2. Plant your strawberries as early in spring as possible, on a cool, cloudy day.
3. It's essential to be sure of your planting depth. The upper two-thirds of the plant's crown needs to remain above ground, and all of the roots should be covered. After watering, check again to make sure all is well.

4. Throughout the planting season, strawberries need regular watering, as roots are near the surface and may dry out during hot weather. This is even more true as the plants begin to send out runners. Until runners have taken root and the new plants are completely independent of their parent, they are totally dependent upon their parents for well-being—especially for water.

5. It's best during the first season to clip off any blossoms that appear. This means that there will be no crop the first year. Pruning the blossoms allows the plant to concentrate its energies on building a strong root system. The second year you'll see the benefit of this technique.

6. Watch for disease and insects, like strawberry crown borer. Remove all infected plants immediately.

7. To encourage pollination by honeybees, plant a patch near a blooming fruit tree.

8. Harvest berries as soon as they are ripe. Pick damaged or overripe berries as well so they won't rot on the vines—since this can lead to the spread of virus.

Succulents

Succulents are among the world's most fascinating and evolved plants, adapting over thousands of years to mostly dry, hostile conditions.

During the process, they have developed amazing growing habits. Some thrive high on barren mountain slopes, in dry conditions and in tropical jungles where most plants wouldn't have a prayer of surviving.

In order to survive long periods of drought, succulents store water in their roots, stems or leaves, or in some combination of the three.

The succulent plants that I suggest below are perfect for a well-lighted spot indoors or out in U.S.D.A. Zones 9 and 10.

Sansevierias are among the most dependable of houseplants, surviving under poor light conditions, as well as dryness.

The pony palm is prized for its swollen, corky trunk and long, slender leaves. Although it can grow outdoors to 30 feet, it makes a dandy slow-growing houseplant as well.

Echeveria is one of the best succulents for creating a bold effect. It forms large, cabbagelike rosettes in shades of blue and pink, and bears elegant pink flowers with yellow centers. If the plant's stems become too leggy, simply cut them off and re-root the head!

Lithops resemble the pebbles that they live among in their South African environment. Grow them in a brightly lighted spot, watering only from spring through summer. In winter, the new growth draws moisture from the old, causing the old leaves to wither.

All the above varieties include many various types, so inquire at your garden center for the best plants suited for your area.

Summer Plantings

To keep fresh produce coming in for weeks after the onset of the first hard frost, you have to use the best vegetables. The seed catalogs are full of 60- to 70-day wonders! Beets, lettuce (all varieties), broccoli, kale, radishes and spinach are some examples. Choose the fast-maturing types, since you'll need to add a week or two to the maturity estimates in the catalogs.

The late summer days, despite the intense heat, simply don't have the growing power of spring days because there is less light. One advantage to fall planting is that vegetables won't bolt in cool weather. They remain tender and sweet in the soil for a good week or more after they ripen. You'll find you can grow some of the best fresh foods you've ever had!

Start seedlings now. The key to starting plants indoors is to provide conditions for germination and growth that don't exist outside. Either in the greenhouse or windowsill, seedlings must be watered twice a day. Don't overwater the seeds. Also, watering properly when setting transplants out in the garden is crucial to the plant's adjustment. The seed-starting medium around the roots of the plant should be wet—not swimming, but a little more than moist.

Prepare for Fall Now

Many vegetables for fall harvest should be sown and transplanted during the summer months. If transplants for crops such as broccoli, cauliflower, collards, cabbage and head lettuce are not available in August, seed packages for them can be sown now in a bed or row. In three or four weeks, they can be transplanted into the garden. Of course, your other fall crops can be seeded directly into their permanent rows.

Planting times should correspond to harvesting crops around the time of the first frost date, October 20. Even though harvest can extend well up to Thanksgiving, don't push your luck. You have to prepare the soil just as you did in the spring, but use only half the fertilizer: 1½ to 2 pounds of 5-10-5 per 100 square feet.

Plant Particulars

- For broccoli, cabbage, cauliflower and collard greens, plant seed by July 30; transplant by August 15–20.
- For kale, kohlrabi, mustard and Swiss chard, plant seed by August 1–20.
- For leaf lettuce, spinach and cress, plant seed by August 1–20; transplant by September 1–10.
- For beets, carrots and turnips, plant seed by August 15 to September 1.
- For radishes, plant seed by September 10.
- For bush beans and peas, plant seed by August 10–20.

These seed and transplant times assume a harvest time of October 20. If frost in your area occurs sooner, move up the transplant time accordingly.

Use only half as much fertilizer in the fall as you do in the spring: 1½ to 2 pounds of 5-10-5 per 100 square feet.

Summer Seeding

Use a cold frame or greenhouse to start perennial seeds in July so you'll have blooming plants next spring and summer. A good one is coralbells. It is good for bouquets and attracts hummingbirds. Other good ones are delphinium, Gloriosa daily and Shasta daisy. Columbine (*Aquilegia*) comes in a mixture of lovely pastel colors, with large flower heads and long spurs, which hummingbirds drink from. For good germination, store seeds in the refrigerator (at 40 degrees) for four or five days.

Summer greenhouse crops require a great deal of ventilation, so keep the fan going. Protect your seedlings by putting screens on doors and vents to keep moths and beetles from flying in and laying eggs.

Biennials are special in that they produce only foliage with their first growing season and then the following year produce a marvelous show of blooms.

Many times the plants will surprise you; they will live over another year and flower once again. Biennials are easily started from seeds now through August. They will grow vigorously during the late summer and fall and will overwinter in cold frames or outdoors. Next spring, the plants will take off as soon as the weather warms up.

Sow the tiny seeds of Sweet William, foxglove (*Digitalis*), Canterbury Bells, pansies and English daisy into properly prepared outdoor beds or flats (use sterile soil). Always keep the rapidly developing plants moist, especially during extended dry spells of summer.

Sunflower Basics

Big, bold and brassy, sunflowers delight everyone during the growing season from summer throughout the fall. And they are among the easiest flowers to grow.

Sunflowers are not demanding; they tolerate any type of soil—and if you give them plenty of water and sun, they will reward you with lush plants and weeks of gorgeous blooms.

Cut sunflowers will continue to open and will last up to two weeks in water if you change the water every day. Strip off all but the top two or three leaves when you cut the flowers so that they don't begin to look limp and wilt.

Growing sunflowers is a cinch. All they need is a sunny location that receives at least three-quarters to a full day of sunshine. Plants that receive inadequate sun will have spindly, weak stems and small blooms.

In areas with mild winters, you can sow sunflowers from March through late July; however, in colder climates wait to plant after all danger of frost has passed. Most varieties bloom in 60 to 90 days. Branching varieties take longer to bloom.

Sow large seeds a half-inch deep, and smaller ones less deep, in well-prepared soil. Carefully follow any planting instructions on the label. Space seeds of full-size types 9 to 12 inches apart.

Keep the ground moist until the seeds germinate and, when watering, do so gently, otherwise the seeds are apt to wash away.

Avoid overwatering. A sprinkler or hose left running can make the ground soggy, so be careful. The roots of mature sunflowers with thin stalks and heavy heads tend to lose their grip and topple over. Staking isn't a bad idea. Some of my favorite varieties are 'Budding Sunflower,' 'Orange King,' 'Sunrich Lemon,' 'Sunrich Orange,' 'Italian White' and 'American Beauty.'

Sweet Corn: The Stalk of the Town

Sweet corn is a native of the Americas and has been enjoyed for 7,000 years. Because of its New World origins, history, popularity and adaptability, the National Garden Bureau celebrated 2000 as the Year of the Sweet Corn.

Corn (or maize) was discovered in Mexico's Tehiacan and spread north to the United States and south to Central and South America. The Native Americans were probably the first breeders of corn, selecting the best plants and saving seed from season to season.

By the time Columbus landed in America in 1492, there were hundreds of types of maize. On his return voyage to Spain a year later, it is believed the explorer brought many varieties of maize back with him.

The Indians had been cultivating flint corn (also known as field corn) for years, sharing many different varieties with the Pilgrims. In 1779, the first recorded sweet corn was collected from the Iroquois Indians of the Susquehanna River Basin. Sweet corn became an American favorite as early as the 1880s.

Sweet corn—also called table corn or sugar corn—is one of the sweetest, most delicious vegetables grown in any garden.

Corn is a monoecious plant. It has male flowers that bear pollen on its tassels. The female flowers (or silks) are at the leaf axis, along the main stem.

Most gardeners who crave fresh corn all summer plant successive crops to harvest over a period of several weeks.

After planting, watering is the most important chore for good corn production. When watering, irrigate the soil—rather than the whole plant—with overhead sprinklers. This will ensure proper pollination. Keep in mind, sweet corn is wind-pollinated—the pollen drifts from the tassel to the silk. If the tassels and pollen are wet with water, the pollen won't leave the tassel and will be washed down to the soil, hampering pollination.

It is critical to water sweet corn just before the appearance of the silks and a couple of weeks after the silks turn brown. During drought conditions, water every ten days to sustain the plants.

Most varieties of sweet corn are ready to ear two and a half to three weeks after pollination. Of course, very hot temperatures can hasten maturity.

The clue to determining when to harvest your corn is to look for brown, dry silks and cobs with round, blunt tips. If the husk fits tight to the cob, go for it—the corn is ready to harvest. If the husks seem soft, allow the kernels to fill out for a few days.

To remove the ear, simply pull it down and twist. After harvesting, store corn in the refrigerator to retain the most flavor. You can also freeze or can it.

Toads

All ancient gardeners thought it their duty to care for the health of toads. Not only do toads eat lots of insects, they are also thought to bring good luck. Therefore, farmers would go to great lengths to get them to stay in their gardens. They would even go to local ponds and catch "friends" for a lone toad that had taken up housekeeping in the cabbage patch, hoping to encourage the small amphibian to stay.

Toads eat three times their weight in insects every day. In fact, one toad will eat tens of thousands of insects a year, including beetles, slugs, flies, grasshoppers, cutworms and ants. That's a lot of bugs!

All you have to do to obtain this remarkable pest control service is let a corner of your garden go a little wild with ferns (for foraging and protection from predators) and a pond for laying of eggs.

Toads are strictly carnivorous, they won't eat plants. They are also the perfect urban amphibian because they like to live around gardens and houses. Leave toads undisturbed and they'll do a fabulous job of helping control the pest population in your garden.

Other insect-loving animals are birds, who hunt by day, and bats, who hunt by night. Bats are particularly good at keeping mosquito populations under control.

Tomatoes: Can We Talk?

Tomato gardeners may talk a different "language" when they discuss their tomato plants with other gardeners. This tomato primer might help you understand the terms.

In most areas of the United States, tomato plants do their best when the seeds are started indoors about six to eight weeks before the last spring frost.

Set, or plant your tomato plants deeper into your garden soil than they were in their pots. In that way, roots form along the stem of the plant to help it grow strong.

Determinate tomato varieties grow to a determined size, then start flowering and fruiting. They bear a heavy yield of fruits just about all at once, but then produce no more. Grow this type if you have a short growing season, or if you want a lot of fruit for canning all at once.

Indeterminate tomato varieties keep growing until frost stops them, vining happily along stakes, up to porch roofs, over fences—and continue bearing flowers and fruit. These are the large fruits and beefsteak types that keep ripening fruit until a frost.

Disease-tolerance is a term that describes the plant's ability to continue to grow and bear fruit in spite of being stricken by disease. Tolerance refers to a relatively low level of ability to perform in the face of disease, a good thing to remember when choosing your seeds.

Disease resistance indicates a stronger response of the plant to thrive in spite of disease.

Note: There is no plant we know of that is disease-proof. If you have a tomato disease in your soil, your plants will most likely be affected, to some degree.

Many hybrid varieties have a greater disease-tolerance or resistance than other "heirloom" varieties show.

A good suggestion is to grow varieties that have disease-tolerance or resistance. This gives you the best chance at a great tomato season. The best way to make sure your plants are vigorous and healthy, with resistance or tolerance to disease, is to choose your variety and grow it from seed. It's not difficult to grow tomato plants from seed. However, always grow what's best for your area.

Paste tomatoes are delicious when eaten fresh. Their flesh is thinner, drier and they have fewer seeds and a rather distinct concentrated flavor. In Mexico the paste tomato, called a "saladette" type, is commonly used fresh for salsa.

Tomato colors are a joy to the eye. Color and flavor are often linked in a tomato-eater's mind. Actually, though, the flavor of a yellow tomato is not necessarily milder than that of a red tomato. Flavor is a subjective topic. Our taste buds may react quite differently to the various compounds and solutions within a tomato, which gives it its distinctive flavor. Many people who describe a tomato as "acidic" would be surprised to learn that their tomato, if analyzed chemically, may show a low sugar content rather than a high acid content.

Flavor is related to a variety's genetic heritage and can be influenced by growing conditions. If you're a flavor nut, try different tomato varieties until you find the one for you. Your neighbor may not agree with you about the flavor of your choice, but your tongue will know. Let your neighbor find his own favorite and that goes for family members, too!

More than 20 different tomato varieties—including the exclusive, new 'Top Sirloin' Hybrid beefsteak tomato—are available for planting.

SOURCE: Ferry-Morse Seeds

Q. *I had some problems last season with my tomato plants. They developed knobby stems soon after they were transplanted into the garden. The plants were stunted and at harvest time very little fruit was edible. What is my problem and how can I keep it from occurring again?*

A. Your problem sounds like adventitious roots, where roots grow somewhere other than where they're supposed to grow, such as the outer surface of the stem. Rest assured your plants are not the only ones to have suffered the same affliction. Adventitious roots usually form on plants that have an excess of lush leaves above and moist ground below.

To control this problem, give your tomato plants ample room to grow so the leaves can dry between rains, never overwater and don't use herbicides. That's a no-no!

Tomatoes, Growing

Follow this easy system and harvest your best tomato crop ever.

To eat the tastiest tomatoes possible, you have to start your own plants from seed. And best of all, when you start from seeds, you can schedule things so that the transplants are ready for the garden when you want them to be.

Start your seeds about eight weeks before you plan to transplant them outdoors, which, of course, will be when the soil and air temperatures are warm and all danger of frost has passed. Otherwise, your little transplants won't grow properly, since they are a warm-weather fruit.

Start seeds in a commercial seed-starting medium where everything is prepared for you.

Temperature: For the best germination, keep the temperature of your seed-starting soil around 80° to 85°F. But once the seeds sprout, turn down the heat to 60° to 75°F. Give your seedlings all the bright light they can get each day.

Practices: When it's time to plant the tomatoes outdoors, plant them deeply—3 inches at least. The buried stem will sprout additional roots which will help feed the growing plant.

Mulch away: Mulch can warm or cool your soil, block pesky weeds and retain moisture. You can use straw, leaves (oak is best), pine needles or bark. In short-season areas, don't add mulch until the soil warms up. But if you live in an area with long, hot summers, mulch cools the soil—a big advantage—so pile it on.

Pruning: Prune your plants but only do it once! Remove all branches (stems) that form at the base of the plant, except those immediately below the first flower cluster. This will encourage fruiting higher up where tomatoes are easier to pick.

Tree Speak

Did you know that trees talk? Not in so many words, but with a chemical alert. For instance, the romantic willow sends a chemical alert to neighbor willows when it is under attack by caterpillars or webworms. This alert stimulates an increase in tannin production that makes willow leaves impossible to digest.

Vegetables

Q. *Why do homegrown vegetables taste so special?*

A. The secret is freshness. Within a few hours after harvesting, the produce usually makes its way to the dining table. On the other hand, most commercial produce must be packed on boats, trucks, railroad cars or planes and shipped hundreds or thousands of miles before it ever reaches the store and, eventually, the table. When it says "fresh" at the supermarket, the produce is at least a few days old, to say the least.

For example, some tender vegetables, such as tomatoes, are harvested green and ripened later in storage. They are too fragile to withstand the rigors of travel and are maybe two or three weeks old before they actually show up in a tossed salad. That makes a huge difference in quality and flavor, whatever way you look at it, because the quality and flavor of garden-grown produce begins to ebb the very moment it's plucked.

Of course, commercial vegetable growers, wholesalers, shippers and retailers do the best they can to bring in quality produce and they do a pretty good job of it. However, time takes its toll, because the flavor of four-day-old produce can't hold a candle to the produce harvested from the garden and delivered directly to the kitchen.

There are three factors that influence flavor: geography, soil and breeding.

Flavor is regional because of the diversity in humidity, temperature and rainfall. Flavor is also affected by the way soil is amended. More than anything else, soil composition accounts for the difference in taste between your beets and your neighbor's. That's why people say organically grown produce tastes better.

It's not the absence of commercial fertilizers and pesticides that makes it better; it's the large amounts of manure, compost and humus that organic gardeners till into the soil. The fluffier and looser the soil, the more easily nutrients, oxygen and water are able to reach roots to nourish plants.

Thriving, well-fed plants, in turn, create more fruit sugars in their foliage, seeds, fruits and roots. Breeding, open-pollinated and heirloom varieties seem to have more flavor, too.

An heirloom is defined as any variety that was in existence before 1940. Most are open-pollinated, which means left to pollination that occurs naturally in the garden and the wild, rather than by the hand of the breeder.

Unlike seeds saved from hybrids (they don't breed true), you can plant open-pollinated seeds and expect the plants to be 90 percent to 95 percent like the parent. This is why most experts prefer open-pollinated and heirloom varieties as their favorites for flavor and not the new hybrids. And the good-tasting varieties get planted year after year.

SOURCE: *The Cook's Garden Catalog; (802) 824-3400.*
Seed Savers International, 3076 N. Winn Road, Decorah, Iowa, 52101.

Vegetables: Midsummer Crops Yield Fall Veggies

Do you stop sowing crops early in the season and then, regretfully, harvest your last few beets, lettuce, corn or cauliflower?

Don't cut yourself short. Plan ahead for fall crops and prolong the harvest of fresh vegetables well into the fall. You can do this by using row-cover production and cold frames.

By planting the following crops in midsummer to early fall, you can enjoy the delicious bounty from your garden while others have to rely on local supermarkets for their produce. Good midsummer crops for you to consider are:

Beans. Plant varieties of 'Provider,' 'Radar' and 'Royalty' in midsummer to produce a fall crop. Disease-resistant varieties are another good choice.

Beets. 'Early Wonder Tall Top' can be planted in late July for a fall harvest of small, tender beets and greens.

Broccoli. Direct seed or transplant 'Emerald City,' 'Green Valiant,' 'Sega' or other varieties in July for a fall crop.

Carrots. For fall and storage carrots, 'Ingot' and 'Rumba' go to 100 days before frost.

Lettuce. Plant lettuce up to early September for a fall harvest. Lettuce can tolerate a light frost with little damage. Some good choices: leaf lettuce, 'Red Salad Bowl,' 'French Crisp.'

Weeding Tales and Tidbits

A recent survey found that most people put weeding at the top of their list of gardening headaches. The majority of respondents (35 percent) said weeding was their least favorite lawn and garden chore.

In another survey, when asked what would make their lives easier, the majority of respondents (31 percent) said a housekeeper or gardener, beating out other answers such as less-stressful job, financial planner and cook or nutritionist.

William Shakespeare hated weeds, describing them as plants that "without profit suck the soil's fertility from wholesome flowers."

In Calgary, Alberta, Canada, neighbors can turn in neighbors for having a yard full of weeds. In fact, many towns have ordinances banning weeds—some ban specific weeds, such as dandelions.

There is an unconfirmed report of a dandelion pulled, using a Weed Hound, that had a root 6 feet long. This, of course, allegedly occurred in Texas.

Some weeds are delicious. Here's a recipe for sautéed dandelions:

SAUTÉED DANDELIONS (4 SERVINGS)

2 pounds fresh dandelion greens, chopped

¼ cup olive oil

2 cloves garlic

Salt, to taste

Pepper, to taste

Chop greens.

Heat olive oil and garlic in saucepan. Add greens, salt and pepper to taste.

Cook 12 minutes or until greens are tender. Serve hot.

SOURCE: *Hound Dog Products Inc.; (800) 694-6863.*

Weeds

No matter how many weeds you till or pull out, let's face it, they are a gardener's nightmare for the simple reason there are countless more waiting to make your life miserable!

Your best bet is to learn to identify the type of weeds that are making their home in your garden. Quackgrass, ragweed and dandelion are among the most common, but hundreds of other less-familiar weeds dwell there, too.

Spotting the culprits is a cinch, since it's a sure bet that anything you didn't plant yourself is a weed! (Unless of course it's a self-sown or volunteer larkspur or poppy!)

Q. *What is a weed?*

A. A weed is a plant out of place. It is a plant that competes successfully against a plant or plants that we wish to grow in our gardens. In another context, Henry David Thoreau said, "A weed is an unloved plant."

Another example: Dandelion (*Taraxacum officinale*) may be a weed in the lawn or flower garden; however, it may be cultivated as a mild diuretic in the herb garden and as a salad or pot herb in the vegetable garden.

Orchard grass (*Dactylis glomerata*) and Timothy hay (*Phleum pratense*) are weeds in the flower or vegetable garden, but they are highly prized as forage grasses in the hay field or pasture for cattle.

Avoid weeding woes: If you'd like to spend more time smelling the flowers instead of weeding between them, you're not alone. In a recent survey of 700 homeowners, more than one-third rated weeding as the most disliked lawn and garden chore. Weeding doesn't have to be a dreadful backbreaking task, because there are solutions to make pulling weeds quicker and easier.

One of the best ways to alleviate weeding woes is to add plenty of sphagnum peat moss to the soil. Peat moss makes pulling weeds easier because it balances the amount of water and air in the soil.

On the list of most-hated lawn and garden chores, dealing with insects and watering rate second and third, respectively. A few simple tips can save time and effort spent on these tasks as well. Some guidelines:

Spread several inches of mulch around to help conserve moisture so you'll water less often. Mulch also will help control weeds.

Use a small pond or bath to attract birds, frogs and toads to your lawn and garden. These animals will happily eliminate many unwanted pests. Insects are their favorite diet.

Periodically add fertilizer to your lawn and garden. Nutritious soil will grow more vigorous plants. The bottom line is this: You need healthy soil. Healthy soil is like an immune system.

Weeds' competitors: The most effective way to prevent weeds is to use desirable plants to out-compete weeds. One of the simplest ways to do this is to heavily over-seed newly planted shrub beds or ground cover areas with fast-growing annual flowers.

They include farewell-to-spring (*Clarkia amonea*), sweet alyssum (*Lobularia maritima*) and scarlet flax (*Linum grandiflorum var. rubrum*).

These attractive temporary fillers germinate quickly and fill the soil spaces between the slower-growing ground covers or shrubs, thus preventing weeds from growing.

The annuals later give way as the more vigorous landscape plants fill in. The occasional weed that does appear can be hand-pulled or cut down. The bottom line, of course, is to recognize that the presence of some weeds is not only inevitable but actually good for the garden. For instance, the common weeds in the sunflower (*Asteraceae*), parsley (*Apiaceae*) and mustard (*Cruciferae*) families are the perfect nectar sources for beneficial insects that attack caterpillars and aphids and other insect pests of the garden.

Many of the "weed" plants are attractive. Sunflower family weeds are English daisy

(*Bellis perennis*), cornflower (*Centaurea cyanus*), yarrow (*Achillea millefolium*) and dandelions (*Taraxicum vulgare*). Parsley family weeds include fennel (*Foeniculum vulgare*), cow parsnip (*Heracleum lanatum*) and wild carrot (*Daucus carota*). Weeds in the mustard family include common mustard (*Brassica arvensis*), hoary cress (*Lepidium draba*) and shepherd's purse (*Capsella bursapastoris*).

Windowboxes

Need a quick, practical way to give your house a facelift? Why not consider windowboxes? They're small investments that pay big returns in beauty and color for the house.

One of the truly amazing characteristics of windowboxes is their versatility. They can have interesting shapes and be designed in a rainbow of colors. They can be filled with plants for every area from sun to shade. Windowboxes should be a statement of personal style, whether they bring a whimsical spot of color to a weekend retreat on the shore or complement the front of a formal apartment in the city.

Installation Tips

Be sure that your windowbox has drainage holes to allow excess water to drain away from delicate plant roots. Cover the drainage holes with fine mesh to keep potting mix from draining out.

The windowbox should extend the entire length of your window. Attach the windowbox to the house using wood screws; include a half-inch spacer to protect your home from moisture. Place the windowbox so that the top edge is just below the windowsill.

The secret of lush windowboxes is overcrowding. The plants like to be jammed together tightly. Arrange plants just like a picture; tall ones in the back, short ones in the front. A well-balanced windowbox will include plants for the back of the box that grow upright, while center plants should have a mounding habit and the front plants should trail.

Water plants well before planting so that the potting medium will cling to roots and bare roots will not be exposed to air. For the first few weeks after planting, make sure that the potting medium is kept moist.

The soil in a windowbox dries out quicker than soil around plants in the ground because a windowbox is exposed to air on most sides. Water by touch, not by sight. If the potting mix feels dry at a depth of 1 inch, it's watering time. After several weeks of watering, plants in windowboxes will benefit from a regular feeding program.

Use a peat-based potting mix because it retains moisture yet allows proper aeration of roots. Watering wands are great for this chore, especially for difficult-to-reach windowboxes.

Traditional wooden windowboxes are usually rectangular in shape and painted to match or complement your house's colors. But it is perfectly acceptable and often more fun to let your imagination run wild and create a windowbox that fits your personality and abode—whether it is a log cabin, cottage, castle or condo. Consider using plywood cut-outs of rabbits, geese or cows to decorate the windowbox of a child's playhouse. Stencil carrots, radishes or herbs for a windowbox on a garden shed. Add sailboats or starfish to the design of a windowbox for the beach house.

Zinnias: Easy to Grow, Fabulous for Show

For many years, zinnias have been the most popular flowering annual for creating fabulous colors throughout the garden and for bouquets. But this wasn't always the case. When the Spanish first saw zinnias in Mexico, they thought the flower was so ugly they called it "sickness of the eye."

Zinnias have improved over the years and have changed in shape, color, plant size and ability to resist disease. The flowers require little maintenance: Just plant them in well-drained soil, water regularly if it doesn't rain and cut them frequently to keep the plants bushy, compact and producing more buds. The less attention zinnias get, the better they do.

If you are planting zinnias in containers, check the soil daily during the hot months of July and August. If the plants are dry, water to a depth of 2 inches or more. When you water, try not to get water on the leaves.

Newer hybrids may be mildew-resistant; however, they are not totally disease-free.

Growing zinnias from seed indoors or out is easy. The seeds of most varieties are a good size, so they're perfect for children to plant. The flowers grow fast, so plan to sow your seeds indoors about four to six weeks before the average last frost date in your area.

For indoor planting, fill a shallow container or individual peat pots with a Pro-Mix commercial soil. Moisten the mix and let it drain. Sow seeds in rows, so they will be easy to separate when it comes to transplanting time. If you are using peat pots, sow three to four seeds in each pot, water to moisten the soil slightly and cover tightly with a plastic bag.

When planting in flats, enclose the seedlings in a sheet of clear plastic wrap or in a plastic bag and close with a twist-tie to keep the mix from drying out while the plants are germinating. Set the flat in a warm spot, but not in sun, until seedlings emerge in six to ten days. At that time, remove the plastic cover and keep the mix evenly moist by watering from the bottom to prevent water from getting on the leaves.

When the seedlings have at least two sets of true leaves, transplant them into individual 2-inch or larger pots. Plenty of sunshine is a must, so the young plants don't get leggy from searching for sun.

You can also plant zinnias directly into the garden when the weather and soil have warmed up, about the same time you plant marigolds, impatiens and peppers. All planting instructions are on the seed packet, so read them carefully.

There are few other garden flowers that are as useful as zinnias for cutting to use in arrangements—dried or fresh. Zinnias have been referred to for years as cut-and-come-again flowers. Cut one flower stem above a pair of leaves and, within a few days, two new stems with buds will have taken its place.

To gather flowers for fresh bouquets, cut them early in the morning, before the sun has a chance to wilt or dry them. Select blooms not fully opened, however, since they will continue to open indoors. Keep in mind that tightly closed buds won't open once cut.

To gather zinnias for use in dried arrangements, cut after the morning dew has evaporated. Dry flowers in a desiccant such as silica gel, which is available in craft stores and garden centers. The flowers should dry in about a week.

fall

HARVEST TIME—another busy season. Your late summer vegetables such as corn, onions, lettuce, cauliflower, string beans, carrots and beets are still filling your kitchen with fresh edibles. Sadly, though, the cooling of the weather means the production of your garden is coming to an end for this year. Soon it will be time to think of garden clean-up. However, fall is also a time for planting. It's also time to plant spring bulbs such as snow drops, crocuses, tulips,

hyacinths and daffodils. Mark in your journal and plan ahead. What flowers do you want to have in the spring or at Easter, for example? Fall is also the time to plant pre-cooled bulbs indoors in preparation for the winter holidays. Planting, cleaning and winter protection is a must, making fall the busiest season of all.

Back-to-School Gardens

During most of the nineteenth and twentieth centuries, many public schools maintained gardens that were an important educational and recreational part of school life.

Gardening was part of the daily life of school back then. For instance, from the late 1800s through the early 1970s, Cleveland had probably the most extensive school gardening system in the country.

Each elementary school throughout the city had a large flower and vegetable garden that the students planted and cultivated. Schools even competed against each other in harvest fairs.

Sadly, beginning in the early 1970s, the gardens began to be dismantled, and they eventually disappeared. One by one these wonderful school gardens were felled by lack of funding, changing school values and new demographics. It was a dreadful loss for Cleveland's schoolchildren and neighborhoods, as it was for many other school districts across the country where today a school garden is only a memory.

Fortunately this decline is being redressed by organizations that promote children's gardening and landscape designs for schoolyards and playgrounds.

Here's where the extension service should play a part, since they are an arm of the agriculture department, supported by taxpayers. In most towns and cities there is an extension service just for this sort of thing. So look them up in the phone book to answer any gardening questions you might have.

As a result of this decline, principals, teachers and community leaders are taking a second look at school grounds. They are realizing that, especially in urban areas, many school grounds are not only barren and ugly but are vastly underutilized for learning. Gardening is such a fabulous pastime for young people—and what better way to keep them occupied and out of harm's way?

I feel traditional gardens are best suited to teach children the basics in everyday gardening: how to sow seed, weed and cultivate, watering practices, climate control, fertilizing, pruning and harvesting.

This should also include focus on creating wildlife habitats to help students learn about the natural history and relationship between the flora and fauna of the area they live in. A number of schools are combining the two types of gardens.

A school garden (in fact, any garden) needs at least one dedicated person to follow through and fuel the commitment and enthusiasm needed for the project to succeed. A little "Eden" for children to enjoy and be proud of.

Resource Information

You don't need to be a teacher to get a school garden started. In fact, some of the best school gardens are cooperative programs between the school, the PTA, community groups, neighborhood volunteers and local garden clubs. Here are some resources and organizations to contact for more information on how to get started.

The Audubon Cooperative, 46 Rarick Road, Selkirk, New York, 12158; (516) 767-9051.

National Gardening Association, 180 Flynn Avenue, Burlington, Vermont, 05410; (802) 863-1308.

Begonia, Tuberous

Q. *What causes the buds of tuberous begonias to dry up at the base without ever opening?*

A. Probably too much dry heat, possibly a change in environment, such as from the controlled atmosphere of a greenhouse to indoors, or merely from more to less light. Tuberous begonias do best with nighttime temperatures in the 60s, up from 80°F on a warm day. They are not exactly the ticket for a heat wave, but other begonias are—the ever-blooming *Begonia semperflorens* types, some of which have individual flowers almost as flashy as the tuberous ones.

Beneficial Insects

You may not be aware of it, but your garden is a place where all creatures, great and small, vie for survival. Some, of course, are beneficial, while others may harm the plants we love and care for.

The big challenge is to attract a diverse population of beneficial creatures that can keep the pests under control, reducing the need for pesticides. When you must use a pesticide, use an insecticide soap spray—and be sure to read the directions on the label carefully. Get to know the beneficial insects as well as the undesirable ones. It's easy: All you need is a magnifying glass, so you can monitor of the population of the "good guys," such as toads, garter snakes, butterflies, spiders, ladybugs, green lacewings and praying mantis, to name a few. Prowl around at night and you'll discover nocturnal pests eating their little hearts out. Handpick and destroy slugs and snails, but wear gloves for this task!

Other good techniques for handling pest invasions is to plant disease-resistant varieties of flowers and vegetables.

Plants are just like people. They have to be clean and healthy to feel good. Since your plants can't get up to take a bubble bath or visit the doctor for a shot of vitamin B12, it's your duty to be something of a nursemaid. Nurture healthy plants, since weak ones that are under stress are usually the ones attacked.

A spring clean-up is an important routine that can eliminate thousands of eggs. Do this by rototilling your garden beds where pests over-winter.

Birds

When your family goes on a trip, you stop several times on the way for a snack, right? And if the trip is long, you find a place to spend the night. Well, every fall, birds do just the same thing: They go south. When days grow short and the temperature dips, birds fly to their winter homes. And in spring, they fly back to nest and raise their families. This round-trip type of travel is called migration.

When migrating birds search around for a quick snack and rest stop, wouldn't it be exciting if your garden was one of their favorite fast-food restaurants?

Of course, some birds don't fly south for the winter. They just stay put year-round. Wouldn't it be fun if your garden was one of their permanent camping grounds?

Many people think that they need to put out bird feed only in the winter. This isn't true. In spring and summer there is very little natural food available to birds. It's not until the fall that birds find the necessary wild seed.

Birds love insects, seeds, berries and fruits. Trees and shrubs are a must for birds since they provide more than food. They are nesting places and shelters, too.

In addition to food, birds appreciate birdbaths (never any deeper than 3 inches) and water. In the winter especially, birds suffer from a lack of water because everything is frozen.

You can easily buy a little birdbath heater that will keep your birds happy and healthy, and the feed you put out will keep them warm in the frozen months of the year.

Feed keeps the birds fat, which insulates their bodies in winter. In my garden, I have several different feed stations and I have several birdhouses, too.

Did you know birds have housing problems just as we do? The Audubon Society (800-274-4201) can help with attractive birdhouses for various kinds of birds. There are big houses and small houses, because all birds can't live together.

Most birds have their own territories because there are always a few big bullies lurking around. Little birds need their little houses to escape such a menace.

There are more than 1,500 kinds of birds in North America, and, of course, they can't all visit your garden. I suggest getting a bird guide and learning to identify your feathered friends.

Stock bird-feeding stations with seeds, suet and water before winter settles in. This way the birds will know who their friends are before the weather makes life difficult. (And keep your cat on the hearth.)

Don't forget, if you feed birds in the winter you must keep it up every day because the birds count on you.

A Few Bird Favorites

- **Big Trees.** Pines, oaks, hemlocks, maples, hackberries.
- **Small Trees.** Hollies, crab apples, cherries, dogwoods, hawthorns.
- **Ground Covers.** Wintergreens, cotoneasters, bunchberries.
- **Shrubs.** Bayberries, viburnums, junipers, sumacs, privets, blueberries.
- **Vines.** Virginia creeper, honeysuckles, grapes, bittersweet, Boston ivy, English ivy.

Backyard Songbirds

One-third of the nation's adult population feeds wild birds in their backyards.

Providing food keeps their little bodies warm, while water and shelter help birds survive. Feeding birds also benefits the entire environment and supplements wild birds' natural diet of weeds, seeds and harmful insects.

Backyard bird-feeding (or any yard, for that matter) is an entertaining, educational and inexpensive pastime enjoyed by children and adults. It provides a break from today's busy lifestyles that often pull many families apart.

Young children are drawn naturally to feeding wild birds. Chickadees, for example, fly from a feeder to a nearby tree. On each trip, they take a single seed and fly to a perch. While holding the seed with their tiny feet, they peck it open and eat the kernel. Kids love it!

Parents enjoy the relaxation and peacefulness of watching birds. Nature serves to relieve the daily stress and can get one's day going on a happy note.

Take the northern cardinal, for example. A fairly common, beautiful bird, the bright-red male and his more camouflaged mate often will be the first ones at the feeder in the morning and the last to leave at night. Mated for life, they will share morsels of sunflower and safflower seeds.

Feeding wild birds in the backyard is an easy hobby to start, and it need not overtax the family budget. It can be as simple as mounting a single feeder outside a window and filling it with a good-quality mix or straight sunflower seeds. This feeder can be a platform or a tubular variety, or one that sticks to the window.

A word of caution, however: In most parts of the country, your first visitor may have four feet and a bushy tail—a squirrel.

For many people, the hobby progresses from there. They discover the relationship between the type and location of feeders, the seed offered and the number and variety of birds attracted.

Parents can challenge an inquisitive child's mind as they explore together these traits in trying to encourage visits by their favorite birds. It also makes an excellent school project.

In fact, bird-feeding can be an excellent teaching tool. Children can assume daily responsibility for cleaning and filling the feeders. It's fun for all involved because different species of birds can be identified. And the activity can be expanded, depending on the interest of the family.

For example, suet products often are put out in little wire baskets to attract woodpeckers, nuthatches and chickadees.

Families can make their own suet, from recipes that include peanuts, raisins and other items in the pantry. Another variation of feeding is to provide sugar water in special (usually red) feeders to attract hummingbirds. These little wonders of nature represent an entire bird study all by themselves.

Bulbs, Beginners and

Do you crave a yard full of spring color, but feel you don't have time to stop to plant the flowers? Are you afraid you don't know how? Do you feel intimidated?

Take heart! Much of gardening isn't as difficult as it looks. In truth, some of nature's most fabulous flowers are "a cinch" even for beginners.

Spring-flowering bulbs such as tulips and daffodils, which are planted in fall, are prime examples.

If you can dig a hole, you can plant flower bulbs such as tulips. That's why bulbs are often recommended for beginner gardens for children. They're big, easy to handle and the flowers are equally big and dramatic. And they work.

Beginners can expect gratification come spring. When planting, make sure the nose of the bulb is pointed toward the sky, not down! A mistake made by many.

Part of this easiness is simply science: Bulbs are not seeds, they are living plants that already have the baby flower growing inside. If you plant them, they will grow and give you beautiful flowers. Certain poetic souls call them "nature's guaranteed miracle."

The following are tips designed for busy gardeners and beginners. Even experienced gardeners may learn a thing or two. These easy steps can be accomplished in just a short time on an autumn afternoon.

Have a Plan

Location: It is likely you want to celebrate the arrival of springtime with a splash of color. So, put your flowers where you or your neighbors can see them: along the driveway, by the front door, outside the kitchen window or around the lamp-post, mailbox or that "great big tree" out front.

Proper planting sites: Wherever you choose to plant, pick a spot where the soil is well-drained. Bulbs love to be watered, but they don't like "wet feet." So avoid low areas where puddles of standing water collect, because soggy soil might cause the bulbs to rot.

When planning where to plant your bulbs, don't worry too much about light. Deciduous trees, the ones that drop their leaves in fall won't have grown their summer greenery (leaves) until after the spring bulbs have bloomed. There will be ample light.

Design: It doesn't matter whether your budget is small or large. Even a single grouping of color can create a pleasing effect. Bulbs can create a great show as a mass planting or as colorful accents to features of your landscape. A mailbox or along a walkway can be especially cheerful. Purple and blue crocuses can be planted right into a lawn to create a magical, fairyland effect next spring. Yellow and white daffodils add a romantic touch along rock or brick walls or along wooded areas.

Color: Here's where you have the most fun. Do you prefer a "look at me" color like hot-to-trot reds, yellows, oranges and purples? Or is soft and subtle more your style with colors such as romantic peaches, pinks, butter tones and lavenders? Decide on the mood you want to set and you can fit the bulbs to match it later. One thing experts all agree upon: There are no mistakes in color choices. Whatever you like is what is right for your garden.

Plant in "visual bouquets": Whether you plant 20 or 200 bulbs, remember that you should plant them in bunches. Lonely tulips, spaced apart in rows like little soldiers, don't have much of an impact. It's far better to create visual bouquets by planting in groupings of 15 or more.

Bulbs, tulips in particular, come in every color of the rainbow. Be creative, let your imagination run wild!

Size in Mind

Strategy: Gardening experts have a rule of thumb: The bigger the bulb, the better the flower. When choosing bulbs, remember that bigger doesn't necessarily mean better. It depends on what you have in mind. Choose the larger bulbs to accent a walkway or plant around a lamp-post (areas that will be seen up close). These will give the most impressive show.

Consider smaller bulbs to create less-expensive mass plantings (especially those designed to be seen from a distance, such as from the road). These are often available in bulk or in collections at very attractive prices, so be an early bird. The small bulbs aren't of lesser quality, they're only a year or so younger.

Value: Many bulbs come back year after year. Others diminish over time. To get the most bang for your buck, look for bulbs marked on their packaging "good for naturalizing." As a rule, "naturalizing" means that the bulbs will multiply and their flowers become a permanent feature in your garden.

Daffodils and other narcissuses, crocuses and grape hyacinths are examples. Alas, most tulips and Dutch hyacinths (the big fragrant kind) diminish after three years.

Using these repeat performers as the basis of your outdoor collection, your planting chores will lessen over the years, and you can also indulge yourself with some additional varieties that provide a dazzling show for one year only.

Bloom time, plant height: Pay attention to the flowering time and the plant height on the packages. Also consider the blooming period. There are three major blooming seasons in spring: early, middle and late. You will want to plant some flowers from each, so that when one batch has finished flowering, another one starts.

How to choose bulbs: High-quality bulbs can be purchased from a wide variety of sources, including local garden centers and nurseries, many home centers and supermarkets. National mail-order sources are also plentiful (look for their ads in gardening magazines).

To judge a bulb's quality, squeeze it. Healthy Dutch bulbs should be firm, not soft. Check for deep scars or cuts and reject those. However, if the papery covering, called the tunic, is torn or missing, don't fret. This is natural and may even help the bulb to root faster.

Planting

You've planned, you've shopped well and you're ready to plant! Everything you need to know to plant your bulbs successfully will be found on the packaging, or on short instructions sheets—here are a few extra guidelines.

Organizing: As with their botanical cousin, the onion, bulbs of the same type look alike. You can't tell a red tulip from a pink one by looking at the bulb. That's why it's best to keep pre-packaged bulbs in their packages with the tags attached until you're ready to plant them. If you buy bulbs loose from bins, keep the little tear-off instruction sheets with the variety written on them in the bag. Before you start digging, lay out your bags near the locations in the yard where they are to be planted.

As a general rule of thumb, smaller bulbs such as crocuses and snowdrops are planted 5 inches deep. Larger bulbs such as tulips and daffodils are planted 8 inches deep.

You can dig small holes just large enough for one or a few bulbs. Or, if you wish to get all your digging over with at once, dig a large trench at the advised spacing and cover them with soil. Whichever method you choose, be sure the bottom of the hole has a couple of inches of loose dirt for drainage and to allow the roots to grow. Remember, bulbs are always planted with the pointed end up, never down!

Food and water: Bulbs by their very nature are natural food storehouses. They come packed with all the food they need for the first season's growth right inside. However, if you want bulbs to come back year after year, it can help to add a little nourishment for the future. Either work some composted cow manure into the soil (you don't need to hunt down a cow—all garden centers have it), or sprinkle in some special controlled-release 9-9-6 bulb food. Steer clear of lawn fertilizers. These are high in nitrogen, which feeds the "green" parts of plants—great for grass but not for flowering plants.

With the bulbs all tucked away in strategic pockets of your yard, give them a good soaking with the hose to help get the roots started. For the most part, nature will do the rest.

You'll be surprised at how quick, how much fun and how satisfying the whole process is. In no time flat, you'll have laid the groundwork for a colorful yard that will give you years of pleasure. Each fall, if you wish, you can improve upon your creation by adding a few more bulbs. When the bulbs have finished flowering at the end of each spring, add a few impatiens or other easy annuals or perennials such as day lilies or black-eyed Susans and voilà!

Happy gardening!

Bulb Border Wisdom

The time to plant a bulb border is in the fall. But before planting anything, cut back your perennials and rake out leaves and debris.

I've also found it easier to scatter and plant larger bulbs such as tulips, lilies and narcissus. Plant these bulbs 5 to 8 inches in the ground (depending on where you live and the variety). Then scatter the smaller bulbs (in the same way as you did the larger bulbs) and plant more shallow, only 3 to 4 inches deep. Somehow these little beauties seem to shift and settle, and find enough room and soil to thrive.

With bulbs, I rarely bother to measure anything out on the ground; instead, I simply figure out the approximate numbers and placement for each area. Then I scatter the bulbs by the handful, similar to sowing grass seed. This technique creates a more natural and informal look. It also saves a lot of time, especially if you're planting bulbs by the hundreds.

How much space I allow between bulbs depends on the variety and the effect I'm looking for. When scattered by the handful, snowdrops, chionodoxas, crocuses and various miniature narcissus usually land 2 to 4 inches apart. If some do end up in a heap, just pick them up and plant where you want them to grow. Plant the larger bulbs, such as tulip, daffodil and narcissus, 4 to 8 inches apart depending on how dense an effect you want to create.

With lilies, I don't use this technique. I place them carefully in the ground, mostly because they seem fragile and cost as much as $6 apiece. The spacing between lilies varies. For example, when planting Asiatics, I will plant them from 3 to 6 inches apart; while the larger, more spectacular Orientals and trumpets I plant anywhere from 10 to 18 to 24 inches apart.

Maintaining a bulb border for spring and summer-blooming bulbs in a perennial border is easy. It's pretty much a matter of leaving them alone. Their leaves die back in an inconspicuous manner, and because the small, early-blooming bulbs are early and low-growing, any yellowing foliage that remains is mostly covered by emerging perennials.

I like to place my bulbs among perennials (like peonies, for instance) with lots of leaves. Otherwise, I just wait until they yellow and wither, then give each stalk a gentle tug. If it still seems firmly attached, I wait a few days and try again. I do the same with lilies, except for the Asiatics, which I simply let go to seed.

After the hybrid tulips are through blooming, I treat them as annuals. I just pull them up (bulb and all) and add them to the compost pile. With narcissus, the foliage must be left until it has matured. When the foliage has turned yellow and withered, I cut them back to the ground.

My borders are now so thick with naturalized bulbs that when perennials need dividing, bulbs are invariably lifted in the process. Once the divisions are planted, I tuck the bulbs back into the ground at the appropriate depth. I usually have extra ones, which I move to other areas or give away to friends for the holidays.

Bulbs, Cut

Q. *Can cut tulips and daffodils coexist in the same container? No, say many flower arrangers, because daffodils exude a compound that poisons the water for tulips and several other flowers, too. Any suggestions?*

A. Here's how to avoid the problem. Keep daffodils in a separate container for 16 to 24 hours after cutting; then rinse their stems with clean water but don't cut them again before transferring them to a container with tulips. Try charcoal powder added to the container water (1 tablespoon per quart). Shake the solution well.

Fall Bulb Planting Guide

NAME	WHEN TO PLANT	PLANTING DEPTH
Anemone	Plant now	3 inches
Begonia	Wait until spring	2 inches
Bleeding heart	Plant now	3 inches
Calla lily	Wait until spring	4 inches
Canna	Wait until spring	6 inches
Crocus	Plant now	4 inches
Daffodil	Plant now	7 inches
Freesia	Plant now	2 inches
Gladiolus	Wait until spring	4 inches
Hyacinth and Grape Hyacinth	Plant now	6 inches
Iris (bearded, Dutch)	Plant now	2–4 inches
Lily (all varieties)	Plant now	6–7 inches
Lily of the valley	Plant now	1 inches
Narcissus	Plant now	5 inches
Peony	Plant now	1 ½ to 2 inches (no deeper)
Ranunculus	Plant now and spring	2 inches
Tuberose	Wait until spring	4 inches
Tulip	Plant now	6–7 inches

Bulbs: Fascinating Facts

Try to answer these true or false statements about growing and using bulbs. The answers may surprise you!

Q. *Bulbs only flower in the spring.*

A. False. Bulbs come in such variety and their growing needs are so varied that gardeners can plan bulb gardens that will bloom all year.

Q. *It's necessary to dig up bulbs each fall and re-plant them in the spring in order for them to continue to bloom.*

A. False. Most bulbs thrive year after year. Some varieties, like caladiums, however, do need to be dug up and stored over winter in colder climates.

Q. *Tulips are the most widely grown bulbs.*

A. True. Tulips are gardeners' favorites.

Q. *More gardeners grow daffodils than petunias.*

A. True. A 1993 National Gardening Association survey of gardeners indicated that daffodils were more popular than the ubiquitous petunias.

Q. *Bulbs don't fare well with other perennials.*

A. False. Bulbs can be interspersed beautifully with a variety of perennials.

Q. *Only experienced gardeners have success growing bulbs.*

A. False. Even beginning gardeners can successfully grow bulbs. Planting bulbs is the perfect project for children to keep their tiny hands out of mischief.

Q. *Experts recommend planting bulbs like tulips or crocus singly, in widely placed rows.*

A. False. To re-create bursts of color and make a splashy impression in the garden, bulbs should be planted in clumps.

Q. *Bulbs need full sun in order to thrive.*

A. False. Like all plants, bulbs have a variety of growing needs.

Q. *Many bulbs provide delightful fragrances.*

A. True. Bulbs provide color, beauty and fragrance.

Q. *It's possible to have flowering bulbs throughout the year—even winter.*

A. True. There are bulbs for all seasons, and they come in every size and color of the rainbow (to please your fancy)—even beginning gardeners can have bulbs flowering throughout the year.

Bulbs, Forcing

Of all flower bulbs, hyacinth, paperwhite narcissus and amaryllis are probably the easiest to bring into flower in an indoor garden. But, if you wish to enjoy the many colors and shapes of the spring garden, you must try some other gems such as tulips, daffodils, crocus, iris reticulate, muscari or scilla.

Coaxing spring-flowering bulbs to bloom in the winter is usually referred to as "indoor forcing." Actually, this is a misnomer; a better way to put it would be "tender, loving care." By the deceptive use of light and temperature, you can cause the bulb to believe that in a period of 12 to 15 weeks it has experienced a total winter-spring span. The requisite climate can be created by placing pots of bulbs in an indoor storage place where the temperature will stay between 40° and 50°F.

Rooting

The potted bulbs need a cold-storage period of at least 12 weeks to develop roots, stem and bud. Rooting should be at temperatures of 40° to 50°F.

Indoor rooting: Place the pots in a cold cellar, old refrigerator, garage or outdoor shed where they won't freeze. Pots rooted indoors must be kept in complete darkness and watered regularly.

Outdoor rooting: Dig a bed deep enough to hold the pots and about 3 inches of sand. Spread an inch of sand or pebbles on the bed bottom for drainage. Set the pots and cover them with 2 inches of sand and a mound of about 5 inches of soil. Dig a small trench around the bed for runoff. Water the bed regularly until freezing weather sets in. The containers can be buried in an outdoor trench, properly protected against excessive cold.

Containers

There are many fabulous containers to choose from; finding some that reflect your decorating tastes should be easy. Metal, ceramic, plastic or clay will all do the job. Use paint, paper, seashells or any other material to transform containers into attractive settings for your flowers. If new clay pots are used, soak them in water 24 hours before you use them. Forced bulbs require well-drained soil. Containers must have a drainage hole and be twice as deep as the bulb. This allows the roots to develop. Bulbs can also be grown in specially designed glass containers that hold the bulb just above the water. Add water as needed to maintain the original level. Small pieces of charcoal will keep water bacteria-free.

Forcing Soil

Light soil is the key, especially for drainage. Combine equal parts of weed-free garden or potting soil, peat and sand. I feel that Pro-Mix commercial soil is best. The soil makes the bulbs thrive, and it is available at most garden centers. (Don't use soil in which bulbs have been grown before.) And don't worry about fertilizer—the bulb contains all its own food. Apply a mulch of hay, straw, evergreen branches, etc., to prevent freezing and heaving.

Flowering

After a minimum of 12 weeks, the bulbs will have roots visible through the drainage hole and sprouts will be 1 to 3 inches tall. At this stage, the containers can be placed in a warmer area. Place rooted pots in a 60°F semi-dark area. After four days, the pots should be transferred to a well-lighted 65° to 70°F area, so buds can bloom. Water regularly and keep pots away from heaters and drafts.

Potted bulbs in bloom prefer cool locations: 60° to 65°F for daffodils and crocus, 60° to 72°F for tulips and hyacinths (warmer temperatures will shorten their bloom). They enjoy full sunlight but should be moved to a cool location at night.

Bulbs: Jewel Tones Are Real Gems

Gardeners who swooned over pastel tulips in recent years are now clamoring for tulips, daffodils and other flowering bulbs in jewel tones.

What people want are punchier colors and more pizzazz—jewel tones like ruby, amethyst, sapphire, topaz, aquamarine and other shimmering colors that interplant nicely with oddball shades of chartreuse, mahogany and oxblood.

The following is a sampler of color combos that I suggest should provide a guide to which bulbs to plant together in order to create complementary bedmates for next spring's garden.

When planting this fall, try these suggested combinations and, just for fun, toss in something unexpected. It's this "something extra" that gives a garden originality, so how you feel and think comes into play here.

Blue and Orange

For a spring garden planted with blues and oranges, try these bulbs that bloom for months on end:

Early season: *Iris reticulata* 'Joyce' (5-inch butterfly-like flowers that pop up sans leaves in early spring, in sky blue marked with orange); with tulip 'Dream Boat' (a luminous, salmon-orange *Greigii* tulip).

Mid-season: Fragrant Hyacinth 'Ostara' (deep violet blue); tulip 'Bestseller' (rich salmon with copper and rose shadings, a sport of much-loved 'Apricot Beauty'); narcissus 'Professor Einstein' (a large-cupped daffodil in clear white with a flat orange cup); and *Fritillaria persica,* with 30-inch spires of pendant dusky plum bell flowers.

Late season: Fragrant tulip 'Ballerina' (a new tangerine-orange lily-flowered tulip); with cobalt blue *Muscari lalifolium.*

Yellow, White and Blue

Cool, clear and crisp, elegant too, that's the look of yellow, white and blue in the spring garden. Where long-distance viewing is a factor, count on this colorful combo to stand out in the landscape. It gives a new look.

Early season: Eranthis (winter *Aconite*) with ground-hugging bright yellow buttercup flowers encircled by a green leafy ruff, with clear blue *Iris reticulata* 'Harmony,' crocus 'Pickwick,' and *Galanthus nivalis* (snowdrop).

Early mid-season: Miniature yellow daffodil 'Tête-à-Tête' with soft porcelain-blue striped squill Puschkinia libanotica.

Mid-season: Muscari armeniacum (long-lasting cobalt blue underplanting), tulip 'Sunray' (clear, light yellow Triumph tulip); narcissus 'Flower Record' (large-cupped daffodil, white with yellow cup, edged in red).

Late season: Tulip 'Françoise' (soft white, flamed with vivid yellow that whitens with maturity); tulip 'West Point' (vivid yellow, lily-flowered).

Red, Yellow and Purple

For royal shades to die for, try a three-season blend of reds, yellow and purple.

Early season: Tulip 'Easter Parade' (rich red and yellow striped Fosteriana tulip, vivid in the early spring garden); tulip 'Sweetheart' (lemon-yellow Fosteriana tulip); *Crocus purpurea* (giant purple crocus).

Mid-season: Tulip 'Monte Carlo' (vivid yellow double early tulip); hyacinth 'Peter Stuyvesant' (deep purple); tulip 'Couleur Cardinale' (single early tulip, scarlet flushed with plum).

Late season: Species *Tulipa linifolia* (low-growing scarlet flowers with deep black heart); tulip 'Georgette' (multiflowering tulip, yellow with ruby-red edge); tulip 'Cum Laude' (single late tulip, deep-violet purple).

All these tulips and many more will help make a glorious spring come true!

Bulbs: Shopping Tips

Q. *Besides bulb size (and in turn flower size), is there any other difference between an average bulb and a better bulb? I see some bulbs for sale very cheap and others quite expensive.*

A. At the auctions in Holland, bulbs are sold by caliber (circumference size). The larger the bulb, the bigger the flower it will produce. In general, larger-caliber bulbs bring a higher price.

Of course, other factors—especially supply and demand—also affect price. As a bulb-buying rule of thumb, consider this: For elegant bed plantings, it's worth buying the bigger, showier bulbs. But smaller-caliber bulbs often sold at very attractive prices can offer a great way of adding color to large areas, or marginal areas of the yard.

Buying large quantities of smaller bulbs can pay off on long-term plantings, such as naturalized narcissus plantings, where the bulbs can "catch up" in size, blooming year after year.

Bulbs, Storing Summer

Many summer-flowering bulbs—such as dahlia, canna, begonia, ismene (peruvia daffodil) and tuberose—should be dug and stored for the winter.

When the leaves turn yellow, use a spading fork to gently lift the bulbs from the ground. Soil that clings to the bulbs should be washed off, except for the bulbs that need to be stored with soil around them.

The soil should remain on achimenes, begonias, canna, caladium, dahlia and ismene bulbs. These bulbs should be stored in clumps on a slightly moistened layer of peat moss or sawdust in a cool area. Simply wash off the soil and separate the bulbs before planting next season.

Discard any undersize, damaged or diseased bulbs. Separate bulbs by variety or species before storing them.

Trays with screen bottoms can be used to store large numbers of bulbs. Never store bulbs more than two or three layers deep. Deep layers can generate heat, which causes decay.

Many of the tender summer-flowering bulbs may also be grown in pots for use on porches and patios. Callas, caladiums, dwarf dahlias and ismene will do well as potted plants that can be taken indoors for the winter.

In the fall, when the foliage begins to fade, reduce watering and allow the bulbs to dry. Store the bulbs in a cool, dry place that is about 60°F.

Be sure to check the specific storage requirements for each variety of bulbs, since some may require watering while others do not.

Bulbs: When to Plant

Q. *How soon should I plant my bulbs after I buy them?*

A. Sometimes you will buy bulbs before you are ready to plant in order to get the best selection. While it is always best to plant your bulbs soon after you receive them, when you have to wait be sure to store the bulbs in a cool, dry place away from direct sunlight. Some people keep their bulbs in their refrigerator crisper drawer, taking care to avoid storing them with ripening fruit. They should be fine for several weeks—even months—if properly handled.

But don't wait too long. Ideally, you should plant six weeks or so prior to a hard frosting, to allow ample time for root development. A tip: The proper time to plant is when the ground temperature is below 60°F at planting depth. While this is not easy for most of us to gauge, it gives you some notion of what is appropriate.

If you don't have six weeks' lead time, plant anyway—even if you have to hack your way through hard, chilled soil. (As always, be sure to water.) The key is that you must plant in the fall to have blooms in spring. Even if planted late, bulbs will spring into action and try to start root growth. They are programmed to grow and will do their best, no matter how late you plant them.

Cactus, Christmas

Q. *A Christmas cactus plant I've had for about two years is blooming beautifully now and is getting big. Should I transplant it and when?*

A. A Christmas cactus ordinarily should be re-potted every two or three years, or whenever the pot is filled with roots and the soil appears to be worn out! Transplant in spring if your cactus is healthy. An unhealthy plant (because of poor root system) may be carefully transplanted at any time and usually transferred to a smaller pot. Note that if buds fall off your Thanksgiving or Christmas cactus, the room is too hot and dry, and the plant is probably suffering from lack of water.

Cannas

Q. *I loved my cannas this year. What do I do with them in fall?*

A. You can either throw them out, having already enjoyed a fabulous season of color, or with a few minutes' effort this fall you can store them over the winter to plant again next spring. Your cannas will not only grow again but also be bigger than before. If your soil was good, a canna can produce more than one rhizome by the end of a summer. Here's what you do to keep your canna vigorous:

Indoors: To the surprise of many gardeners, cannas can make interesting indoor houseplants if given sufficient sunlight and an occasional cutback. The gorgeous foliage of many variegated types makes them particularly attractive in indoor settings. Place potted canna in good strong sunlight. Fertilize with a general fertilizer periodically. Do not over-water. If leaves get tatty, cut the stalk back to about 4 inches. A new stalk will come up.

Warmer zones: Lucky you: Cannas are winter-hardy in your area. You can lift your cannas to re-plant the next season or leave them where they are. If winter frosts are a problem, a light blanket of mulch is a good idea over winter.

Colder zones: Leave the cannas in the ground until frost blackens the foliage. (This is true for all tender summer bulbs, except for tuberous begonias, which should be dealt with before frost.)

Then cut down the stems to about 4 inches. Carefully dig up bulbs, brush off the soil and then divide the rhizomes by breaking them apart or cutting them, making sure that each one has at least one place where a leaf can be seen growing.

Place them out to air-dry in a cool, dry place. Be careful not to bruise the rhizomes as this promotes mold. Label different varieties because they'll all look pretty much the same once the leaves dry up.

After drying, cut off any remaining foliage and pack the bulbs in a few layers of clean vermiculite, peat moss or excelsior. Store in a cool, dry place until spring.

Next spring, pot up canna indoors to get a jump on the summer garden season. By starting growth eight weeks prior to your usual planting-out date (after the threat of last frost), you gain months of summer growth! While you're at it, start up your caladiums, elephant ears, dahlias and begonias early, too. This helps you hit the deck running in the summer garden, with plants ready to go once the weather warms up.

Chamomile, Growing Conditions

Q. *This year I planted some perennial chamomile in my herb garden but the plants all seemed to just burn up. What culture do they need to grow best?*

A. Perennial chamomile prefers full sun but will tolerate a little shade. Chamomile likes a well-aerated, rich but gritty and slightly acid soil.

It's hard for me to say why your plants died since this plant is quite hardy and tolerant of most garden conditions. Nevertheless, chamomile can fail to thrive when subjected to extremes of dryness or moisture. If your soil is very heavy clay, which neither holds water well nor drains quickly when overwatered, your plants may have suffered from both.

Herbs usually die if waterlogged in winter. Maybe you overfertilized or accidentally sprayed them with a herbicide. If so, chuck out all herbicides and use an insecticide soap spray for insect control.

Chilling Requirements

As outdoor temperatures gradually fall, the chilling process for most plants slowly begins. Plants require a chilling period that is quite long. Few require less than two months. Most plants need ten to 16 weeks of cool temperatures before growth can resume or before flowers and seeds can be produced.

Understanding chilling requirements helps gardeners meet their plants' needs. The chilling of plants can harm or help them, since they react to cool temperatures in many ways.

For instance, some plants, such as the tropical-foliage types, show severe damage if exposed to temperatures below 40°F, even though they are not frozen. Leaves usually drop suddenly, turn yellow or develop brown margins.

Many varieties of plants do best in cool temperatures, including herbaceous, perennials, biennials, shrubs, mature trees, seeds and flowering bulbs.

Hydrangeas and azaleas are two flowering houseplants that require a chilling treatment since both form flower buds during the late summer and fall if they have been kept outdoors. Both should be moved indoors into a cool place before freezing weather arrives.

Azaleas will chill beautifully in low light since they don't shed their foliage.

Hydrangeas will chill after leaves have dropped off, so they should be placed in a cool, dark spot to promote leaf drop. Both varieties should be kept slightly damp during the chilling period.

Spring bulbs such as hyacinths, daffodils and tulips also require chilling before flowering can occur. So as soon as bulbs are available they should be potted immediately and placed in a cool, dark spot in early October for flowering indoors in late winter.

Of course, for outdoor flowering, chilling occurs naturally over the winter. Chilling in the soil takes place after planting. Usually the soil remains too warm for chilling immediately after planting; nevertheless, roots begin to form anyway. Chilling begins as soil temperatures drop into the mid-40°F range and this continues until the soil freezes when the chilling process slows.

In the spring, as soil warms again, some chilling may still occur until the flower stems elongate and growth resumes. Most spring-flowering bulbs need ten to 14 weeks for proper chilling, although there is a great deal of fluctuation among varieties.

In seeds, dormancy not only requires chilling but moisture during the chilling process. Therefore, many seeds should not be allowed to dry excessively before chilling. They should be planted soon after harvest, and if they can't be planted, placed in moist peat moss and refrigerated for three months or more.

If in doubt about the length of chilling, use a longer rather than shorter length of time. Some seeds, such as viburnum and peony, require high temperatures followed by low ones before germination can occur.

Chrysanthemums

Q. *Last year I bought six chrysanthemum plants that I planted outside. In the fall I had bouquets of color inside. How should I treat the plants outside so they will come up next year?*

A. Hardy chrysanthemums need to be divided and re-set every second or third year and kept well fertilized and free of disease and insect pests. Considerable care should be given to the selection of varieties for outdoor planting. There are many kinds in the trade but only a few of these bloom early enough in the fall, or are sufficiently hardy where winters are severe. Cover your plants after the first killing frost and when the soil is slightly frozen. Use evergreen branches and dry leaves.

Beautiful Versatility

Chrysanthemums are America's most popular fall flowers because of their many versatile uses.

Bedding plants are superb for use as specimens in foundation plantings, massed in beds or grouped in plantings of three or five for colorful and dramatic focal points in the landscape. They can be planted either as young plants in the spring or as flowering plants in the fall.

Hanging baskets add a finishing touch to any patio or porch or tennis court they decorate. Garden-mum hanging baskets can be started in the late spring or early summer from young plants or purchased in bloom for a fabulous display of beauty.

Since garden mums grow into wonderful mounds of flowers, they are perfect for use in containers. Use these lovely mums on decks, patios, front-door steps, windowboxes, by the pool or tennis court. Mums are easily planted while in bud and bloom into urns, barrels and other types of containers.

Planting Guidelines

Plant young plants in a sunny spot where they will receive at least half a day of sun.

Plant in fertile well-drained soil. Improve soil by adding compost, such as peat moss or other organic matter.

Space garden mums far enough apart based on plant size. Young mum plants planted in spring should be spaced 18 to 24 inches apart.

Watering

Rainfall in many areas is sufficient to keep your garden mums growing well. During dry spells, water as needed to keep plants from wilting.

Freshly planted mums should be thoroughly watered every two to three days if there is no rainfall.

Garden mums planted outdoors in the fall do not need any fertilizer until the following growing season, spring.

Winter Protection

Keep your soil moist as winter approaches. No pruning is needed until the following spring.

After several hard frosts, protect your plants with straw or evergreen branches.

In the spring, remove any old mum stems—a rake works well—and as the weather warms, remove the mulch.

Fertilizing

During the growing season in spring, incorporate into the soil a general, all-purpose fertilizer at the rate of ½ to 1 pound per 100 square feet. Repeat monthly until August. A liquid fertilizer can also be used. If you plant in fall, don't fertilize!

Pinching

To encourage branching and development of compact bushy plants, it's most important to pinch back your mums in the spring as soon as the new growth is 4 to 6 inches tall. Simply use thumbnail and index finger to pinch about one-third of the new growth at the top of each and every shoot.

Repeat this procedure throughout the summer whenever new shoots are 3 to 5 inches long. In northern states, stop pinching about July 10 to 15. In southern states, stop pinching about July 20 to August 1.

Chrysanthemums: Medicinal Benefits of

Legend tells us that chrysanthemums originated in China centuries ago—even before reaching Japanese shores—so it comes as no surprise to learn that the Chinese to this day believe in the medicinal value of mums.

In traditional Chinese medicine, chrysanthemums are supposedly used to treat headaches, fever, hepatitis and swollen and painful eyes.

Among therapeutic benefits attributed to the plants are improved eyesight, detoxification, lower blood pressure and a soothing effect.

A soothing effect is the primary therapeutic benefit most gardeners get from seeing beautiful mums in their garden. Although *chrysanthemum* means "golden flower" in Greek, garden mums are no longer just golden and come in a multitude of eye-pleasing colors as a result of years of scientific breeding.

Of the six basic garden mum flower forms bred by the Yoder firm, one flower, the "pompom," got its name centuries ago from the French because its rounded shape reminded them of the wool pompoms on their soldier's hats. The other flower forms are daisy, decorative, anemone, button and spider. Some garden mums come in a combination of flower forms, such as spoon-tipped daisies or quilled decoratives.

On top of the medicinal benefits ascribed to them by the ancient Chinese, chrysanthemums have been found to be an environmentally safe insecticide. There are two on the market. One is made with "botanical pyrethrins from chrysanthemum flowers" and another from the "dried and crushed chrysanthemum heads."

One advantage they are supposed to have over other insecticides is that they can be used on edible fruits and vegetables up to the day of the harvest, and the produce will still be safe for consumption.

Chrysanthemums, New Varieties

Garden mum season doesn't always exactly kick off over the Labor Day weekend, but it does start at about the same time as the football season. Like the football season, mum season is being lengthened with fabulous new varieties available in most garden centers.

People want their garden mums just like they want their football, and the good thing about gardening and garden mums is that you don't have to be a genius to be a green-thumb gardener.

While it may be too much to expect the garden mum season to extend into January, the way football does, garden mums have been blooming longer with new extender varieties.

Before these new varieties were introduced, the garden mum season typically ran from mid-September to early October. Now it stretches from around Labor Day to Halloween in northern states, and in the south the season can run through November.

As the fall garden mum season progresses, here are a few great new varieties to look for:

'Autumn Kimberly': A fine companion for the growing list of extender varieties. Mauve-red daisy flowers range to 1 ½ inches in diameter with good lasting color.

'Blushing Christine': Gardeners love Christine; they will find this apricot-pink beauty irresistible.

'Bold Christine': Another enticing variety of the popular Christine with red-coral decorative flowers.

'Felicia': A lavender daisy with the best flower and foliage quality and large flowers ranging to 1 ¾ inches in diameter.

'Foxy Valerie': A stunning, vibrant-red decorative mum with dark-green, glossy leaves.

'Gentle Kimberly': A lively orange-bronze daisy that extends the garden mum season into October. Very prolific and long-lasting flowers.

'Glowing Lynn': Bright orange decorative flowers that broaden and improve the orange color among garden mums.

'Helen': An early flowering red decorative mum that is rich in color, a number-one-selling garden mum.

'Janice': Golden-yellow decorative flowers with richer flower color and better early flowering. The number-two-selling yellow garden mum.

'Laurie': An outstanding honey-bronze mum with large flowers up to 2 ¼ inches in diameter, extends fall flowering season with elegance and beauty.

'Stunning Lynn': A stunning new color combination to expand the look of garden mums, one of the most popular ever introduced. Dusty rose outer ray petals of 'Stunning Lynn's' decorative flowers are highlighted by dark raspberry-red center petals. A beauty!

'Yellow Ginger': Adorned with bright yellow flowers, 'Yellow Ginger's' easy-to-grow plants are an ideal companion to the two-toned bronze 'Ginger.'

Compost, Prevent Rotting

Q. *Usually I turn my compost pile every week. Lately I've been a little tardy and now I have two 5-foot-diameter bins loaded with a mix of fresh grass clippings and matted, smelly, moldy older clippings. What do you suggest?*

A. I think the easiest way to deal with your problem would be to make a new pile from the fresh grass clippings and incorporate the older, matted clippings directly into the garden. The matted clippings are no doubt too heavy to easily mix into a new pile, so I suggest putting them in the garden as is and till them into the soil. Left on the soil surface, they'll dry out and form a crust that water simply can't penetrate.

Use the fresh clippings to start a new pile. If you can't turn the pile regularly, mix in materials high in carbon, such as hay and dried leaves (oak is best) to create a better balance of nitrogen and carbon. To prevent rotting and matting, cover the pile—you won't want the same problem to happen again.

Corn-Husk Dolls

The American Indians were the first to make corn-husk dolls. Corn husks were dried, tied and fashioned into chiefs, warriors and women. Then faces were painted, and sometimes sticks were added for arms and legs.

The doll is created with corn husks and yarn and—when correctly tied—will include all the body features.

You can use other materials to create clothing; it's best to attach facial features with glue. To begin the project:

- Gather 12 corn husks, yarn or string and scissors.
- Tie husks tightly together at one end with yarn or string.
- To make the head, tie the husks a little way down from the top knot. Gather three of the husks and tie them together halfway down for an arm. Gather and tie three more husks at the opposite side of the doll to form the other arm. Cut away most of the excess corn husk that is beyond the arm knots.
- To make the body, tie the remaining corn husks halfway between the head and their ends.
- Make one leg by taking three husks and tying them together a little up from their ends. Make the other leg the same way.
- Now that your doll is finished, use your imagination in decorating.

Cover Crops

There's a difference between a green-manure crop and a cover crop. Green-manure crops are planted with the garden plants; cover crops are planted after the garden crop has been removed.

A cover crop can improve your garden soil. It's not new; the Chinese, Greeks and Romans all did it to improve their soil.

Home gardens can be planned so that a third of the area is in early-maturing crops. This can then be sown with a cover crop. Change the area for early crops each year so that a cover crop can be planted every third year.

Crab Apples

Q. *On our west-facing lawn we have two crab-apple trees that are just gorgeous when in blossom, even though they bear little fruit. There are about a dozen slender shoots growing from the base of one of the trees; how and when can these be safely separated and transplanted so that one day they can give as much beauty as the parent plant?*

A. My dear, you have "suckers" growing on your trees! Cut them off immediately. They are wild and no good for transplanting; they will only sap your trees of energy. Fertilize the trees in the spring with 5-10-5 and keep them well mulched for the hot, dry summer months.

Daffodils, Fertilizing

Q. *I have noticed the instructions for growing daffodils in my bulb book say to add a half-pound of nitrogen, phosphorus and potassium fertilizer per 100-foot area. I have a bag of 10-10-10 fertilizer (What do the numbers mean?). How much should I add?*

A. It's very easy to explain what the numbers stand for: The "10-10-10" numbers on your fertilizer bag means that the fertilizer contains 10 percent nitrogen (always the first number), 10 percent phosphorus (always the second number) and 10 percent potassium (always the last number).

To find out how much actual nitrogen, phosphorus and potassium you have, simply multiply the percentage of each nutrient by the weight of the bag.

For example, if you have a 40-pound bag of 10-10-10 and you applied the entire bag of fertilizer, you'd be adding 4 pounds of nitrogen, 4 pounds of phosphorus and 4 pounds of potassium.

You only need a half-pound of actual "N-P-K" in a 100-foot bed, which is one-eighth of the 4 pounds of each nutrient in the whole bag. So simply divide the 40 pounds total weight of the bag by eight and you get 5 pounds of 10-10-10 fertilizer to add to the bed.

My dear readers, it's only simple arithmetic. Daffodils are not heavy feeders, so broadcasting a half- pound of 10-10-10 over a 100-foot area, plus adding a handful of compost or composted manure per planting hole, should last the bulbs for many, many years.

I've grown daffodils in one area for eight years, adding fertilizer to the planting hole only once, and they still bloom marvelously well.

Daffodils, Splitting Bulbs

Q. *When planting daffodil bulbs, I've noticed that many of the larger bulbs have one or two side bulbs attached. Shall I plant the bulbs with these bulblets attached, or can I split them apart and plant each one separately? Please explain to me each system.*

A. You can split your daffodil bulbs apart and plant them separately. Many of the smaller ones will bloom next season while some will not. The other system: If you plant the daffodils with the side bulbs attached, they'll still grow and flower but, before long, the planting area will become overcrowded. When that happens, you'll simply have to dig up the bulbs, separate them and re-plant them.

Day lilies

Americans are re-discovering the beauty of perennials. Bursting back onto the scene with gusto are day lilies, a diverse group of perennial flowers unsurpassed for versatility in the landscape.

Anyone who associated the day lily exclusively with yellow or orange star-shape blooms might wonder what all the excitement is about. The news is that this old-fashioned flower has a great new look. Blossoms now come in all colors of the rainbow: pink, purple, red, peach, apricot and all shades in between, including dramatic color combinations. Petals may be ruffled, twirled or flecked with eye-catching glitter called "diamond dust."

And there are lots of new sizes and shapes, ranging from giant spidery blooms a full 12 inches wide to biscuit-shape miniatures barely 2 inches across.

Day lily plants may rise to a height of 4 feet or remain as short as 12 inches. The taller varieties make marvelous additions to traditional perennial borders, while low-growing varieties perform beautifully as ground covers. Day lilies can also be planted in naturalistic drifts in lawns, where they will multiply and spread like wildflowers.

The scientific name for day lily is *Hemerocallis,* meaning "beauty for a day." Although individual blooms are short-lived, opening and fading the very same day, individual plants continue to blossom for weeks. Flower stalks of modern cultivars carry an average of 20 to 30 buds. On a given day, anywhere from one to six buds may unfurl. As one flower stalk becomes depleted, another takes its place, either immediately or a few weeks later.

With the advent of early, mid-season and late-blooming varieties, gardeners now can have continuous blooms from spring into autumn. In fact, day lilies flourish with little care in almost every part of the country.

The old rule of thumb used to be that evergreen varieties do best in the South and dormant varieties do best in the North, but nowadays the vast majority of modern evergreens and dormants do well just about everywhere. Evergreen day lilies retain their foliage throughout the year, while the tops of dormant varieties die to the ground each autumn.

The day lily is probably one of the most carefree perennials you could choose. The plant will grow well in average soil as long as it drains properly, and it will bloom from dawn until dusk if touched by a few hours of morning sunlight. Day lilies are great flowers to have around the house because they come in all sizes and colors, especially the new hybrids (often *Hemerocallis*). The ones you see along the road have escaped cultivation and become wildflowers. Some of the fancier ones come in gorgeous colors: brilliant reds and pink, dark wine and amethyst, butterscotch, peach, lemon, chartreuse, melon or ivory. The rare and unusual day lilies also come in fancy prices, stud plants going for $100 or more! But don't worry—you don't have to have the rare ones to have magnificent beauty. You can pick up a wide range of colors at around $3 per division.

The tuber-like roots can be planted in spring or fall, preferably in spots receiving at least six hours of direct sunlight daily. Day lilies are not fussy about soil, although a well-drained loam is best. If soil is heavy, mix in some peat moss or compost at planting time. While it is best to plant the roots immediately upon arrival, they can be stored out of sun in a cool, dry area or in damp sand for a week or two. They should not be left in standing water for more than a few hours.

Day lilies should not be planted too deep. Instead of digging a hole, my method is to loosen the soil to a depth of 1 foot and then plant a cone barely below ground level. After spreading the roots over the cone, I cover them with about 1 ½ inches of soil and water thoroughly.

Spacing, of course, varies according to how they are used in the landscape. Whenever I do any mass planting, say with 20 or more day lilies per bed, I space the roots 12 to 15 inches apart. But when I want a dazzling display, I plant in groups of four or five, leaving just 6 inches between individuals.

Don't fertilize newly planted day lilies for at least four to six weeks after planting. However, established plants should be fed with a low-nitrogen fertilizer (use half the amount recommended on the label) and only in the early spring and again in fall, when temperatures are cool.

New plantings should be kept moist for the first month. Although established day lilies are drought-resistant, they perform best if watered whenever the soil becomes dry. Beyond this, little care is needed. Every three to five years, day lilies become root-bound and should be divided. Simply dig up any overgrown clumps in spring or fall, shake off the loose dirt and then separate each clump by hand, or with a knife, into a few individual plants.

The divisions can be re-planted or given away to friends. The roots are extremely hardy and do not have to be dug and stored for winter, even in the coldest climates.

I have a special tip on how to use day lilies as cut flowers. Pick individual blooms early in the day, when they are freshest, and then put them in the refrigerator to delay closing. Bring them out just before they are needed and pop each one in a waterpick inside the arrangement. Day lilies arranged at dinnertime will last until midnight.

Dormant Season

The roots of many shrubs and trees continue to grow in the late fall and winter, although the branches and stems may be dormant and without leaves. Nutrients applied now through mid-December, when the soil temperature is still above 40°F degrees, are easily absorbed by the roots, moving upward to the above-ground stems.

All plants supplied with nutrients in the fall are more resistant to winter cold than plants without them. Fertilizer applied early in the spring is generally not available to the plant until the soil warms, then is absorbed at a reduced rate because of cold soil.

Use a well-balanced fertilizer such as 5-10-5 and be certain your plants have been thoroughly watered prior to its application; if not they may be damaged from high salt accumulation.

Drip Irrigation

As gardeners across the country join the effort to conserve our most precious resource—water—they are discovering the many benefits of drip irrigation.

So, what exactly is drip irrigation?

Drip is the delivery of a deliberate and exact amount of water to specific plantings. Using flexible plastic tubing and drippers (emitters), drip irrigation enables water to be delivered very slowly, efficiently and directly to the roots of a plant. That means the moisture isn't evaporated by the sun or blown away by the wind, nor is any wasted on non-growing areas, such as patios, walkways and rock gardens, where water is neither wanted nor needed.

The slow application of water over extended periods of time helps develop deeper, stronger roots and, ultimately, more abundant foliage and better fruits and vegetables. A simple starter system, such as a drip-watering kit, features all the tubing, drippers and other accessories needed to cover 200 feet. After a gardener understands the basics, other accessories, including extra tubing and emitters, fittings, fertilizer applicators and battery-operated timers are available that will permit the expansion of an existing drip system to cover up to 5,000 square feet.

Drip irrigation offers many benefits over traditional sprinklers. As already noted, water delivered by a drip-irrigation system goes directly to where it is needed and with no waste or evaporation.

Drip irrigation, as a result, is far more cost-effective than sprinklers because a drip system will dispense about a gallon of water per hour, while sprinklers distribute gallons of water per minute. That's a major difference that will be felt every time a water bill arrives over the course of a long, hot summer.

For those gardeners who are still most comfortable with sprinklers, the technology of drip irrigation offers an ideal compromise. There are also microsprinkler kits available that operate on the same principal as drip, but rely on microsprinkler "heads" rather than emitters to disperse water.

Drip-irrigation equipment, from kits to accessories, is readily available at most major garden centers, retailers and chain stores and the systems are easy to install because no glue or tools are needed. The various tubes, drippers and fittings can all be connected by simply "squashing" them together like you would the tubing for a fish-tank filter to an air pump.

To ensure that you get the most out of your drip system, be sure to carefully read and follow the instructions that come with whatever drip-irrigation equipment you decide to buy.

These days, with water resources at an all-time low and water bills at an all-time high, it's time to look for smart, cost-effective watering practices. With all of its benefits, it's easy to see why drip irrigation is becoming more and more popular with home gardeners.

Earth-Friendly Mulching and Composting

Mounting concern for the environment has everyone looking for ways to step up recycling efforts around the home and in the yard. The solution? Mulching and composting are two easy methods that homeowners can rely on to drastically reduce the amount of yard debris dumped in public landfills, while helping to develop healthy soil for their lawns and gardens.

Healthy, conditioned soil is essential to successful gardening. In many gardens, adding a mulch may be the only step necessary to keep things in balance.

Composed of organic or inorganic materials such as wood chips, bark, straw and gravel, mulch cushions plants against the adverse effects of wind, sun and rain. It moderates soil temperatures, deters weeds and improves the overall soil structure.

Shredding yard and garden material into mulch is easy with the new-and-improved Flowtron chipper/shredder and mulcher (model CS3500). Quick and efficient, this three-stage chipping system reduces piles of lawn clippings, thatch, trimmings and branches up to 2 ½ inches in diameter into decorative and useful garden mulch.

Leaves can be recycled into mulch as well, with a lightweight and inexpensive electric leaf eater. This durable machine reduces eight bags of wet or dry leaves into one bag of

valuable mulch. The bagged leaf shreds should then be spread in 4 to 6 inch layers over soil and under trees and shrubs.

The mulch acts as a protective cover for the soil and roots. When mixed into the soil, mulch introduces nutrients that promote root growth. During dry spells, mulch helps protect the soil from the evaporative effects of sun and wind, and keeps the soil from drying out and hardening.

Ideally, mulch should be loose and airy when placed over the soil, rather than compacted. In the event of heavy rains, mulch also prevents the leaching of plant nutrients and reduces the effects of soil erosion.

While mulch is primarily used as a top dressing, compost is considered one of the ultimate soil conditioners. Compost is made from just about anything organic, such as vegetable and fruit rinds, hedge trimmings, sawdust, leaves, eggshells, etc.

Avoid fatty meat scraps and similar waste because they decompose at a slower rate, create odor and often attract dogs and rodents to your compost pile. Because smaller pieces compost faster, it is also wise to avoid material thicker than a quarter of an inch.

Once the materials are gathered, the simplest way to make compost is in a pile or in special bins designed specifically for this purpose. Whatever you choose, for best results it is important to select a convenient, well-drained spot without direct sunlight.

The best compost piles are formed in layers. Start with a bottom layer of brush to support the pile and help aerate it. Continue adding alternating but equal layers of slow-decaying material such as leaves, clippings and food wastes. Then add a compost activator and a 2-inch layer of garden soil. Remember to moisten each layer thoroughly as it is added to speed the decomposition process.

As the compost begins to break down and create heat, care must be taken to systematically turn the pile. Turning the compost with a pitchfork every few days moves composted material away from the center of the pile and replaces it with partially composted material.

Fall Clean-up

Fall is the time to start thinking about putting your garden bed to sleep for the winter. Here are ten tips to help you get a jump on garden clean-up and the end of the gardening season:

1. Rake and remove leaves from under your rose bushes. This will help remove the breeding ground for insects and fungus that may harm your roses. Add the leaves to your compost bin.
2. Pick up and remove fallen fruit from under your fruit trees to prevent wintering of insects that could cause problems next spring. You can add fruit to the compost pile, too.
3. Remove weeds before they produce seeds—and more weeding chores for you next spring.
4. Take cuttings of tender plants such as geraniums before frost kills them. This is a great way to start plants for next year.
5. Pull up annuals after they've been downed by the first hard frost. You can shred them with a chipper/shredder and add them to your compost pile.
6. Dig and store summer bulbs such as dahlias, cannas, gladiolus and callas. Clip off the green tops and store them in a cool, dry place for winter.
7. Wrap trees to prevent winter injuries from rodents or deer.
8. Buy a pond de-icer for your water garden if you want to keep your goldfish alive in the pond all winter.
9. Mulch around the bases of perennials to help protect them from changes of temperature in the fall and winter.
10. Fill your bird feeders with plenty of snacks. Birds, especially those winging South, look for feeding places along their route.

Fall Gardening

Tips for Perennials

With summer nearing an end, it's time to start thinking about fall gardening chores. Here are some timely tips for your perennials.

1. Plant four to six weeks ahead of the projected killing frost date in your area, to allow plants to get established.

2. Keep plants watered well throughout the fall, until the ground freezes. This promotes good root development. Keep up general garden care, such as weeding and pest control.

3. Fall is a good time to rearrange plants in beds or start new beds and to plant container-grown perennials and shrubs. It is also time to divide many perennials that have finished flowering. Early spring bloomers should not be divided in fall.

4. Have your soil tested and correct pH imbalances. However, don't add fertilizer until spring when new growth begins. During December, January and February, shorter periods of daylight allow plants to rest and gather energy for the coming season.

5. Dig and store tender bulbs, such as dahlias, when the foliage of the plant shrivels.

6. Cover tender plants at night when frost is expected.

7. Put your garden to bed clean. Pick up all leaves and debris so insects can't over-winter. Put your garden to bed as you would your child—with tender loving care—and you'll have less work in the garden come spring.

8. Water perennial beds thoroughly before they go dormant.

9. After the ground freezes, mulch the plants with 2 or 3 inches of straw, shredded bark, composted leaves, evergreen branches, etc.

10. Remove dead foliage and stems. It is not necessary to cut everything back in the fall. Standing stems help hold mulch in place and provide interest and color in the garden throughout the winter. Compost the garden debris.

Gardening Checklist

Rake the leaves for the compost pile, or shred them to use for mulch.

Fall is serious garden clean-up time! Rake up all debris so there are no hiding places for insects over winter. Chopped-up pine needles and oak leaves are perfect cover for tender plants, such as strawberries and perennials, that need winter protection.

Remove diseased, broken or damaged branches from shrubs and trees.

If a live Christmas tree is your fancy, dig its hole before the ground freezes and mulch well.

Keep feeding the birds with suet and seeds and provide water. To keep the water from freezing, use a heater. The winter months are often a desperate time for our feathered friends. So, once you start to feed them, don't stop.

Fall Leaf Color

Q. *Why do leaves change color in the fall?*

A. When the warm summer days begin to wane, the shorter days and cool weather cause the trees to stop producing chlorophyll. In other words, deciduous trees (the ones that lose their leaves in fall) slow down at the end of the growing season and start storing food in the roots instead of concentrating on making leaves. It's as if the trees know they soon will lose their leaves.

Different varieties of trees turn various shades of color, and it's this dazzling combination that makes the fall season so spectacular. Most of the intense color is supplied by only a few trees, such as sugar and red maples, sumac, dogwood, black gum, birches, hickory, beeches and oak trees.

The beginning of autumn is around September 20, and by the time the "frost is on the pumpkin," most trees are bare.

Fallen leaves are known as "nature's jewels" or "nature's fertilizer." They cover the forest floor with valuable nutrients, so use them to improve your soil.

Oak leaves are best for mulching and for covering shrubs and plants for winter protection because they are loaded with nutrients.

Fall Planting

Right now, during the fall season, is one of the best times of the year for planting shrubs, trees, bulbs and fall-flowering perennial plants.

Plants set out now have a chance to establish better root systems over winter, which should result in better top growth and healthier plants next year.

Speaking of planting, it's time to set out spring-flowering tulips, daffodils, hyacinths and crocus. Check with your local nursery, landscape or garden center, however, for exact timing and planting conditions for your area. For the best selection, choose these bulbs early.

If you're looking for colorful plants to add to the garden, now that the summer annuals and perennials have bloomed, this is a good time to plant flowering kale, flowering cabbage or winter-flowering pansies. Winter pansies are ideal to plant with your bulbs because the pansies reach their peak of beauty at the same time that the bulbs flower in springtime.

Whether you're planting trees, shrubs, bulbs or fall and winter flowering plants, be sure to select the right location. Ask the professionals at your local nursery or garden center whether they grow in full sunlight, partial sunlight, shade or full shade. Most plants will require good drainage.

One of the most important steps is to prepare the soil properly when planting any shrub, tree or flowering perennial plant. Always make the planting hole at least twice as wide and deep as the actual size of the plant. For example, if the root ball is a foot wide and a foot deep, make the planting hole 2 feet wide and 2 feet deep. Pour a bucket of water into the planting hole to check drainage. If the water sits in the hole, you will need to provide additional drainage either by making a sump hole next to the planting hole or tilling away the excess moisture.

Next, prepare the planting soil at the bottom of the hole by thoroughly mixing peat moss, compost or processed manure with your existing soil.

Be certain to set the plant at exactly the same depth as it was planted previously. In the case of bare-root shrubs and trees, there's often a soil mark on the stem or truck to use as a planting guide. Plants such as rhododendrons, camellias, azaleas and heather can be planted so the top of the root ball is level with the soil surface. Plant bulbs three times deeper than their diameter, with their pointed ends up.

Water thoroughly after planting; never depend on Mother Nature to do the job. Large trees or shrubs should be staked to prevent them from wind-whipping during strong fall, winter or early spring storms. Tender plants should be mulched over the root system to provide winter protection.

Fall Tips

As leaves start falling, add them to your compost pile. The resulting leaf mold is excellent for soil improvement and potting.

Remember that proper proportions of nitrogen and moisture are necessary to get the pile to "heat up," which is best done if the pile is built in a week or two. The addition of fresh green fodder—such as cut grass or young tender weeds—and a turning of the pile can usually get the friendly bacteria in a compost pile quickly working.

It's still possible to plant cool-weather crops: lettuce, spinach, kale and radishes—in fact, the taste of some actually benefit from the cooler temperatures. You might consider putting in new rose plants now. Although they will see little root growth this season, the soil will settle firmly around the roots through the fall and the plants will be well established and ready to start active growth as soon as the ground and air reach growing temperatures.

Most gardeners have far more time to properly prepare their rose beds now than in the hustle and bustle of spring.

This is the time to divide day lilies and phlox once they have flowered. It's also time to harvest and remove eggplant, tomatoes, corn, pepper and squash plants.

And don't forget to harvest herbs for drying just when the first few flowers open. Pick off 4 or 5 inches of tender new growth tips, wash in cold water, pat dry, tie the shoots loosely in small bunches and hang to dry in a cool, airy spot.

Although cold treatment is not necessary for paperwhites, you'll get better blooms by putting them in a cool, dark place for three weeks after potting them in pebbles and keeping the water around the lower half of the bulbs at all times. Then, bring into a bright spot to bloom.

If you use a cold frame for forcing bulbs, invert a pot over the top of the bulbs to keep out rodents. Set the potted bulbs down into the soil, up to the rim; then cover with a thick mulch of straw or leaves.

When potting tulips, place bulbs so the flat side of the bulb is toward the edge of the pot. Leaves fan out from this side and hide the skinny stems.

If you still have vegetables in the garden, it is important to watch for signs of frost. If frost seems imminent, harvest or cover your most frost-sensitive vegetables immediately, by flashlight if necessary.

Periodically check vegetables that you have in storage and remove swiftly any that show signs of spoilage.

A solution of non-detergent soap (2 tablespoons of flakes to 1 gallon of water) acts as a mild insecticide against scales and aphids on your houseplants. Sponge the leaves carefully; don't forget the underside—they make a dandy hiding place for insects.

Flea Beetles

Flea beetles may be hard to see, but you'll know when they've been dining on your plants. The leaves will be riddled with tiny holes. When these ravenous pests get a whiff of their favorite vegetables, your garden becomes their meal ticket. A flea beetle is tiny—only one-eighth to one-fifth of an inch long—but what an appetite!

Brussels sprouts, broccoli, cabbage, turnip, eggplant, tomato, potato, mustard and many other crops are their favorite snacks. Just like the "big 7" other pests that attack your garden, flea beetles are attracted to their particular plant by its odor. Although no cousin to fleas, they can leap explosively (better than a lizard) and do a vanishing act at the smallest disturbance.

What to do with a bug you can hardly see? One key is to understand its life cycle. I will let you in on a flea secret: The biggest damage comes after the adults have spent a delightful winter in your garden, hiding in plant residues, under leaves or even in the soil. When the warm days of spring arrive, they crawl out and begin feeding on whatever is available.

As voracious as the beetles are, you can make it hard for them to find their targets by diversifying your garden patch. Using mixed cropping, growing small gardens and using natural weed growth help mask odors that attract flea beetles.

Whatever control you use—herbs, clover mulch or intercropping—at the end of each season, clean up your garden properly; don't leave any flea meals around or supply your pests with comfortable winter quarters.

Geraniums

Q. *How should I over-winter my geraniums that I planted around my house?*

A. One way is to take cuttings by snapping off stems 2 to 3 inches long and stripping each stem of all but three or four of the top leaves.

Leave the stems exposed to air in the shade for a day or so to help form a callous on the end and to keep them from rotting. As an extra precaution against disease, dip the callused cuttings in rooting powder. Set each stem in moist, sterilized soil packed lightly and keep the soil moist, but never soggy.

After the roots develop (in about three weeks), place the pot in a bright, sunny window, but let the soil dry out between waterings and fertilize after new growth appears. Once your little plants are 5 inches tall, pinch back the stem tips to encourage branching so the plant develops into a lovely bushy specimen. In about four to five months, under proper growing conditions, the plants should start flowering.

Herb Pillows

Scented herb pillows are having a renaissance, and they make great holiday presents. After a day's work at the office or in the house, we can again enjoy that Victorian pleasure of a scented pillow to help ease our cares.

Choose the combination of herbs you wish for your pillow. Dry them well and add a fixative such as orris root (1 tablespoon of orris root to a pint of dried ingredients) and, naturally, a few drops of essential oil to achieve your favorite fragrance.

If you are creative, use up scraps of fabrics and trims for your herb pillow.

Cut two pieces of cloth 4 to 5 inches square; join pieces by sewing them together on three sides. Fill the pillow with your herbal combination and sew the remaining side. Slip the herb pillow inside your bed pillow—and, if you have a penchant for fantasy, sweet dreams!

Herbs, Harvesting and Using

To dry seeds such as anise, dill and caraway, pick the seed heads when mature but still green. If you wait for the seed to turn brown on the plant, many seeds will be lost when you pick them.

Make bundles of seed heads, as if they were regular herbs. Enclose them in a paper bag so that if they are jarred the seeds will fall into the bag.

Determining when herbs are dry enough can be tricky. There is no set time, since relative humidity and the amount of moisture in the leaves varies. You simply have to develop a feel for when the time is right. When the leaves are crinkly, usually they are ready.

To preserve color, herbs should be dried in as dark a place as quickly as possible.

The location for drying herbs is most important. A hot, dry upstairs room or attic is ideal. Avoid basements, since they are often damp.

You can also dry herbs in a garage—but if cars are parked there, the herbs should be placed in paper bags to prevent dust and fumes from settling on the leaves.

Leaf herbs—such as thyme, rosemary, basil and sage—should be picked before the plant begins to flower. If a plant is allowed to flower, the essential oils that provide the flavor in the leaves are diverted to flower and seed production. The result is herbs with a lot less zip.

The time of day you pick your herbs is important—in fact, it is the key. Wait for the sun to dry the morning dew, but don't wait too long, since the sun tends to vaporize the essential oils as the day goes on.

There are many ways to use your herbs in the kitchen. For instance, you can add a pinch of thyme, marjoram or oregano to a sauce before combining it with vegetables. Chop herbs fine so the flavoring oils can escape.

Herbs Indoors

Q. *I would like to grow some herbs indoors this winter on my windowsill. Which ones grow best during the winter months?*

A. The list of herbs that do not grow well indoors is short, such as summer savory, sweet basil, tarragon and lemon verbena. All are poor choices because they either go dormant or shed their leaves continually. Most other herbs do very well in a South-facing window. Sage, parsley and oregano can be grown in tiny pots and trimmed as needed for the kitchen. Other good selections, which need more growing space, are pots of sweet bay and rosemary.

In the onion family, chives, garlic cloves and onion sets can be started in pots and the emerging leaves clipped when a couple of inches high. If you have only an Eastern- or Western-facing window, try such candidates as lemon balm, peppermint and spearmint.

If you are bringing in herbs that have been summering outdoors, be sure that you're not importing white flies or other pests. For a potting medium, indoor herbs do best in a mixture of two parts potting soil to one part coarse sand or petite. I like to set my pots on trays lined with gravel to keep them from getting wet feet, should you overwater. Cool temperatures, around 60°F, especially at night, will keep your herbs at their very best.

Herbs, Winter

Before frost, pot up some parsley, chives and mint. Set in a cold frame, allow to freeze for four to six weeks, then bring to a sunny window. They will grow well all winter if given this period of chilling beforehand. Also be sure to bring indoors potted specimens of sweet bay, rosemary and myrtle before freezing.

Houseplants

Outdoors, frost and other inclement weather take away much of the garden at least once a year. Indoors, we have to simulate this natural cycle and not be afraid to pitch out seasonal flowers that are past their prime—poinsettias, paperwhites and florist chrysanthemums, for instance.

If houseplants have been outdoors for the summer, bring them inside when the temperature drops below 60°F. Check for bugs and slugs.

For a party, dress up your container plants, indoors or outdoors. Mulch the soil surface with moss, wood chips or pine needles. Gently wash the leaves with a little soap and water—we all like to look our best!

For nonstop bloom in a bright window or near a sunny one, group pots of African violets, *Begonia semperflorens* and hybrid Cape primroses (*Streptocarpus*). Keep the soil evenly moist and be sure temperatures range between 60°F and 75°F during the winter heating season (cold and hot drafts prevent bloom).

Hyacinths

No flower in the spring garden has quite the deliciously fragrant scent of hyacinths. To walk along a hyacinth-bordered path on a dew-kissed morning is to breathe in spring itself. No wonder they have been prized throughout history.

Hyacinths, it is believed, were first cultivated in Europe by the ancient Greeks and Romans. Both Homer and Virgil described their fragrance. In eighteenth-century France, Madame de Pompadour, mistress to King Louis XV, filled the gardens of Versailles with them. Inside, she forced hundreds of lush hyacinths "on glasses" to sweeten the palace air in midwinter.

The hyacinth enjoyed a vogue in Europe in the later eighteenth and early nineteenth centuries, grown not only indoors and out, but used as ornaments for women's fashions and even as a pharmaceutical. Labeled "the scourge of the Arabs," hyacinth juice mixed with wine was touted as a retardant of beard growth.

Europeans remain heady of hyacinths. And today, Americans, too, are gaining interest in this delightful garden treat.

Hyacinths are prized in the garden, especially along walks and near doors where their fragrance can be enjoyed.

Plant them in the fall. They're also easy to grow indoors. Hyacinths can even be grown indoors without soil in special hourglass-shaped glasses filled with water. Look to mail-order catalogs, garden centers and even supermarkets to find everything you need to grow these fragrant favorites.

Hydrangea: Drying the Flowers

Q. *This year, my hydrangeas (*H. macrophylla*) were amazing. Beautiful flowers in blue and pink. What do I do to preserve them so I can enjoy the flowers indoors during the winter months?*

A. It's not so simple a task to dry hydrangea flowers and prevent them from shattering without using special drying materials and special techniques. Follow my procedure or your hydrangea flowers will naturally dry to a brownish color which, by the way, isn't bad!

Cut the stems when the flowers are in full bloom and place them in a plastic container filled with ample silica gel to cover and dry the flowers. Silica gel is available at most hobby stores, craft stores and even at some pharmacies. Seal the container for ten to 14 days. The flowers may lose some of their color when dried. Be careful. You must handle them gently, because they'll be very fragile.

If you want the flowers to last for years, immerse the dry heads in a liquid foliage preserver called Forever Natural Foliage Preserver for seven to ten days. The finished flowers will be pliable and will not break. Craft stores sell these products, too. Good luck!

Iris

The iris has always been one of my favorite flowers because of its exquisite form and color. They can be easily divided and planted in different areas of your garden. Of course, the ideal time to do this is in the late summer or early fall, after the plants have bloomed. This can easily be accomplished, providing the roots are kept out of the sun and they are re-planted immediately.

Iris should be divided and transplanted whenever the rhizomes are growing over one another because of overcrowding.

Dividing an iris is easy, but there are a few basic steps for you to follow.

Select the clump you wish to divide; then cut the foliage down to a height of about 6 to 8 inches.

Next dig up the clump, but do so carefully, taking care not to break up the rhizomes or roots. Wash the roots and rhizomes thoroughly but be sure not to let the roots dry out while separating. Using a sharp knife, separate into clumps of three or four fans. Now the fans are ready for planting.

Prepare your soil to a depth of 10 to 12 inches with compost or peat moss. Be sure to dig a hole large enough so that the roots are not overcrowded. The rhizomes should be planted just below the soil surface.

Finally, cover the iris, making sure the rhizome is tightly packed and the soil is evenly moist, not soggy.

Don't make the iris divisions too small—it delays blooming.

Iris, Bearded

Q. *My bearded irises looked awful last summer so, thinking they were overcrowded, I decided to divide them. However, when I dug them up I was surprised to see a number of holes in the rhizomes, obviously the dirty work of iris borers. What do you suggest I do to control these borers?*

A. Iris rhizomes that are badly infested are best chucked out. Irises that are not infested can be salvaged by digging out the pinkish larvae (use a pocket knife) and trimming away any damaged areas. I always soak damaged rhizomes for half an hour in a 10 percent solution of household bleach and water. Then dust them with powdered sulfur and let the cut surfaces air-dry in a shady area for several hours before replanting.

For best results, clean up dried iris stems, leaves and other debris in the fall. This will help eliminate any over-wintering eggs. If you miss any, they will hatch by late spring. The tiny larvae crawl up the young iris leaves and feed, producing telltale notches. They then enter the leaves, producing pinpoint holes. As the larvae slowly work their way down toward the rhizomes, they leave a ragged, water-soaked tunnel in their wake. When you spot such a tunnel, simply squash the borer inside by pressing the leaf between the thumb and forefinger. When the leaves of your iris are 5 to 6 inches tall, spray with an all-natural insecticide.

Japanese Beetles

Q. *What is the best way to keep Japanese beetles off roses, especially white roses? A friend told me that if you put a white bowl filled with water near the plants, the beetles will all race there to mate. Is this really the only way to keep these pests away? Somehow it would seem to compound rather than solve the problem—unless they get so carried away they drown!*

A. The Japanese beetle (*Papillia japonica*) is a native of Japan and was first found in the United States in 1916, in Cimmaminson, New Jersey. When introduced to uninfested areas, these beetles increase very quickly over a period of about three years, then decrease again to a point where control is possible. Until this devastating plague passes, though, the best method I know of is to pick the little devils off by hand. The water trick will also work if there is a layer of kerosene on top. By the way, beetles prefer a yellow bowl!

Kalanchoe

Q. *Why won't my kalanchoe bloom again? I received a gorgeous plant in full bloom last January, but since then I haven't had a single flower. I grow it under fluorescent lights (two 40-watt tubes) with my African violets. It gets dry between watering and I fertilize about once a month. What's my problem?*

A. Like another holiday plant, the poinsettia, holiday kalanchoe needs short days in order to set buds and bloom. Although you don't say how long you keep the fluorescent light on, my guess is they're on too long. Kalanchoe needs six weeks of short days (at least 14 hours of complete darkness) in order to flower. If the fluorescent lights are on longer than this, or if you turn on room lamps at night during the six weeks of short days, the plant simply won't bloom. During this short-day period (in the fall, late September), put your plant in a dark closet or room for 14 hours each day.

Keep the plant in a warm, sunny spot during the day. Water normally, but do not fertilize. Fertilizer should be given only during periods of active growth—never during bud set and bloom.

Landscape Fabric

More than just an ugly eyesore, weeds battle with plants, shrubs and trees for water and essential nutrients. Gardeners and professional landscapers alike used to fight weeds the time-tested way, with a hoe or spade, or even more painstakingly, with their bare hands.

Then, plastic bags were laid on top of the soil, but this proved a poor substitute. Plastic allowed too much water runoff and interrupted the flow of air and water. Poor, soured soil often resulted. Worse, plastic only blocked weeds temporarily, as it tore easily and soon disintegrated.

Finally, as the environment and its well-being transformed from a minor concern into an international issue, homeowners, municipal park managers and landscapers alike realized there had to be a more effective, safer way. That better way turned out to be landscape fabrics.

Landscape fabrics, barriers designed to prevent the growth of weeds in the soil, are produced either by weaving fibers together at right angles or by bonding short or continuously spun fibers together through heat bonding, needle-punching, spin bonding or other processes (nonwoven). The result is a fabric with the ability to block weeds and harmful sunlight without disturbing Mother Nature.

Today's multipurpose landscape fabrics, available at most major garden centers, are easy to cut with a pair of scissors or a knife, don't unravel and can last for several years despite direct exposure to the sun.

Commercial landscapers have been using fabrics successfully for years as a weed deterrent and are continually finding new places to use them. Fabrics are often utilized by professionals when transplanting or installing new plants in a landscape formation and when erecting or repairing walkways, patios and decks.

Today many do-it-yourself gardeners have also discovered the fabric's many applications and its cost effectiveness. According to recent studies, people who purchase the fabrics report great results and note that they would buy the product again.

A well-made fabric is ideal for weed control anywhere, including around trees, plants and shrubs and even in potted plants. Although more costly than the black plastic sheeting many people still buy, landscape fabrics are resistant to tears, and because they "breathe" (meaning that air and water can pass through), decorative mulches laid atop the fabric won't wash away with the water buildup caused by rain, hose watering or sprinklers.

Because fabrics help soil to retain moisture by blocking sunlight and slowing down the evaporation process, covered areas require less watering, an important factor in drought-stricken areas where rain and water are limited.

If you want to achieve results similar to those of a professional when caring for your own yard, look to landscape fabrics. They are readily available at local garden centers, hardware stores and chain retailers.

Lawns: Fall Feeding

Late fall (late November/early December) lawn fertilization promotes root and rhizome development without producing excessive top growth. Top growth is best supported by a healthy and extensive root system. Concurrently, a good root system allows for better nutrient intake, increased turf density and spring growth.

Furthermore, less water and fertilizer are required with a deep-root system. This application fills the need for any early spring feeding of turf.

The type of fertilizer to be applied at this time is important to note. A complete, slow-growth, controlled-release type is a must!

With a quick-release one, the nitrogen component can readily leach past the root zone and ultimately into the ground water. The amount to use is 1 pound of actual nitrogen per 1,000 square feet of lawn.

If your soil has not been tested for pH in the last few years, take it to your local cooperative extension office now and beat the spring rush.

Leaf Management

Autumn leaves and grass clippings make up 3 percent of the trash Americans send to landfills each year. Faced with shrinking space and rising costs, many towns have already begun charging for curbside pickup—as much as $1 per bag or more—and others are expected to follow suit.

For homeowners already affected, this represents a significant expense. But even where free pickup is still offered, throwing away bagged, unprocessed leaves and grass clippings is burdensome on the town and the environment. It's also a waste of good raw material for your garden. Leaves and grass clippings are nature's way of replenishing the soil.

The availability of lightweight, inexpensive electric shredders has made it possible for anyone to process their own yard debris for compact disposal or, better yet, to use as compost and mulch.

The best machine around for the purpose is called a Leaf Eater and it's available at local retailers everywhere.

The machine shreds grass clippings and fallen leaves (wet or dry) as fast as they can be loaded into its roomy hopper. In seconds, leaves are reduced to a fraction of their original volume—in other words, what used to fill eight bags now fits in one.

Once you've shredded leaves and grass clippings, you can put them to good use

around the yard. A 4- to 6-inch layer of shredded leaves or grass will protect tender plants over winter and help preserve soil moisture, reducing the need to water.

Leaf mulch is excellent for roses and evergreens, especially shallow-rooted rhododendrons and azaleas. Use it on bulb beds to prevent alternate thawing and freezing, which can heave bulbs out of the ground. As mulch decomposes it will improve the soil.

It's advisable to add a little garden lime to areas where leaf mulch is used. This will offset the acidic condition created.

Composted leaves and grass clippings make wonderful soil enrichers. Composting is easy, odorless, takes little space and is one of the most responsible approaches to the growing disposal problem.

Layers of shredded leaves, grass clippings, vegetable leftovers from the kitchen and other organic debris will break down in a compost pile over a season, even faster in one of the new compost tumblers.

Shredders and Leaf Eaters are available at hardware stores, garden centers and other chain retailers around the country.

Lettuce

As soon as the worst of summer heat is over, plant a variety of leaf lettuce for salads in autumn. Plant either in the garden or in cold frames, right up to killing frost.

Lily Multiplication

Q. *A friend of mine gave me seeds and "scales" (the outer layers of the bulb) from a prized Oriental lily. What must I do to get the same flowers my friend has to bloom?*

A. To be certain to get the same flower, plant only the scales. Unfortunately, seeds of hybrid lilies will not come true to type and will only produce a mixture of colors.

If the lily is not a hybrid, it's a different story. You can use either scales or seeds to grow new plants. From seeds or scales, the technique or procedure to grow new lily plants is the same. Both need cold treatment; however, if you put the scales outdoors, they may not germinate in autumn. During the fall, sow both seeds and scales in flats filled with damp vermiculite and cover with a clear plastic bag. Place the flats in a 70-degree room for two months or until you see growth shooting through the soil.

Oriental lilies then need a cool treatment to induce dormancy. Place the flats in the fridge for six to eight weeks. When you remove them, place them under grow lights until May; then plant them in a nursery bed of well-drained, fertile soil. Keep the plants shaded and well watered. Plants grown from seed will flower in three to four years, while plants grown from scales should flower in two years.

Lily of the Valley

If your lily of the valley bed is too crowded, now is the time to dig, divide and replant. First replenish the soil by spading in 2 inches or 3 inches of compost and sphagnum peat moss, plus a sprinkling of bone meal.

Marigolds

Q. *Last summer my marigolds bloomed beautifully. However, by August the leaves and flowers began, one by one, to turn brown and die. I noticed small webs on the leaves. What's this all about?*

A. The webs, of course, are the telltale sign that you have an advanced stage of spider-mite infestation. Always keep in mind (during fall clean-up) that spider mites winter on plant debris in the soil and attack many garden plants when the temperatures are hot and the humidity low. Marigolds are one of the mites' favorite dishes. They reproduce every two weeks throughout the summer, becoming a major problem in the flowerbed.

To control spider mites, clean up and destroy plant debris in the fall. (I am repeating myself because it's the key to success.) During the growing season, remove all dead bottom leaves where mites love to hide. If you buy transplants, start with healthy ones; keep them stress-free and, most important, make sure the plants are properly watered.

Although spider mites are hard to see without using a magnifying glass, early signs are pale-colored leaves with tiny white holes, indicating those devils are feeding. By the time you see webbing, it's usually too late for control.

Once you have spider mites in the garden, spray your plants twice a week with insecticidal soap, making sure to cover the leaf tops and bottoms. Spraying keeps leaves moist and kills the spider mites by suffocation.

Q. *I would like to know how to make seeds from my marigolds and how to store seed for use next year.*

A. Usually it does not pay to collect the seeds of annual flowers. Keep in mind the fact that cross-pollination can occur in your garden and some seeds may actually be hybrids and so will not produce plants identical with the parent. When seeds are to be held for any length of time, they should be stored in a dry place with a range of temperature varying from 45° to 50°F. The viability depends upon seed variety, but storage conditions are a major factor in preserving quality seeds successfully.

Mulching

A mulch is a covering applied to the surface of the soil to increase crop yield, prevent weeds, retain soil moisture and restrict the chance of lawn-mower damage to tree trunks. There is a great variety of mulch materials used by gardeners with varying success;

however, you must always mulch with what works best for you.

Which mulch material you use depends on appearance, uniformity, cost, availability, ease of handling and rate of breakdown. The mulch material used in landscape planting should not look out of place or compete with your precious plants. Dull, dark materials look best, although light-colored stones are attractive with dark plant stems and dark-green grass.

Useful mulches should be available in quantity to ensure a supply. Cost and availability are, naturally, the key. The thickness of the mulch layer and unit cost determine the overall expense.

Mulches should be easy to apply. Plastic films are easy to lay before planting but difficult to apply among established plants, especially if the wind is blowing. Granular or lumpy materials are easy to spread from a bag, while stringy materials in bales may be hard to separate and apply evenly. The best value of mulches is secured by even application.

Mulches should last at least for the season, which may be only once in the annual flower garden. After this one season, rapid disintegration after incorporating into the soil is best.

In landscape plantings, a more durable cover is needed. Organic mulches that break down rapidly need supplemental applications of nitrogen to compensate for decay.

Rain, wind, children, pets and other animals can displace a mulch. Light materials can easily be blown away, so it is helpful to water down immediately after applying.

Where flooding or surface erosion is likely, use a mulch that will allow moisture to go into the soil and not easily float away. Coarse materials, such as stones, always invite children to pick them up and throw them onto the lawn, driveway or even at windows— so don't use these mulches where children can easily get their tiny hands on them. They're too inviting.

Mulches can control weeds by their smothering growth. The larger the weeds, the thicker or more resistant to penetration the mulch layer should be. Some perennial weeds are very difficult to control once they are established, so be an early bird and apply mulch as soon as possible.

Distributing soil moisture evenly is another benefit of mulches. Mulch reduces water loss by evaporation from the soil surface. The advantage of thin layers of mulch is that rain or irrigation water penetrates the soil more easily, replenishing the soil lost by evaporation or plant use.

Mulches act as an insulating layer and reduce fluctuations in soil temperature. A mulch can keep soil cooler during the summer and warmer during the winter.

Mulches used around trunks of trees and shrubs help prevent damage from lawn mowers. Continual injury to the bark of trees can eventually cause the tree to die.

As organic mulches decompose, they improve the soil structure and add nutrients to the surrounding soil, increasing your crop harvest.

Here's how to make the most of the organic matter in your garden:
- Don't till to create a clean-looking surface with fine tilth. Mix the organic material into the top 6 inches, then stop.
- Shredded or chopped leaves or stalks require less tillage than unshredded ones. Compost needn't be tilled in at all.
- Don't till routinely for weed control; instead, use mulches and constant hoeing.
- In fall, leave residues on the surface where they rot more slowly and prevent erosion.

Paperwhite Narcissus

Plant paperwhite narcissus bulbs in shallow bowls of pebbles and water, or simply in well-moistened sphagnum peat moss. Set to root for two or three weeks in a cool, dark place. Then bring to a bright, sunny window and watch them grow. They'll start to bloom in just a few weeks. Start some every seven to ten days and you'll have sweet flowers to smell over a long season.

Q. *When and how should I plant paperwhite narcissus bulbs in order to have flowers for the December holidays?*

A. Timing can be tricky, owing to variable temperatures from year to year. Generally speaking, a period of two to three weeks is needed in a cool (60°-70°F), dark place for the bulbs to form a thrifty root system. It takes another two to three weeks in a sunny, cool place for the leaves to grow and the flower buds to turn into clusters of deliciously sweet-smelling blooms. Incidentally, you can grow paperwhites the time-honored way, in pebbles and water, but many of us now find it easier to plant them and the similar yellow-flowered Soleil d'Or in shallow pots or flats filled with well-moistened sphagnum peat moss. More important than the kind of medium is supplying the roots with moisture at all times; if they dry out, blooms will dry up without ever opening. Forced bulbs can't be brought to bloom again in pots. Hardy types such as tulips, daffodils and hyacinths can be planted in a mixed perennial border or half-wild garden outdoors. Tender bulbs such as the paperwhites are best discarded after flowering.

Peonies, Transplanting

Q. *My cousin's house—that's next door—is going to be demolished, along with some 25 peony bushes. I long to save them, but how would I transplant such large bushes?*

A. Fall is the ideal time to divide and re-plant peonies. The easiest way to move them and create new plants at the same time is to divide the old bushes first. A 30-year-old peony, for example, may have a root ball 3 feet in diameter, so you can create ten to 15 divisions. However, each division should have three to eight eyes, or upward-pointing new growths, on their brown roots.

Once the root ball has been divided, plant divisions in full sun in well-drained soil. Set the eyes no deeper than 2 inches below the soil surface. Keep the peonies well-watered the first several years and mulch with a 2- to 4-inch layer of bark. Snip off any flower buds that form the first year to encourage strong root growth. Let the peonies flower the second year, but don't be surprised if it takes at least several years to get full-size flowers with the color and shape that you remembered from the mother plant.

Perennial Flowers

Q. *Do you have to water dormant perennial flowers in winter, or do you just cover them?*

A. No watering at that time is needed; your plants are dormant (sleeping). Simply cover them after the ground is frozen. I like to use pine needles for a covering because I always have so many in the fall.

Perennial Flowers: Dividing

Fall is the time to divide perennials.

It's the new math of gardening: You can multiply your plants by dividing them. Dividing your perennials (also called propagating) allows you to create smaller plants to fill in other areas of your garden.

But perennial division isn't simply a way to get more plants. It's also the best method for keeping your perennials in top shape. That's because most perennials need to be divided every several years to bloom to their full potential. For spring and summer bloomers, fall is the best time to divide.

Why do perennials need a break? They need to be divided for the same reason you need that cup of coffee in the morning—for the rejuvenating effect. Perennials get bigger and better each year, but can grow too big for their own good and overcrowd other plants. And, if you don't divide some perennials, they'll stop blooming.

For example, when peonies need dividing, they no longer expend energy on producing blooms, though the foliage comes up every year. Other plants, such as lamb's ears or coreopsis, die in the center but continue to grow outward.

The plants that divide best are those perennials that grow in big clumps with fleshy root stocks, such as day lilies and peonies. Other division candidates include tuberous plants, such as irises, and perennials that develop crowns, such as heuchera and ajuga.

Here are ten easy steps for dividing perennials:

1. Dig up the area around the plant with a sharp border spade. You are going to sever some of the roots, so brace yourself—the plant will survive.
2. Gently remove the clump from the ground and set it on top of a cloth or hauling bag.
3. Place two pitchforks, back to back, on the center of the clump.
4. Pry apart the clump into two pieces.
5. Continue dividing each of the pieces, making sure each division section has a shoot to grow upward and roots to grow downward.
6. Remove any dead or woody parts of the plant. Also, clip back about half of the foliage on the plant.
7. Immediately plant the divisions. You can place the mother plant back in the same spot she occupied before the division.
8. Water and fertilize each division well.
9. In areas that get frost, mulch around the base of the plant with shredded bark or leaves.
10. Continue to water well to help roots grow strong until the ground freezes.

Perennials from Fall-Sown Seeds

Many plants that are native to temperate areas of the world have seeds that need a moist, cold period before they sprout.

You can grow these seeds by sowing them in pots and setting them out in late fall or winter. This is a popular pastime for many green-fingered gardeners all over the world. This treatment is known as stratification, because it replicates the natural environment the seeds need to germinate.

This method works beautifully for starting seeds of many favorite perennials, such as glove flower, colchicum, bleeding heart, monkshood and garden phlox. It's useful, too, for starting the seeds of many fall-ripening shrubs and trees, such as lilacs, dogwoods, viburnums and some species of roses.

Here is the process you should follow to start your seed in order to ensure success.

Sow the seeds: You can use flats or pots for this project (4-inch pots are best). Use a Pro-Mix commercial potting soil. It has all the nutrients to make seeds grow to perfection.

Moisten the soil and fill the containers, tamping down to a half-inch of the rims. Sow seeds a half-inch apart and cover with a thin layer of soil.

Label each container with the plant name so you know which one is which. Water the pots well to ensure proper moisture, which is a necessary prelude to the chilling period.

Have patience—wait for germination: Check your seedlings often and water frequently if the top of the soil mix feels dry.

As days get longer and spring approaches, you should see signs of growth. Of course, different varieties will germinate at different times. For example, some may appear in early spring, while others do so in late spring. Some may even take up to a year or more to appear.

As the seedlings sprout, move them to an area where they'll receive bright but indirect sun.

Watch for snails or slugs. They have voracious appetites and can devour all your seedlings overnight.

Transport or thin seedlings: When seedlings have grown their second set of true leaves, transplant or thin them to prevent overcrowding.

If you don't need many plants, simply transplant them, one per container, into a 3-inch wide pot filled with moist potting mix. Use a fork to gently lift the seedlings out of their original containers and tease them apart gently.

To avoid damaging their stems, handle the seedlings by their leaves. Water the seedlings and place them in direct sun for a few days to recover.

After a week or so, place seedlings where they receive morning sun. Start fertilizing once a week.

Finally, into the garden: By late summer or early autumn, many of your treasures will be large enough and strong enough to be set out in the garden. Transplant on a cool day and water gently for a few weeks afterward, until they are well established.

Some of your slower-growing varieties may not be large enough to move yet so keep them in a cold frame over the winter and move them outdoors come spring.

Perovskia (Russian Sage)

The Perennial Plant Association has recently selected perovskia as the Perennial Plant of the Year. Commonly called Russian sage, perovskia has silver stems and small, gray foliage. It reaches heights of nearly 4 feet and is categorized as a sub-shrub with a woody base. The leaves are barely toothed, 1 ½ inches long and, when crushed, have the scent of sage. Small, light blue to lavender flowers are arranged in whorls along the stem and the spikes are often 12 inches long or more. Perovskia begins flowering in July and often lasts throughout September. In winter, Russian sage provides interest in the garden with its silver-gray foliage and stems.

Although there are seven species of perovskia, only a few are cultivated and available. *Perovskia atriplicifolia,* the most readily available, is native to Afghanistan and Tibet and is a member of the mint family. However, the *Perovskia atriplicifolia* currently sold in the U.S. has been identified as a hybrid between *P. atriplicifolia* and *P. abrotanoides,* and appears to be identical with *Perovskia* 'Blue Spire.'

Perovskia atriplicifolia grows best in sunny, dry locations and is one of the most heat- and drought-resistant perennials available. It is easily grown in hardiness Zones 3 through 8, but it will perform best in areas with consistently warm summers, even when the humidity is high. In shaded areas, plants will grow, but tend to be leggy and sprawling. The only condition that perovskia resents is poor drainage, especially in winter. For best results, plants should be cut back nearly to the ground each spring before new growth begins.

Perovskia is most easily propagated by 3- to 4-inch-long stem cuttings that root easily in sand or in an equal volume mixture of peat moss and perlite. If placed under mist, remove immediately after roots begin to form since cuttings will be lost if they remain moist for too long. To avoid the use of mist altogether, plastic may be placed over the cuttings to maintain humidity. Rooting generally occurs in two to three weeks. Propagation by division is possible, but slow, or by seed. Seeds require a short cold treatment of about 30 days. Rooted cuttings or seedlings should be planted out in the spring or early enough in the fall to allow sufficient root development before winter freezing. They grow best in neutral to alkaline soils.

Perovskia is normally purchased as a potted plant. At planting, loosen the soil in an area two to three times the diameter of the pot. Thoroughly work in a complete fertilizer like 10-6-4 or a 10-10-10 at the rate of 2 to 3 pounds per 100 square feet into the top 6 inches to 8 inches of soil in the planting area. In addition, 4 inches to 6 inches of leaf mold or other organic compost can be spread over the planting area and thoroughly worked into the soil to a depth of 6 to 8 inches. Composts are particularly valuable in improving soil structure and water-holding capacity. Finally, remove the plant from the pot and set it at the same depth as in the pot. Firm the soil around the plant and water it thoroughly.

Commonly available perovskia cultivars are: 'Blue Mist,' 'Blue Haze,' 'Blue Spire,' and 'Longing.' The earliest flowering cultivar is 'Blue Mist' which, along with 'Blue Haze,' has lighter-blue flowers than the species. 'Blue Spire' has deep-purple flowers and larger panicles. 'Longing' has stiff, upright stems and a more formal appearance than the species. A new cultivar, 'Filigran,' has deeply cut foliage, bright-blue flowers and is more compact than other cultivars.

In the landscape, perovskia's bright-blue flowers are particularly striking when planted along with white-flowered species like *Phlox paniculata* 'Mt. Fuji.' And, besides its attributes as a landscape plant, perovskia is also a reasonably good cut flower. Other landscape uses include massing or filler in the border as well as being used to separate dominant colors.

Pine Trees

Q. *I have four 8-year-old Monterey pine trees whose needles are turning brown, and I notice many small round holes in the bark. How can I solve this problem? I live in Walnut Creek, California.*

A. The California five-spined bark beetles (*Ipspapa confusus*) is the culprit. The area you live in is outside the native coastal range of Monterey pines and the hot summers and cold winters there stress the trees. Once a bark beetle finds a stressed Monterey pine, forget it—the tree is usually dead within a year.

Bark beetles are active year-round in California. The adult males drill very small holes in pine tree trunks and emit a pheromone that attracts female beetles, which, in turn, lay eggs under the bark of the tree.

Both adults and larvae are thought to carry a fungus that clogs the tree's conductive tissue, causing the tree to die.

Once your tree is home to the bark beetles there is absolutely nothing you can do to stop the infestation.

If your pine needles are red, lime-green or yellow and you notice the holes, you might just as well cut the tree down because death is imminent.

I suggest growing similar pines that are better adapted to the heat and cold of Walnut Creek and not so susceptible to bark-beetle infestation. Good choices for planting are Allepo pine, Canary Island pine and Italian stone pine. If you have Monterey pines that are not yet infested, keep the trees well-watered and only prune between November and February when beetles are less active. For some reason, tree pruning attracts the beetles.

Pollinators

Q. *Just what types of plants need to be pollinated?*

A. Any crop that you eat the fruit of, such as melons, beans, tomatoes, cucumbers, peppers, squash, apples and berries, is pollinated by bees.

Pumpkins and other cucurbits (zucchini, squash and the like) will not form fruits at all unless their pollen is spread from flower to flower by insects, simply because the male (pollen) and the female (the ovary that eventually becomes a fruit) parts are in separate flowers and their pollen is just too sticky and heavy to be carried from male flower to female flower by the wind.

Of course, the pollen of many weeds is carried by the wind. Under these circumstances, the pollinator for the above crops mentioned is a solitary bee known as the squash bee.

Cucumbers need to be pollinated by insects (mostly by bees) or they will not set fruit just like squash. The more bees that visit your cucumber flowers, the bigger and better cucumbers for the table.

Watermelons, cantaloupes and melons can set a few fruits without the help of insects, but once again the best pollinators are bees, which mean more fruit.

Eggplants, peppers and tomatoes can also form fruit without the help of insects. But with the help of insects, especially bumblebees, these fabulous crops yield even more.

Researchers have found that the more pollen a tomato flower receives, the faster the fruit develops, which means it gets to the table before you know it.

Why are bees the most important pollinators in the world? Simply because they are specially equipped to pollinate certain plants. They have fuzzy bodies that pollen clings to, and even their tiny hind legs are equipped for carrying loads of pollen. Their reward, of course, is the food they gather (nectar and pollen that contain nutrients).

Many people think the purpose of a garden flower's beauty is to provide delight to the gardener; alas, that's not so. The truth is that the beautiful markings are there for the pollinators: bees, flies and other bugs.

The colors are guidelines for the pollinators, like lights on an airfield or lighthouse.

Some flower colors reflect ultraviolet light in wavelengths that are only visible to pollinating insects, but invisible to the human eye.

Even the form of a flower can be geared toward its pollinator. For example, look into the delicate blossoms of flowers like Queen Anne's lace and you can see there's a drop of nectar in the bottom of the flower; this allows flies, wasps, sweat bees, beetles and ants with short "proboscises" (a sort of tongue) to reach the nectar and move pollen around while feeding.

Flowers that are trumpet-shape or deep-cut, such as a trumpet vine, are designed so that only creatures with long proboscises like bumblebees, honeybees, moths, butterflies and hummingbirds can reach the nectar in these flowers and pollinate them.

The way a flower is shaped often forces its pollinator to perform some gymnastics to get to the nectar. Thus, while doing so, the pollinator will have to brush up against the part of the plant containing its pollen.

Bees have to be very adaptable, sometimes hanging upside down in a flower to enjoy a tasty snack; and as they do, their "rummies" are sprinkled with pollen as they shake the flower.

And when hummingbirds gently flutter in front of a fuchsia flower, their tiny feathers get wet with sticky pollen from the anthers (the pollen-producing parts) sticking out of the flower.

Be good to your pollinators by helping them as much as you can. Without them our gardens would be forlorn.

Pond Gardening

If you have a fish pond you have been enjoying all summer, now is the time to put it to bed for the winter. It's relatively easy to accomplish, if a few important steps are followed:

- If the pool is in-ground and at least 16 inches deep, it should be kept full of water over the winter.
- Pumps and filters can be left in their place for the winter, either running or not.
- Fish can be removed or left in over the winter; the latter is easier. Continue feeding them two days a week through the middle of October and one day a week until the end of November. After that, nothing at all (poor dears!).
- It is important to keep all falling leaves out of a pool that contains fish. The gasses

emitted from decomposing leaves are deadly and are the prime cause of death to fish.

- If you have tropical waterlilies, annual replacement is a must. These flowers are beautiful; they bloom profusely all summer and come in fantastic colors. But they are tender and should have been discarded by now. Some people say that tropical waterlilies can be brought into a greenhouse for the winter and returned to the pool next spring. This is not true. However, hardy waterlilies can be left where they are all winter. If the container in which they're planted is raised near the surface of the water, put it back down into the deep end of the pool so that the roots do not freeze as the pool freezes.

Once the deep freeze sets in, the pool is set for winter—and nothing more needs to be done until April or early May.

Pots, Terra-cotta

Q. *Can terra-cotta pots be left outdoors over the winter?*

A. Terra-cotta flower pots will weather severe winters; however, you may risk losing yours to flaking and frost cracks. Clay pots absorb water easily but when the water in the pot freezes, it expands and the pot may be damaged. If you have an area like an attached garage where temperatures don't drop below freezing, I suggest placing your pots inside during the cold winter months.

Pumpkins

Q. *What does the "frost is on the pumpkin" mean?*

A. The "frost is on the pumpkin" is a saying that means the end of the year has come and it is harvest time. The saying has been used to symbolize the end of life, but I like to think that it simply refers to a time of year. To quote a part of the famous poem by James Whitcomb Riley, "When the Frost is on the Punkin": "The strawstack in the medder, and the reaper in the shed / The hosses in they're stalls below—the clover overhead! / O, it sets my hart a-clickin' like the tickin' of a clock / When the frost is on the punkin and the fodder's in the shock!"

Q. *Please let me know what kind of pumpkins are edible, and which make the best pies.*

A. The best pumpkins for making pies, soups, breads, puddings and whatever else you want are 'Lady Godiva,' 'Triple Treat,' 'Spirit Hybrid' or 'Autumn Gold Hybrid.' The fleshy fruit of these varieties makes for delicious eating!

Q. *How do people manage to get the whole pumpkin seed out of its shell in one piece?*

A. A raw pumpkin seed has a tough, leathery outer coating and a very soft, moist inner seed. If you try to rip or smash the shell, you are sure to damage the delicate embryo. Therefore, in order to get the whole pumpkin seed out in one piece, you must first let it dry thoroughly. Put the seeds out in the sun for at least a week, until the exterior becomes crisp and brittle. At the same time, the interior will dry and shrink slightly. Then you can easily crack the shell and remove the dried seed.

Raspberry Health

Q. *My red raspberries have always been healthy, but this year some of the leaves are curling with brown blotches on the tops and yellow powdery spots on the undersides. What causes this sort of problem?*

A. Your raspberries appear to have a fungus, "yellow rust." This ordinary disease over-winters on the canes and old leaves on the ground. A severe infestation of this fungus disease lowers production and weakens the canes.

To control yellow rust, clean up and destroy old leaves in fall, including leaves that have not fallen from the canes. One application of lime-sulfur spray in spring, when the tender buds are showing green—but before the new growth is a half-inch long—will help control the disease for the entire summer. Next time you plant red raspberries, try growing a yellow, rust-tolerant variety called 'Chilli-wack.'

Rhubarb

After frost, mulch beds of rhubarb and asparagus with 3 to 4 inches of compost or well-rotted manure. It will improve your crop next spring.

Romantic Garden

Since that long-ago dawn when the first spring flower bloomed, the garden has been associated with love and romance. In literature and in landscaping, the garden has endured as a perfect setting for lovers to meet.

For modern romantics, fall is the perfect time to see how their garden measures up. It is then—as the garden is still green—when you can see where romantic possibilities lie. Perhaps a lily pond could go here, or a shaded grove or a snug gazebo there. Fall is also time to plant shrubs and trees and tulips, daffodils and other bulbs that bloom in spring.

Sense of Privacy

I feel that privacy is an important element in creating a sense of romance in the garden. For discretion, it can be a natural barrier such as a hedge or a fence. Ideally, I would want an arbor over the entrance or exit or both, with the entire garden guarded by lovely hedges, such as yews.

I feel that a romantic garden should delight the senses—the eyes, the nose and the ears. The sound of running water is incredibly soothing. It makes you feel cool and refreshed (it also masks the intrusive sounds of the outside world). In a romantic garden, a pond with a waterfall or burbling fountain is a must.

Fragrant plantings that fill the air are perfect for mood setters. Some hints: scented hyacinths planted along a walk in spring; perfumed lilies in the summer; and, of course, fragrant roses are a must.

To add color, spring-flowering bulbs offer a marvelous choice. Spring is the season of romance. I prefer the dreamy softness of pastel shades.

I think some of the exotic tulips would be perfect, say parrot tulips such as 'Estella Rijnveld.' Multiflowering tulips such as 'Georgette' (red-flecked yellow) and peony-flowered 'Angelique' (pale pink) would be perfect, too.

As a companion to tulip plantings, try fragrant catmint and nepeta; they are wonderful 8-inch plants with spikes of tiny blue flowers and foliage shaped like a pinky nail. Other companions should include hardy pansies and sweet alyssum, either blue, white or pink, or better yet, mixed.

The romantic garden should have surprises—paths that twist and turn, with something to delight the senses around every corner. I think memory is really what inspires a person's sense of romance. I have girlhood memories of riding my pony past daffodil fields on Sunday morning family outings.

To re-create that romantic-nostalgic feeling in a garden, I suggest a profusion of plants. There would have to be lots of vines and climbing roses, including lots of flowers, waves of tulips and daffodils, and an abundance of honeysuckle and morning glories for summer.

In spring, a sense of depth would be essential to creating the romantic effect. I would mix plants of various heights and plan for successive waves of color that would feature fragrant JanBos hyacinths. These are very deep fuchsia with extremely plump plumes, and next would bloom the tulips that would be planted in droves. These would likely be rich pastel favorites such as pink 'Elizabeth Arden' and peachy 'Apricot Beauty.' Their blooms would be followed by waves of alliums.

I'm mad for purple, blue and yellow alliums. To me they look like stars and clouds. I especially love *Allium christophii*. It has an enormous blue umbel on top of a sturdy stalk and florets that are spread out, forming sort of loose, fluffy balls.

My companion plantings would include yellow alchemilla and old-fashioned double-orange pansies. These look great below magenta-purple "drumstick" alliums.

For the holidays, create a romantic garden indoors by forcing bulbs for the holidays and late-winter blooms. Buy bulbs that are marked "good for forcing" (pre-cooled), and plant pots and containers with these fragrant beauties. 'Tête-à-Tête' daffodils are fabulous on a windowsill. 'Little Jack Snipe' daffodils are also great. They're so jaunty looking, like a miniature chorus, each one trumpeting in the same direction.

However, no matter what your personal vision of a lovers' paradise might be, fall is the perfect season to plan and plant a garden for a romantic setting in your future. Above all, the garden is a living thing, and a romantic garden must be a sensual place!

Roses, and Black Spot

Q. *Please, the name of the rose that is immune to the "black spot" plague? Could it be American Heritage? I have tried sprays for five years; no luck. Thanks for any assistance.*

A. Black spot is not serious except in wet seasons when it may be controlled by spraying with Bordeaux mixture.

Picking off infected leaves and cleaning up old stalks and debris in autumn is the key to disease-free roses. During the summer months when cultivating the beds, take up all fallen leaves.

There is no rose completely immune to black spot (and resistant to other fungal diseases) that I know of except 'Bonica' and 'Flower Carpet.' Both are pink roses, perfect for any garden.

Roses, Cut

Spray and water roses early in the day—also the best time to cut for bouquets. Plunge the stems immediately in warm water up to their necks. Place in a cool, shady spot for a few hours. They'll last longer that way.

Roses: Dried and True

I recommend drying roses in silica gel, available at craft stores and florists, instead of freeze-drying them.

Bury the blooms in a dry silica gel (for starters, try putting them in a show box) without letting them touch each other. Leave them there for up to two weeks, depending on their density and size.

Even open flowers can be dried successfully using this technique. The flowers retain their shape and form, and the petals won't shrink as they do when they are air-dried. After drying, spray the blooms with a dried-flower saver.

Roses, Fall Planting of

Fall-planted roses make little or no root growth during that season because the plants are becoming dormant. As they are planted, their dormancy deepens.

The advantage of planting roses in the fall (aside from the availability of the gardener's time) is that the soil will settle firmly about the roots throughout the fall, allowing the plants to become more established and ready to start active growth by early spring, usually long before most spring roses are available.

Most gardeners have far more time to properly prepare their rose beds and do a good planting job in the fall than in the hustle and bustle of the spring.

Roses, Preparing for Winter

One of the chief reasons roses need winter protection is their ability to bloom over and over again. Hybrid teas and their cousins—grandifloras and floribundas—simply don't know when the party is over and when they should prepare for their long winter's snooze. This reluctance to go dormant exposes new growth to harsh, drying winter winds, sudden freezes and even spells of sub-zero weather.

The gardener's first job in preparing roses for winter is to discourage new growth and further bloom. Keep in mind, pruning and feeding encourages growth and flowering, so stop these activities immediately after the flush of fall flowering (in the northern zone, late August). However, keep watering because roses need lots of water, especially in autumn as the bushes get ready for the dry winter season.

If you live in an area where winter means extended periods of sub-freezing weather (and especially if your thermometer ever dips below zero), your roses probably need winter covering. This step should be taken after the ground freezes solid (usually early December), which is generally after several nights of below 20°F temperatures.

A covering of leaf mulch or bark works well, but the best insulation cover of all is good black dirt mounded up around the base of each rose bush to a depth of about 12 inches. Don't use soil already in the garden because this risks unearthing the rose's roots and exposing them to the elements. By bringing in fresh earth, you are also top-dressing the plants for next spring.

A final way you can help your roses survive the rigors of winter is by choosing rose plants carefully. Not all roses are equally fit for winter survival. Some can survive with precious little outside help, and others are truly tender blossoms. Hardiness is one of the criteria in evaluating new rose varieties. And since test gardens span the country (with locations in cold-weather climates of Minnesota, Wisconsin and Colorado), the All-America Selection winners have proven themselves in the toughest climates. The AARS green-and-white tag on a rosebush not only predicts seasons of lovely flowers, it also means that the rose was bred for hardiness and growing success in your garden.

Always buy roses for the area you live in. For example, a rose that thrives in Maine may not be good for Southern zones.

Q. *For the past several years I have protected my tree roses in the winter by building a burlap screen and packing mulch around the tree. This was satisfactory until last year, when rodents got into several of the enclosures and caused severe damage. Is there a better way to winter my tree roses?*

A. Have you ever heard of Microfoam? It is a material that in the past has primarily been used to package sensitive instruments, fragile articles and fine furniture. However, it has recently been found effective as an insulating material for various plants and trees, and it was tested in the New York City area with a high degree of success. Tree roses were wrapped with the Microfoam, a white, light-weight, Styrofoam-like material that remains flexible even at low temperatures. The entire trunk and main canes were wrapped by spiraling the Microfoam tape starting at the soil line and working up to the top graft union, overlapping slightly each time around. The Microfoam strip was held in place with masking tape. In the spring the Microfoam was removed, and the tree roses were pruned and fertilized. They broke bud as normal and produced an abundance of flowers despite a terrible winter! The use of Microfoam to protect plants is new, but judging from the results of these preliminary studies, I think it may be the wave of the future. Check with your local garden center.

Q. *How should one handle roses to give them the best chance of living through the winter in a New Jersey climate?*

A. First of all, as winter approaches, prepare your roses by cutting the bushes down to about 2 feet high. (There are differing opinions on when to prune—I only "cut back" in the fall and do my major "pruning" in the spring.) Make a mound of soil 12 inches or more high over the bud union of each bush; the soil should come from a different part of the garden. After mounds freeze, cover them with straw to keep them frozen and thus protect the bushes through the winter. If you have climbers, protect them as you do your bushes by building a mound of soil around the base. Blanket the remaining plant with straw wrapped in burlap. Come spring, your bushes and climbers will be ready to go!

The National Garden Bureau suggests burying banana peels (only three peels per bush) around rosebushes to produce better blooms and stronger stems. They will also increase the yield of eggplant, peppers and tomatoes. Banana peels contain phosphorus and potash, and roses just love them!

Slugs

Q. *Do you happen to know any flowers that slugs avoid?*

A. In the unofficial Slug Capital of the World, Seattle, a group of green-thumb gardeners have found three dozen or so flowers to be mostly slug-resistant. Keep in mind the list is based solely on personal observations, so here goes. To name a few: alyssum, achillea, aster, astilbe, cosmos, dianthus, dicentra, lobelia, nasturtium, paeonia, phlox, poppies, sedum, verbena, vinca, viola and zinnia.

Soil pH

Q. *What should I add to the soil to lower its pH?*

A. To lower the pH of 100 square feet of soil from 7.0 to 6.0, cultivate into the soil 2 to 5 pounds of aluminum sulfate. The best time to do this is in the fall, but if this is not possible, work aluminum sulfate into the soil in early spring as far ahead of planting in the area as possible. Mixing peat moss with the soil will also lower soil pH, but of course more slowly.

You neglected to say what your current pH is or why you want to make your soil more acidic. However, I've given you some general guidelines.

If you are still not satisfied, call the extension service; they will test your soil.

Squash: Winter Storage

Q. *Every fall I harvest my winter squash and store them in a basket in the garage. Unfortunately, most of them rot by Thanksgiving. I thought that squash was supposed to last all winter. Please help me to store my squash correctly.*

A. Winter squash should keep for several months after harvest; that is, providing it's stored properly. Here are some guidelines for you to follow:

Pick the squash from the vine when it is mature, leaving some stem. The deep-colored fruit should be full size and have a hard rind that resists piercing with a thumbnail.

Cure the rind by exposing the fruit to full sun for at least seven to ten days.

Cover the squash in the evening if frost is expected during this hardening-off period. Listen to the weather report in the evening.

Once the rind is cured, handle the fruit gently because any injury to the rind will make the squash store poorly.

Stack the squash in a single layer in crates, placing crumpled newspapers between them.

Store them in a warm protected area between 50° and 60°F. Colder temperatures can cause injury, so avoid storing the squash in your garage.

You can expect to store acorn squash for five to eight weeks, butternut squash for two to three months, and Hubbards for up to six months.

Squirrels, and Bulbs

Q. *How do I keep squirrels from digging up bulbs?*

A. Squirrels can be pests. They won't bother daffodils and other narcissus bulbs (which taste terrible to them), but they find tulips and crocus, in particular, to be delicious.

The only surefire way to protect tulips and crocuses and other tasty bulb treats from squirrels is to lay wire mesh, such as chicken wire, on top of the bed. The squirrels can't dig through the mesh and the flowers will grow perfectly through the holes.

Bulbs are most vulnerable in fall, immediately after planting, when the soil is still soft and worked up. Digging then is easy.

Squirrels often "chance" upon bulbs when burying their nuts in soft ground, or they are attracted by planting debris such as bits of papery bulb tunic and other bulb-scented tidbits from the bulb bags. Don't advertise your plantings—clean up and keep those squirrels guessing.

Here's one neat trick that I've found works beautifully: After planting new areas, lay old window screens in frames on the ground, covering the newly turned soil. The screen weighs enough to foil the squirrel, but allows air to circulate and rain to seep in. Once the ground has settled, remove the screens and store for future use.

Another remedy that some find successful is to actually feed the squirrels during the fall and winter. The theory is that the squirrel population, when offered a handy plate of peanuts or other easy-to-get treats, will leave your bulbs alone. At the White House, the gardeners put out six peanut-filled feeding boxes to appease the hungry denizens there—it reduced squirrel damage on bulb beds by 95 percent.

Many gardeners claim success with commercial repellents, but these are often sticky and unpleasant to deal with, or wash away in the rain.

Home remedies include sowing cayenne pepper into the soil or on the bulbs before planting and scattering mothball flakes on the ground. You will find advocates and detractors of both techniques. A favorite Dutch remedy is to interplant *Fritillaria imperialis.* This tall, dramatic plant gives off an odor that squirrels (and deer, too) find repellent.

Sunflower Seed Harvest

Q. *I planted giant sunflowers all around my garden as a windbreak. What's the best way to separate seeds from the heads?*

A. When the back of the sunflower head turns from green to a light yellow, the seeds are mature, but the flavor will be best if you leave the heads on the plants until their backs turn brown. To keep birds from eating the seeds before you do, enclose the heads either in paper bags or cheesecloth. When you have cut the stalks, you can remove the seeds by brushing the head with your fingertips or a stiff brush. Then let the seeds dry for a few days before packing them up in airtight glass jars and refrigerating them to retain the flavor and freshness. Sunflower seeds are delicious any way you choose to eat them. You can eat them raw or you can roast them in a shallow pan at 300°F for 15 minutes.

Tomatoes at Frost

If tomato vines are heavy with fruit in various stages of ripeness the day a killing frost is predicted, pull them up and hang them upside down in a frost-free, cool place. You'll be amazed at how many will ripen over a period of several weeks.

Topiary

One of the oldest forms of gardening is becoming once again extremely popular in the U.S. Topiary, the art of shaping plants into decorative forms, can be enjoyed outdoors or can be brought into the house during the cooler months of late fall and water (January, February, March), or for special occasions, even as a table centerpiece.

There are any number of topiary shapes to suit everyone—from greenery trained into spirals and balls for the holidays to animals, frames and arches. Best of all, no special skills are required for this rewarding pastime. You either train, cut and trim the plant into an ornamental shape, or you can use a frame for the plant to grow into a specific shape.

To train foliage without a frame, always begin with a plant that has a sturdy, straight stem. The container should have enough weight to counterbalance the top when the plant matures. Topiary for the terrace can be fashioned from houseplants, herbs, or hardy garden plants. When the plant reaches the height you want, pinch off the tip so that a head is formed. If it happens to be a small-leafed plant, you can start pinching earlier than one with large leaves. If side leaves grow on the main stem before the crown develops, don't disturb them but lower branches should be removed.

While growing, the plant needs good light and a stake tied to the main stem to keep it straight. Later, when pinching off the top, new shoots will grow a few inches and these should also be pinched just above the leaf nodes. Eventually, the crown will be full and lush but you must have patience!

Should you choose to grow a plant over a frame, you can purchase all sorts of sizes and shapes at most garden centers. You may even find rust-resistant wires around the house that can be shaped into intricate animals and birds, or shaped into single hoops and hearts. If the frame is two-dimensional, you will be training the leaves to follow the shape of the frame—likewise with three-dimensional sculptures, which also allow you to fill the form with moss and potting mix for a fuller look and more immediate results. To keep the frame upright in the container, it can be held in position with a U-shaped wire or long pins. Some frames even have spikes to stick into the soil. Topiary gardening can lead to years of enjoyment caring for your whimsical creatures.

Tree Care in the Fall

Horticultural oil: Horticultural oil has been used by gardeners for scale insects, spider mites and other pests for years. Although oil has experienced many changes and has improved significantly over the years, today's horticultural oil is more highly refined, contains fewer impurities and is safer to use on plants than its ancestors.

Oil is now used during the dormant as well as growing season, making it our most widely used treatment for insect pests. One reason for its popularity is safety to humans and pets. Oil is highly effective against many plant pests but has minimal impact on beneficial insects and other non-target organisms.

Late fall is an ideal time to apply dormant treatments of horticultural oil. Favorable weather conditions, equipment availability and effectiveness make autumn an excellent time to apply oil to your trees and shrubs.

Cabling and bracing: Fall is a good time to have your trees inspected for structural weaknesses that could lead to breakage during storms. Narrow branch attachments ("V" crotches), multiple upright stems, cracked limbs and long horizontal branches are primary concerns.

The risk of failure from these structural weaknesses can be reduced through pruning, cabling and bracing. Cabling involves installing steel cables from weak to strong limbs to provide additional support. Cables are anchored to eye bolts that are inserted through limbs. Bracing rods are threaded bolts inserted through cracked limbs, stems or weak crotches to provide rigid support.

It's best to hire trained arborists to detect structural weakness and to properly install cable and brace supports.

Trees: Pruning

For many homeowners, the first step in tree pruning is reaching for the phone to call a landscape professional.

But tree pruning doesn't have to be an overwhelming chore left only to specialists. With the proper tools and techniques, it is an easy task many homeowners can master.

Consider first the necessary equipment. There are many different types of tree pruners available today, such as pole pruners, blade saws, or gas-powered, extended pruners. Before purchasing equipment, homeowners should evaluate a product's performance, productivity and safety.

Homeowners need lightweight pruners that are easy to handle and give top performance when trimming limbs and branches. Equipment that enables operators to easily crop tree branches more than 12 to 15 feet overhead while remaining on the ground is highly recommended by most garden experts. That way, you are able to ensure safety by visualizing cutting areas and avoiding falling branches. Industry experts also advocate using equipment specially designed to distance users from the cutting chain.

But even with the proper tools like a Power Pruner (Black & Decker)—an extended, gas-powered pruner that reaches up to 15 feet overhead—some homeowners are still nervous to make that first cut for fear of harming a tree. But pruning is essential to invigorate a tree, improve its health and manage its growth. When trying to direct the growth of a young tree, homeowners must understand that low branches stay at their original height and just grow larger in diameter. Therefore, branches that are too low to the ground to produce adequate light or prohibit people from walking underneath should be removed immediately.

Additionally, professional tree experts have found it important to remove all dead, diseased or insect-infested limbs or branches to prevent further infection. But over-pruning can kill or damage a tree, so be certain to maintain at least two-thirds of the live tree when pruning. And, when cutting out dead wood, always cut back to healthy wood.

Homeowners wanting to better manage tree growth should consider that pruning during summer months actually slows down a tree's growth rate, while pruning during the winter months, or while the tree is dormant, stimulates the roots and encourages a burst of new growth come spring.

There are times when professionals should be called in for consultation, however. This should be done when a tree is too large and when pruning requires extensive equipment like a bucket truck. You should also bring in a pro when a tree is located near a utility line, building or highway. Safety and good judgment should always prevail when tree pruning.

Tulips

Q. *My tulips grew green leaves, but not flowers this year. Why?*

A. If tulips produce leaves, but no flowers, there are generally two reasons for this.

If the tulips were planted just last fall and this happens, it probably means the bulbs were exposed to a fertilizer with a very high nitrogen content, such as a lawn fertilizer. Nitrogen promotes vigorous green growth, and too much can inhibit flowering. In the fall, always use a fertilizer with a low first number for slow growth.

If the bulbs were planted several years ago, it just may be natural regression that causes this. Technically speaking, tulips are perennials which means they should come back each spring, year after year. But actually, most tulips naturally only behave this way when grown under climatic conditions similar to the rather severe climatic conditions—cold winters, hot dry summers—of their original native habitats in the steppes of Russia, northern Turkey and elsewhere.

In most home gardens in the United States, tulips do not find these conditions. Thus, tulips here are generally considered annuals and need to be re-planted or replenished every year. Occasionally tulips acclimate to different settings and come back. Also, certain varieties or types of tulips are inherently more adaptable and thus more likely to perennialize than others. These easygoing types are often sold as perennial tulips and can come back nicely to re-bloom for three or more years.

Q. *I adore tulips. They are my favorite bulbs, but I simply don't have space for them. Would it be possible to plant them in a whiskey barrel, right now, and leave them outdoors for the winter?*

A. Of course, but the tulip bulbs need winter protection their first winter, and by the second time around you'll probably need to re-plant new ones. Container tulips bloom well for only one or two seasons before needing to be replaced. That's because the warming rays of the sun during cold winter days stimulate bulb growth before temperatures are consistently warm. When the sun goes down, temperatures drop and the new bulb growth is usually damaged, alas!

To get your fall-planted bulbs through the first winter, cover them with leaves, soft hay or bark mulch after the deep freeze sets in, or move the barrel to an unheated area such as a garage or the shady north side of the house. Whiskey barrels just don't hold enough soil to nourish the tulips with the nutrition needed to come back and bloom each year. Green-thumb gardeners do this: They plant tetraploid single late varieties or Darwin varieties, and transplant 2-year-old bulbs into a garden bed to rejuvenate for the coming years.

Tulips, Black

Q. *When can I buy the rare black tulip?*

A. Actually, black tulips are not rare—black tulips do not exist. However, there are some very deep-purple tulips, some of which appear almost black. The search for the fabled black tulip has been an epic quest for centuries. In 1850, Alexander Dumas—famed French author of *The Count of Monte Cristo, The Three Musketeers* and *The Man in the Iron Mask*—captured the popular fancy with *The Black Tulip*, a romantic tale in which a fictional black tulip figures in a love story laced with murder, torture, greed and bizarre surprises.

Today, the lure of a black tulip still exists. Dutch tulip breeders have achieved some deep purples. 'Queen of Night,' for example, is officially listed as 'deep velvety maroon' and is very, very dark in color. But achieving a truly black tulip is not possible yet, so have a little patience.

Until then, I suggest planting 'Burgundy' (deep purple-violet), 'Black Parrot' (violet-black) or 'Black Diamond' (deep mahogany).

Tulips, Lily-flowered

Q. *I am a big fan of lily-flowered tulips. Can you suggest some good ones to try?*

A. Lily-flowered tulips are indeed a lovely tulip class. Unlike those with the traditional tulip shape, these 'liliflora' varieties have pointy petals that resemble their summer-blooming cousins. Compared with other varieties, there are relatively few varieties. Here are a few you might look for:

'Aladdin'	deep red, yellow-edged
'Ballade'	bright violet, white-edged
'China Pink'	luminous carmine pink
'Elegant Lady'	creamy-yellow, violet-red-edged
'Jacqueline'	tender pink
'Mariette'	pure pink
'Maytime'	bright violet, white-edged
'Queen of Sheba'	red, yellow-edged
'Red Shine'	bright red
'White Triumphator'	pure white

Tulip Tip

The depth tulip bulbs are planted plays an important part in the final blossoming results. The farther north you live, the deeper the planting. In the Northern United States, you will find that by planting tulips 12 inches deep, the bed lasts longer and doesn't run out. Also, they come up later and avoid frost and rabbit damage. As you move South, plant shallower.

Vegetable Garden: Fall Tips

Tilling

Shallow tilling in late fall is an easy way to destroy large numbers of grasshopper eggs by exposing them to the elements and predators.

Storage

If you do not have a root cellar, carrots, Brussels sprouts, parsnips and Jerusalem artichokes can be left in the garden into the winter. Just before the soil freezes hard, cover the plants with an 8-to-10-inch hay mulch. This will keep the soil workable and soft so you can dig out your crop as needed. Sprouts and kale can endure extreme cold. For best taste, cook them before they thaw. Frost will magically transform the flavor of Brussels sprouts.

The best time to harvest horseradish is as the soil cools. Plant each spring to avoid a tangle of roots and save some of the pencil-thin roots for a new crop.

Plant a cover crop as soon as a main crop finishes, unless vegetables are slated to go in the same spot. You can even sow the succeeding cover crop before the maturing first crop is out of the way.

When harvesting pumpkins and winter squash, remember to leave 4 to 5 inches of stem attached for better keeping. Store them in a dark, dry place on boards or wooden shelves, never touching them. Store at 50°F to 60°F, except acorn squash, which stores best at 55°F.

"Humified" grapes remaining on the vine are usually a sign of black rot. Pick them off immediately, take up fallen leaves and destroy them to prevent spreading (of rot) next season.

Root crops (carrots, onions, etc.) need high humidity in storage (so skins won't shrivel and darken) and temperatures of 32°F to 40°F. Cut off the green tops to about 1 inch in length.

Your garden can also be a fabulous storage place for your root crops such as beets and carrots. In fact, it's a whole lot easier leaving them in the ground than harvesting and storing.

If you live in an area that really gets cold, the key is to heavily mulch root crops.

Straw works best to prevent the ground from freezing solid, making it impossible for you to dig out your produce.

If you plan to do a lot of winter picking, I suggest placing a tarp over your mulch because if the mulch gets wet and freezes it will be hard to remove. Simply anchor the tarp with rocks so it doesn't blow away.

Vegetables for Cold Weather

Pull on your sweater along with your gardening gloves—there's no reason to stop enjoying garden-fresh vegetables at the summer harvest. With timely and successive plantings throughout the summer and early fall, several crops—ranging from lettuce, leafy greens and peas, to broccoli, carrots and cabbage—can provide a bounty of fresh vegetables to serve throughout the winter. All you need is basic knowledge of cool-weather crops suitable for fall-weather planting.

Lettuce: A cool-weather crop that tolerates light frosts and summer heat, the leafy vegetable can be successively sown every two to three weeks from spring to late summer in order to assure a continual harvest up to several weeks after the first fall frost.

'North Pole,' a compact, butterhead lettuce, is extremely cold-resistant. 'Reine des Glaces' (Queen of the Ices), grows very well in the cold and has a rich flavor and crispy texture.

Broccoli, cabbage and kale: These crops have two optimum planting times—early spring and midsummer. Plant seeds 12 to 14 weeks before the first fall frost and transplant the seedlings into your garden five to eight weeks before the first frost.

'DeCicco' broccoli, an old Italian variety, is great for fall gardens. At maturity, the 18- to 24-inch plants produce a primary head with lots of tender side shoots.

'Earliana Green' cabbage is perfect for home gardens. An early ballhead type, it produces compact heads of 2 to 2 ½ pounds.

'Red Ursa' kale is an extremely hardy new variety that is a cross between 'Red Russian' and 'True Siberian.' Its deep purple-red leaves have excellent flavor.

Carrots: The orange vegetable lends itself to successive plantings throughout the spring and summer, but late plantings to be much sweeter due to exposure to light frosts. 'Scarlet Nantes' is a nearly coreless, sweet, juicy carrot that produces roots that are ideal for bunching, eating fresh or for storing.

Chard: A crop you can continue to harvest from the same plant, chard is easy to grow and harvest well into winter. 'Broadstem Green' produces large, generous green leaves with white, succulent mid-ribs and stems that are tender, tasty and even more nutritious than the leaves.

Peas: Peas can be planted in either early spring or late summer. 'Cascadia Snap Bush' peas produce green pods containing five or six peas per pod and have a sweet flavor. 'Sugar Pod 1' is an edible-podded snow pea that produces thick, succulent and juicy pods that yield two per node.

Radishes: Some radish varieties, such as 'Cherry Belle' (tasty, round, red outer skin with crisp white flesh), are quick-growing and can be planted throughout the summer until two to four weeks before the first fall frost. Others such as the long-rooted Japanese 'Tokinashi Daikon' (a popular long, mild-flavored white radish with crisp, white flesh that is perfect for eating raw in salads or pickling) can be sown in any month that the temperature stays above freezing.

Spinach: Spinach prefers cooler weather and can be planted late summer for a fall harvest. 'Bloomsdale' is a savoy-leafed spinach with tasty, thick, dark green leaves. 'America' is a thick, deep green, savoy-leafed variety that grows to a foot in width.

Venus Flytrap

Among wildflowers, this plant is truly amazing. It is an endangered species in the wild but readily available for domestic cultivation as a houseplant.

All of the known populations of the Venus flytrap (*Dianaea muscipula*) are found growing within 50 miles of Wilmington, North Carolina, along the coastal bogs. Despite its being picked nearly to extinction, this fascinating plant is still under review by the U.S. Fish and Wildlife Service for possible future protection! Can you believe it?

The feeding habits of this carnivorous plant are a marvel of botanical engineering accounting for its popularity in the drawing room. ("Watch what happens when I put a dead fly right here.") The plant feeds through its leaves, which are spread out on the ground, circling the single stem. Each leaf comprises two identical blades ringed with comb-like teeth and hinged along one side. The bright color of the inside of the leaf is caused by thousands of glands which secrete enzymes and absorb nutrients.

When insects are attracted by the flytrap's sugary nectar and brush along the sensitive hairs on the edge of the leaf, it slams shut, teeth interlock and the prey is doomed. Enzymes break down the insect's tissues and several days later the plant digests its meal. That accomplished, the leaf opens once again, the remains are blown away and the trap is reset.

If this plant appeals to you, it is readily available from reputable retail nurseries, so leave the wild Venus flytrap in the wild! Please!

Waste Management

Q. *My town is now enforcing strict guidelines for the disposal of garden and yard waste. Because of this, many homeowners are turning to composting. Just what is compost?*

A. Compost, also called humus, is a rich, natural substance that results from the decomposition of organic matter. Leaves, kitchen scraps (no fats!), grass clippings, vegetables, fruit peels and even eggshells (never fish, meat or chicken leftovers) are recommended for composting.

Compost allows these natural materials to be returned to the earth providing improved soil structure and fertility. Compost also helps control weeds, retain moisture, reduce soil erosion and release precious plant nutrients.

Whiteflies

If you have fuchsias, lantanas and heliotropes, watch out for whiteflies. The best spray for them is Resmethrin, a synthetic pyrethrin. If you prefer an organic method, spread molasses on a piece of wood painted bright yellow; the color attracts whiteflies, and the sticky syrup traps them.

Winterize Your Garden

The severity of past winters has caused us to seriously consider the need for winter protection in our landscapes and gardens. While the vagaries of Mother Nature are beyond our reach, there are things we can do to minimize plant damage when she deals us a bad hand from the deck of winter cards.

Our first consideration is the hardiness of our plants. We have enjoyed some exceptionally mild winters and this has tempted us to fill our gardens with borderline hardy plants. Unfortunately, these plants suffer severe damage when the temperature drops suddenly or remains very cold for long periods.

If you are a plant collector and enjoy experimenting with tender plants, continue to do so, but with the understanding that you will often suffer severe losses.

If you want a trouble-free garden, read the plant hardiness lists and stick with those plants that have proven themselves to be reliably hardy over a long period of time in the climatic zone of your residence.

Most of us have become a generation of gardeners addicted to container plants. Geraniums, begonias, trees and shrubs in containers add much to our patios, decks, malls and plazas.

While most deciduous trees suitable for planting will survive in exposed containers, during the winter, most broadleaf evergreens will suffer damage. The hardy coniferous evergreens, such as pines and spruces, may also suffer from windburn or lack of water, so when there's a winter thaw, water them thoroughly.

It seems that the roots of most plants, especially broadleaf evergreens, are unable to withstand cold temperatures as well as their tops.

Plants such as ilex have a temperature differential as great as 20 degrees. In other words, their tops can withstand temperatures 20 degrees colder than their roots.

While some plants may survive at zero degrees when planted in the ground, their roots will be damaged or killed when planted in above-ground containers.

Such plants must be wintered in a protected cold frame or unheated building where the temperature will not become as cold. If small enough to be easily handled, they can also be plunged into holes dug in the ground in a well-drained location and mulched.

The needle-bearing evergreens, although supposedly hardier, will be less apt to burn if placed out of the winter sun and wind. A major cause of winter damage with evergreens planted in the ground is lack of water. Their leaves lose water through transpiration whenever they're not frozen. If the soil is dry or frozen, the roots are unable to replace the lost water and the leaves will "burn." Exposure to sun and strong winds further aggravates the problem.

One way to prevent this damage is to water the soil thoroughly before it freezes to ensure an adequate moisture supply.

Winter mulches of leaves, pine needles, straw or pine boughs around such plants as rhododendrons, azaleas and hydrangeas will reduce the depth of freezing and allow the roots to utilize the available moisture. Don't apply the mulch too early, especially with young plants, or they may not mature properly and suffer stem damage.

It used to be the rule of thumb that broadleaf evergreens were planted where they had protection from the winter sun and winds. This pattern is still practiced in colder climates such as New Hampshire and Maine.

We have become careless as the result of past mild winters and have planted our evergreens with full exposure to obtain better flowering and a more compact look.

Such plants would have sustained much less damage in recent cold winters if they had been planted on the East side, or Northeast side, of a building, or where they had overhead protection, such as from a tall linden tree.

If your evergreens are not planted in protected areas, the best thing to do is provide cover for them with shades and windscreens of burlap or snow fencing. Perhaps you should consider extending this protection to other tender plants.

Hybrid roses do need winter protection. The polystyrene cones that are used to cover roses in colder climates are unnecessary and may even be harmful. As spring approaches, the temperature may build up under the cone and result in premature growth and/or the development of damaging fungi. It is usually sufficient to mound a few shovels full of soil over the base of the plant to a depth of 8 to 12 inches. Some gardeners prefer to add a layer of salt hay, once the soil has frozen, to minimize temperature fluctuation. I like to use rotten manure.

Herbaceous perennials and strawberries are more often damaged by frost heaving than from cold temperatures. A winter mulch applied after the soil is lightly frozen will stabilize the soil temperature and prevent heaving. Several inches of salt hay, straw or pine boughs will do the job.

I would like to mention, and can't stress enough, the importance of the general health of plants at this time. The hardiest rhododendron or yew may suffer winter damage if its roots have been damaged by taxus weevil or other insects, by summer drought or from having been planted in a poorly drained location. Winter protection will be of little help to these plants if the weather is really severe.

If your plants are reliably hardy, in good health and well protected but still damaged, take consolation in knowing you have done everything you could to help them.

Consider such damage as one of the challenges of gardening in a cold winter climate. Keep in mind that snow is the poor man's fertilizer (loaded with nitrogen) and acts as a cozy thermal blanket to keep plants protected and warm.

Winterize Your Yard

Believe it or not, fall is already upon us and, before we know it, winter will hit us from behind. As the seasons change once again, gardeners will witness the slow and inevitable end of spring and summer. This year, however, why not take a few simple steps in fall to prepare your yard for the coming cold weather and ensure a much healthier appearance next spring.

As weather conditions change and time passes, trees and shrubs will naturally acquire their share of dead twigs and broken branches. So perhaps one of the easiest and most important steps you can take to help rejuvenate the natural beauty of your landscape is to prune.

To start, remove all of the dead or injured branches using pruning shears, being sure to trim any weak, spindly growths. If a shrub is seriously overgrown and needs to be cut back dramatically, additional trimming may be necessary. A "thinning" cut removes old limbs at the base of the shrub, allowing light to reach the interior of the plant and encouraging new growth. A "heading" cut takes the branch only as far back as the bud, which stimulates side branching, enabling the plant to grow compactly.

Winter Watering

As temperatures continue to drop and the ground begins to freeze, evergreens begin to acquire brown needles, an indication that thirsty plant roots are not receiving water.

Although all plant life suffers from winter conditions, evergreens tend to be hit the hardest.

Trees and shrubs transpire year-round, meaning they release water through pores in their leaves—water that continually needs to be replaced. Plants depend on the soil for this moisture supply, yet encounter difficulty when faced with frozen conditions. To help your plants survive, water the soil several feet deep in late fall. Deeply watered soil tends not to freeze all the way through, allowing roots to reach needed moisture, which will protect your shrubs from becoming dehydrated.

Landscape Fabrics

In the search for a product that helps protect and maintain landscapes through the winter months, more and more gardeners are turning to landscape fabrics available in most garden centers. Landscape fabrics are designed to help prevent weed growth while at the same time working to retain moisture in the soil. More important, landscape fabrics reduce the amount of water lost to evaporation and help moderate temperature fluctuations, making it more difficult for the soil to freeze. Landscape fabrics are inexpensive and easy to use.

Simply lay overlapping strips of the fabric over the prepared area. Then, using scissors or a knife, cut holes or X's in the appropriate spots and pull the fabric down around the plants, pushing the loose fabric back under the plants. Landscape fabrics will last many years and will save you hours of time that would otherwise be spent fighting weeds and watering your plants.

Mulch

After installing landscape fabric, many gardeners apply 2 to 3 inches of mulch around the plants. This provides a decorative look to the garden and helps prolong the life of the fabric. Whether it's pine bark or shredded leaves, mulch helps keep soil, plants, trees and shrubs moist. Like a warm blanket, mulch helps protect plant roots against the damaging effects of severe winter weather.

This year, don't let Old Man Winter get the best of your plants. By following these few guidelines, you can help your plants, trees and shrubs survive even the most harsh winter conditions. The effort and time you put in this fall by putting your plants to bed properly for winter will leave you with less to do next spring.

holidays

FOR ME, THE HOLIDAYS START with Thanksgiving. This is a fantastic celebration because it is so uniquely American. Even though it falls in late November, Thanksgiving is still a gardener's delight to decorate because Mother Nature continues to provide abundantly at this time of year. Not only does a gardener plan for decorations but also for some of the food that can be served at the Thanksgiving table: pumpkin soup and pumpkin pie, cornbread, winter squash and green beans. And, of course, the decorations with pumpkins, gourds and corn stalks, in the American tradition of using things that were on the table when the Indians helped the Pilgrims after

that first long winter at Plymouth Rock in 1620.

The next big one, Christmas, takes a lot more decorative planning because by December winter has really set in. Christmas flowers of red and white must be planted indoors by October in order to be blooming for the holidays. Amaryllis and narcissus, as well as many others, are discussed in Winter. And that brings us to springtime and Easter. Again the planning and planting for this festive celebration has to be done well in advance. Colors, types of flowers and Easter table decorations will be fun to read about on the following pages.

African Violets

Q. *How do I keep African violets blooming in winter?*

A. As winter days grow shorter, the same windowsill where your violets flowered all summer long may not provide enough light to keep them flowering. To flower, violets need bright, reflected light all day or full morning sun two to five hours daily. (Be watchful—just like us, violets can suffer from sunburn.)

If you can't move your violet to a brighter location, add artificial light. Cool white fluorescent lights are the most economical and work well as long as they are no farther than 18 inches from the plant. Special plant-growing fluorescent lamps and a variety of decorative incandescent spotlights can supplement natural daylight to boost your bashful violets back into bloom.

Lukewarm water should *always* be used when watering, because cold water dropped on all fuzzy-leafed type plants causes ugly spots on the leaves.

Amaryllis

If you love fresh flowers for the holidays, then consider amaryllis. You don't need a degree in horticulture to grow these beautiful flowers. In fact, even a toddler can plant them and get great results. Simply drop them into some Pro-Mix soil, give them a good drink and stand back. In four to six weeks, you'll be rewarded with a spectacular display of bloom. Unlike other forced bulbs, amaryllis require no pre-cooling in order to bloom. They're ready to go right after you buy them.

At first glance, an amaryllis bulb, with its flaky brown skin and gnarled roots, doesn't look like it holds much promise. But once it starts to grow, this ugly duckling turns into a swan. Tall, graceful stalks rise from the bulb producing huge, lilylike blossoms in an assortment of spectacular colors. Each flower stalk develops a cluster of three or more giant blooms—a single flower may measure ten inches or more in diameter. But the flower show doesn't end there: A second amaryllis can provide still more blooms. And they're very versatile flowers, too. Individual amaryllis make strikingly beautiful plants, but you can increase the magic by grouping two or three bulbs together in a large pot. In addition, amaryllis are also excellent long-lasting cut flowers.

Planting an amaryllis bulb is about as easy as gardening gets. When your bulb arrives in the mail, remove it from the box and gently untangle and separate the roots. Soak the roots in lukewarm water for three or four hours before planting the bulb. You'll want to select a pot that is 2 or 3 inches wider than the top of the bulb. Fill the pot with rich, well-drained potting soil. Set the bulb in the soil, leaving about two-thirds of it above the soil line. If you are planting more than one bulb at a time, mark the variety name on a plant marker so that you can keep track of your favorites. Water the bulbs generously, but avoid getting them wet. You'll want to place the pot near a sunny window or in a warm room (day temperature at least 70°F) that is filled with bright, indirect light.

To suit your fancy, amaryllis are available in a wide variety of colors, including white, pink, red, salmon, pale-yellow and bicolors. For the holidays, consider these elegant single-blooming varieties: the snow white 'Christmas Gift' or the cheery red-and-white striped 'Peppermint Stick.' Double amaryllis have twice the bloom of the singles and are exotically beautiful, yet they're as easy to grow as their single-flowered cousins. Popular double varieties include the 'Red Peacock,' the soft-pink 'Rozetta,' and the pristine 'Double Jewel,' all wonderful choices for your holiday arrangements.

Q. *What care should I give an amaryllis that came already potted and about to bloom?*

A. Give your amaryllis bright light but shield the flowers from hot, direct sun. It does well at temperatures comfortable for you, about 70°F in the daytime and into the 60s at night. Keep the soil evenly moist (mulching with florist sheet moss gives a nice finishing touch and also conserves moisture). When the petals wither, cut off the bloom stalk where it emerged from the bulb and set to grow in a sunny, warm window. Water freely and make regular applications of a flowering houseplant fertilizer during the spring and summer. The idea is to promote as many big, healthy leaves as possible during this period. If you can sink the pot to its rim in a partly sunny place outdoors, so much the better. In September, or before frost outdoors, bring the amaryllis inside.

Autumn is the time to withhold all water and fertilizer; set the pot in a cool (60°F), dark place. When the leaves dry up, remove them. Anytime after two months of resting, flower buds may show. Bring to a warm, sunny window and resume watering—but not too much—until there are obvious signs of growth. Not all amaryllis bulbs bloom the second time around but, if not, give them one more season of sun, warmth, water and fertilizer, and flowers are almost certain.

Ashes, Charcoal

Q. *Are the ashes from charcoal briquettes safe to use in the garden?*

A. Briquettes are composed mostly of wood, but they contain coal with wheat or corn as a binder. The problem lies with the coal. Some coals have high sulfur and/or heavy metal content, in particular high lead and cadmium levels that are absorbed by plants. Sulfur combines with water to produce sulfuric acid which lowers the pH. Of course, not all coals contain dangerous levels of heavy metals and sulfur; but since there's no way of telling without a chemical analysis, it's a no-no!

Birds

Q. *During my two-week winter break this February, I won't be able to put out birdseed every day as I usually do. I am worried that some birds will starve during my absence because a great variety depend upon my feeder.*

A. Don't worry—if a feeder suddenly becomes empty, birds are self-reliant and find other sources of food. If you live in a remote area where there are no other feeders, your birds will be put on the same footing as wild ones who have never had the benefit of human handouts. Keep in mind, most feeder-habituated birds forage for 75 to 80 percent of their diet, with commercial birdseed accounting for the rest.

When you get home, you'll have fewer birds visiting your yard. Have patience—it takes a little time for them to re-establish themselves.

Birds' Christmas

If you find it impossible to attract birds to your feeders because you have no cover (trees or bushes nearby to protect them), create your own shelter by driving three 5-foot steel fence posts into the ground and tying discarded Christmas trees to them. If you can fine long-needled trees, they are best, since they retain the needles throughout the winter. Within a few days your new "sanctuary" will become a thriving feeding station.

Birds, and Kids

Children don't have to hibernate from outdoor fun in fall and winter, they can learn about nature right in their own backyard.

Fall and winter are crucial seasons to provide food and shelter for birds. Migrating birds may pass through your yard on a thousand-mile trek, faced with diminished food snacks and freezing temperatures. Children can have fun and feel good about a project that helps feed, shelter and maintain birds.

For starters, children love making pine-cone feeders. You'll need plenty of pine cones, Crisco shortening, a plastic knife, birdseed and yarn or string. Peanut butter is optional.

It's easy. Spread Crisco and peanut butter in the cone's ridges, then roll in birdseed. Help kids suspend the cone with a length of string or yarn. (Brightly colored yarn may be more noticeable to the birds.) Hang the treats outdoors in the garden so the birds can start eating.

A scooped-out orange or grapefruit half is another fun, temporary bird feeder. Hang the fruit cup from sturdy string and fill with seed.

Want a more permanent structure? Long winter evenings are the perfect time to build a bird feeder or birdhouse together. Many garden centers sell books of plans. If you're not the do-it-yourself type, you can shop for a feeder or birdhouse. Garden centers usually offer a wide selection of both.

Holidays are an opportunity to give something back to the environment. Children will love to decorate a Christmas tree with edible ornaments for the birds. Here's a place to use your pine cone and orange cup feeders, as well as garlands of popcorn and cranberries.

Love the idea, but don't have the time for homemade treats? Some garden centers sell ready-made birdseed bells and stars as well as suet cakes.

Live Christmas trees make nice winter shelters for birds and small wildlife. When the holidays are over, have children help you move the tree to a corner of your yard where it can remain. It's a lesson in both recycling and providing wildlife habitat and protection from icy and snowy weather.

Hollies, winter berries, beeches and hemlocks are a few examples of trees and shrubs that offer food and shelter for birds. Ask your nursery professional for suggestions of what you and your child can plant together. Your efforts will make a permanent contribution to the wildlife in your garden while setting an example for other children in the neighborhood.

Bulbs: How to Chill

Q. *How do I grow spring-flowering bulbs in warm climates?*

A. It's possible to grow spring-flowering bulbs in climates as warm as Zones 9 and 10. However, the blooming season in these zones is much earlier than in cooler zones.

Some spring-flowering bulbs recommended for Zone 9 can be planted with no pre-cooling. Others will need a special cold treatment before planting.

No pre-chilling needed: amaryllis, allium, neapolitanum, *Allium rosenbachianum,* Anemone de Caen and Anemone St. Brigid, *Brodiaea laxa, Crocus chrysanthus* (snow crocus), Dutch iris, freesia, ixias, lilies, all narcissus/daffodils, *Ornithogalum umbellatum,* ranunculus, *Scilla campanulata* (wood hyacinth), sparaxis, *Triteleia uniflora* and tritonia.

Pre-chilling needed: tulips, hyacinths, crocus and the other spring-flowering bulb favorites.

Here are some warm-winter tips: First, choose cultivars that have proven well in warmer climates. For a list, look up www.bulb.com, document "Some Like It Hot," which appears in the "Spring-Flowering Bulbs" section under In Warm Climates.

Cold-hardy bulbs that need pre-cooling in warm winter regions must be treated as annuals, and new bulbs must be planted the following fall. Pre-chill the bulbs for a minimum of six to eight weeks in a refrigerator at a temperature of around 40° to 45°F (the temperature of most home refrigerators).

If you use a refrigerator, be sure not to store any apples or other fruits alongside your bulbs. Ripening fruit naturally gives off ethylene gas which will kill the bulbs. Don't worry if you bought the bulbs early in the season and need to store them for several months before planting.

Keep them chilling, even up to 16 weeks if necessary, until it is time to plant. For best results, the bulbs should be put in the ground in December or early January. Plant tulips about 6 to 8 inches deep, water well and protect with a layer of mulch to retain moisture and heat.

When bulbs do not receive sufficient weeks of cold treatment, they bloom too close to the ground and on too-short stems.

Bulbs, Winter Storage

Q. *What is the best way to store bulbs and tender tubers for the winter?*

A. Tender tubers and bulbs should be dug up and stored for the winter before the frost hits in your area; while tuberous begonias, dahlias and cannas should be dug after the frost has blackened the leaves.

Be very careful when lifting these beauties to avoid bruising and allow them to dry well before storage. Most tubers take about two weeks to "cure." Store at 40° to 50°F in sand and check occasionally during winter to make sure they stay in shape.

Unfortunately, once out of the soil most tubers and bulbs look pretty much like one another, making identification of variety and color difficult. Here's what I do to solve the dilemma. If you label your plants during the summer, it's easy to transfer the name or color of the variety directly onto the tuber using a felt-tipped pen. So come spring, it's a cinch to plant the right dahlia in the right spot!

Cactus, Holiday

Q. *Can you explain to me the difference between these cactus species: Thanksgiving, Christmas and Easter? I am confused about which is which.*

A. These species are all part of the same family. The Easter cactus (*Rhipsalidopsis gaertneri*) blooms in spring as the days grow longer, while the flowering of both Thanksgiving (*Schlumbergera truncata*) and Christmas cactus (*Schlumbergera bridgesii*) seems regulated by day length and temperature conditions. If grown in cold frames, the Thanksgiving and Christmas species will flower with the shorter fall days and cold nights (55°F). The Thanksgiving cactus will have visible flowers by the end of October. To ensure a December crop for Christmas cactus, plants should be given short (nine-hour) days by covering them with black cloth for the other 15 hours, starting in late September. All three species can be propagated from leaf cuttings.

Cactus, Softening

Q. *I have a ball cactus—notocactus, I think—that was fine. It has gold spines and a nice shape. I was told not to water it during the winter and give it good light. It's starting to get soft and shrivel at the bottom. Will I lose it? Do I need to water it?*

A. I don't think your cactus is in danger, or at least not yet! Notocactuses tend to have spreading-root systems and are best in shallow, wide pots. The soil should drain freely, but not be too coarse. As with most cactuses, don't water them during the winter or water very lightly to prevent the plant from shriveling. Generally, a two-month rest period of cool temperatures and no water is sufficient for notocactuses, but don't increase the water you give the plant dramatically until it shows a growth pattern.

If your plant is in too large a pot, the soil could easily be staying too wet, and the plant is rotting. If the plant is in too small a pot, it could easily be shriveling because it's too dry. If you haven't watered it in several months, then, yes, you need to water it. As a side note, winter shriveling of cactus isn't necessarily a bad thing. In fact, it's normal for many types of cactuses to shrink during the dormant season. A little water helps the plant, but increase watering and soil moisture gradually. It's easier to kill a plant with too much water than not enough.

Tip from a Reader

"I've discovered that the stems of my holiday cacti that hang closest to the window set buds first, and if I rotate the plant every few days to expose each side to the cold window the plant becomes symmetrical and fully fabulous!

"In the spring, when the temperature doesn't fall below 50°F at night, my plants go outdoors under an overhang and they come back indoors when the temperature dips into the low 40s. This early move avoids transfer shock. My holiday cacti are awesome!"

Christmas Decorating

After Thanksgiving, the decorative mood changes. The geese are honking their way South, and the cold air hints of snow—winter is here. I change the color scheme in my house from fall bronzes and golds to festive red and white and Christmas greenery. Christmas flowers for me include poinsettias, amaryllis, lilies of the valley, orchids and a small army of paperwhite narcissus.

Pre-cooled bulbs of paperwhite narcissus and amaryllis take from about four to ten weeks to flower from potting up depending on variety. The simplest method for forcing these is to use Pro-Mix, a commercially prepared "soil-less" medium comprised of sphagnum peat moss, perlite, vermiculite and other goodies; it's clean and convenient and seems to nurture healthy roots and tops. If you stagger bulb plantings every week or so, you'll have them continually through the holiday season, for Thanksgiving, Christmas and Near Year's.

I start my Christmas decorating by placing a big wreath (balsam fir, because it does not shed) on the front door. The wreath dates back to ancient Greece where it was worn by brides as a symbol of good luck and happiness. The circular shape, having neither beginning nor end, symbolized eternity. The pine cones on a wreath were used by the guardian spirits of Babylon for the daily ritual of sprinkling the tree of life, to keep demons from attacking. The scent of the pine wreath was thought to drive away evil spirits from the house at Christmas time. Holly is another good-luck piece of Christmas greenery. The ancient Romans thought it to have the ability to ward off lightening, evil spells and poison.

If a holly tree grows in your garden, you have another piece of good fortune. Pruning of fruiting hollies is best done just before Christmas, and why not use the short branches for your own decorations? All other pruning at this time should be limited to taking out diseased or dead wood and crossed branches. (Trimming to make the trees compact in habit or dense can also be done during early spring before growth starts.) And by the way, on a more modern note, George Washington was a famous horticulturist who appreciated holly. He recorded in his diary that in the early part of the year 1785 he spent several days planting holly trees at Mt. Vernon. His set of false teeth were reported to have been made of the white, hard-grained holly wood.

Every Christmas I get everyone in our house into the spirit by hanging mistletoe in a couple of doorways. Kissing beneath the mistletoe is an old custom that dates back to the Druids. The plant was believed to symbolize purity and strength and to bring happiness and peace, and promote romance. Enemies meeting beneath a sprig of mistletoe were said to become disarmed and kept their truce throughout the day.

Lastly is our beautiful Christmas tree. The tree, always an evergreen, is regarded as a symbol of everlasting life. The lights that are put on a Christmas tree were originally meant to help rekindle the sun's light to bring the family warmth through the holiday season.

Knowing these customs gives Christmas a special meaning to me and my family. As we decorate, we have a feeling of peace and happiness and love.

My Christmas dinner table is always red and white and green—red candles, garlands of greenery and bowl of paperwhite narcissus, which have a fragrance that is out of this world.

For the week after Christmas, I like to keep the same festive colors throughout the house. The paperwhite narcissus will last two weeks if they are kept in a cool place.

The poinsettia is the most popular plant for the Christmas holidays. It was discovered, made popular and named after our first ambassador to Mexico, Joel Poinsett. If given proper care, your poinsettia can bloom again the following year and for years to come. The requirements are not difficult: proper watering is most important; just keep it moist and not soggy. If you are lucky, it could be blooming until Easter! When the blooms fade, withhold water and place out of the light; it goes into a dormant stage and what it really needs is a rest!

In early May, trim the plant back to two or three nodes (small swellings on the stem), start watering and put in direct sunlight. When the frost is gone, just put your plant anywhere in your garden that has good sun; plunge pot and all into the ground. Fertilize occasionally and water during the hot summer months. Now comes the important part. In September, when the nights get cool, bring in your poinsettia; it must get 14 hours of total darkness every night, either by covering or closeting the plant. Be sure it gets no light from sundown to sun-up until Thanksgiving (not even a ray). Any light during that period will interfere with its cycle and it won't bloom. However, during the daytime it can have full light; but when darkness falls, back to bed again. Come Christmas, your poinsettia should be full of buds.

When January arrives and the New Year's celebration is over, it is time to unwind with a feeling of fatigue and a little sadness. Time to put all the Christmas tree ornaments back in their boxes for another year. I always get a *live* Christmas tree (the roots balled and covered) and immediately after the first of the year I plant it in a pre-dug hole. Plan ahead—you can have a great Christmas tree for the holidays and then have a wonderful new tree for your property. The hole should be dug before the ground freezes and should be one-third filled with mulch from your fall clean-up. This will keep the bottom of the hole from freezing so that it will be ready to receive your tree.

It gives me great pleasure to be able to plant the tree after the holidays. As with everything in the garden, it means the continuous renewal of life. Now that the year is over, I putter around the greenhouse—everything is resting. It is the quiet time. The seed catalogs arrive in the mail and I start to get excited thinking and planning for my great new garden next spring. Soon I will start sowing flats.

Christmas Potpourri

A treat for all of you who love potpourri: What more delightful way to usher in the holidays than with a round of aromatic herbs. If you've never made a potpourri before, you'll be amazed at how easy, fun and satisfying it is. And if you're an old hand at this ancient craft, I bet this recipe of combined scents will tempt you!

3	cups balsam or spruce needles
½	cup dried orange peel (broken into tiny pieces)
5	cups dried rose petals
2	cups dried lemon verbena
1½	tsp frankincense
1½	tsp myrrh
2	tsp orris root
½	cup assorted dried flowers
½	cup dried marigold petals
	Few drops of balsam-spruce oil
	Few drops of rose oil

Mix the ingredients and allow to mellow and age for at least four to five weeks. For best results, shake and turn daily. After two weeks, check the fragrance. Add oil and adjust the scent by adding more of one of the dry ingredients if needed.

Can you think of a better present for a friend than a sachet of Christmas potpourri?

Christmas Rose

The flower so often referred to as Christmas rose is not even a rose at all but a helle-bore, *Helleborus niger*. Botanically it belongs to the buttercup family and rarely (if ever) blooms at Christmastime—more likely in March. The flowers of this lovely plant are large ivory-white buttercups that are 2 to 3 inches wide. As they age, the flowers take on a curi-ous rose-green color. For hellebores to thrive, provide them with well-drained soil that has ample moisture. Mulch with pine needles for winter protection. A well-established colony of hellebores is well worth cultivating, a plus in any garden.

Planting is best in spring when the weather warms up, but never during the dry sum-mer period when the hellebores are usually dormant.

Christmas Tree Care

Q. *It is customary in our family to buy, put up and trim the Christmas tree two weeks before Christmas. We leave it up through New Year's. Unfortunately, by the time January 1 gets here, our tree is as dry as a bone with half the needles already fallen on the floor.*

I keep it in a stand with water, but this doesn't seem to help. Do you have any suggestions for making our Christmas tree last longer?

A. It really is a problem keeping a tree fresh through the holiday season. Not only are the dead fallen needles unsightly, but a dried-out tree can be a real fire hazard.

Most trees are cut in bulk, then shipped to where they are sold. Your tree can be any-where from a few days to two weeks cut when you buy it and probably is already starting to die before you even get it up. I have a suggestion that will help, plus you can make it a fun family adventure.

Go to a tree farm and cut your own tree. Start in the morning so you can cut your tree in daylight. Bring a tape measure because trees look smaller outdoors and take a saw for cutting the tree (an ax might slip loose and cut your leg).

Cut the tree near the ground; the lower branches can be used for wreaths. Be sure to bring some string for tying the tree to the car. When you get the tree home, make a new cut diagonally across the base of the trunk. Then put it in a container that holds water. This freshly cut tree should last you well through the holiday season.

Tips for Tending Trees

With all the fun and activity the Christmas season brings, don't forget to care properly for the loveliest of holiday decorations—the Christmas tree. Here is my checklist for easy tree care:

1. To improve water intake, make a fresh cut ¼-inch up the tree trunk. For potted trees, keep the root ball moist but not dripping wet. Remember to water your tree regularly because it will absorb several quarts of water each week.

2. Test all lights and check for frayed wires before you start trimming the tree. On living trees, use lights that don't give off heat. Never use candles and, if you do, don't leave them burning if no one is in the room. Place the tree away from extreme heat, such as a fireplace or heater.

3. Acclimate live trees to the outdoors gradually when the holidays are over. Mulch the ground before planting and don't remove the root-ball covering unless it's plastic, but be sure to cut any string from around the trunk and peel back the burlap.

After planting, mulch well and water as needed. Stake your live tree to help it withstand the harsh winter winds.

Christmas Tree, Choosing a

What would Christmas be without the sight and smell of a beautifully trimmed tree! This charming custom came from England, where the tradition was borrowed from German religious plays featuring a lovely Christbaum, or wreath, decorated with roses, wafers and apples.

There are about 40 different types of Christmas trees, but the most popular are white pine (balsam), fir, spruce and Scotch pine.

Here are some pointers to keep in mind when selecting a fresh Christmas tree:

1. Naturally, the shape is important. The traditional Christmas tree tapers from a broad, bushy base to a conical top.

2. The tree should be a healthy green color with no brown patches and should exude the fresh fragrance of evergreen. Red pine, white pine and Scotch pine, Douglas fir, balsam fir and white fir are best for needle retention and longevity.

3. To test for freshness, gently bend the needles back; if they break, the tree is too

dry. Run your hand across the bottom of the stump. Usually it will be wet and sticky if the tree has been freshly cut.

4. When you are ready to bring the tree inside, place it in a stand that has a well for water. Never let the container run dry! Water helps replace the moisture given off by needles in a warm room.

5. If you choose a living tree, or an uncut tree that has been dug and burlapped, remember to dig a hole for it before the ground freezes and cover the hole with insulating material, such as straw or leaves. Do not keep it in the house for more than a few days, and then place it in a cool basement or garage to harden off before transplanting. A direct transfer from a warm house to freezing temperatures outside can kill a tree. Proper planting will have to wait until the ground thaws in spring.

Christmas Tree Farming

The concept of a cut Christmas tree often makes environmentally conscientious people uncomfortable, but let me explain. Christmas trees are grown in rural areas, usually on hillsides. These areas are often unsuitable for farming but can become productive with Christmas trees. The trees continually provide animal habitats, help control soil erosion and aid in directing run-off water into underground reservoirs. Keep in mind, once an area is harvested it's immediately re-planted the following spring. These rural areas benefit from employment the industry brings to it.

Christmas Tree, Living

More and more families are choosing live, balled and burlapped trees at Christmastime. Whether the trend reflects a motivation to do something positive for the environment or a desire for the freshest tree possible, keeping a live tree green and growing all year is a simple matter. Just follow my guidelines.

Site selection: Christmas trees are evergreens and therefore grow best in full sun and well-drained soil. Choose a planting site and dig the hole well before the ground freezes. Mulch the hole after digging to keep the ground workable until you get a chance to plant your tree.

Digging the hole: Make sure the hole is twice the width but only as deep as the tree's root ball. Keep the soil you dig out in the garage or basement to prevent freezing. You'll need it when you plant.

Acclimate your tree gradually. Avoid temperature shock. After bringing your tree home from the nursery or garden center, give it a few days in your garage, porch or other sheltered area. After you have enjoyed its fragrance and beauty throughout the holidays, gradually acclimate it to outdoor temperatures. Again, a porch or garage offers the shelter and intermediate temperatures your tree requires right now.

Tree placement and decoration: Heat sources such as radiators, television sets and fire-places dry out a tree. While checking your electric lights for worn or frayed wires, make sure they don't emit too much heat. Turn lights off when you leave the house and before retiring in the evening.

Watering your tree: Never let water levels become depleted on a live tree; the root ball must stay sufficiently moist. Most live trees require a larger, sturdier container than the traditional tree stand. Garden centers carry all sizes.

Planting your tree: When it's time to introduce your tree to its permanent home, position the root ball in the pre-dug hole, keeping the soil line on the trunk level with or slightly above the top of the hole. Remove the string and roll back the burlap to expose the top of the root ball. Back-fill around the root ball with the soil you saved earlier. Water thoroughly. If your climate doesn't receive much snow, your newly planted tree may need periodic watering.

Follow these simple guidelines, and a live Christmas tree with provide enjoyment and beauty far beyond the holiday season.

Q. *Is it a good thing to have a living Christmas tree? We'd like to have one each year, then plant it on our property in the country.*

A. If you mean in an apartment that is hot and dry, the answer is no, but if you can situate the containerized or balled-and-burlapped tree in a place where temperatures will be mostly below 70°F, insulate it from hot, dry drafts of air and keep the roots moist at all times; yes, you may succeed with your plan—a charming one. I know of a couple in Westchester County, New York, who have Christmas trees representing more than 25 holidays they've shared together, planted as the backdrop for their beautiful flower borders and vegetable gardens.

Christmas Trees, Recycling

Each holiday season, millions of Christmas trees end up destined for the town dump—from holiday treasure to trash literally overnight!

Why waste a tree and especially your tree, a symbol of life, giving and hope when it can be put to good use?

Buy a balled or burlapped or a potted tree and plant it after the holidays. Living trees are more expensive than cut ones, but they will be enjoyed for years to come rather than for a few short days. When ready to plant (prepare a hole before), be careful not to move the tree directly from a warm area into freezing temperatures. First, take it to a sheltered spot for several days so it can adjust to colder temperatures.

Old Christmas trees (live, cut ones), can take on new life. They may be chipped and shredded and can be recycled into mulch. Or you could cut off the boughs and place them on your perennial beds for added protection.

> ## Decorating Idea
>
> Try decorating your Christmas tree with cut flowers, some fragrant, all in water picks, which your florist can supply (you can save them to use on other special occasions).

If you have a chipper/shredder, try turning your tree into mulch. Make sure to remove all decorations, lights, tinsel, attached stands or any nails used in the base of the trunk. It's not a good idea to shred holiday trees that have been painted or flocked.

If you want to keep your tree outside in the garden for a little color, decorate it for the birds with orange slices, suet balls and small hanging seed feeders. The birds will flock in for treats and use the branches for shelter and cover.

Many cities have tree-recycling programs that involve residential collection, drop-off locations and even a weekend chipping event (that will produce lots of mulch). Check with your local department of public works for information about tree recycling in your area.

Some communities are using discarded Christmas trees to make barriers to help curb sand and soil erosion on beaches and riverbeds. Old conifers are also sunk into private ponds where they provide protection and a feeding area for pond fish.

One thing you should not use your Christmas tree for is firewood. Burning your old tree may contribute to creosote buildup in your chimney—nobody needs that!

Christmas Tree Safety Tips

To minimize the risk of Christmas tree fire, remember:

1. A dry tree is a fire hazard. Before purchasing a cut tree, strike the butt against the ground sharply. A shower of needles means the tree has already dried out.
2. Before placing the tree in water, make a fresh cut at the trunk to expose new wood for better water uptake.
3. Keep the water container of your tree always full. A fresh tree can drink several gallons of water in the first few days in the home.
4. Never place a tree near a fireplace, radiator or other heat source. Keep the room cool to minimize drying.
5. Keep your tree fresh as long as possible and reduce fire hazard by spraying the entire tree thoroughly with an antidessicant like Safer's ForEverGreen.
6. Check each set of lights, new or old, for broken or cracked sockets, frayed or bare wires, or loose connections. Discard any damaged lights or repair before usage.
7. Use no more than three standard-size sets of lights per single extension cord.
8. Never use lighted candles on or near a tree or other evergreens.
9. Don't burn Christmas greens in your fireplace. The sparks they throw are a real fire hazard.
10. Plan for safety. Always look for and eliminate what common sense tells you is a potential danger.

Christmas Trees for Small Spaces

People living in apartments, small houses and mobile homes often have little space to set up large Christmas trees for the holiday season. Although table-size trees may solve the dilemma, they may be too dear.

Of course, one answer to this predicament would be an artificial tree, but they lack, of course, the fragrance and natural beauty of the real thing. Sound hopeless? Not quite. The solution is to create a small Christmas tree with all the trimmings of evergreen trees and shrubs.

A Christmas tree about a foot tall can be easily constructed at home. One item needed as the trunk of a Christmas tree in the project is a block of Oasis, a material used by florists in making flower arrangements. The block can be set on end in a plastic hold-er, also available at garden shops.

The top end of the block should be trimmed to about 1 ½ inches in diameter, any excess cut off with a sharp knife. Form the block so that it resembles a cone; be sure to do this before wetting the block.

Trimmings from fragrant white cedar, Douglas fir and balsam fir are best. Boxwood and juniper are good, too. Hemlock and spruce shed needles quickly when dry, but the moist Oasis block that forms the trunk of the tree supplies moisture to the trimmings, thus allowing them to hold their needles longer.

Most important for success before putting together a tree is to soak the Oasis in water for several minutes. It absorbs a large amount of water, thus providing moisture to the greens for about a week. In a warm room the Oasis may need watering twice a week or more often, so just pour water into the holder and the Oasis will pick it up.

The next step is the construction of the tree itself. Insert the evergreen trimmings from the bottom up, using the longest pieces (6 to 8 inches) first to make a bottom circle of greens. Using progressively shorter pieces, build circles of trimmings toward the top, tilt-ing them slightly. The pieces near the top should be almost vertical.

Now the fun begins, decorating your little tree. Let your imagination go wild by using all sorts of tiny tree lights and miniature ornaments and anything else that strikes your fancy!

Merry Christmas!

Chrysanthemum Cascades

Whether buying or propagating a mum, it is possible to grow breathtaking cascades like those featured in botanical gardens around the United States. Here are ten tips to help you grow a successful cascade that will be the envy of your friends.

1. To stop early blooming, mums need at least 16 hours of light daily. If possible, break up nighttime hours with four hours of light, 10:00 P.M. to 2:00 A.M.
2. As the cutting/plant grows, tie the main stem to a stake to keep it straight. Pinch the lateral shoots (approximately every ten days), leaving only two sets of leaves. This continual pinching forces the main stem to grow fast and makes the plant fuller since the pinched laterals will grow additional branches.

3. Water when the soil feels dry but don't let the plant wilt. Use a liquid fertilizer once a week. A 20-10-20 mix is suitable.

4. Re-pot to a larger container every four to five weeks. When the plant is 2 to 3 feet long, repot for the last time in a 7-gallon container.

5. Place three plants in a row at the edge of your 7-gallon container, gently bending the main stem downward and tying them with twist ties to a wire frame.

6. Place the mums outside (around May 15) and continue pinching. As the days get longer, nighttime lighting becomes unnecessary. Tying down main stems and pinching the lateral and bilateral shoots are still important if a full plant is preferred.

7. Pinch the mums until late August or early September when budding should begin. Make the last pinch about eight weeks before the "show," but continue to water and fertilize faithfully until color begins to appear. Discontinue fertilizer at this time. A 7-gallon pot of mums should produce approximately 1,000 blooms. New blooms will continue opening for about two weeks, and flowers will last about six weeks.

8. Elevate the container so the mums can cascade to the ground. Porch rails are ideal.

9. When the blooms begin to die, trim them off the plant. Begin again the following February with cuttings from this cascade. (Original plants can actually be trimmed back and retrained, but better cascades will result from new cuttings.)

10. Enjoy the chrysanthemums; they are a fabulous plant.

Citrus Indoors

Q. *I would like some advice on growing citrus indoors, especially what to do with them during the winter months. Can I start my own trees from seed?*

A. The best varieties for indoor culture are lemons, limes, kumquats, satsuma mandarin and calamondin. If sufficient room is available, oranges, tangerines, tangelos and grapefruit will also do well.

For citrus, proper soil is critical for good growth. They need a soil that is well drained. A pre-mixed potting soil is satisfactory, but if it's rather slow to dry add sand and/or perlite to it. Water thoroughly and don't let the pot sit in a saucer of water. Also, allow the soil surface to dry before watering again.

A second important key to growing citrus successfully is light. Citrus needs full sun or as much light as possible for growth, flowering and fruiting. During the winter indoors, place it in as much light as possible. Also, citrus needs warm temperatures to thrive. During the winter, citrus will show very little growth in cool indoor conditions, so decrease watering and fertilizing accordingly. For citrus, any equally balanced fertilizer (10-10-10, i.e.) containing minor elements is fine. Just be sure to read directions on the label carefully.

When buying a citrus tree for indoor or patio culture, you'll usually buy a plant that was rooted from a cutting. Grafted or budded trees on dwarfing rootstocks are also a good choice. The cheapest way to start a citrus tree is from seed. This works well for calamondin, lime and some lemons, but most other citrus varieties may not flower or fruit for several years if grown from seed.

Cold Frames

A cold frame is usually a rectangular, bottomless box with soil—almost always with a cover of some sort—often transparent, or at least translucent.

A cold frame is very different from a hot bed in that a cold frame receives no artificial heat. Frames with bottoms derive heat from the earth; the deeper, the warmer.

The wind can be trouble because it blows covers away, even when secure. It also injures tender parts of plants when covers are lifted. It's best to build your frame with some protection from prevailing winds, both the cold winds of winter and the dry ones of summer. A fence, hedge or building is best, as long as it doesn't block out the sunlight.

Compost, and Sick Plants

Q. *Can "sick" material such as blighted peony flowers or diseased tomato vines be added to my compost pile? What about seed-laden debris from noxious weeds?*

A. It all depends on how hot your pile gets as it composts. If your compost is piled in large heaps and is turned often, weed seeds and pathogens are usually destroyed. But if you're a lazy composter, you've probably got a cold pile and you shouldn't throw anything sick on it. Keep in mind, diseases are killed by heat, but to destroy most weed seeds the compost pile must reach high temperatures of 140° to 160°F on the inside of the pile for at least three days. I feel if plants are heavily infested or if the disease in question has been a persistent problem in your garden, keep that plant out of the compost pile—it's just not worth the risk.

Never build a pile heavily laden with sick plants or weeds, for that matter. And, remember, in winter no compost pile heats up as it does in the summer months.

Container Gardening

One of the most versatile and easy ways to grow bushels of colorful annual flowers is in containers. The fast-growing popularity of containers is proof that Americans like container growing, whether they do it themselves or have someone else prepare it for them.

If It Will Hold Soil, It Is a Container

While many people think primarily of terra cotta, plastic pots, glazed pots or half-barrels as likely containers for plants, just about any container is a possible candidate. Car tires, old shoes, coffee pots, raw bags of growing mix and just about anything imaginable can be used to grow plants. If whimsy is your style, don't be afraid to try it. The basics always remain the same.

The Benefits

Container growing offers many benefits, not the least of which is that you can put a "garden" just about anywhere you choose. Cement balconies on a high-rise building can become urban gardens, or splashes of color can be put on a backyard deck or patio. And, providing the containers are not too heavy, potted plants can be moved and rearranged whenever the need or mood arises.

Without doubt, container gardens require less weeding than in-ground counterparts, making them ideal for busy people who love gardening but have limited time. However, watering has to be watched more closely. Containers in hot sun can dry out quickly, and even a gentle summer breeze will steal moisture from plants. Be prepared to water daily or even twice daily during the long, hot dry spells of July and August.

Start with a Plan

Where would you like to put your containers, and what would you like to grow? If an area receives full sun most of the day, you can choose from a wide selection of sun-loving flowers. If the area receives limited sun, choose plants that tolerate less light, and shady areas, of course, call for shade-loving plants. With containers, one of the advantages is that you can move them to keep them in the sun if you have the time.

Once you know where you want to grow, choosing what to grow is the next big step. No matter what you grow, plan out each container or grouping of containers, making notes of what you would like where. For appealing groupings, include plants of different heights, colors and textures, keeping in mind that plants taller than 1 ½ times the height of the container may look unbalanced.

For maximum interest and to create depth, plan groupings of three to five different sized containers—for example, one to two large pots with plants reaching about 2 or 3 feet tall, one with 18-inch plants, and two with 12-inch or smaller plants. When grouped, these plants will give a three-dimensional look to your mini-garden.

One common mistake made with container gardens is choosing the wrong combination of plants. Don't mix shade-loving plants with sun-loving plants in the same container or in the same grouping. Shade plants will not perform as well in full sun, and full-sun plants will not perform their best in limited light. Even if mixed and put in partial sun and partial shade, neither type will give its best, so stick to one type in a container and in a grouping.

You can also create a garden that you can vary quickly by planting masses of one color and variety in separate containers and then grouping and re-grouping them as you like; one pot of trailing flowers or one of a mass flower such as marigolds is a good choice, for example.

Container Basics

Choose a container deep enough for the root systems of the plants you will be growing, and one that will hold ample soil for both support and water retention. A good container will have a drainage hole at the bottom. Before adding soil, put some gravel or pieces of broken pots over the hole to prevent the soil from washing out with each watering. Good drainage can prevent soggy soil that limits a plant's uptake of needed oxygen. Overwatering is more of a problem with plants grown in the shade than with plants grown in full sun. If you want to use a decorative container that doesn't have a drainage hole, consider placing a pot in a pot. Put a few inches of gravel in the bottom of the decorative pot to hold the flowering pot off the bottom.

Use a good, sterile, porous potting medium for filling your containers. A Pro-Mix soil is best because it contains all the nutrients needed for proper plant growth.

There are three ways to grow plants for your containers. You can sow seed directly into the containers to start them. If you do this, follow the germinating instructions on the seed packet and be prepared to thin out the plants when they are young. You can also start from seed using a starter kit and then transplant the seedlings to the containers when they are ready. Or, you can purchase started bedding plants at your local garden center or nursery and plant those in the containers.

How many plants per container? If you provide enough soil and water, you can space plants closer together than the usual recommendations. In a larger pot, you could plant 8 to 12 transplants of flowers, depending on how spreading they are. Be careful not to overplant or when the plants mature they will overpower and overshadow one another and look too crowded.

Designing a Container Garden

Color, texture and flower form are the basic elements in designing a container garden. With color today, anything goes. Gone are the days when pink and scarlet clashed—today you can combine any colors you want in a pot or in a grouping.

Texture is often best brought out by including foliage plants such as leather-leafed ferns, or asparagus sprengeri with its long lacy fronds. Let trailing plants spill over the edges of the containers to soften and deformalize plantings. Some perennial ground covers offer interesting textures and can be dug up and re-planted in the garden in fall when the annuals have died back.

Flower forms can be grouped into three basic shapes. Linear forms like *Salvia spendens* or snap dragons are tall and spiky. Mass forms such as daisies, petunias or marigolds have many small or large flowers. Focus forms such as African marigolds or a spectacular geranium plant are characterized by large or distinctive flowers.

One example of combining these forms would be a large container of red salvia (upright and tall), pale-blue petunias (round masses of flowers, medium height) and white alyssum (small lacy flowers, low and trailing). Or use tall blue lavender for height and white petunias and red creeping phlox for color.

Plant individual pots of one type (all salvia for example) or combine one or two types in a larger pot (salvia and sprengeri) depending on the look you want for your grouping. The idea is to combine color, texture and varying heights in a grouping of containers.

Container Garden Care

Keep your containers well watered and watch for any silting when the wind blows.

Container growing isn't that much different than growing plants in a garden plot, but can offer more versatility and a lot less weeding work; do this when needed.

Cranberries

Cranberry country extends from Newfoundland to North Carolina and as far west as Minnesota and Arkansas. Other important commercial cranberry states include New Jersey, Wisconsin, Oregon and Washington. But no other state surpasses Massachusetts, where commercial production began in 1820. Massachusetts produces almost half the world's supply of cranberries—over 800,000 barrels annually. Harvest time in cranberry country is a six-week frenzy that begins in late September. Bogs for miles around are flooded and transformed into lakes of luscious red berries as waterwheels churn the water and dislodge the berries from their vines. The growers, wearing chest-high rubber waders, step into the bogs and corral tons and tons of floating berries to where they can be propelled by elevators into waiting trucks to be processed for the market.

Cranberries were among the first presents the Indians brought to the Pilgrims back in 1620. The Indians relished fresh berries, dried them and mixed them with dried deer meat and fat to make pemmican. Cranberry juice was often used as a dye and crushed berries as a poultice for wounds. The word *cranberry* was a contraction for craneberry, because the pale-pink fruit blossoms resembled the head of cranes. In the fall, these delicious ripe berries are the main food for cranes.

Even though the lowlands are called bogs, cranberries don't grow in water, only on swampland near a water supply where the water provides frost protection and irrigation. When new plantations for the harvest are needed, swamp areas are carefully cleared of brush and trees, and water is drained to a depth of 18 inches. The peat soil is spread with sand and cranberry cuttings and planted deeply. The vines spread very much like strawberry plants. Once the berries were handpicked but, like most everything else, the harvest is now mechanical.

Eating cranberries at holiday time has been an American tradition for years; in fact, well over 300. Luckily the berry is thriving and still the same marvelous fruit. For weight-watchers, cranberries are a low-calorie fruit—one cup contains only 4.6 calories—besides being a source of vitamin C and iron.

For a tangy relish, two cups of ground cranberries can be combined with a cup of chopped celery and a cup of chopped apple. Fresh chopped cranberries can be added to coleslaw for another holiday treat.

Cyclamen

When you're ready for spring as winter drags on, some indoor color can keep you going until you can get back to your outdoor annuals. Cyclamen can continue blooming up to four months under ideal conditions. Beautiful butterfly-like blossoms last two to three weeks in white, pink, lavender or red.

Bright diffused light helps buds to develop and bloom. Cool nights (50° to 60°F) extend the flowering period. Check watering needs frequently since wilting can damage buds. Water thoroughly when just the soil surface is dry to the touch, taking care not to let water stand in the crown of the plant since this encourages rotting.

C.Z.'s Special Holiday Toddy

Start with a big pot of apple cider, add 3 or 4 cinnamon sticks and about a dozen cloves. Heat slowly. Don't boil. When it's steaming hot, ladle this mixture into a mug and add as much rum as you dare! Be sure not to get any loose cloves in the mug.

You can leave the spiced cider simmering on the stove all day and the aroma that fills your kitchen is divine! So any time you feel like a little taste of holiday cheer, just grab the ladle and the rum.

Happy holidays!

December Gardening Tips

The first priority this month is winterizing the garden so it will be in good shape for next year. Clear all remaining plant refuse from the garden and add it to the leaves in the compost heap. Shallow tilling is an excellent way to destroy large numbers of insect eggs by exposing them to the sun, weather, birds and other predators. Your garden must be put to bed spick-and-span if it is to be prepared for next spring's plantings.

If possible, blanket the whole garden with freshly fallen leaves and pine needles. (This is what I do.) It is an essential time for your plants to rest and restore their energy for next year. Just make your garden cozy; blanket it and protect it as if it were your child.

Fall applications of fertilizer should be made on dormant shrubs and trees, easily accomplished after the leaves have fallen. Since the soil is still relatively warm (above 40°F), the roots will absorb the nutrients more readily than in early spring.

The holiday season will soon begin, to make sure bulbs have been planted, such as aristocratic amaryllis and fragrant paperwhite narcissus. Set narcissus bulbs in shallow bowls of pebbles and water and put them in a dark place to root. After two or three weeks they'll do best in a stronger light. When flower shoots are 6 to 7 inches high, bring to a bright window, but not into direct sunlight. You'll have a glorious display in about five weeks.

Once the earth has frozen hard, it's a good idea to mulch beds of perennials and bulbs with 4 to 6 inches of light material, like straw or evergreen branches. Your plants will thank you next spring for the thoughtfulness.

December Tips

- Pot up herbs to grow on sunny windowsills.
- Prune evergreens for indoor holiday decorations. Do it with care so as not to destroy the beauty of your tree.
- Feed the birds; it keeps their little bodies warm.
- To prolong the color of poinsettias, put them where they can enjoy 72°F temperatures by day and 62°F for nighttime. And keep the soil moist, not wet.
- For holiday favorites such as Christmas cactus, kalanchoe, cyclamen and poinsettia, place them in full sun but away from household heat. Never put a plant on top of a radiator or in a draft.

The Big Sleep

Unlike most animals, plants sleep not so much to rest but to avoid adverse environmental conditions such as bitter cold, draft or excessive heat. Often plants go dormant simply to await favorable conditions to their liking, such as germination.

Entering dormancy requires a combined effort among different plant parts. Take deciduous trees, for example—oak, maples, willows, fruit trees to name a few. In the fall, when the days shorten and cooler temperatures arrive, trees shed their leaves. Growth all but shuts down (except for the roots) so the cells inside the woody plants must generate their own "antifreeze" to keep from freezing and bursting.

Dormancy lasts until the arrival of warm temperatures and longer days—a signal to the sleeping buds to break dormancy and emerge. Roses start to prepare for dormancy at the end of August; therefore, no fertilizing is needed after the second week of that month.

Nature is often contrary. Sometimes during long, warm falls dormancy is delayed. It plays havoc with some fruit-tree varieties because they require a minimum number of days of dormancy to produce flower buds and fruit. A fruitless year can be due to a warm fall, a mild winter or an early spring.

Dormancy is basically a period that protects the plant from the elements, not a suspension of growth. Always keep in mind that the roots of plants never stop growing—when they stop growing, the plant dies.

Decoration Recycling

Old Christmas wreaths made from evergreens and wound with wire or twine make dandy mulch-retaining rings when placed around azaleas, blueberry bushes and other small acid-loving shrubs. Just work the wreath down over the tops of the bushes to the ground. It will hold mulch, compost and moisture together. Eventually it will decompose its nutrients into the soil.

Check Christmas tree sales after Christmas. Some dealers will give away unsold trees. They are perfect for bird shelters.

Old holiday greenery makes a perfect covering for the perennial bed, newly planted bulbs and other plants in need of protection due to freezing and thawing of the soil.

Make the tree a winter bird feeder. Put up strings of cranberries along with pine cones stuffed with peanut butter and rolled in bird seed.

Flowers, Best Gifts

Running out of ideas—and time—for finding that perfect holiday present? Fresh-cut flowers are "in," one of the most appreciated of gifts for both personal and business giving.

I offer these guidelines to help you create a floral present or wreath for those special people on your holiday list.

Greeting: A florist can help you convey a special greeting for each person on your list. Provide information such as recipient's gender, personality type, as well as business, personal or family ties.

Colors: Specific colors such as green, white or red are typically associated with the holiday season but, outside of tradition, you may want to complement colors of the recipient's house or office. Certain colors may have special meaning to the individual since most flowers complement each other. I favor using a single-color scheme—all white, for example, can be striking. Arrangements of mixed colors are always festive and reflect the way flowers grow in nature.

Style: Certain buzzwords conjure up images of particular floral styles. Here are some words that florists often use that may help you to describe your favorite floral style: masculine/feminine; formal/informal; nostalgic/contemporary; loose; bold; dramatic; unusual; seasonal; ikebana (Japanese style). I say let your own imagination run wild!

Price: The price of a floral gift is determined by several factors. Usually the more flowers the higher the price. During the holiday season, good flower buys can be found in chrysanthemums, carnations and roses. Flowers in non-holiday colors are particularly good values.

Accessories: Wine, balloons, stuffed animals, fruit candies and, of course, the most festive drink of all, champagne, add to the cost of an arrangement. The total price will usually include a design fee unless you're purchasing loose stems to arrange at home. And, for a small additional fee, floral wire services also offer the convenience of ordering a floral gift for delivery across the country. Flower containers come in all price ranges, from inexpensive plastic bowls to clay pots to crystal vases. Be sure to ask about all charges (including delivery) before finalizing your holiday purchases.

Frostbite

The American Medical Association warns frostbite can be very dangerous and painful. A prickly feeling of "pins and needles" is the first sign of frostbite. Get the person immediately indoors. Do not rub or massage the frozen part; treat it gently and get medical help as quickly as possible.

Fruit Trees

I'd like to relate a technique used for successfully growing fruit trees in very cold winter areas. Often the problem of growing fruit trees in cold areas is not the tree's lack of winter hardiness but the tree's susceptibility to frost. Early blooming fruit trees can lose their entire crop to an untimely spring frost. Often late winter or early spring brings violent snow storms, and this is the precise moment to protect your trees. Using a snow blower, shovel or tractor to pile snow around the fruit trees, extend a base of snow around the trunk as wide as the tree is tall. The snow pile will last late into spring, creating the perfect temperature around the tree and roots.

By trying to control the weather, most frost protection techniques work by delaying bloom at least seven to 10 days.

Fruit Trees from Seed

Q. *Is it possible to start plum, peach and apricot trees from seed?*

A. You can grow these trees by planting their fruit pits, but I don't recommend it because the fruit they bear won't be as good as that of the original tree. Fruit from seed-grown trees is usually green and small.

Your best bet to obtain good, productive fruit trees is to go to a reliable nursery and buy grafted trees, which combine root stocks that are pest- and disease-resistant with scions (fruiting branches) of varieties that bear super fruit.

However, not to discourage you from using your own fruit pits, here's how you can grow root-stock from your own grafting attempts.

Clean the pits, then dry and store them in a cool spot with low humidity where they won't become moldy or dry out. When soil temperatures fall to about 40°F, plant the pits outside about 6 inches apart and 2 inches deep in well-drained soil. They need about 120 days of temperatures of 40°F before they will sprout. About 50 percent will germinate.

To protect against rodent damage, use wire mesh, but remove the mesh in about April before the seeds begin to sprout. Don't fertilize too much, but water the seedlings well, letting them grow through one complete season. Then graft the kind of fruit you want on them.

Garden Gloves

Q. *I received a pair of luscious leather gardening gloves for Christmas. As this is a rare and special treat, I want to do right by them! How do I take care of them after each gardening season?*

A. Rub a little lanolin on the gloves and, while you're at it, give your hands a good rub, too! Don't expose the gloves to the sun; shade is the key here while they are conditioning with the lanolin.

Gifts for Gardeners

Q. *I have many friends and neighbors who garden, and I would like to give them presents that would suit their hobby. Can you help me out with some ideas?*

A. The possibilities are practically endless because there are so many fabulous gardening items on the market. Of course, at this time of year (the holiday season), some people find it difficult to locate gardening products since most garden centers and nurseries are stocked with holiday trimmings and Christmas trees. However, most places have the items but not on prominent display, so just ask. Being so late in the season, you might even get the product at a reduction.

Consider a nursery gift certificate for a shrub, tree or lawn mower; they could pick it up next spring. Gardening equipment is another possibility; it ranges from large to small and from expensive to moderately priced. Tools are another consideration, or equipment such as an electric hedger, leaf blower, nozzle, sprinkler or wheelbarrow. I think a hose is one of the best items.

Stocking stuffers: Small hand tools, clippers, a bulb planter, summer flowering bulbs, pre-cooled bulbs, amaryllis and hardy chrysanthemums are all nifty presents.

A pine-cone three-wicked candle makes a great centerpiece or hostess gift. A flickering flame turns any dinner into an event, and a large centerpiece candle filled with dried botanicals will really help to set the holiday mood.

Inspired by the bounty of the garden, give your favorite green thumb a set of collectible garden ornaments made of mouth-blown glass in the Old World tradition: a trio of pomegranates, a whole and half pear duo and a green and red chili pepper pair.

Holiday greens by mail are the perfect way to send the sentiments of the season in style. You can buy wreaths, garlands and even trees, freshly harvested and fully fragrant. Noble fir and eucalyptus wreaths and cedar garlands are just a few of the selections available at your garden center.

Glastonbury Thorn

About 50 years ago, a New York City physician, Dr. Thomas Everett, brought a Glastonbury thorn from England to his house in Brooklyn, then donated it to the New York Botanical Garden in the Bronx, where it has been growing happily ever since. Each late fall, as well as May, this amazing plant's fragrant white blossoms smell to high heaven and unfold to admiring viewers. One of the rarest trees of the Botanical Garden's collection, the Glastonbury thorn is rooted in a biblical myth.

The Glastonbury legend began in 31 A.D., when Joseph of Arimathea, an uncle of Jesus, worn by his pilgrimage from the Holy Land, climbed to the summit of Wearyall Hill at Glastonbury, a small town in England. There he thrust his staff into the ground as a sign that his wanderings were over. He left his staff, which was made of wood, in the soil.

Soon afterward, the staff put out roots and leaf branches. In the course of time, the holy thorn blossomed, not only in the spring, but also on Christmas Eve. Thus, the tree that sprang from St. Joseph's staff is the holy thorn of Glastonbury which, over the years, has become known as the Glastonbury thorn.

The thorn grew where St. Joseph had planted it until the time of the Puritan rebellion against Charles I, when it was cut to a stump by one who believed it was idolatrous. Nevertheless, the stump survived until the middle of the eighteenth century, and its site is now marked with a stone reading "Joseph of Arimathea."

Cuttings have been taken from the tree and established elsewhere in England. They, as well as the tree at Glastonbury, were regarded as the holy thorn, and the vandalism that destroyed Joseph's planting served only to demonstrate the immortality of trees and legends.

Not only is the tree still flowering, but in parts of England people still gather on Christmas Eve to wait for its blossoming. The Christmas Eve of the Julian calendar (January 5) is when the thorn is believed to bloom. The tree's heaviest bloom occurs in May, but the blossoms of October are equally as ravishing and, in either case, they honor the birth of Jesus Christ.

The Glastonbury thorn is located immediately adjacent to the Museum Building at the garden.

Holiday Bulb Flowers

Anticipating the holidays is fun, as anyone can tell you, and anticipating holiday plants as gifts and decorations is smart, as every hostess knows.

Now is the time to plan and plant flower bulbs for the holidays for both gifts and decorations. You can start from scratch by assembling your own forced bulb kit, or buying ready-grown bulbs at a garden center or florist and popping them (plastic or clay pot and all) into a more decorative container of your choosing (the container makes a great second gift in itself!).

For the do-it-yourself person, bulbs are a perfect choice. Assembling a planting gift kit is easy, requiring only bulbs, soil or other planting medium, a pot and some decorative doodads, such as moss, ivy and ribbons.

Anything expensive, like a bowl or pot, is not essential. Some of the best buys are flea market finds. Most people like to receive bulbs at the planting stage. Watching bulbs grow is half the fun, but for those who prefer instant gratification, give the gift when blooming.

Some bulbs, such as amaryllis and paperwhites, can readily be brought into flower in time for the winter holidays if you start about five to six weeks in advance. Even some tulips, such as Brilliant Star, Christmas Marvel and Flair, can be brought to flower in December, though tulips require pre-cooling and are among the trickier bulbs to force successfully. Even easier are hyacinths which can be bought partially pre-cooled and therefore more quickly brought to flower.

Guidelines for Forcing Flower Bulbs

The term "forcing" means fooling—for what you really do is fool the bulb into thinking that winter is over and it's time to flower. There's nothing wrong with that. Following is a list of bulbs for forcing and some forcing tips.

Easiest Indoor Bulbs

Paperwhites are especially easy to grow. They can be bought as loose bulbs or in a pre-packaged forcing kit. They are often found in displays along with gravel, containers and other bulbs for forcing. Paperwhites are best grown in a shallow pot or bowl with drainage holes in the bottom.

Fill the pot two-thirds full with gravel, stones or even fun things like colored beads or marbles. Place as many bulbs as will fit on the gravel with the pointed side—or the nose side—up. Then fill in gravel around them, leaving the top half of the bulb exposed.

Add water up to the base of the bulbs and maintain water at this level. Place the container in a cool place. Within days, strong roots will appear. As they grow, they will sometimes push the bulbs upward. If so, just push them back into the soil.

When the green shoots appear, move your plant to a cool, sunny spot. The shoots will develop rapidly and, in about three more weeks, you'll have masses of fragrant white flowers.

Amaryllis bulbs are very large but very easy to grow. These big bulbs are normally planted one to a pot and are also available in complete pre-packaged kits. To be successful, begin six weeks in advance, as amaryllis can be easily brought to flower for the holiday season. By starting a new pot every few weeks, it's possible to have amaryllis blooming in the house from December through April.

Choose a pot only slightly bigger around than your bulb, but be sure it has a drainage hole (and a saucer to catch the water that drains). Always empty the saucer of water; otherwise it will rot the roots. Add several inches of soil and place the bulbs in the pot, pointed end up with the neck and bare shoulders of the bulb just peeking over the top of the container.

Fill in with soil and gently pat down, leaving the neck and shoulders of the bulb exposed. Water well. Place in a cool sunny spot. Water sparingly at first. After the first tiny flower bulb appears (about two weeks), water often. In four to six more weeks, you or your recipient will be proud to show off huge, exotic-looking flowers of velvety red, pink, white, peach, orange or even multicolored.

For a big statement, plant three bulbs together in a pot more broad than tall (again slightly larger around than all three bulbs positioned in a circle, but not touching).

Magnificent amaryllis grow tall and often top-heavy. So stake the stem as it grows to keep it upright as it blooms. Try double-potting by using a lightweight flower pot placed inside a heavier decorative container or cache pot. Another option is to place several pots within a basket, filling in around each with pine cones, moss or holiday decorations. Three bulbs in a broad-based pot will naturally be less tippy.

Bulbs That Need the Cold Treatment

Forcing many other bulbs—especially hyacinths, tulips, crocuses, grape hyacinths (muscari), dwarf irises and daffodils (narcissus)—is also easy, but may take a bit longer and require some free space in a refrigerator or in an unheated garage or storeroom.

Spring-flowering bulbs normally spend the winter underground outdoors because they require a period of cold temperatures below 48°F to kick off a biochemical reaction inside that starts the bulb to grow and flower. Indoor forcing induces that reaction artificially.

Most bulbs cannot be brought to bloom in time for the holidays (only pre-cooled ones) but still can make marvelous gifts (clearly on their way to blooming) in a nice container with a colorful ribbon. Placed on a shelf in their new home, they will grow quickly with very little care. They are literally the "gift that keeps on growing" weeks and weeks after the holidays have passed.

When forcing bulbs that require cold treatments, it is important to look for varieties that will force easily. This information is usually provided on the packaging when you buy bulbs.

- Use regular flower pots or other containers with drainage holes.
- Add a layer of potting soil to a depth of 2 or more inches.
- Use as many bulbs as will fit in the container; then fill in with enough soil so just the tops of the bulbs are visible, with the soil line about half an inch below the pot rim.
- Water thoroughly. Wait two days, then water again.
- Put a piece of tape with the date written on it on each pot so you'll know the blooming time.
- Place your pots in a refrigerator or dark cool place (between 40° and 50°F) and water regularly for ten to 15 weeks, depending on the type and variety).
- When the cold period is over, move the pots to a warmer area in indirect or low light. Keep them there a week or two; then move them to a cool, sunny area where they should flower—to everyone's joy—in just two to three weeks.

The Holiday Hyacinth

Of all the bulbs that need cold treatment, hyacinths are special. There are pre-cooled hyacinths for forcing available. The pre-cooling process trims about two weeks off the time needed for the bulbs to flower. This makes it possible to have hyacinths for the holidays if you begin by late fall. Hyacinths are also special because they can be grown without any soil or gravel. Special hourglass-shaped hyacinth glasses are available from many catalogs and retail stores. Such containers allow you to grow these fragrant flowers suspended just above (but not touching) the water.

The growing roots, which can be seen clearly through the glass, add a special interest. Whether you buy bulbs professionally forced or as a last-minute gift or make them your special holiday project, forced bulbs are thoughtful and appreciated holiday gifts that keep on growing, brightening the dreary days of winter for weeks on end.

Holiday Decorating

Christmas pickings from the woods (wilds): For a wild Christmas wreath, try using flexible honeysuckle or grape vines to form a base. Twist the vine four or five times over, letting its kinks entangle with one another, binding into a circle. Just keep weaving in and out until you have a tight mat of interwoven vines. Poke dried flowers, berries, or whatever into this home-fashioned frame. Let your imagination carry you beyond tradition, all the more festive!

Many of the plants growing in the garden and woods (yard) have attractive seed pods, foliage or fruit that can be used for the Christmas season. Decorations made at home will have a special meaning to you and the children and, besides, it's fun to use your imagination making holiday festoons.

Items that can be used: Holly, berries, hemlock, spruces, cedars, pines. Each tree offers a distinctive pattern of branches, needles and cones. Traditional wreathing materials.

A popular Christmas present is a potted flowering plant. For poinsettias, keep the soil a little drier than what is recommended for most foliage plants. For other potted plants, keep most and place in a room with natural light, preferably a room that is relatively cool. No over-watering, please!

Garden tools and gadgets make wonderful Christmas presents. If you have a friend who "has everything," think about his feathered friends and give a bird bath or birdhouse. There's always a housing shortage!

Holiday Favorites

Q. *What are your favorite fall holiday decorations?*

A. I always prepare for the fall holidays early by planting in the summer. Come the end of October, I am reaping my harvest of fancy gourds of every shape, size and color, bumpy and smooth. I let the gourds dry, then coat with a clear acrylic spray or varnish. This treatment keeps the gourds beautiful all winter long. They make a great table or mantle decoration. I use them on my Halloween table on either side of a jack-o-lantern.

For Thanksgiving and an added touch of fall beauty, I sometimes place a few color-ful autumn leaves around the gourds. With these materials you can decorate your whole house and create a real holiday spirit!

Holiday Greenery, Preservation of

While holiday foliage, wreaths and Christmas trees brighten the festive season with their natural beauty, evergreens, once in the house, often shed their dried needles and leaves, causing a terrible mess.

To better preserve holiday foliage and prevent it from losing its luster, I recommend spraying trees and other greenery with Safer's ForEverGreen. Because the product is non-toxic and non-flammable, it's safe to use around children, pets and holiday lights.

This all-season plant protectant extends the life of the holiday foliage by helping to prevent water loss. When sprayed on a plant, ForEverGreen forms an invisible protective coating over the surface of the leaves or needles, sealing in the moisture and preventing the loss of valuable fluids that causes leaves to shed.

By simply spraying the upper and lower surfaces of the needles or leaves, Christmas trees, wreaths and outdoor plants can safely be protected from indoor dryness and winter cold.

ForEverGreen can be found at lawn and garden centers and other stores, including selected discount chains throughout the country.

One application of ForEverGreen will last four to six months, so go with it!

Holiday Plant Shopping Tips

Avoid plants that were left wrapped in their shipping wrappers because many plants deteriorate quickly when left this way, especially blooming potted plants.

Before leaving the nursery or store, wrap the plant properly with paper or plastic. Wrapping the plant protects it from temperature extremes and helps prevent torn leaves, knocked-off buds and other damage. Do not leave the plant in the car where it will be exposed to extreme cold or heat.

Holiday Spirit

Pies baking in the oven, bayberry candles, spice, cinnamon and hot toddies . . . these are the delicious aromas of the holiday season.

Add to that the fragrance of narcissus, lilies of the valley, fresh-cut balsam, holly, wreaths and mistletoe, and you'll see why the tradition of bringing nature's outdoor beauty into our homes is the best part of the holiday season.

Visit your local garden center for new decorating ideas. Maybe this is the year to change the look of your holiday decorating scheme. If so, designers are continually creating beautiful handmade (fresh or otherwise) decorated wreaths, swags and wall hangings in many different styles. In some shops, you can even bring in swatches of fabrics and wallpaper to create something especially for you. There are new styles of natural tabletop Christmas trees that designers can customize.

Holly

Q. *When should American hollies be pruned? Is cutting boughs at Christmastime good or bad for the trees?*

A. No harm is done by cutting branches for Christmas. In fact, the best time to prune them is mid-December through mid-March when they are dormant. During dormancy, the branches can be pruned heavily since new growth will emerge in the spring.

Horseradish

Q. *I've been growing horseradish for several years and usually have a mild crop. When is the best time of year to harvest the roots, and what can I do to get them to taste hot?*

A. For the best flavor and hotness, horseradish can be harvested after a few hard frosts, in the fall through early spring.

To harvest, remove whole roots and store them as you would carrots, packed in damp sand in the basement with temperatures between 32° to 40°F. Be careful handling the roots because any wounds or bruises will shorten their storage life.

To over-winter horseradish in the garden, mulch the plants after the ground has frozen to keep them from thawing. Save the lateral root cuttings of six to eight inches, or larger, to re-plant for next year's crop. Store them in moist sand in a cellar if they can't be re-planted immediately, or in the refrigerator.

Houseplant Perils

SYMPTOMS	CAUSES
Leaf yellowing, stunted growth or small leaves	• Root rot • Pot-bound roots • Insufficient light • Nutrient deficiency
Browning of leaf tips or margins	• Hot or dry air • Root rot • Nutrient deficiency
Wilting of entire plant	• Too little water • Root rot
Loss of leaves	• Environment change • Root rot
Bottom leaves turn yellow and drop off	• Nutrient deficiency • Pot-bound roots • Natural on mature plants
Spots on leaves	• Environmental problems • Fungus leaf spot
White patches appear on leaves and flowers	• Powdery mildew

Houseplant Soil

Q. *Can you tell me what the best soil for houseplants is?*

A. Here is a good potting mixture that I use:

1 part good potting soil
1 part good vermiculite or perlite
½ part coarse builder's sand
A little cow or sheep manure

Mix and add the following for each 6-inch pot you use:

1 tbsp dolomite lime
1 tbsp Osmocote fertilizer
1 tbsp bone meal

Another good choice, too, is ready-to-go sterile Pro-Mix potting soil available at nurseries and garden centers around the country. Everything you'll ever need for plants is in this mixture, so all you have to do is pot up your tiny treasures.

Houseplants: Decorating

A green plant is probably the most useful and least expensive item one can put in a room. Plants brighten the indoors, refresh the air we breathe and generally improve the quality of our lives just by their presence. They are especially nice for apartment dwellers. You can use plants as accents and room dividers, in place of wall hangings, curtains, also to frame an entrance or soften a harsh angle. You can even grow your own fancy salad greens and culinary herbs indoors.

When using plants indoors, take a tip from ikebana, the Japanese art of flower-arranging, and display plants in odd-numbered groups. Two or four plants together can have an unnatural, staged appearance. But three or five of varying heights, colors and textures will make a harmonious grouping. Remember that dark greens tend to recede, while lighter shades leap out of the background. Combine glossy-leafed foliage with softer, fuzzy-leafed plants for an interesting effect or, better still, simply let your imagination run wild!

Bright Ideas for Dark Spots

Poor lighting conditions have discouraged many an apartment dweller, but there are a number of attractive plants that don't need bright light. Try a broad-leafed cane (*Dieffenbachia picta*), palmlike dracaena (*Dracaena marginata*), leathery cast-iron plant (*Aspidistra elatior*), Chinese evergreen (*Aglaonema commutatum*), or the old favorite, snake plant (*Sansevieria trifasciata*). Many ferns will also tolerate deep shade.

Container Camouflage

Most plants, especially large ones, come from the store in temporary-looking pots. These can be set into a larger clay container or stray basket that complements your decorating scheme. Group several smaller plants in a single basket and cover the tops of the pots with sphagnum or Spanish moss (sold in packages at the garden center) for an attractive arrangement.

Salad Greens and Herbs Indoors

If you have a window that gets five to six hours of daily sunshine, you can grow the makings for gourmet meals. Parsley, chives, oregano, rosemary, thyme and other aromatic kitchen herbs are easy to grow in small pots on a windowsill.

Fancy loose-leaf lettuces and other salad greens need larger pots but also will do well in a sunny spot. All can be started from seed in a Pro-Mix moist potting soil. Hint: Make a temporary greenhouse by covering pots with plastic wrap while seeds sprout.

Keeping Houseplants Healthy

As a general rule of thumb, water houseplants when the top half-inch soil feels dry to the touch and give them a thorough soaking. Most plants also will benefit from a monthly feeding with a complete fertilizer for houseplants used according to the package directions.

Glossy-leafed plants will appreciate an occasional bath with a clean sponge and lukewarm water. Others, especially ferns, may be set in the shower for a few minutes. This will remove accumulated dust and certain pests and refresh the whole plant.

If insects become a problem, avoid harsh chemical insecticides, especially on edible greens. Control insect pests with a non-toxic insecticidal soap for houseplants. The spray kills insects on contact, but is harmless to people, pets and the environment.

Houseplants: Extending Life

Q. *How can I extend the life of my flowering pot plants?*

A. Many beautiful flowering plants such as cyclamen, hydrangea, azalea, cineraria and calceolaria (also known as pocketbook plant) will not re-flower indoors on their own. However, you can extend their bloom time by turning the light up and heat down.

These plants prefer bright window locations and cool temperatures (60° to 65°F) in the daytime, and 55° to 60°F at night. Moving them to a cool porch or basement at night can significantly extend bloom time. The popular chrysanthemum, with its many flower forms, does well in more moderate temperatures up to 75°F days and 70°F nights. Keep in mind, most flowering plants rest during the winter months (December, January and February) and need little or no fertilizing.

Houseplants: Fertilizing

Q. *How frequently should I fertilize my houseplants?*

A. With the wide variety of fertilizer types and forms on the market, it's easy to get confused. But always remember that more problems are caused by too much fertilizer than by too little. Don't exceed the dosage recommended on the package. Fertilizer will not cure an ailing plant and could even make it worse by burning plant roots.

Slow-growing plants need less fertilizer than fast-growing ones. You can gauge feeding by the type of plant and also by season. Plants grow faster in the spring and summer when they get more light during the longer days.

Fertilizer salts can build up and form a crusty white residue on the soil surface which may harm your plant. Wash these salts out of the soil by "leaching"—watering the plant heavily and allowing the excess water and fertilizer residue to drain out.

During the winter months, let your plants rest, *no fertilizing*, please!

Houseplants: Flowers for Winter

Q. *What flowering plants can brighten my home during dreary winter?*

A. Chrysanthemums mean variety in both color and shape. They can be white, gold, yellow, pink, lavender, bronze or red. The common decorative flower shape is a tuft of many curving petals—but that's only the beginning. There are single, daisylike flowers; small, globular pompoms; "spoon mums" with spoon-shaped petals; as well as quill and spider types with tubular petals. Cool nights extend the three-week flowering period. Buds need bright light to open. Once in full bloom, mums can tolerate lower light.

Kalanchoes are the perfect choice for the forgetful waterer, since these colorful succulents like to be kept on the dry side. They come in red, pink, salmon, white, orange or yellow blooms with thick decorative leaves that make them attractive foliage plants even after their two- to six-week blooming period is over. A sunny location helps keep their colors bright. Pale or bicolored flowers indicate too-low light.

Houseplant Tips

This is a slow time of year for your houseplants; many are resting in a dormant period. Plants that are resting should be kept damp and without fertilizer; it's good for their diets. Pinch off the yellow leaves; new ones are on the way. If you have trouble with spider mites, you must control it before damage becomes severe. When applying an insecticide soap spray, a second spraying may be necessary within six days because mites are able to complete their life cycle in seven to ten days. Being so small, they are tough pests to get rid of. They are usually more numerous on the underside of the leaves. Infested plants should be isolated immediately from all other plants.

Easy Houseplants

If you like indoor greenery but have little time for gardening, here's a list of the easiest indoor houseplants to grow: philodendron, spider plant, grape ivy, ferns, snake plant, wax plant and wandering Jew.

Houseplants: Watering

Q. *How frequently should I water my houseplants?*

A. As often as they need it! But how do you tell? Consult your garden center, florist or plant-care tag to determine if your plant is one of the watering exceptions that either needs to dry out between waterings or be kept constantly moist. The vast majority of houseplants need water when the surface feels dry to the touch.

Other ways to gauge watering needs include: lifting the pot; the lighter the pot, the drier the soil. Inserting a probe; if soil crumbs cling, the lower soil is still moist. Tapping the pot; hollow rings mean dry soil.

Remember, plant roots need air, too. Overwatering is a common mistake that damages roots and causes yellowing and dropping of lower leaves. Water thoroughly so water runs out the pot's drainage holes—but empty the saucers so that your plants don't develop overwatering symptoms from sitting in water for extended periods of time; they're not fish! For some reason, people think that plants have to be swimming in water. They must have a day or two to dry out or they'll drown. Do as I do; water only three times a week. Of course, in the winter they need even less watering.

Houseplants: Winter Tips

Buy those houseplants that are easy to care for and can tolerate the normally difficult growing conditions found in most apartments and houses.

Poinsettias that have finished flowering should be allowed to dry out. Store them on their sides on a greenhouse bench or in a cool cellar (55° to 60°F) and cut back sparingly.

Cinerarias and greenhouse primulas should be fertilized weekly the minute they show buds and their pots are filled with roots.

During the cold winter months, be sure to water plants with room-temperature water, especially African violets. Do it early in the day so they can dry off before night. Violets won't bloom if temperatures fall below 60°F, or if they get insufficient light.

Keep cyclamen moist (and I don't mean soggy) because, if you don't, they will plop over completely if allowed to go dry. To revive a dry plant, set the pot in a pan of warm water up to its rim and put in a cool room for about one hour. The plant should perk up immediately unless it's been allowed to remain dry for an intolerable length of time.

Hydrangeas

Q. *I have two large hydrangea bushes on the Northwest side of my house and for the past three years a few of the flowers open slightly and the rest remain dormant. I plan to cut them back this fall and feed them. Please explain why this happens.*

A. Poor soil, too much shade, over-fertilization, improper pruning and winter injury are some of the important factors that effect the flowering of hydrangeas. Pruning at the wrong time of year (fall or spring) will prevent flowering by removing the flower buds. Prune immediately after blooming (late July). Give your hydrangeas more winter protection by covering them with leaves, held in place by chicken wire.

Q. *I am confused (like a great many others) about when and how to prune my 10-foot-tall white-flowering hydrangea shrub. One book says to prune hydrangeas to the ground each fall. Another advises to remove only spent blossoms in spring and not to prune in fall. Which course is correct? I'm in a quandary.*

A. Generally, you prune hydrangeas after flowering, so exactly when depends on the variety of hydrangea you have. I suspect a 10-foot hydrangea is probably the PeeGee hydrangea (*Hydrangea paniculata grandiflora*). Your book that recommends cutting the plants all the way to the ground each fall is referring to a different variety, probably *H. arborescens,* a shorter plant that spreads by underground stems.

PeeGee hydrangeas flower in July and the flowers remain on the shrub until fall, eventually turning a lovely rust color. You can prune off flowers anytime after July, but the best time is just before the plant leafs out in spring. Hydrangeas set their flower buds on the new growth, so don't prune after growth starts or you'll risk losing that year's flowers.

Your other reference, which recommends removing only spent blossoms in spring, is probably PeeGee hydrangeas, but you may want to remove more than just the dried flowerheads because the plants can get 12 to 15 feet tall!

You don't say how you want to manage your 10-foot plant. I think PeeGees do their best kept to about 6 feet tall. They produce the best size and quality flowers when pruned to an umbrella shape with no more than five or six primary branches coming up from the base.

To shorten your plant, remove the tallest one or two basal branches every year which will bring the plant down to size in about three years. Or else, cut the trunks to a side shoot or branch at about 4 feet above the ground.

Both methods will require several seasons to get the tree to its ideal shape. After that, maintenance pruning will be a simple matter.

Mealybugs on Houseplants

Q. *What can I do about mealybugs on my houseplants?*

A. Mealybugs are tiny, whitish-pink, crawling, sucking insects that form a white, cottony mass as they mature. They are often found on the leaf stems and crevices. Since they can quickly spread from one plant to infest your whole collection, you must isolate the affected plant, observing other plants frequently to be sure they are not affected.

There are several methods of control. You can wash the plant gently but thoroughly with warm, soapy water, or use an insecticide soap and then rinse with clean water. Dabbing the mealybugs with an alcohol-soaked cotton swab is also effective.

Orchid, Cymbidium

Q. *How should I care for a cymbidium orchid plant received in full bloom?*

A. Tenderly! Which is to say, give it cool temperatures (nothing over 70°F), bright light but little or no direct sun, and protect it from drafts of hot, dry air, as from the furnace or fireplace. Water often enough to keep the roots moist. When the blooms fade, the best place for your cymbidium is a cool greenhouse or sun porch. It can't tolerate overheated rooms and dry air. Cymbidiums summer well outdoors; they should be left there until just before frost so that nighttime chilling can set next season's flowers, then brought to that cool, airy, moist place indoors.

Poinsettia

Q. *Can I re-flower my poinsettia?*

A. Yes, of course you can! This challenging project will help you appreciate the gorgeous poinsettias produced by professional growers under scientific greenhouse conditions.

Continue to care for your poinsettia during the winter and early spring. When danger of frost is past, cut back the stems, leaving only a few lower leaves, and re-pot the plant in a slightly larger pot. Place the plant outdoors where the increased light will stimulate growth.

Autumn is the time to create your own "scientific greenhouse environment." Before night temperatures fall to 40°F, bring your poinsettia back indoors for the dark/light treatment that will bring those green bracts back to color. (Poinsettia "petals" are really modified leaves, called "bracts.")

Starting October 1, put your poinsettia in complete, uninterrupted darkness for 14 hours, followed by 10 hours of bright light each day. Shutting your plant in a dark closet or covering it with a large box are effective ways to create a dark world. Place "move-the-poinsettia" daily reminders for yourself since a plant in the closet is easy to forget! At all times, keep your plant well-watered.

Once the bracts start to change color, you can return your plant to normal indoor conditions. Your re-flowered poinsettia may not be as attractive as the original, professionally grown plant; however, it's a holiday accomplishment you can display with pride.

Q. *My poinsettia is losing all its blooms and leaves. What should I do with it now? Can it be cut back?*

A. Drafts and overwatering often cause leaf drop. Remember, poinsettias are heat lovers. They thrive outdoors during the summer, but require a constant temperature of about 60°F after early September. Without this and high humidity, the leaves will drop. With proper care your poinsettia can bloom again next year and for years to come. Proper watering is most important. Just keep it moist, not soggy. When the blooms fade, withhold water and place out of the light as the plant becomes dormant. In early May, trim back the plant to two or three nodes (small swellings on the stem), start watering and put in direct sunlight. When the frost is gone, plunge your plant—pot and all—into a sunny spot in your garden. Fertilize occasionally and water during the hot summer months. In September, when the nights get cool, bring in your poinsettia and cover or closet it. Be sure it gets no light from sundown to sunup until Thanksgiving. Any light during that dark period will interfere with its cycle, and it won't bloom. However, during the daytime it can have full light. Come Christmas, your poinsettia should be full of buds.

Poinsettia Myth

Old myths die hard—but I'll say it just one more time—poinsettias are not poisonous.

It's hard for me to believe that many people are tempted to eat one of these favorite holiday plants—even so, it hasn't kept them from being one of the garden trade's hottest items. A recent survey found that 50 percent of Americans believe poinsettias are toxic. Twelve percent know that's not true, and the rest simply don't give a damn!

Let's be sensible; the poinsettia was never intended to be eaten. Therefore, it's a fact that those who do eat parts of the plant (and wish they hadn't) will find some degree of discomfort (a bellyache)! I recommend ice cream or milk to soothe the ache, and keep all non-edible houseplants away from tiny hands and pets!

Poisonous Plants

The winter holidays are rich in festive plant traditions: Christmas trees, poinsettias, holly, mistletoe and many other holiday plants are used to enliven otherwise drab winter households. But in houses with small children, parents need to be careful in the selection of the plants they bring indoors. The toxicity of some of the most common holiday plants is important to know, so here are suggestions on colorful alternate plants that are safe around tiny children.

Poinsettias (**Euphorbia pulcherrima**): For years, articles have appeared in the popular press claiming that poinsettias are dangerous, even lethal, if ingested by children. These can be traced back to just one reported fatality early in this century, they say. That report has never been confirmed, and recently poinsettias have been the subject of repeated scientific testing. Laboratory rats used in that testing not only did not die; in some cases, they actually gained weight on a diet of poinsettias. Still, poison control centers occasionally report that poinsettias cause mild nausea and skin irritation, so they are best displayed out of reach of tiny hands.

Christmas cactus (**Schlumbergera bridgesil**)*:* This plant is a good holiday choice in homes with small children. There is no evidence that it is toxic.

Evergreens: Millions of pines and firs are used in wreaths in Christmas trees every year, largely without incident. They contain turpenes (related to turpentine) which may cause gastric upset if eaten in great quantity. But, in general, pines and firs may be considered safe. Yews (members of the *Taxus* genus), however, are another story. They contain highly toxic alkaloids that can cause heart and respiration problems and have resulted in deaths. Do not use yews in holiday greenery and take care when children are around them outdoors.

Mistletoe (**Phoradendron serotinum**)*:* Both the leaves and berries of this plant can cause vomiting and diarrhea if ingested, and at least one death has been reported. This plant is best displayed well out of reach.

Holly (**Ilex opaca**—*American holly, and* **Ilex aquifolium**—*English holly):* The leaves, and especially the berries, of these plants contain a potent brew of several toxins. These can cause persistent vomiting and sometimes diarrhea and may also have an effect on the nervous system. Some deaths from holly berry ingestion have been recorded. But, in 1988, according to the American Association of Poison Control centers, there were 2,000 cases of accidental ingestion of holly with no deaths. Bright holly berries will attract young children, so keep these plants on a high shelf out of reach and take steps to prevent berries from falling within reach.

Jerusalem cherry (**Solanum pseudocapsicum**)*:* This member of the Nightshade family contains highly toxic alkaloids that can cause burning sensations in the mouth and throat, vomiting, diarrhea, fever and, in severe poisonings, heart and respiration disturbances and, occasionally, death. Its bright fruits will attract children, so keep it well out of reach.

How do you generate festive holiday color without putting children at risk? I say that there are many safe and colorful alternatives to traditional plants. For instance, the Bromeliad or Pineapple family contain many plants with brilliant and long-lasting red, pink and orange leaves and bracts, and many are available in plant stores through the holiday season. Some specifics: 'Earth Star' (*Cryptanthus acaulis*) is available in a star-shaped plant that is brilliant pink. 'Scarlet Star' (*Guzmania lingulata* 'Cardinalis') has brilliant scarlet bracts. Blushing Cup (*Nidularium fulgens*) has leaves that blush brilliant red just before the plant flowers.

Call your nearest Poison Control Center if you have a problem.

Potatoes: New Ways to Store

If you want to help your potatoes do better while placed in storage, try putting some rosemary, sage and lavender in with them. Researchers have found that the essential oils in those herbs suppress sprouting and inhibit the bacteria that cause potatoes to rot in storage.

To make sure the process worked, Green scientists tested this process in two ways. Some spuds were stored with the essential oils of the herbs while other spuds were simply stored alongside the dried herbs. In both instances, the potatoes sprouted much more slowly than control spuds that were stored under identical conditions but without herbs. When the herbs were removed, the potatoes sprouted normally.

Home researchers have also learned that another herb, Greek oregano, inhibits the growth of bacteria that will cause potatoes to spoil. The taste of the potatoes was not affected by any of the herbs. Sounds like a good idea.

Potting Benches: A Must

It's the usual story. Just when home gardeners think they're ready to begin planting, they discover they've forgotten their trowels or spades and must run back to the potting shed, basement or garage to retrieve them. Or when gardeners begin to fill flowerpots with soil, they find themselves spending more time cleaning up than actually accomplishing their mission.

Home gardeners have found versatile potting benches to be the efficient storage solution for storing everything from tools to flowerpots.

Home gardeners need plenty of room to work and should look for a bench that has many capabilities, such as a soil bin and potting sink, which is a practical way to ease clean-up and save soil.

A potting bench should also be versatile and be at the proper height for the person using it. P.S. They make great gifts!

Presents That Live

For those considering presents of living plants for the holidays, the American Association of Nurserymen has advice worth heeding.

Plants, inside or outside, keep memories of the occasion fresh for years to come. Of course, like any present the selection should be personal, with the recipient's likes, dislikes and lifestyle in mind. For example, if the recipient is a beginner at caring for indoor plants, easy-to-maintain plants such as philodendron, Ponytail or jade plants would be the proper choice. On the other hand, if the present is going to a "green thumb," something new and exotic would be a challenge.

A very busy household with little time for chores will prefer a plant that requires almost no care and infrequent watering, while a person alone at home much of the day will enjoy the need to pamper the growing plant.

Rosemary

Rosemary, the Christmas herb, is the symbol of fidelity, friendship, remembrance and the primary European traditional gift of appreciation. It has been used in the celebration of Christmas since the sixteenth century, making it the most traditional of all Christmas plants.

Rosemary trees and topiaries can be used to grace a table or in front of a window as a festive Christmas welcoming. In the kitchen, the rosemary leaves are the perfect flavoring to add to turkey, chicken, lamb, pork or shellfish.

Here are four basic steps to keep rosemary happy through the winter:

1. Don't bring it indoors too early. It likes to be cool and will sustain frost. This will put it into dormancy.
2. Bring it into the coolest room you have. Rosemary is happy with nighttime temperatures in the 40s.
3. Give rosemary as much light as possible during the day. A bright bay window is perfect.
4. Don't keep it too wet, but don't ever let it dry out.

If your rosemary should develop a fungus during the winter months, simply put the rosemary outside on your doorstep during days when the temperature is above freezing. Air and light circulation cure the fungus. That's all there is to it!

Shrubs and Evergreens from Cuttings

November and December are the two best months of the year for starting flowering shrubs and evergreens from cuttings. Just when most people think the gardening season is coming to an end, smart gardeners are beginning to reap the best harvest Mother Nature has to offer: free landscape plants from your own plants!

Almost all amateur gardeners have at one time or another tried to reproduce their favorite plant from a cutting, usually without success. After a few unsuccessful tries, they give up, believing that it cannot be done without a greenhouse and all kinds of special equipment, when really all they had wrong was their timing.

For the amateur gardener working at home, the best time to reproduce favorite plants from cuttings is when they are dormant. Once dormancy occurs, the tops of the plants are resting quietly for the winter (during the short days), but root activity can still take place. Taking a cutting from a plant that is dormant does not cause the plant or the cutting any undue stress, and therefore the cutting will immediately start to replace the roots it lost when you removed it from the parent plant.

Cuttings of evergreens such as taxus, junipers and arborvitae can be taken anytime after Thanksgiving. Take a cutting 4 inches long, strip the needles from the lower two-thirds of the cutting, dip the cutting in a rooting compound and stick it outdoors in a bed of coarse sand.

The sand bed should be in a well-drained and shaded area. Water the sand bed thoroughly and keep it watered next spring and summer. By fall, your evergreens should be rooted and ready to transplant.

Deciduous shrubs such as forsythia, red-twig dogwood, mock orange and privet should also be done in the late fall or early winter. Once the shrubs have completely lost their leaves (defoliated), 6-inch cuttings can be taken. Make your cut just below a node. (Nodes are the bumps on the stem where the buds will appear next year.)

Take as many cuttings as you would like, dip them in a rooting compound and then tie them all in a bundle with the butt ends even. Dig a hole about 18 inches deep and bury the entire bundle upside down (butt ends up). Pack some moist peat moss over the butt ends and then completely fill the hole in. Mark it with a stake so you can find your cuttings in the spring. Leave them buried until late spring.

Snow, and Other Cold Hard Facts

Snow covers 50 percent of the earth's land in winter—more than 6 million square miles!

To dig out a 50-foot two-car driveway after a 4-inch snowfall, you'll have to remove four tons of snow. No wonder 40 percent of homeowners in the Northern zones (snow belt) own snow throwers.

Snow Fertilizers

Snow absorbs nitrates, sulfates and calcium from the atmosphere and releases them into the soil—worth $120 per acre in the Midwestern part of the country. Snow is known as the poor man's fertilizer because of its nitrogen content.

Wet Snow Blocks Radar

In avalanches, snow can flow like liquid! So, skiers beware!

Snow control accounts for one-sixth of the world's annual consumption of salt. Average uses ranges from 400 to 1,200 pounds per mile of road.

U.S. record annual snowfall: 1,000 inches in Paradise, Washington.

Snow Blower

Q. *What's the safest way to unclog a snow blower? I'm concerned about sticking my hand down the discharge chute.*

A. Never, but never, stick your hand into a discharge chute while the engine is still running. Severe injury is possible; in fact, unavoidable! The best and safest way to unclog the machine is to shut off the engine and disconnect the spark-plug lead. Then, use an old broom handle to clear the chute and loosen packed snow around all the nooks and crannies of the machine, especially the "auger."

Soil, Sandy

The most important way to build your sandy soil into fertile crop-producing loam is lots of organic matter. You can't overdo it. Rotten plant material such as leaves, wood chips, grass clippings, straw, hay or bark should be worked into the soil. Sandy soil can be mulched anytime, but spring is best, right after a rain.

Stephanotis

Q. *I have had one of my favorite plants, a stephanotis (*S. floribunda*) for three years—no flowers, only masses of shoots. It's located in a Southwest-facing room with a night temperature of 60°F. Every time I cut the shoots, I get more growth. How can I get it to produce those fabulous fragrant flowers?*

A. Stephanotis flowers buds are produced on the current season's growth, so you may have pruned your plant at the wrong time! You should trim and thin the vine in late winter, before new growth begins. If you prune in spring or summer, you run the risk of removing the flower bud stems.

Perhaps you've been over-fertilizing. If so, stop, because your plant seems to be growing vigorously already. Excessive feeding, especially with nitrogen, produces vegetative shoots at the expense of flowering ones.

Tools: How to Sharpen

Q. *I find it more and more difficult to dig in the soil each year. I can't decide if it's just me getting "long in the tooth," or if my shovel needs a good sharpening. Is it possible to sharpen* *it, or do I just need a nice, new lightweight one? (Since I can't get a new body, it will have to be the shovel.)*

A. Dull tools make miserable chores out of the most satisfying work. When we talk about sharpening garden tools—pruning shears, hedge clippers and lawn mower blades come to mind, but few people realize that digging tools like shovels and hoes need to be sharpened regularly to keep them in tip-top shape and easy to use.

Most garden tools have single-bevel edges like the blade of a chisel. These are sharpened by filing only one side of the blade. Rather than a fine edge, a shovel should have a tough edge that can slam into rocks and roots without bending. The wider the bevel angle, the thicker the metal right behind the cutting edge and the stronger the edge. The more acute the angle, the thinner the metal right behind the cutting edge and the sharper and more fragile the edge.

Clean the blade by scrubbing the metal with dry steel wool. Then inspect the edge. If it is chipped or broken, you will need to have the tool ground. Grinding is for professionals, so thank goodness many small, old-time hardware stores still exist (not the large chain stores) that grind and sharpen tools.

If the edge of your shovel is in fairly good condition, you can sharpen it yourself. You will need a 10-inch mill bastard file and a file card. A file card is a type of wire brush used for cleaning filings from between the file's teeth. Using a file card is the key to keeping a file sharp.

On a tool that has a short, straight edge like a hoe or spade, one straight filing stroke will usually take you across the width of the blade. With a shovel, file one side then the other, rather than trying to make one stroke go all the way around.

Use a rag to coat all the metal surfaces of your garden tools with oil. Inspect the wooden handles for rough spots, then smooth them out with sandpaper and coat the wood with linseed oil. Who needs splinters?

Sharpen all your gardening tools in the fall and put them away clean so you'll be all set to start working once more in the garden come spring.

Trees from Seed

Just when most people think the gardening season is coming to an end, the smart green-thumb gardeners are just beginning to reap the best harvest Mother Nature has to offer: new plants at no or very little cost.

Flowering dogwoods and Japanese maples are easily grown from seeds. Seeds collected in the fall can be planted outdoors in the fall in a bed of peat moss or potting soil.

Japanese-maple seeds should be soaked in water for 48 hours to soften the hard outer coating and initiate germination before planting them ¼ inch deep. Dogwoods must be soaked in water until the seed can easily be removed from the pulp. These, too, can be planted outdoors in the fall in a bed of potting soil or peat moss at a depth of ¼ inch. Cover all seed beds with a screen or chicken wire to keep chipmunks and squirrels and other night poachers from eating your seeds.

For the amateur gardener working at home, the best time to reproduce landscape plants from seeds or cuttings is in the fall, when the plants are dormant or almost dormant. Taking a cutting from a plant that is dormant does not cause the plant or the cutting any undue stress, and therefore the cutting will immediately start to replace the roots it lost when it was removed from the parent plant.

Trees: Winter Concerns

Unlike people, trees can't step indoors to avoid the harsh winter and enjoy a hot toddy by the fire. However, homeowners can help their trees survive the brutality of the cold months by taking a few simple precautionary steps.

Trees are often left to fend for themselves during the winter because people think they hibernate. Not true! Trees protect food reserves and carefully conserve energy until spring beckons renewal. Most of a tree's growth areas are shielded inside jackets called buds. Any hungry creature needing a meal chews and nibbles on the resting buds and twigs, leaving trees in grave danger.

People should think of tree care as an investment and help their valuable trees stave off animals and inclement weather. A healthy tree increases in value with age—paying big dividends by beautifying surroundings, purifying air and increasing property value.

Here are six critical guidelines for protecting trees during winter:
1. *Compost:* Add a thin layer of composted organic mulch that blankets the soil surface. Mulch protects and conserves tree resources and recycles valuable materials.
2. *Wrap trees:* Properly wrap new trees that have not developed a corky bark and could easily be damaged. This will help keep animals from damaging a tree.
3. *Remove deadwood:* Remove or correct clearly visible structural faults and deadwood. Try to make small pruning cuts that minimize the exposure of a branch's central heartwood core.

4. *Lightly prune:* Perform limited greenwood pruning of declining and poorly placed branches. Pruning should conserve as many living branches as possible with only a few selective cuts.

5. *Fertilize:* Fertilize in small quantities. Adding essential elements over a mulch layer will help provide a healthy soil environment for root growth.

6. *Strategically water:* Water where soils and trees are cool but not frozen and where there has been little precipitation. Winter droughts need water treatment the same as summer droughts. However, it is easy to overwater in winter, so be careful.

The International Society of Arboriculture offers a complete set of brochures covering many of the basic principles of proper tree care to help you. To order these brochures, or to locate an arborist in your area, contact ISA at *P.O. Box 3126, Champaign, Illinois, 61826-3129.*

Leafless Trees

One of the best and most accurate ways to inspect a tree for injury and defects is simply to look at it. But that's easier said than done during most of the year when trees are blanketed in leaves. Even so, many property owners wait until the spring to think about tree maintenance.

Winter—after deciduous trees have shed their leaves—is the perfect time to look for injury and certain diseases, including decay. Leafless trees also reveal structural problems in trees. Ideally, a tree's branches will be evenly distributed along the tree's trunk, creating an even "scaffold" effect. Angles that are tight or V-shaped where branches meet the trunk can be a sign of instability in the tree.

A professional arborist will be able to identify potential problems and suggest remedies. In many parts of the country, winter is a slow time for arborists, so they might have more time to devote to your trees and the price is usually right.

Identifying tree-care problems and scheduling work during the winter can help keep you one step ahead of the crowd when it comes to the busy springtime tree-care system.

To receive a list of the arborists closest to you who are members of the National Association of Arborists, call (800) 733-2622.

Q. *The evergreens on my property are still recovering from staggering snow and ice storms of several years ago. What can I do to protect my plants from now on?*

A. Ice and snow accumulation can damage evergreens in two ways: by weight and careless methods of removal. Either way can lead to broken or cracked branches, which is an invitation to canker-producing fungi.

Snow should always be removed from branches carefully and gently, and it is best to do it several times during a snowstorm rather than to wait until the plants are already bent down almost to the ground.

When you clear walks and driveways, avoid snow-blowing or piling snow around shrubs where it will overload the branches and produce flooded soil when it melts. Ice spells trouble because it can't be easily removed. Instead, wait for it to melt naturally.

Small plants, especially those planted under the eaves of a house, can be sheltered with wooden A-frames or slatted boxes set over them. The stems and branches of larger plants can be tied up with spirals of twine or bicycle-tire inner tubes or anything else that will prevent the plant from being splayed open by the weight of ice and snow. For a plant with a single delicate stem, a bamboo pole can be tied along the stem's length for reinforcement.

At winter's end, examine all your plants and prune off any damaged limbs. Cut back to within a quarter of an inch of a live bud, or just outside a branch collar. Take your time inspecting your plants; do not rush to remove branches that simply appear to be winter-killed. Try this if you're not sure: Scrape the bark with your thumbnail, and if the tissue beneath is still green it's alive. It's best then to wait to see if new growth emerges.

Tulips: Re-flowering Potted

Q. *Can I re-flower potted tulips?*

A. Yes—but not indoors. Flowering bulbs, including tulips, hyacinths, narcissus and crocus, are forced to bloom out of season in response to controlled environmental conditions in the greenhouse. To bloom again, they require a rest period and natural outdoor environmental conditions.

To re-flower your bulb plants, remove the faded blooms and keep the plants watered in a cool, bright location until the foliage matures and dries out. Plant the bulbs outdoors after danger of frost is past, two to three times deeper than their diameter. Have patience; they should bloom in a year or two during their normal spring season.

Witch Hazel

Q. *I am looking for a plant that will dress up my winter landscape. A neighbor suggested witch hazel. What do you think?*

A. Witch hazels are deciduous winter-blooming small trees or shrubs and are the perfect plants for your situation. There are two native species: the common witch hazel (*Hamamelis virginiana*) and the vernal witch hazel (*H. vernalis*) that bloom in the fall and mid-winter, respectively, while the Asian varieties—the Chinese *H. mollis* and the Japanese *H. japonica*—bloom in late winter and early spring. Witch hazels are pollinated by winter-flying moths and have colors that vary from clear yellow to orange to maroon. Some of the best choices for the garden are the hybrids between the Asian species (*H. X. intermedia*). These produce the showiest flowers and grow into very large shrubs—I should say, trees—ranging from 6 to 15 feet high.

Among the two dozen cultivars, some of the best are the late-blooming yellow 'Arnold Promise' and 'Jelena,' with their orange-red autumn leaves and copper-colored blossoms; and the primrose yellow-flowered 'Primavera' and 'Ruby Glow,' with copper-red flowers that mature to reddish-brown. Depending on the species, witch hazels are hardy and are best sited in a moist, well-drained spot in full sun to partial shade.

Wreath, How to Make

1. Buy a wire frame or form a coat hanger into a circle.
2. You will need ample greens (at least a bushel). Cut all greens to 3 to 6 inches before starting.
3. To bind greens on the frame you'll need a spool of florist's wire.
4. Drape a group of three or four sprigs of greens along the frame with the tips faing away from you and the cut ends toward you.
5. Bind the greens onto the frame with three or four turns of the wire.
6. Add the next bundle of greens with their tips overlapping the bound ends of the first bundle. Bind them into place.
7. Keep continuing the procedure around the frame until you finish; be sure to tie it securely.
8. Now comes the fun part. Add trimmings such as pods, seeds, berries, "bunting" cones, and why not let your imagination go?

Best greens to use: pine, hemlock, spruce, holly, laurel, juniper, balsam.

index